The Gopal–Rakhal Dialectic

Colonialism and Children's Literature in Bengal

Gaganendranath Tagore, *Where East Meets West: 'Deadly Sensitivity'*

The Gopal–Rakhal Dialectic

Colonialism and Children's Literature in Bengal

SIBAJI BANDYOPADHYAY

TRANSLATED BY
RANI RAY & NIVEDITA SEN

Tulika Books

Published by
Tulika Books
35 A/1 Shahpur Jat, New Delhi 110 049

First published in India in 2015

ISBN: 978-93-82381-55-6 (hardback)

Printed at Chaman Offset, Delhi 110 002

To

MANABENDRA BANDYOPADHYAY
without whose inspiration and urging
this book would not have been written
– with all my respect

Contents

Foreword

(to the 2013 Bengali edition)

Some time in the early 80s, at one of the regular *adda* sessions of some teachers of Jadavpur University, Manabendra Bandyopadhyay declared happily that a bright young student had shown up in their department (Department of Comparative Literature). Along with this, he also made it known that the student had in the meanwhile shored up much argument against the writings of those very teachers present in the *adda*, which they would undoubtedly get to know at the right time.

And, indeed, many did come to know of all that. The shy and sharp student, frail yet full of intelligence, could often be seen in the constant company of Manabendra, almost always involved in some argument or the other. We were all as much enlightened by his invaluable companionship as we had been by Manabendra's. And within a short time, taking us all by surprise, an essay written by him as an M.A. term paper came out in the shape of a slender book in 1983: *Prasanga Jibanananda* (*On Jibanananda*). The book provided us with an analysis based on a radically new understanding of the poet, clearing the cobwebs of obscure and unfounded notions that had clouded our judgment about Jibanananda for the last thirty years or so since the poet's death – all of this done by a rather young man. And to some of us what appeared as a highly significant moment was that a young Marxian youth had managed to acknowledge Jibanananda as a major literary figure at a time when the general tendency in the Marxist literary critical circles had been to dismiss him outright.

And that young man soon emerged as a teacher in the same department, surrounded at all times by a bevy of students – female and male – eagerly looking up to him as a source of inspiration. A teacher who could at each moment imbue them with a sense of life and thought. And that teacher published yet another book in 1991 – a thesis on Bengali children's literature – while remaining immersed in study and debate, in discourse and disquisition, wit and confabulation, ensconced among his friends and disciples. It is not that that no one had written on the subject before him; there were in fact quite a few books already existing on the topic. But our age-old children's literature found a new spokesperson, its study took a new direction, with the publication of Sibaji Bandyopadhyay's *Gopal–Rakhal Dvandasamas*. No, it would also not be fair to say that the book gave a new direction to the study of children's literature – rather, it ought to be emphatically stated that it offered a new way of reading literature itself. In the field of Bengali literary criticism we may regard the book as an advent, as a harbinger of ways of thinking about literature proper to our age. We, as readers, were taken aback when we saw in it a most startling analysis of hidden aspects of the psyche of both authors and readers. Some of us began to utter in a half-mocking tone that we were afraid to read lest another frightful image of the author, or indeed of ourselves, be revealed therein! The book uncovered – at regular intervals – how deeply buried in the recesses of our mind lay the hidden forms of patriarchy, how all our notions of child-rearing were implicated within matrices of power, and how distorted our ideas of the 'life-world' of the black men under the imperceptible influence of the white rulers were. Under the light of such revelation we learnt how to read not only Bengali children's literature (the writer had incorporated the educational primers into the corpus of literature), but also many well-known English novels in a radically new way.

Several strange new ideas were afloat when Sibaji was writing. Words such as postmodernism, structuralism, post-structuralism, deconstruction, along with the names of their theorists had begun to circulate in the four corners of the world. We cannot say that the fall-out of such a maelstrom of thought was always beneficial – many a time, inundated by theory, the central idea of the discourse was lost. But despite a strong theoretical strain, or perhaps because of it, Sibaji Bandyopadhyay's book never lost a certain lightness of touch; theoretical speculations came to him naturally, as it were, much like breathing. And it was because of this that the entire *Gopal–Rakhal Dvandasamas* – the novelty of the name itself – became synonymous with an effortless and pleasing narration, full of lucid reasoning and sparkling wit.

Generations of Bengalis have grown up under the aegis of *Barna Parichay*'s infallible wisdom: 'Gopal is a good boy, Rakhal is not; everybody should be like Gopal, not like Rakhal.' And Sibaji goes on to show how these two prototypes, in different disguises and in different names, have been intrinsic to our children's literature – rather, our entire society. To validate this, Sibaji finds it necessary to dwell upon the evolution of educational policies in India under colonial rule, to reveal the 'true face' of institutions such as the family and the school, to scrutinize the significance of obedience and discipline in relation to those institutions.

The good boys, otherwise 'Gopals', try hard to keep the naughty boys like 'Rakhal' outside the domain of literature and society, but at the end are not always successful. As Sibaji shows, this is because no 'Gopal' can remain a pure entity of goodness. As 'Rakhal' of necessity must contain a bit of 'Gopal', so also a bit of 'Rakhal' is latent in 'Gopal'. Centering on one text after another, the book goes on to demonstrate how the inner division or ceaseless antagonism between 'Gopal' and 'Rakhal' gets played out, how a dialectics is thus construed.

In order to clarify what makes 'Gopal' what he is, Sibaji submits before us the entire colonial administrative arrangement and the imperial greed for expansion of the empire underlying it. In this context, the relationship between the ruler and ruled becomes just that of a master and a slave; it is a relationship that is inherently patriarchal. And thus a certain kind of structural duality comes into being: the child, the woman, the slave and the black man on one side, and the school, the master of the house and the white man on the other. The model of ideal parenthood guides the relationship between the black man and his white counterpart. The subservient black feels no compunction in obeying the command of the master/father. Sibaji culls the picture of such a relationship from some English novels and proceeds to show that we are so attuned to the wisdom received through the prism of the white man that within our consciousness too, Africa becomes the Dark Continent, violent and frightening.

In his analysis, Sibaji's reasoning has been aided by his very personal mode of language. I have already pointed to the lucidity and sharpness of his prose; what I wish to add is the way he introduces a new turn into the very structure of established discourse. Thus, in his style of writing, everyday parlance cohabits with dense thoughts and phrases. All of a sudden he drops a word or two of Arabic or Persian, a style almost non-existent in current Bengali prose. Or, by twisting a couple of lines from some well-known poem, Sibaji tries to make a statement all his own. He can write quite nonchalantly how the Bengali will accept a social system gifted by the British by removing 'the venom of antagonism from his heart'; or, the rulers were thinking that unless religiosity does not return to the Hindus and Muslims, 'darkness born out of the skilful artistry of lies would soon descend'. Sibaji does not have to resort to the niceties of word use by keeping them separate and apart, as in '*tar theke*' ('from that'), but conjoins them as they would be in everyday speech, conflating the sounds as in '*tattheke*'. This and other examples of such language use make us aware of the personality of the writer as inherently both rebellious and witty [These are impossible to render into English here for linguistic reasons – Translators]. Or, as I had suggested earlier, he adds a new flavour to speech by combining a formally serious word with one of habitual conversation [Examples abound of such usages that resist all attempts at successful translation – Translators]. Such rebellious usage makes us wonder further about the slight half-smile with which they were undoubtedly written. We understand that Sibaji's attack is directed not simply at his subject of analysis, but also towards language itself.

I do hope that no reader will regard these few words of mine as any sort of

Introduction to this book. Truly, I do not possess the competence to attempt such an endeavour. These few words remain as a testimony of my admiration, both for dear Sibaji and for this canonical book.

Kolkata
September 2013

SANKHA GHOSH

Author's Preface

(to the 2013 Bengali edition)

Twenty-five years seem to have gone by so quickly. In 1991, Papyrus Publishers brought out *Gopal–Rakhal Dvandasamas: Bangla Shishusahitya o Upanibeshbad* (*Gopal–Rakhal Dialectic: Colonialism and Bengali Children's Literature*). I wrote the book between 1988 and 1990, during the three years that I was a research fellow in pursuit of a doctoral degree in the Department of Comparative Literature, Jadavpur University. A reworked and augmented version of *Gopal–Rakhal Dvandasamas* is being published now (2013). Although it has not been altered from top to bottom (the chapterization and organization remaining the same), there is certainly a distinction between the original and the current versions of the book. The journey that started in 1988 and ended in 2013 is punctuated by two other books of mine – *Abar Shishushiksha* (*Pedagogy Again*, 2005; 2010) and *Bangla Shishusahityer Chhoto Meyera* (*The Little Girls of Bengali Children's Literature*, 2007). There is no doubt that both in re-reading *Gopal–Rakhal Dvandasamas* after so many years, and in refashioning it, it has not been possible for me to free myself from my attachment to these two books. However, despite this unavoidable constraint, I have tried to reproduce and retain as far as possible the imprinted reminiscences of the theoretical–social–political–ideological ambience of the1980s within which *Gopal–Rakhal Dvandasamas* had initially unfurled.

In the colonial era, a new genre called 'children's literature' was constructed within the domain of Bengali literature. Immediately after, that literature crossed the restricted terrain of children's primers and child-friendly moral homilies to evolve into a laboratory for several nationalist themes and structures. In fact, from the middle of the nineteenth century, even in the domain of primers that was generally looked down upon as having merely a functional agenda, there was evidence of a conscious artistry. Bengali primers became a large archive of verses composed in diverse rhymes and meters pleasing to the ear, and also competent prose that was embellished with accurate punctuation. Moreover, it was a storehouse of various technical matters like decisions about fonts, determination of the sequence of the script and decoration of the alphabets. In *Gouriya Byakaran* (*Bengali Grammar*), printed in 1833, Rammohun Roy had earnestly appealed for the use of the phonetic script. It was this that led to the birth of numerous textbooks that were conceptualized as introductions to reading and writing for children. Along with writers who were child-sensitive by profession but also defenders of tradition, exceptional litterateurs like Madanmohan Tarkalankar, Ishwarchandra Vidyasagar, Bankimchandra Chattopadhyay, Jogindranath Sarkar, Rabindranath Tagore and others came forward to make the child's entry into the world of letters in Bengali a pleasant and smooth experience. Thanks to this collective journey, within a short span a wonderful surplus, in the definitive sense of the term, accumulated in the universe of Bengali primers. Instead of getting exhausted in the training of language-forms like the alphabet, rules of spelling and composition of sentences, but certainly in collaboration with those exercises, diverse signs of compromise with colonial modernity surfaced in them. An epoch does not necessarily end with the advent of another; one has to realize the new through conscious efforts. The new Bengali primer was soaked in this rare sense of history. And because of this very reason, this genre, generally neglected by virtue of being textbooks for little children, demands the special attention of literary writers as well as social scientists.

During the period of British rule, due to their novel methods of appropriation with the two-fold power acquired through the spread of capital and perpetual land-grabbing, everybody in our native state acquired a new ageist title: *shishu* ('child'). The attitude seemed to be that without the nurturing provided by the wise foreigners, Indians would never be able to cross the threshold of childhood. According to this perspective, the educational atmosphere that the English administrators had built, specifically since the age of Macaulay, beginning in 1835, was predicated, as it were, on this context of primers, with the noble intention of civilizing and enabling Indians who had not gone beyond childhood, were indifferent about the phenomenal universe and a repository of blind superstitions. And such a recourse was the primary capital of all Bengali children's teachers after the mid-nineteenth century vis-à-vis their reflections on the first stage of life. However, there are many illustrations of the case of the master/servant, in which the cost–benefit calculation did not reach an expected solution. Somewhere in between, it got derailed from its predetermined trajectory. In the Bengali primer, one got solid proof of following up the unfinished plan of modernity befitting the so-called stunted intelligence of backward Indians that was formed under the supervision of the British mentor; yet, if one listened carefully, at many places, the resonances were disjointed. The humble arrogance of the disciple was, in fact, the sign of his desire for his own rights. The passion to construct a theory of childhood in keeping with the approbation of present times can be closely discerned in Madanmohan's

Shishushiksha, Vidyasagar's *Barna Parichay*, Jogindranath's *Hashi Khushi*, Rabindranath's *Sahaj Path*, Bankimchandra's *Sahaj Rachanashiksha*, and even in Madhusudan Mukhopadhyay's *Sushilar Upakhyan*. That passion one can see only in the writings of those who were reluctant to adhere to received knowledge-traditions. Rather than be dominated by the traditions and views of history that were imposed by others, rather than sacrificing one's own selfhood, the eagerness to construct an alternative was crucial evidence that there was a group of native learned men who were gradually moving towards shaping themselves. It is beyond debate that that incentive – whether it was an ideological objective, a pleasant sense of execution or a documented scholarship – was in no aspect of the same value at all places. Moreover, on the highway of history, most of the zeal of self-aggrandizement was being expended with the agenda of reinforcing the expansion of the rising English-educated *bhadralok* society. All things considered, it was an exceedingly complex *swadeshi* educational ideal by the merging of two opposing tendencies. During this sorry state of affairs in the colonial age, the Bengali primer was a document that recorded the presence of mind in investing whatever advantages one could extract from the benevolence of the master after altering and improving upon it according to one's needs. Likewise, it was the deed proceeding to establish the supremacy of the middle class over the lower strata after assimilating the authority of upper-class society. At the same time, the primers were also signifiers of the structural inadequacy of exercising hierarchical domination.

It is well known that no matter how tight the knot, there will always be loose ends. It is of great satisfaction that the book in which this dangerous signal is most clear is a text meant for children. This book – immensely popular and blessed in the support it got from people – was *Barna Parichay* (1855) by Vidyasagar. In it there is Gopal, the representative of the disciplined, focused, modest, patient body of students. And all about him is Rakhal, the representative of the undisciplined, inattentive, restless, riotous group of students. This very Rakhal is a relic of the inadequacy and restrictedness of the intelligence of respectable grown-ups in the discourse of constructing a colonial gentleman. There is not the slightest doubt of the impossibility of determining beforehand what expression Rakhal's 'Rakhalness' would assume, and what its political trajectory would be. Rakhal is not incarcerated in any static image because he is embedded in a possible narrative of *contingency* rather than in a historicist narrative of *becoming*. Actually, Rakhal's image is so much a thing of the future, so fragile in its constitution, so malleable, that it can be made to appear time and again on the stage of history in different masks and garbs.

It is no wonder, therefore, that in 1895, during a revolutionary moment of turnabout in Swadeshi thought, paying his due respect to Vidyasagar wholeheartedly, Rabindranath vehemently rejected the much eulogized Gopal of *Barna Parichay* in favour of warmly welcoming the much-maligned Rakhal. He said:

'There is no doubt that the good, well brought up boys will pass out, get good jobs, and earn lots of dowry during their marriage. But we can expect a lot more from bad, disobedient, restless boys [like Rakhal] for the sake of their country.'

There is nothing to be surprised about even sociologist Benoy Ghosh having written, in *Bidyasagar o Bangali Samaj* (1957–59), that in the Gopal–Rakhal story of *Barna Parichay* lies concealed an important link that serves as an introduction to that society. One can claim that there has been a continual expansion of the very 'link' about which Benoy Ghosh had given an indistinct hint. Its manifest evidence is Jogindranath Sarkar's *Hashi Khushi* (Part 1, 1897; Part 2, 1904); Rabindranath's three primers *Sanskritshiksha* (1896), *Ingreji Sahajshiksha* (1930), *Sahaj Paath* (1930); and elsewhere, a direct battle with *Barna Parichay.* There is an affectionate indulgence towards the unruliness of the transparent Rakhals, and a comprehensive critique of the servility of the frank Gopal-like boys. Apart from this, an added accomplishment was the innumerable manifest evidences of the 'link' on the subject of 'introducing society' in the Gopal–Rakhal story. All this is distributed across Bengali literature that has been composed for children.

Reflecting a little, one can sense the covert references to the dual stars, Gopal and Rakhal, in the nooks and crannies of this repository. In the defence as well as in the critique of the *bhadra* 'moral economy', one comes across citations of Vidyasagar's Janus-faced construct. This binary opposition is the mainstay of the narrative intended for the moral uplift of the childlike subjects of the colonies. However, strangely, precisely because of that, many wondrous things happened in the domain of Bengali 'children's literature'. For instance:

1. Although *shishu sahitya* is a synonym for children's literature, the intended readers of Bengali children's literature are not just 'children'. It warmly welcomes everyone from boys and girls, young men and women to old men and women. In this context, Buddhadeb Basu observes that one often realizes that although the writer has written primarily or ostensibly for children, even mature readers are not beyond their intended readership ('Bangla Shishusahitya', *Sahityacharcha*, 1954).
2. In the modern Bengali language, the interface of a hard and fast demarcation between the writings marked 'adult' and 'children' is quite fragile and blurred. Its glaring proof is that there is no writer in Bengali who has not tried her/his hand at composing rhymes, poems, essays, stories, plays and novels for so-called immature readers. Besides, most writers worth their salt were dedicated to writing chiefly for the entertainment of children and adolescents. Who is not there in that long list?

   Let us prepare a catalogue (years and dates are jumbled): Gyanandanandini Debi, Rabindranath Tagore, Akshay Kumar Dutta, Sibnath Shastri, Dakshinaranjan Mitra Majumdar, Upendra Kishore Roy Choudhury, Jagadananda Roy, Jogindranath Sarkar, Sukumar Roy, Sukhalata Rao,

Lila Majumdar, Anandashankar Ray, Sibram Chakraborty, Kuladaranjan Ray, Kazi Nazrul Islam, Jaladhar Sen, Girindrasekhar Basu, Premendra Mitra, Buddhadeb Basu, Kamakshi Prasad Chattopadhyay, Narendranath Mitra, Banaphul, Achintya Kumar Sen Gupta, Ashapurna Debi, Narayan Gangopadhyay, Sunirmal Basu, Gaganendranath Tagore, Syed Mustafa Ali, Bibhutibhushan Bandyopadhyay, Saratchandra Chattopadhyay, Tarashankar Bandyopadhyay, Manik Bandyopadhyay, Khagendranath Mitra, Dhirendralal Dhar, Manoranjan Bhattacharya, Hemendra Kumar Roy, Shailajanandan Mukhopadhyay, Narendra Deb, Kshitindranath Bhattacharya, Hemendralal Roy, Sourindra Mohan Mukhopadhyay, Prabhavati Debi Saraswati, Manabendra Bandyopadhyay, Gita Bandyopadhyay, Sisir Kumar Das, Manilal Gangopadhyay, Mohanlal Gangopadhyay, Trailokyanath Mukhopadhyay, Nabaneeta Deb Sen, Bande Ali Mian, Gajendra Kumar Mitra, Ajit Krishna Basu, Nripendra Krishna Chattopadhyay, Nihar Ranjan Gupta, Bidhayak Bhattacharya, Sukumar De Sarkar, Nalini Das, Shailesh Ghosh, Saradindu Bandyopadhyay, Mahasweta Devi, Syed Mustafa Siraj, Shirshendu Mukhopadhyay, Amarendra Chakraborty, Sunil Gangopadhyay, Tarapada Ray, Sankha Ghosh, Subhash Mukhopadhyay, P.C. Sarkar, Satyajit Ray, Abanindranath Thakur . . . to place a full stop to that inventory is impossible.

Alongside, it is also worth our attention that those who undertook the task of illustration or book designing in order to amuse and entertain the little ones were also not negligible in either numbers or in artistic talent. Even if all of them are not equally gifted, who can leave out the following from the list of illustrators (though chronologically jumbled again)? Upendrakishore Roy Chowdhury, Dakshinaranjan Mitra Majumdar, Rabindranath Tagore, Nandalal Basu, Purnachandra Chakrabarti, Krishnendu Chaki, Purnachandra Ghosh, Abanindranath Tagore, Asit Kumar Haldar, Subrata Choudhuri, Harishchandra Haldar, Ramkinkar Baij, Benodebihari Mukherjee, Pratulchandra Lahiri (Kafi Khan), Sukumar Roy, Ahibhushan Malik, Debabrata Ghosh, Shaila Chakrabarti, Phani Gupta, Samar De, Makhan Datta Gupta, Pratul Bandyopadhyay, Anup Ray, Jatindra Kumar Sen, Debashish Deb, Narayan Debnath, Mayukh Choudhury, Sudhir Maitra, Samir Sarkar, Subrata Gangopadhyay, Sayan Chattopadhyay, Bimal Das, Jayanta Ghosh, Raghunath Goswami, Purnendu Patri, Satyajit Ray, Ganesh Pyne.

3. Bengali children's literature is not controlled by a group of professional writers. Consequently, it has never been presented in different kinds of packaging based on computing figures related to the respective age of readers, and taking into consideration predetermined theories about childlike sensibilities. For this very reason, that literature has not really needed a plain and simple style of narration customized to entertain imaginary lit-

tle boys and girls. It has not had to put up too much with the unbearable onslaught of linguistic mollycoddling and the most cloying of sickly-sweet styles of narration. Because the fluidity of language is not arrested, an extended context has easily been attained there that is also represented in poetry and narratives composed for the consumption of adults. For this reason, Nirendranath Chakrabarti has said: 'One has to think of the Bengali language as a great exception because unlike other literatures, there has never been an attempt to artificially divide our literature into children's writers and adult writers' ('Amader Shishusahitya o Nabaneeta', *Chhotoder Galpa Samagra* by Nabaneeta Deb Sen, 2004). Thanks to there being no trace of that insulting artificiality in the delightful poems in Rabindranath's *Shishu* (*The Child*), there is no dearth of poems in Bengali which do *not* undermine their little adressees. In the works of the brilliant Lila Majumdar, Ashapurna Debi, Khagendranath Mitra and others, there is an unbiased discussion of the duplicitous practices and conventions of the adult world that go against any logic that children can perceive. In the works of the vivacious Premendra Mitra, Kshitindranath Bhattacharya, Satyajit Ray and others, there are interesting investigations of scientific myths. In the works of the exceptional Narayan Gangopadhyay, Kamakshiprasad Chattopadhyay, Rabindralal Ray, Manoranjan Bhattacharya, Sunirmal Basu and others, there is provision for chatty, relaxed, clean entertainment, although the perspective, in many cases, is critical. And, most amazing, under that very canopy is spread a no-holds-barred exhibition, at times bared in all its irrepressibility, of every kind of twisting and beating, trimming and expansion, pulling and wrenching and reverse runs of prose actions and verse movements in the creative anthologies of Rabindranath's *Shishu Bholanath – Shey – Galpashalpa – Chhelebela*, or Abanindranath's *Jatrapala*, or the collections of Sibram Chakraborty's nonsense stories, or Sukumar Roy's *Khai-Khai – Abol Tabol – Ha-Ja-ba-ra-la – Chalachittachanchari*. One cannot amuse children by imaginary tales that are meant to delude. In fact meaningless obstacles are placed in the way of their growth and development by these. This commandment is so interiorized in a fraction of Bengali children's literature that it is not difficult for Lila Majumdar to comment: 'Those children's books that do not get the approval of mature adults are not first-rate children's literature. Adults should also like good children's books. In fact, this is the real test of children's books' (*Sukumar Roy*, 1981).

The net result is that in the incipient years of colonialism, in one segment of Bengali children's literature, in a hurry to fashion respectable adults out of children, we have a repository of heaps of good counsel on improving their mental health; on the other hand, in its other and stronger segment, there are innumerable examples of audacious Rakhaldom that can shock out of their complacency the Gopals who are absorbed in the difficult project of growing into well-brought-up adults. So many examples – or one may say bad examples – of straying from the norm give rise to a kind of curiosity. What form do all those crowds of people, unknown customs and rituals, other lifestyles, etc., towards which there exists either cold contempt or, at best, an enforced civil tolerance (and a genuine middle-class sensibility is unimaginable without these), acquire in Rakhal-centric narratives? What impact does the dynamic weaving of the home and the world, thanks to which the abstract image of the woman has been embedded at the essential core of Bengali modernity, have on girls in stories that are saturated with Rakhals? Although directly confronting or secretly resisting complacent *bhadralok*dom, despite many radically propitious suggestions, for the most part of Bengali children's literature there is no compromise, apparent or oblique, between the good boy Gopal and the unruly Rakhal. The spectral presence of Gopal-in-the-guise-of-Rakhal does not, in fact, accompany the phantom of the anarchic onslaught of Rakhal-in-the-garb-of-Gopal. A question that follows from this is whether it is due to the unconscious repercussion of that hidden *entente* that we forget that there was the suggestion of a new dawn even within the construction of the image of Gopal? Gopal is emblematic of the forces that countered the *babu*, the species sponsored by the East India Company and its Permanent Settlement Act of 1793, a species that drew its sustenance by severely oppressing the peasants. In short, Gopal represents the *bhadralok* class positioned against the *babu*s. Gopal, therefore, stands for people who are contesting the claims of birth, and so-called destinies, on the strength of education alone. It is redundant to say that this education became mechanical very soon and the blue-bloodedness of the newborn *bhadralok* quickly posed innumerable obstructive barricades at every turn of the path of social mobility for others. Along with this, there is a deeper anxiety about whether the many liberal Rakhals of Bengali children's literature are not partners in the same ritual of obstruction. Politically relevant to date, this anxiety is at the root of *Gopal–Rakhal*.

The discussion of *Gopal–Rakhal Dvandasamas* is limited to the colonial age; many of the writers mentioned above, therefore, do not find a place in it. Even after independence and partition, there was a growing market for children's literature in West Bengal for quite a few decades. But when I started writing *Gopal–Rakhal* at the end of the 1980s, it was quite evident that the market was on the decline. And today, at least in the upper-class Bengali society that is well-versed in English, the sub-genre of Bengali children's literature has become virtually extinct. In the twilight years of the colony, child-centric practices suggested a modern catalogue of performances that was a self-representation provoked by self-contradiction. Right now, it seems somewhat that at least in the higher reaches of society, in the temptation to become 'global', in the successively anxious and intense obsessive love with the universal language English, not even a trace of that agenda remains. In order to filter and absorb this heartrending emptiness, perhaps we will have to take recourse to neocolonial psychological theories. Irrespective of how we assess the damage, there is not the slightest doubt that what Rabindranath had written regretfully 117 years ago, in the sixth lesson of the primer *Sanskritshiksha, Part II* (1896) – 'Only Gopal returns. Others do not' – is a regret that is bereft of meaning now. Today's Gopal, bereft of closeness to the devious Rakhal and having been rendered historically irrelevant, is such an unadulterated and independent Gopal that no matter how he might have multiplied in number, no similarly intense and conflicting dramatic situation can be scripted around him.

Behind this revised edition of *Gopal–Rakhal Dvandasamas* lies the assistance and encouragement of many people. Among those who are in the ranks of my mentors are Manabendra Bandyopadhyay, Amiya Deb, Malini Bhattacharya, Sourin Bhattacharya, Himani Bandyopadhyay, Subir Roy Choudhury, Ratnabali Chattopadhyay, Jasodhara Bagchi, Swapan Majumdar, Nabaneeta Deb Sen, Hayat Mahmood, Tirthankar Chattopadhyay, Sankha Ghosh and Ashok Sen. I am privileged in having poet-professor Sankha Ghosh write the Foreword which has been appended to this edition. By formally thanking him, I would certainly discredit the honour I have gained by that graceful gesture.

The preliminary drafts of quite a few chapters in the book were printed in *Baromaas*, edited by Ashok Sen and *Prama*, edited by Surajit Ghosh. The indulgence and generosity of the two editors is unforgettable. The post-script section is a modest testimonial that after its publication, apart from being subjected to several candid critiques, *Gopal–Rakhal Dvandasamas* has received its share of acclaim from several people. [This section has not been included in the English translation, but a selection from here has been reproduced on the back of the book's jacket – Translators.]

The index for the first edition had been prepared by Subimal Lahiri; for the second edition, it has been done by my student Agniv Ghosh. The list of people to whom I am grateful is quite long. I must have left out many; even so, I mention a few of those who were involved with the Papyrus and Karigar editions: Aparup Ukil, Abhijit Sen, Arijit Kumar, Arjun Sen Gupta, Ananda Mukhopadhyay, Indranil Mukhopadhyay, Kasturi Chakrabarti, Nandita Sen, Maharghya Chakraborty, Anirban Mallik, Nandini Kundu, Sankha Bandyopadhyay, Satyaki Kundu, Shobhan Tarafdar and Suchetana Chattopadhyay. It would, of course, be ungrateful of me not to mention the names of Debashish Sau of Karigar, and my friend Somnath Ghosh, the artist and cover designer for the current edition.

August 2013 SIBAJI BANDYOPADHYAY

Translators' Note & Acknowledgements

Like many others who have read this mammoth, pathbreaking treatise in the original Bengali, we thought it deserves to have a readership beyond the Bengali-reading coterie that it was originally meant for, and undertook the daunting task of jointly translating it. But this work would never have got going without the unqualified confidence reposed in us as the book's translators by Sibaji Bandyopadhyay, its author. Through all the vicissitudes that the translation has undergone, Sibaji has responded to every doubt or query we have raised, and shown us light at the end of the tunnel when we have occasionally been cluelessly groping in the dark. He has relentlessly and rigorously worked at reshaping the text according to the Bengali edition that came out in 2013, midway through our translatory enterprise. But even Sibaji could not have done all this within his hectic academic schedule without the constant support, cooperation and assistance of Maharghya Chakraborty and Agniv Ghosh, Ph.D. scholars attached to the Centre for Studies in Social Sciences, Calcutta. A warm thank you to both of them for their painstaking contribution to the English text. We are honoured to have the cover of the book designed by the eminent artist Sankha Banerjee, with the able assistance of Rajarshi Dutta. We also thank Somnath Ghosh, another reputed artist, for procuring the visuals reproduced in the text.

Indu Chandrasekhar of Tulika Books readily agreed to publish the work without once questioning or vetting our competence as translators. Ever since she took on the project, she has patiently guided us at every step apropos the logistics of producing this kind of text, and how it can be made reader-friendly for a wide network of non-Bengali readers, even those who are unacquainted with the language at all. We are very grateful to Arun Kirketta of Tulika who bore with our demands for the last two years, and did a thorough job of formatting, typesetting and correcting the manuscript according to our instructions.

This book could never have seen the light of day in its present form without the original inspiration and translation of a major portion of chapter 5 by Rimli Bhattacharya. It was in 2003 that Rimli requested me (Nivedita) to jointly translate with her chapter 5 of this book, for the annual journal of the Department of English, Delhi University. That is what got the ball rolling, and eventually made us want to rewrite Sibaji's text in English for a number of scholars, critics and academics who have been craving to read it. Needless to say, Rimli's translation of a sizeable section of that chapter has been retained here virtually with no alterations. She has been extremely generous in letting us use that excerpt without actually being acknowledged as a translator of this work; herein we are exceedingly grateful to her, and credit her for rendering our effort that much easier and swifter.

New Delhi
July 2015

RANI RAY & NIVEDITA SEN

Prologue

> Gopal is a conscientious boy; he does whatever his parents tell him to do . . . he does not play on the streets while going to school; arriving at school he takes his own seat in class, listens attentively to the new lessons his teacher introduces. . . . He never neglects his studies. . . . [Gopal] does not for a single day quarrel or have a fight with anyone . . . whosoever comes across him immediately takes to him. All children ought to be like Gopal.
>
> Rakhal is not inclined to be as responsible as Gopal. He does what he likes; does not listen to what his parents tell him; plays on the streets on his way to take lessons. Rakhal is very inattentive when it comes to learning. He does not put his mind to his books even for a single day and cannot repeat his lessons even once. He starts a quarrel with everyone and beats people up when it is time to play. Nobody loves Rakhal; nobody ought to be like him. If one becomes like him one will never learn how to read or write.[1]

Gopal and Rakhal appear time and again, by other names, in Parts 1 and 2 of Ishwarchandra Vidyasagar's Bengali primer, *Barna Parichay*; Sushil and Yadav, Ram and Bhuvan are their kin. And we may easily regard the ideal, good boy Gopal and the ill-natured, naughty Rakhal as representative prototypes of each other's complementary selves.

As the perimeters of the prototypes are definite, so too the division between the two is distinct. It is well-nigh impossible for these children of the world of *Barna Parichay* to inhabit, permanently and at the same time, each other's universe. As much as there is a laying out of a perfect pattern – or exact conditions – for the observance of rules that would make a child deserving of the honour of the appellation 'good', so too it is clearly stated as to who will have the absolute authority of judging in such cases. Primarily and most importantly, the conditions are two-fold: the ideal child should be deserving of the confidence of his parents on the one hand, and his teachers on the other.

Elders always do what is good for children. Guided by this *a priori* truth, and reposing trust in the wisdom, circumspection and goodwill of their mentors, children should blindly follow all the commands and advice doled out to them. Among the many conditions laid out in Vidyasagar's text, it is possible to identify the above two as more important for their recurrent allusion. In Vidyasagar's understanding, the relationship between the young and the elders is a type of social contract as it were. The young are quite helpless; there is no other way for them but to rely on their parents' compassion. Therefore, in return for the parents' goodwill and maintenance, blind devotion and unqualified obedience are demanded of the young. Thus: 'If they do not out of pity give you shelter, provide you with food and clothing, your misery would have no end. Therefore, you must never ever disobey your parents.' If one digs a little deeper into the implications of such injunctions, it becomes apparent that compared to the father's role, that of the mother is relatively insignificant. In the arena of domestic politics the father reigns supreme; it is to him that one is liable to give explanations in case of any breach of contract. But there is one other who is most powerfully present in the universe of the children of *Barna Parichay*, and that is the father-like figure of the teacher. Like the father, the teacher too keeps a strict vigil so that the rules laid down as a necessary foundation for becoming a good girl/boy in the future are properly complied with.

All the conditions imposed on the young of the universe of *Barna Parichay* are infallible, irrevocable and without exception. The whys and wherefores of an offence are not matters of adjudication; and, in the eyes of the authorities, any failure to strictly abide by the given rules and commands is an unforgivable dereliction. Not even a minor deviation on the part of the young escapes the notice of the authorities in this rigid and compact system. The father and the teacher together hold a tight rein over the family and the school – the two distinct arenas under their control.

However, it is possible for the children of *Barna Parichay* – either Gopal or Rakhal as the case may be – to change places and to become the other; the thoroughfare between these two prototypes is forever open. It is possible for Gopal to forget his true calling and become a Rakhal, and for Rakhal to ascend to Gopal's world through exercises in self-improvement. And Vidyasagar has provided us with quite a few instances of such transformation in Jadab or Nabin. Noticeably, neither caste nor class is an impediment in the crossing over to Gopal's world.

Of course, fear and a sense of insecurity rather than any strong desire to be good urge the minds of the young of *Barna Parichay*: an apprehension that in case of a breach of contract, the other may not be willing to confess her/his culpability. And that such apprehensions are not totally unfounded is borne out by the abundance of examples provided by several sections of *Barna Parichay*. Madhab is a thrilling example of the fall from the condition of Gopal into the state of Rakhal. At the beginning Madhab is quiet and good like Gopal; but soon there is a change in his mentality and, driven out by both father and teacher as a result, he suffers untold misery. Tormented by acute hunger, he goes from door to door crying out for food; but no one shows him any sympathy or compassion. The two main monitors of the young, father and teacher, have the power to both banish the guilty for dereliction of duty and reward the obedient with hope of bounty. Therefore, both the expectation of being rewarded and the fear of being rusticated reside in the minds of the children of *Barna Parichay*.

Time and again Vidyasagar reminds us that those who study hard live happily ever after. It is no wonder, then, that out of 239 verb forms (both transitive and intransitive) in *Barna Parichay*, about 25 are forms of the infinitive 'to read'. And yet Vidyasagar does not give us any reasonable explanation for this happiness. On the contrary, he shows that if one is unmindful of this *a priori* truth, then one would have to bear the entire burden of its consequences; that one would have to suffer terrible misfortune if one does not follow, literally word for word, the necessary rules for the practices of learning, and in the end become like Madhab or Bhuban – marginalized outcasts of society. As if the world of *Barna Parichay* is a *tabula rasa* carrying no traces of history, no signs of hearkening back to the past – only the promise of setting out anew.

'Gopal' and 'Rakhal' appear not only in Vidyasagar's *Barna Parichay*; they are omnipresent in the entire corpus of Bengali children's literature. They appear and reappear in different names, in different shapes and in different guises. And the conflict between the two prototypes remains one of the most discussed and staple subjects of nineteenth- and twentieth-century children's literature in Bengal. Therefore, if one does not care to know the identifiable characteristics of the good boy and the bad boy, one will not be able to analyse the characteristics, or the reach, scope and variety, of that literature. Therefore, in what ensues, our two main queries are:

(1) Are the two prototypes of Gopal and Rakhal true of all places and for all times, or are they only relevant for a particular historical time and a specific society?

(2) What is the mutual relationship between Gopal and Rakhal?

The first chapter of this book deals with the impulse and creativity behind myth formation. The word 'myth' is used not to denote a kind of historical narrative but to refer to a de-historicized form of utterance. A discussion of the processes and uses of myth formation is followed by the subject of the deconstruction of myth, which could become an impossible task if one fails to unearth the hidden linkages between myth and history, or situate myth in the context of time and space. In continuance of the exploration of the social, political and economic scenario of colonial Bengal (in the concluding pages of chapter 1), chapter 2 discusses *Thakurmar Jhuli* and *Thakurdadar Jhuli*, two major collections of contemporary Bengali folktales, with a focus on their context and content as well as the response they elicited from their upper-class readers. Chapter 3 charts the evolution of the policy of education under British rule, highlighting stories written around the institution of the school. Literary representations of interpersonal relationships between family members, inclusive of servants, within the domestic space are taken up next, in chapter 4. Broadening the canvas, chapter 5 includes an analysis of both English and Bengali tales of adventures experienced by the young as they move beyond the jurisdiction of the family. Chapter 6 discusses how in the literary works of Rabindranath Tagore, Abanindranath Tagore, Sukumar Roy and Sibram Chakraborty – especially for children – the language is infused with humour produced by the play of sounds. The epilogue is concerned with a detailed discussion of Rabindranath Tagore's *Sahaj Path*.

Notes and References

[1] Ishwarchandra Vidyasagar, *Barna Parichay, Part 1*, in *Bidyasagar Rachanasamagra* (*Collected Works of Vidyasagar*), Calcutta, 1987, p. 22.

[2] Ibid., pp. 22–23.

[3] Pabitra Sarkar, 'Barnaparichay theke Kishalay: Banglar Primarer Nanadik', in *Bhasha Desh Kal*, Calcutta, 1392 (Bengali calendar), p. 110.

1

Myth and History

I

The world is sonorous dear, deathly arrows will strike you, coming from the very direction you have plugged off the sounds.[1]

– Rabindranath Tagore

Man is by nature a wordsmith. He goes on weaving words, one word over another word, word coalescing with word, entangled with yet another – and this eternal weaving of words only complicates the pattern. Words are produced in different shapes, created in different ways – at times by sounds, tunes and lines, at times by gestures. The exchange of words carried on by men among themselves, either openly or unobserved, is also diverse in manner. It is well-nigh impossible to analyse such diversity by the help of certain clues, even though, in the context of words or language, a thousand and one opinions have been manufactured. I have chosen from among these two opposing opinions that are contextual to my argument.

The Contradiction between Language and *Langue* (or Linguistics)

There has been in currency for a long time a certain notion regarding 'language', both generally and in a specific branch of linguistic analysis. According to this widely circulated and popularized opinion, language is nothing more than a vehicle for personal utterance. This notion developed under the aegis of a certain philosophy of individualism which, by valorizing personal freedom, has influenced the entire world. According to this philosophy, unbounded creativity is natural to the self and this form of creativity is as applicable to language as it is to other forms of artistic activity. In other words, there are no fundamental differences between the practitioners of language and art, the only difference being one of degree. To the proponents of this view, the immense creative potential of language is inextricably linked to individual expressiveness. Consequently, they do not feel the need to look beyond individual taste and ideology when attempting to understand the 'whats' and 'whys' of a plethora of utterances. They feel that it is possible to use the same structure of arguments in order to explain both individual psychology and linguistic character. There is, however, a simple argument against such a simplistic methodological assumption, which is that every individual is unique; and in their zealous quest to give this truth its due respect, these philosophers forget that human beings do not exist *ab nihilio* – cut off from all social relations. Having forgotten this plain truth, they render the human being into a disembodied concept divorced from reality. The self-regulated, self-sufficient, isolated individual whose valorization is endemic to Romanticism has much in common with the subject of this asymptotic individualistic linguistics. The problem being that, at least in the sphere of language, there is no longer an easy way to combat the audacious claim that all utterances are personal. The paradox is that these complications have been created by a school of linguistics which itself is anti-Romantic.

A second branch of linguistic analysis, on the other hand, refuses to admit the plentitude of utterances as a subject of analysis. For the proponents of this view, utterances are engendered in such numbers and so relentlessly that their documentation/ recording is endless and hence rather pointless. Thus no idea can be formed about the rules and regulations of language if one only follows the apparently whimsical, subjective *parole*. Their advice to all who wish to explore the science of language is to disregard random individual utterances and concentrate on a more general pattern; to be wary of the nebulous, confusing terrain of varied utterances and, instead, take cautious stock of the notion of *structure*. Structuralism is central to this point of view. No matter the diversity in individual utterances, no matter how arbitrary and subjective their movements, all this is ultimately bounded by certain fixed rules and, apparently, free utterances are slave to certain limits: *parole* is always pre-determined by *langue*. Thus, individual utterance is a surface phenomenon that is always already regulated by the *meta-language* of the *langue*. In a way, the *langue–parole* binary resembles the famous binary of the immutable, eternal 'soul' and the mutable, transient 'body'. Consequently, *langue* is nothing but an accretion of certain general and already ascertained rules, like those of customs, rituals and fixed patterns, and the rules and regulations of grammar. In other words, *langue* is an assimilation of certain ideal and identical language forms. Since it is the host for all established and limiting norms, no utterance can escape its silent vigilance. Much like the 'Permanent Settlement' (of Bengal), language must pay its taxes to *langue*. Even if the speaker is not an inactive, helpless agent, or a mere tool, in the last instance, all subjective utterances are but distorted semblances of the ideal language form that is *langue*.

In 1929, V.N. Vološinov (1895–1936), a contemporary of the celebrated thinker Mikhail Bakhtin (1895–1975), published the book *Marxism and the Philosophy of Language*. Vološinov did not deny the fact that humanity possesses many streams of thought regarding language. Still, for purposes of explication, he chose the two aforementioned schools. He did this not for the sake of arriving at an easy summary but because of two contradictory points of view being exemplary by dint of their proponents. Due to their relentless use in the arena of language, these two schools – Romantic and anti-Romantic – have now emerged as paradigms, with all other modern views emerging from their conflict.

Vološinov identified Wilhelm von Humboldt (1767–1835) – theorist of law, historian, classical linguist, a leading figure in the comparative study of ancient languages, the first exponent of the philosophical intervention of the *Gita* in the west – as the ideologue of the Romantic trend. In the thought-system of the German savant Humboldt, Vološinov found the germ of an individualistic language science. On the other hand, Vološinov chose Ferdinand de Saussure (1857–1913) as the chief figure of the anti-Romantic structuralist trend. It was Saussure's book, *Course in General Linguistics* (posthumously published in 1916) – in which was anthologized the remarkable theorem of Saussure, the Swiss linguist who was well-versed in Sanskrit and Panini – that was considered the most topical among the Russian linguists of the 1920s.

Vološinov termed the two trends, one set in motion by Humboldt and the other by Saussure, as 'individualistic subjectivism' and 'abstract objectivism' respectively. One of Vološinov's central observations was that in spite of differences in approach, these two trends are indistinguishable in the field of the theory of knowledge. Since the subjectivists are capable of regarding language as an activity, they are also capable of giving due importance to the history of language itself. Thus, no matter whether other equations upset the applecart, the point of view of subjectivism faces no difficulty in exploring mobility, sequence and complex changes in language. That is, in the subjectivist trend, the stress is on the temporal dimension of language and not the spatial. On the other hand, since the supporters of objectivism are more concerned with the inner workings of language than with its substance, obviously neither the slow movement of the said substance nor the behavioural changes of language come to their attention. That is, in the objectivist trend, it is not the temporal but the spatial that is stressed.[2]

Vološinov's complaint, following the mind–matter split proposed by French mathematician–philosopher René Descartes (1596–1650), is that this separation between the temporal and the spatial has rendered the notions of subject and subjectivity similarly dualistic. Even if the two streams have numerous dissonances, they are ultimately reflections of each other: while the first displays 'voluntarism' in excess, the second valorizes determinism. What thus remains unacknowledged is either the individual's social relations or the social being's individualism.

Therefore, for Vološinov, language is neither a mobile, self-sufficient entity, an aggregate of multiple individual realizations, nor an object bounded by the dictums of *langue*. Rather, a new linguistics must be thought of that takes both the spatial and the temporal into account without a split between them – much like the time–space continuum advocated in physics by Albert Einstein (1879–1955). *Marxism and the Philosophy of Language* presented a rough draft of this idea in 1929. Unfortunately, Vološinov fell foul of the orthodox Marxists of the Soviet Union of that time and, like many others in the third decade of the twentieth century, he was sacrificed at the ruthless altar of Stalinist silencing. *Marxism and the Philosophy of Language* almost disappeared from the public eye. Only members of the Prague Linguistic Circle of Czechoslovakia, outside the Soviet Union, managed to keep Vološinov's fading memory alive. In 1973, when the English translation of the book was published, a wider circle of readers became aware of his alternative thought. By then Structuralism had firmly established itself; in fact, Post-structuralism was gradually strengthening its foothold. And, in spite of the immense gap in time, perhaps due to the new atmosphere of thought, the value of Vološinov's revolutionary thinking became enhanced.

Vološinov's central assertion is that language itself is deconstructive; it is a kind of exchange system where there is an indissoluble link between the narrator and the audience, the sender and the addressee of a message. For this reason, it is not the detached 'sentence' but the 'utterance' that may be regarded as an individual unit for linguistic analysis. The significance of the utterance being determined by the respective social situations and perspectives of both the sender and the addressee, and by their continuing subject of discussion, goes to mean that all utterances are dualistic in nature. To say something is to say it to someone else. No utterance is totally aimless. Even when man thinks to himself, he is not totally disassociated in all those inner, intimate self-reflexive moments; his monologues are actually directed outside of self. Since conversation and dialogue are the main resorts of language, it is not possible in any situation to do away with all links to the external world. Besides, there is no qualitative difference between the inner and the outer world of man. This is because of a long-standing cultural habit which similarly compels us to regard the home and the world as separate and independent spaces. However, language is both the primary repository of the psyche and an image of social relationships for it must contain the indelible print of social interchange. Language not only bestows expressive form to experience, it also helps to shape that experience. It is also not the exclusive property of a class or a section of society. All men included in the family of language exert their rights over it – to a smaller or larger degree. For this reason, language turns into a battlefield for class conflict and for all kinds of clashes taking place continuously, either openly or away from public gaze. It is not that there is a clear indication of this at any historical juncture or at certain moments of crisis, but even in its so-called quiet and languid chapter, language carries imprints of many conflicts and ideological differences. Unless one remains alert and sensitive to issues, one will not be able to cognize the various discordant voices, the blows and counter-blows of the oppositional forces embedded in language.

We are now entering the arena of a special kind of speech and we will see that even though all the general qualities pertaining to language also apply to it, at first glance (taking off from Vološinov), this is not how it may appear.

The Construction of Myth

It must be declared at the very outset that we are not using the word *myth* here in terms of a conventional plot such as in the ancient epic, but in terms of its special use as a type of speech or 'utterance', or, more especially, as it holds in the Levi-Strauss/Barthian way of thinking. The subject of our discussion is the multifarious uses and purpose of the construction of myth. But first, what is myth?

Myth as Speech against Itself

A dialogue cannot be carried on meaningfully if equal theoretical importance is not given to both the sender and the addressee of the message. If the path connecting the two does not remain free and open, the dialogue cannot develop in stages but must come to a sudden halt at one place or another. And if there are no interchanges between the two parties, the dialogue cannot develop; rather, it might produce discontinuity in a continuous field and result in speech that is fixed and unchanging – a kind of speech that is not amenable to deconstruction and therefore not befitting dialogue. We bestow the appellation *myth* to this kind of unilateral, univocal speech. Myth is by its nature inflexible and exceptional, reluctant to entertain any alternate voice. It would not be possible for myth to preserve its orderly/skilful patterning if it did not consign to oblivion the idea of the real world as multilayered, and as pervaded by conflicting and contradictory voices; if it did not completely ignore the possibility that an opinion or an attitude is always subjective. If we go a step further, this means that speech carrying the nomenclature 'myth' is at its roots self-contradictory and open to deconstruction. In spite of being a kind of utterance, it step by step dismisses its primary condition, brushing under the carpet the question of the shareholding relation or the partnership between sender and addressee that any utterance would necessarily signify. And, because of this, the world of myth can never become multivocal and variegated. Myth is synonymous with authoritative – *a priori*, closed or fixed – speech or even a slogan. It may take different shapes but at rock bottom, its basic pattern or arrangement never alters. It is almost impossible for one to enter the universe of myth unless one is willing to accept, without a murmur, some of its absolute conditions and unchanging truths. In that universe there may exist dispute or inequality between the sender and the addressee; the first party may entangle the second in an unequal relationship of power, but even the sender would remain to the last a mere bearer of a message and nothing more than that.

According to the terminology of Roland Barthes (1915–1980), myth is a kind of second language, a kind of weed growing around the basic language.[3] All signs are products of the 'sound-image' or 'signifier', and 'object' or 'signified'. The relationship between the signifier and the signified is entirely arbitrary. This Saussurian postulation takes on bizarre dimensions in the case of myth. Take, for example, the term 'black man': the two words have come to signify people of a certain colour. In the realm of myth, this sign becomes a signifier which, coming together with a new signified, produces a new mythic sign. In colonial times the 'black man' did not remain just a 'black man' but implied all kinds of illiteracy and barbarity. The power of the mythic sign is such that it makes it impossible to recognize the original sign. Myth is polysemic in the coexistence of several meanings, and although it dilutes the original meaning of the sign, it does not have any inhibitions in this regard and is forever hospitable to even an original sign that may cross over to its territory. It is also possible to find that a combination of several myths may have been the *fons et origo* of an original sign. But in all cases, the signified gains precedence or the upper hand over the signifier, and the dominance of the signified over the signifier is one of the necessary conditions of myth formation. Myth is not a mere sign, it is also an unalterable signal. And the relation between signifier and signified is so fast, so inseparable, that the mythic signified is transcendental, unalterable.

If myth is on the one hand against itself, on the other it is inclined towards domination. Its second role is rather conspicuous in societies comparatively less complex. There, *a priori* truths hallowed by memory take on the role of different social directives. In order for the same edicts to remain socially operative for ages to come, or for the idea of the normative right to be and for the sense of propriety to remain eternally in force in social consciousness, a relentless recitation of incantatory speeches is called for. And sentences encasing such presumptive truths keep warning us against moral turpitude. Thus the objective reality slips away from the material world in the same proportion as myth takes over its realm.

Myth as Self-sufficient Speech

We have seen that in the world of myth there is no place for utterance in its own right – to say anything at all in the context of myth is merely to repeat an already ordered speech. Both the sender and the addressee have no role except to identify their respective predetermined places within a fixed verbal pattern – as if myth were a self-sufficient entity detached from the outside world and it is not necessary to step outside its perimeter in order to evaluate its status; as if myth is regulated by myth itself and all other computations do not hold; as if the universe of myths radiates with their own independent selfhoods in all their significance and glory. All this taken together makes myth a self-sufficient, self-regulative, self-directed and self-referential meaning system. But alongside, since myth as speech is both against itself and self-destructive, it is obliged to alter under external pressure as much as it tends to remain irrevocable. Which means that despite all assurances of stability, no myth can remain intact or unscathed; caught in the skirmishes and conflicts of the real world, it cannot preserve its so-called stable form. Now, let us identify the skill of execution that has produced this tight, unitary system.

Repeated utterance or tautology

Since the movement of myth is from the signified to the signifier and not its opposite, there is no other way but to take recourse to a counter-argument. It becomes necessary to manufacture a counterfeit semblance of causality in order to create the delusion of infallibility. If A happens, then B has to be; any scrutiny of an elaboration of such reasoning would reveal that there is no necessary connection between the two, that the gap between A and B can only be bridged if one resorts to blind faith, and that only a belief in divine intervention exceeding all rational explanation can lead one to draw a line linking the two. We would see that no matter what the intention of the mythic speech, there is no predictable causal relation between its subject and predicate. And where the rightful outcome or that which is properly anticipated does not exist, we may presume that the consequence remains within the jurisdiction of intention – in other words, as already enveloped within it. This would call for a special kind of speech or this wondrous possibility would not be. Like, for example, a flower is a flower (or a rose is a rose). There is no question that the predicate of the speech is contained in the subject or the intention itself. Nevertheless the speech does not tell us anything; it merely reiterates, it is a tautology. There is no doubt that to state that a flower is a flower is to state the unexceptional and the infallible, but it does not tell us anything about what makes the flower a flower. In terms of the theory of logic, such speech is defective for its repetitiveness and for being a tautology. Mythical speech is also structurally a repetition. And because of this, by the force of its application, even variable or conjectural truth acquires an aspect of a neutral, inviolable verity. What in the real world is just a chance, a mere possibility, becomes inevitable and ordained in the world of myth. What in the material world is subject to proof is, in the world of myth, surpassing evidence and axiomatic. Because myth is the unalterable truth, all impassioned truths are in its possession.

There are many ways in which such tautological speeches are composed, one popular way being the long practice of correlating a bunch of contrary words. If '*kha*' is the negative of '*ka*', then it would not be possible to recognize either of them separately as they do not exist separately. Then '*ka*' is only '*ka*' because it is not a negative of itself. Thus light can only be light because it is not darknesss.

Assimilation: relationship between the self and the other

Moreover, if we assume one can prove that '*kha*' is stronger than '*ka*', then, according to the corollary logic, it can be easily said that '*kha*' has nothing called originality and is but the opposite of '*ka*'. '*Ka*' then becomes oppositional to the recently demoted '*kha*'. Countless glaring examples of this can be gleaned from diverse places: colonial discourse regarding the ruler and the ruled, racist discourse on the white and the black man, and sociological discourse on man and woman are but some of them. If the 'other' can be moulded in the shape of the 'self' as it so desires, then the distinct identity and separateness of the 'other' is bound to be lost. And this self-produced self-image would be reduced to becoming a mere reflection of the 'self' or an act of interpolation. The 'other' would no longer remain the 'other'; it would have no separate identity and would not be known by any special category to which it may belong. Rather, the 'other' would become an inversion of the 'self', having lost its distinct perceptible form and being relegated to a disembodied, abstract idea originating in the mind. This 'other' – inhabiting the self-centred regime of sign – can never attain the status of subject, remaining forever a mere object. In such circumstances, the 'other' would have no conceivable role to play except as a prop to bolster self-recognition. A skilful execution of assimilation and self-absorption bestowing a certain kind of security to the 'self' would preempt any need to question the order and the propriety of its internal patterning, or to ascertain its authenticity by external standards of evaluation. In this 'self–other' relationship, ultimately, neither is the subject. Since the 'self' desires to see only itself in the mirror of the 'other', its self-identity remains primarily a negative one. By inversing the inverse order, it can succeed only in reaching the originary centre of the self – in reality, a hollow and empty entity. That is, the west is mighty because the east is not, 'white' is always civilized because 'black' never is; and man is 'intelligent' because he is not like the stupid 'woman'.

Assimilation: part and whole

If a part of the whole is passed off as its complete state, the remaining fragments would be naturally either suppressed or ignored. These would be dominated, then, by an excessive importance given to a fragment. We would not cognize the whole for its wholeness or its collectivity as the identity or separateness of every other distinct and individual segment would disappear owing to the extraordinary force of an emphasized fragment. That is why, if one wants to hold up only an individual segment of the composite as possessing its significant value, then, of necessity, one would have to disregard the distinct aspects of individual parts and consider them as redundant, or insist that they are identical or homomorphic and not to be distinguished by any distinct sign. This is assimilation: an instance of segregation whence a fragment of society achieves power in the name of everybody, the entire society buckling under owing to an extraordinary skill of execution whereby the signifiers of the suppressed parts seamlessly merge into the sign of the dominant fragment. This kind of myth, by means of such spurious populism, leads to the formation of false collective consciousness; and, by the help of a hidden ideology, the interests of a particular class or a segment of society rather than that of the entire populace is served.

Assimilation: order–disorder–order

There is a kind of myth which inspires the human heart by upholding a picture of calm reassurance against the intolerable nature of the present – as if there is no other recourse but to resign ourselves to the contemplation of the distant image of a pure past in order to escape from the disordered present. And if one were not able to revisit that sublime originary moment or match the present with the golden past, one would not be able to resolve the present crisis or bring to an end the dichotomy between virtue and desire. The past is illumined by its own radiance; it does not behove us to submit it to any present standards of judging. The present crisis is the outcome of a disregard for the continuation of an inherited tradition; the present predicament is the result of slipping away from the strict and narrow path of religion. Therefore, if one wants to come out of the disorder and misrule of this intermediate period, the future will have to acquiesce to the past. In the unalterable pattern of past–present–future, the future will have to become homologous with the past. And if these two do not coalesce, one will not be able to reach the ultimate moment – and the unbelted strains of the eternal music of the sublime will remain forever unheard. That is, if you wish to go forward, go backwards, walk against time, in order to reach that juncture beyond time whence one might discover an indication of the way to the future. In this schema, the disordered present becomes harmonious, effects a reversal to the perfect proportion of the past; and by reversing that reversal, we are able to reach an aspired future – a future where order is again intact and all differences with the past are dissolved in the completion of a circle. The more this myth extends its hold on society, the more relentless becomes the attraction of a fantastic, pre-mythological past.

It is possible to map the movement of the progress of time in another way. According to such a design, human history is an instance of pure effort without human agency. The logic of evolution enables humans to reach their destination one day or another. A myth that bestows to humans an end that is certain and inevitable gives the hope or belief that no matter how crooked, complex and rocky the journey across time might be, at the end, quiet resolution and ultimate satisfaction awaits them. As if the destiny, memory and future of humans are so inextricably tied together by a hidden thread that mankind has no choice but to move steadily to that still moment – has no option but to bow to the order of the glorious, final stage of human civilization and to the radiance of that ultimate moment.

Assimilation: the wheel of time

A special example of such mythic speech may be discovered in the philosophical notions embedded in our everyday conversations, whose sway has been extensive. The original form of mythic speech is captured in a well-known philosophical proposition: the circular movement of time with a beginning and an end engulfs all that is material, divisive and finite. Because of the relentless movement of time, everything in this world is always subject to change: rise is accompanied by fall, happiness by sorrow, birth by death; there is nothing that remains eternally static in the world. But, at the same time, if one has to admit that time moves in circles, one would have to concede that there is nothing called progress in this world. In fact, the idea of progress is itself an illusion; only those who are immersed in cultivating ignorance drown in such foolish dreams. So that unless one constantly reiterates the axiom that going forward is not going anywhere at all but a return to an earlier position, one cannot hope to escape the all-destroying, blinding darkness. Consequently, the narrative of social life has long since ceased to exist and now all utterance is mere reiteration – all sound a mere aphasic echo. Even if there exists the possibility of transformation, no alteration can be envisaged either in the degree or the quality of experience. In such a dispensation, a cluster of opposing signs can attach itself to any group of signs. As a result, although there may exist some tension between themselves, at a higher level all of that gets cancelled out and leaves behind a void.

Myth as Ahistorical Speech

From its many characteristics, it would become clear that myth is not willing to tolerate history in any sense. Thus mythic speech presents itself to its addressee in the mask of neutrality, as if its reach were unlimited, its acceptability and power for all times and for all peoples. There is no basis for any discrepancy or any reason for complaint; for the addressee, this is indeed good news. Myth as the messenger of eternal truth is not dependent on the vagaries of actual history; its perfect design is not jeopardized by any turn of event; it has no connection whatsoever with the flow of life or with the nascent earth. As if all sundry doubts about truth have already been resolved at some secret space existing outside history; as if myth were an attendant to the hidden primordial power of an absent lord.

The grammar of myth contains no verbs – which is to say, myth trades only with ideas outside history. It is possible that in the actual world there are traces of a pure idea, but the appearances of those empty, imaginary shapes are mere distortions of the original; they are but shadows of the truth. And if one gets mesmerized by these shadowy forms, one may never be able to discover one's supreme or primordial existence, or come to know one's essential identity. Rather, one would rotate endlessly in the worldly maze: as if myth wrings out the secret thread of connection from among the many differences in an apparent reality and reaches to man this essential significance uncontaminated by history. A reversal of the mythic results in establishing social construction as natural – with history becoming but another name for the rule of nature.

That history's point of departure is in many cases not an act of blind pursuit, that change or revolutions or the commencement of a new future age could be made by drawing a strict line of continuity from the past and the present, is something that mythic utterance is not willing to entertain or adhere to. In the words of Roland Barthes, myth is that kind of speech which totally erases all marks of history and politics.[4] And to come under the sway of such speech is to become reduced to an idle plaything. Finally, then, myth is also a kind of metaphysics; man observes the world from its metaphysical orbit, from a distance, whence not even a minute stir of movement is caught by his steadfast unblinking eyes. And it seems as if there is no need to come to terms or enter into any arrangement with the world, no reason at all for getting agitated or distressed.

Myth effects a separation between subject and object in two different ways. In the deterministic perspective, the significance of the subject can be suppressed completely; on the other hand, by celebrating volunteerism, one can safely leave aside the question of the reality principle or the limits on consciousness imposed by the material world. In the first dispensation, the sociality of the external world is ignored; in the second, because of the unchecked tyranny of the subject, the materiality of the universe is reduced to nothing. We have discussed two linguistic theories earlier; these two ways of myth formation that I mention here can be singled out in both these theories.

The Deconstruction of Myth

Myth is not discerning; it can happily ensconce itself in any discourse. It can also build up a new discourse amalgamating several different myths. Alternatively, the power of the mythic discourse would depend upon to what extent and by which means myth is able to suppress dissident voices.[5] The opposition is cornered and rendered voiceless to the same degree by which the discourse extends its influence. And those who are outcasts, living on the margins of society – those lapsed individuals – their opinions do not matter at all; and who does not know this? Therefore, in order to make the system work, maintain stability and keep in place the hierarchical order, it is necessary to obfuscate all notions related to contradictions in society through the force of a special kind of discourse. Even a child knows what Karl Marx (1818–1883) had posited so many years ago: that no production can continue for more than a year unless its conditions of production are reproduced.[6] Since the condition of production is a necessary reproduction of those very same conditions, in an unequal situation, men have to render their social coordinates immovable. Several complementary discourses come together to create the dominant ideology of society, an ideology that purports that the language and value system of the ruling class with regard to life is not only correct, but also the one and only. Which means that the reproductive practice of ideology makes it certain that it is in place, simultaneously weakening the possibility of revolutionary practice.

But is the practice of myth exclusively a matter of ideology? Does it not have a wider implication? Is it enough for us just to pronounce that myth is de-historicized and de-politicized speech, and to stop thereon? Is it not necessary, in such a context, to be aware particularly of the suppression of political intent? If it were so that only the dominant ideology reigned in the mind of society, there would be no need to raise such a question. But in actual fact there exist in society many levels of ideology, various strands, and in their continuous mutual interactions, the total picture of society does not remain static.[7] Then again, myth may exist hidden in the interstices of the socialized world, the languages of which are either in opposition or function as rival discourses. At times, a myth is refuted by means of another myth; at others, myth itself becomes the main instrument in combating myth-making. Even if the skill of execution is the same, it does not follow that the political impulses in the construction of myths are necessarily identical. The ruling class has to, time and again, look for clues towards the resolution of problems arising out of internal social contradictions or in confrontation with an opposing power. And because of this, there always remains a gap between the power of the ruling class and the power of the state. Thus many variants of myth are dispersed among the many ideologies in this rather complex situation. And if one were to deconstruct all those constructions, there would be no other way but to take recourse to history. We would have to attack and demolish myth's ability to erase history in order to comprehend the secret of its executionary skills – counter a single, goal-oriented myth with varieties of historical aims. This does not mean that one can change the world by effecting change in the consciousness or by the sheer power of theoretical arguments; nevertheless this remains one way of waging such a battle.

It is better to be wary that we do not fall into the trap of the 'mythical' while discussing the myth-laden children's literature of colonial times. We therefore start by asking ten questions. Who writes? What is written? For whom is it written? How is it written? Why is it written? Where and when are the writer and the reader situated? By what means is the text despatched to the reader by the writer? In other words, we would like to know the details about the producer of the material – the consumer – the subject matter – the means of production – ideology – conditions of production – conditions of consumption – the system of circulation and distribution of the material. Although, for the sake of analysis, we disconnect these various components or features, the traces of their combined influences nevertheless remain in the text. Just as, for the sake of argument, reference to the separate, to the individual class–gender–race–community identities of the producer and consumer become extremely relevant, similarly, it is necessary to maintain an overall picture of the same. If we distinguish between readers in order to judge them on an individual basis, we will discover that the relationship forged between the sender and the addressee, on the basis of the text, is rather a fuzzy one. One way to deal with that fuzziness is to try and understand the arrangement of exchange and distribution. We know that the writer and the reader of modern Bengali literature are, by and large, the educated *bhadralok* class. Exceptions, if there are any, are not worth making a note of. Can we not also extract a faint idea of the quality of that literature by taking into consideration the range of the literary production, and the conditions governing its demand and supply? Besides, if we were to look a little deeper, we would find that in many instances the writer creates, either consciously or unconsciously, an ideal reader – with whom he is engaged, as if in direct verbal communication. As a consequence, we would have to find a place for this 'virtual reader' alongside the 'actual reader' in any discussion of a literary text. Singularly, on the basis of an analysis of the readerly material, no clear notion of the subject, method and ideology can be arrived at. For that, one would have to have some precise information about the 'genre' to which the literary production belongs.

If we were aware of these ten questions heretofore posed, we could avoid the pitfalls of the many theoretical traps. One, because we have to consider, separately or apart, (a) the distinct ideologies of the producer and the consumer; (b) the dominant world view at the time of writing and reading; and (c) the ideology of the text. Consequently, we cannot dispense with the question of ideology in one or two sentences, nor can we confuse the intention of the text with the intention of the author. Despite their interrelatedness, these five aforementioned views or beliefs continue to be separate or apart, not in the least losing their distinctiveness. Two, by no means ought we to regard the text as a closed system. Since we are bound to concede the importance of the role played by the receiver along with the sender, the ways of creating a new text by splitting open an existing one always remains a distinct possibility. And three, within this theoretical framework, the text is not a mere printed book or an inert object; it is directly implicated in history.

II

Man makes his own history but not of his own choosing

– Karl Marx[8]

In his essay 'Bangadesher Krishak' ('The Peasants of Bengal', in *Collected Essays*, Vol. II, 1872), Bankimchandra Chattopadhyay (1838–1894), one of the chief architects of Bengali modernity, had clearly stated:

> We are not zamindar haters, the zamindars have wrought us no harm. Rather we consider many zamindars as worthy of our special praise, the zamindars are among those whose love and affection we count as the chief boon in our society. The zamindars are the acme of the Bengali race, who does not aspire to deserve their love and friendship?[9]

It is worth noting that the quoted passage is bound within the use of the first person plural. And the manner of address makes it abundantly clear that Bankim is speaking not on behalf of himself but as the representative of a social group. He seems to have taken for granted that there are no reasons for any difference of view between himself and his readers; neither of them are zamindar 'haters'. And by invoking the pronoun 'we', he is offering the reader entry into a secret pact and marking a common, albeit inconspicuous, meeting ground.

But at the same time, dispersed in this essay are descriptions of untold atrocities committed by the zamindars on the peasants and ordinary folk, as if despite not being a zamindar hater, for the sake of truth and justice, Bankim is obliged to divulge the sordid happenings. And it seems that if this truth results in a break-up of his ties with that class or losing their affection, then so be it. The essay opens with a risky question:

> Nowadays one hears much talk about an increase in the country's prosperity. All this time our country was hurtling towards its ruin, now under the skilful administration of the British we are becoming civilized, the country benefiting. In all this claim about the profusion of our prosperity and well being the thing to ask is: 'Who is actually benefiting from this disbursement of largesse?'

The twenty-six-year-old Marcus Tullius Cicero (106–93 BC), renowned Roman orator, senator and constitutionalist, had made a series of arguments defending an innocent man who had been charged with treason by the state. The tract became famous as *Pro Roscio Amerino*. In this tract Cicero mentions the instance of the renowned Lucius Cassius, whom the Roman citizens considered an honest and wise judge, having the habit of repeatedly asking, '*cui bono*?' The Latin phrase *cui bono* means 'to whose benefit?' / 'as a benefit to whom?' Undoubtedly, there exists a fond familiarity between Cicero's *cui bono* or 'to whose benefit?', and Bankim's question, 'who is actually benefiting?'[10] Thus, the more we read, the more we discover that Bankim has gone on to show that the ordinary peasants are not party to the so-called increase in the country's prosperity – that there is not the slightest evidence that the Hashim Shaikhs and the Rama Kaibartyas of Bengali society have benefited even a jot from it. Rather, the hard-earned wealth of the peasants has somehow or the other gone to fill the coffers of the zamindars – as if the relationship between the ryot and the zamindar is not one of protector and protected but of predator and prey. 'Living beings are the greatest enemy of other living beings, men of other men, and the enemy of the Bengali ryots are the Bengali landholders. The big man going by the name of zamindar feeds on the small man called the peasant.'[11] After this stern declaration, within the interval of a bare paragraph, Bankim writes:

> We would like to make a special mention that what we say here does not apply exclusively to the zamindar class. And those who claim that the zamindars as a class are tyrants and torturers, they are downright liars. There are many zamindars who are amiable, devoted to their tenants and the votaries of truth. Therefore, the remarks made in this essay do not quite fit them. The essay is directed against the ones who are oppressive.[12]

In which case, should we take it that, according to Bankim, there is no fundamental flaw in the zamindari system, and that he is only trying to draw his reader's attention to some of its failings? Yet, on the other hand, it is Bankim himself who constructs a character like Paran Mandal: 'Paran Mandal is an imaginary character. Our intention', he says, 'is to narrate the many atrocities committed by the naturally cruel zamindars on peasants like the imagined Paran Mandal.'[13] Let us assume that there is no progress towards prosperity in the land of Hashim Shaikh or Rama Kaibartya; Paran Mandal is their representative, he is a symbol of the entire peasant community of Bengal.

How, then, is it that one could imagine a single individual as representative of an entire community when it came to the ryots but not the zamindars? Why this discrepancy in the ruling? Besides, if on the one hand an insinuation is made against the landlords in the essay, there is, on the other, a showering of praise over the same, especially the big zamindars. At places, Bankim is bitter and angry; at others, gentle and compassionate. How does one explain this vacillation? Why does he make a retreat after pursuing his argument thus far, expunge the sharp words over and over again? Is there not, therefore, a sufficient hint in his writings that Bankim would want to gag his own voice and suspend the reprint of his 'Peasants of Bengal' for many years? In the essay itself, one of Bankim's statements becomes entangled with another contradictory statement, a counter-statement abolishes an earlier one – and by this intimate ebb and flow is created a strange play of addressal and refutation.

Did Bankim enter into a debate with himself – a debate that would finally remain inconclusive?

In order to earn the favour of the zamindars, he says at one place in the essay: 'The ryot-tenants of many zamindars are also not good. They don't pay taxes unless pressured.'[14] And in the 'Introduction' to the reprint published in 1892, twenty-five long years after its publication in the journal *Bangadarshan*, this comment reappears in a new garb: 'In many instances we may note that it is the ryots who are the persecutors, the zamindars are weak people.'[15] How and by what means does Bankim reconcile these two contradictory threads of his argument: the zamindar as the oppressor of the ryots, and the ryot as the tormentor of the zamindars? For an answer to this dilemma, one would have to glance again at those about whom he had earlier proposed, 'We are not among those who have been harmed by the zamindars.' Thus, in the gap between the zamindar clan and the Paran Mandals reside these unidentified 'we'. And it is on their behalf that Bankim pronounces his moral message:

> The peasants of Bengal are helpless, stricken with adversity, they do not even know how to express their sorrow socially. And if I do not expend a few words to mitigate the abject condition of those mute people, then I would be committing a grievous sin . . . let the voice be silenced which has not expressed pain for those who have suffered; let those writings that have not been written to help the afflicted fail.[16]

Nevertheless, this 'we' is also not that indeterminate, as right at the beginning of the essay Bankim had asked his assumed reader: 'O you bespectacled gentleman, what good have you done to these peasants? What have you done to improve their condition after acquiring so much learning?'[17] Of course, Bankim is himself one such bespectacled gentleman. Therefore, whether he likes it or not, consciously or unconsciously, he becomes the target of his own sarcasm. Underlying the discussion of the zamindar–ryot relationship, an alternative discourse is constructed – the self-criticism of a conscience-driven, morally propelled *bhadralok*. 'The Peasants of Bengal' is not a mere treatise of social theory, an objective analysis of the agrarian system; it is Babu Bankimchandra's personal deposition.

Speaking of the unending misery of the peasants of Bengal, Bankim writes:

> For the first time in history, misfortune has struck the peasants of Bengal in the British Empire. This 'Permanent Settlement' is but a permanent settlement for the ruin of Bengal – nothing will make it return to its former state. This scandal of the British is to last forever as the arrangement is a permanent one.[18]

If one calculated, one would see that the beginning of the ruin of Bengal was during the administration of Lord Cornwallis (1738–1805), the then Governor-General and head of the British East India Company – on 22 March 1793, to be exact. The 'Permanent Settlement' was introduced that very year and as a result, the face of Bengali society underwent a complete alteration; a new pattern of an unequal relationship came into being between the zamindars, the ryots and of course 'us'. But prior to this arrangement lay the history of the long preparation for this, the brutal narrative of how the rule of traders gave way to the rule of the emperor. The history of the establishment of the rule of foreign power can be traced back to the 'battle' that was fought in the mangroves of Plassey in Bengal on 23 June 1757, between the armies of Lord Clive and Nawab Siraj-ud-daula, in which the English lost only twenty-nine lives among whom sixteen were native soldiers. Prior to that, the East India Company, set up in the year 1600, with a security capital of 70,000 pounds, was a mere business establishment. It was in the same year, on 31 December, that the Company was able to get permission from England's Queen Elizabeth I to trade with the several countries in the eastern part of the world beyond the Cape of Good Hope. In 1639 the Company established the Fort of Saint George in Madras; in 1678 it bought the island of Bombay off King Charles II; in 1700 it established Calcutta as its centre in Bengal. This gradual spread of power was not only an Indian phenomenon, it could be witnessed all over the world. A new imperialism made its presence felt in human history, altering the face of the world. In 1914, the year of the First World War, Rabindranath Tagore (1861–1941), seeking to explain the reasons behind this radical alteration, wrote in the essay 'Laraier Mul' ('Why War?', *Sabuj Patra*, Poush 1321 [Bengali calendar]):

> Currently the world is witnessing the rule of the merchant class. Trade today does not signify mere exchange of goods, it has long since entered into an unholy pact with imperialism. At one time goods were what the merchants possessed, now they own human beings . . . there is not another instance of such large ownership in the world. For Europe, the area of domination is Asia and Africa.[19]

Because of this union between trade and empire despite the intervening distance of the 'seven seas', a handful of Western European countries began to determine the fate of almost all the countries of the world. It is a record, on the one hand, of extraordinary accomplishment, and on the other, of a commensurate laundering of wealth and prosperity. The robbed riches of the colonies provided fuel for the newly emergent European capitalism, for the wealth garnered thus turned into capital. Through this 'primitive accumulation of Capital',[20] the more powerful Europe became, the weaker the colonial countries were rendered. There was a ceaseless flow of raw material, food, fuel and human beings from the colonies. In many countries – in India, for example – the money that the English invested did not come from England. There was reinvestment of money the English had robbed India of, or the profit they had made or even their salary savings. India was caught, so to speak, in a vicious circle of being garbed in the very vestments robbed off its own back.

In the words of the historian Romesh Chandra Dutt, author of *The Economic History of India*, 'The Indian empire was established, several wars were fought, all with the money of the Indian people – the British did not have to spend a penny.'[21] Now let us examine what form this history of playing with the fate of the human beings took in Bengal.

Right on the heels of 1757, in the year 1764, Mir Kasim threw the final challenge to Company rule on behalf of the now totally obsolescent feudal system. But after Mir Kasim's defeat at Buxar, no possibility remained of any resistance coming from the Nawabs. Traitors like Mir Jafar, entangled in conspiracies of their own making, were unable to help improve the situation; power simply passed into the hands of the English. Within a period of five years from 1759–60, when they first acquired landholdings in the 24 Parganas and were given the responsibility of collecting taxes in the districts of Midnapur, Chittagong and Burdwan, the Company acquired the lease of the provinces of Bengal–Bihar and Orissa from the Mughal emperor Shah Alam in 1765. And thus began the dual administration of India. However, up till 1772, the burden of collecting taxes lay with the Nawabs and the Diwans. The Company explored ways of increasing the revenue using Mohammad Reza Khan as a shield. In order to increase the total revenue collected, it resorted to auctioneering and leasing out the charge for the collection of local revenue, appointed several committees like the district 'Revenue Supervisor' in 1770, the 'Revenue Council' in Murshidabad and Patna, the Calcutta 'Controlling Committee' in 1771, etc.[22] According to the lease agreement of the Company with the feudal establishment, the Mughal emperor was entitled to Rs 26 lakhs per annum and the Nawab of Bengal to Rs 32 lakhs of the revenue collected – the rest was deposited in the Company's treasury.

The age of dual administration was also an age of ultimate anarchy. On the eve of the 'transfer of power', the people of Bengal–Bihar and Orissa were subjected to unqualified oppression – after which the high-ranking officials of the Company were given all kinds of benefits and perquisites to facilitate easy and shameless profiteering from Company rule. For example, in the year 1765, an unofficial trade consortium was established under Lord Clive's patronage, and a writ to the effect that only that company would enjoy a total monopoly over the salt trade was procured from the puppet Nawab. By 1772, however, the business came under the total jurisdiction of the administration. This, in short, was the general pattern of unflinching arrogance of the new rulers at that time.[23]

In 1769, over and above all kinds of pressures exerted on the ordinary man, there was an additional one of natural calamity. The collusion of man and nature in ensuring the appearance of drought and famine led to countless deaths. In the famine, popularly known as '*Chhiatorer Manantor*', more than one-third of the population died of disease and starvation. Yet, despite such calamity, the percentage of tax collected did not go down; rather, it increased. Whereas the tax collected in 1768, the year before the famine, was 1,52,04,856 *taka*, in 1771, the year after the calamity, tax collection went up to 1,57,26,576 *taka*. These are not mere numbers but reliable evidence of the unbounded oppression practised on the peasantry during that time. Apart from such indices of extortion, there exists the actual confession of none less than the Governor-General of Bengal, Sir Warren Hastings. In a letter to the Company Directors in 1772, he wrote:

> Despite the loss of one-third of the population of the state and the resultant decline of agricultural produce, the net tax collection was higher in 1771 than in the year 1768. It would have been natural for any person to assume that given the situation of great national disaster, the tax collection would have been lower. The reason why this did not happen is that taxes were collected using utmost force.[24]

The policy of the Company took yet another turn in 1772, in a phase that was to continue till the year 1786. By 1771–72, it was decided that henceforth the Company itself would bear the entire responsibility of the Diwani; consequently, the regime of the native Nawabs and Diwans (rent collectors) ended then and there. The treasury of the central government was transferred to Calcutta from Murshidabad. From 1772 onwards, the Company began to depend more on the pre-Company landholders, taking attention away from those who had been given land lease for two years. This did not mean that provisions for convenient auctioneering were dropped as it was only such arrangements that were found to be conducive for simplifying the taxation system. The Directors of the Company turned to the old landholders who were adept in tax collection. The lease agreement was consequently increased to a five-year settlement. After the five-year contract came to an end, the system for a yearly contract was introduced in 1777. An agreement was reached with the landlords about the share of gains on the basis of taxes collected for three years. This was accompanied by many kinds of bureaucratic reshuffling in an increased attempt to make the machinery for tax fixation more powerful. In Calcutta, a 'Controlling Council of Revenue', 'Revenue Board', 'Committee of Revenue' and, last but not the least, 'Board of Revenue' were established.[25] The era of Warren Hastings (1732–1818) was even more interesting. It is but obvious that the rule of the same Hastings who was responsible for the first translations from Sanskrit to English, under whose aegis the Company officer Charles Wilkinson (1749–1836) translated the *Bhagavadgita* which was published by the East India Company in 1785, and who was indicted just a year before this by the British Parliament on charges of fraud, would be nothing short of colourful. Hastings abruptly cancelled the Company's agreement with the Mughal emperor and stopped the despatch of yearly rent to him.

In 1773, the British Parliament adopted the 'Regulating Act', keeping in mind the interest in 'improving the conditions in India.' On 13 August 1784, Pitt's India Law 'came into operation – according to which the British Imperial power appointed two commissioners for the supervision of matters civil, military and for rent collection'. And in this way, the control of the Parliament over the Company administration gradually increased. Warren Hastings bid farewell to India the year after Pitt's India Law came into operation. The next year, in 1786, Lord Cornwallis occupied the vacated seat. From 1786 to 1793, several experiments with the land tenure system were conducted, and according to a new scheme of 1789, a ten-year agreement with the zamindars was arrived at by Lord Cornwallis. But knowing that this would not permanently solve the problems or fulfil their ultimate aims, on 22 March 1793, the 'Permanent Settlement' was promulgated. In this way – after one-year, five-year and ten-year agreements – a firm relationship between the zamindars and the English was finally established, and a permanent understanding and friendship grew between the two parties.

According to this 'peace accord': (a) the 1789–90 revenue payable to the British, approximately ten-elevenths of the tax paid to the landlord by the ryots, was taken to be the permanent arrangement, and there was no provision for any further alteration in the amount of money involved; (b) the zamindars who managed to successfully submit the Company's share of profit on time to the Company coffers would never again have to worry about their progeny. The 'good' zamindars would have the right to enjoy, hereditarily, exclusive ownership of the property. In this new dispensation the fixed amount due as tax to the Company from Bengal came to Rs 2 crores and 68 lakhs – or 34 lakh pounds. Although the pressure on the zamindars for collection was initially pretty hard, it was reduced as the income went up. One can see from the 1880 accounts that whereas the zamindars earned 2 crore pounds from land tax, only 40 lakh pounds were remitted to the government treasury. However, because of the excessive land duties of the initial period, many landholdings changed hands and the places vacated by the original aristocrats came swiftly under the control of the upstart rich denizens of the city of Calcutta. It did not take long for these subservient, flattering tradesmen-agents of the Company to completely graft themselves to the new arrangement. During the years 1793–1815, some 40 per cent of zamindaris changed hands.

But why did the Company of its own accord suffocate one of its most substantial means of income? Was it because the revenue collection was continuously falling due to the ineptitude and lack of skill of the Directors of the Company? Considerable contribution by certain theorists of the day was behind the gradual evolution of the Permanent Settlement. Chief among them were the Physiocrats, who monopolized early modern economic theory in Europe, among whom the names of Henri P., Philip Francis and Thomas Law are worth mentioning.[26] Their main slogans were: let the capitalist mode of production be introduced in the agriculture of Bengal, the cultivation of crops increased by the touch of the magic wand of private ownership of land, and the spineless serfs emerge as hard-working tenants. But it was discovered shortly after that the exact transcription of all the rules and regulations that had operated so easily in capitalist England could not be made to sow their seeds on the soil of its colonies; and this was also because they did not serve the interests of the British. Did not Henri P. himself say that the more the Bengalis realized the benefits of individual ownership of property, the more they would learn to appreciate the value and greatness of the British way of life and its related benefits, and this, consequently, would open doors to new investments.[27] Whatever might have been the original impetus, such intention was prone to get distorted and bound to face radical alteration under the colonial condition. The Permanent Settlement in Bengal did not usher in a capitalist mode of production in its entirety of the kind that is described in books on political economy. Rather, it created a strange mixture of a pre-capitalist and capitalist accumulation of wealth, and in this dual mode of production there grew two different kinds of social systems. Because of this arrangement, the cultivation of practically one-third of the land in Bengal that had lain fallow after the famine of 1867 did not lead to much improvement in the production and investment in agriculture, in spite of the increase in the income of the zamindars.

Although the agricultural system changed from one that was traditional to one that entailed individual ownership of land, and despite the enormous amount of wealth in the hands of the new rich, this wealth did not get transformed into capital. This failure was mainly due to the fact that the Company held a total monopoly of the industrial sector. Although the monopoly somewhat disappeared after 1813 owing to the pressure exerted by the proponents of free trade and open market in England, the situation of the wealthy Bengalis remained as it was. Of course, by that time there were no traces left of the initiatives and enterprises undertaken by wealthy Bengalis like Dwarakanath Tagore (1794–1846) during the first phase of the Company's rule. A useless class, comprising those who possessed a huge amount of unearned wealth, the so-called new aristocrats, and absentee landlords unconnected with the business of administering the tenure system – in other words, a redundant class – came into being. It was this class that gave birth to a culture of decadence (the so-called '*babu* culture') and transformed Calcutta into its pleasure palace; it was as if this curse of lack of manliness and this condition of mental feebleness were inevitable. Because of the discrepancy of power between the centre and the periphery, and as a direct result of the industrialization of England, the underdevelopment of Bengalis was almost a given; and it was also foretold that Bengal would march towards increased underdevelopment under the pressure of England's further progress.

In 1872, England started printing calico; the next year, muslin was produced in Manchester. In 1786, the Company's investment in indigenous cotton production reached zero, and by 1860, the weaving industry in Bengal had virtually collapsed. The weavers gave up their traditional profession and became either tillers of land or left the countryside. There is no doubt that no matter what they professed regarding free trade, the British regarded Bengal – a banner-raising picture of success in commerce – as nothing more than an extended market for British commodities. It did not take long for the so-called exponents of freedom to realize that if the inhabitants of the colonies became directly involved in the processes of production instead of remaining inactive consumers, England's free trade would not remain free. During the years 1815–16 and again in 1832–33, the export of cotton goods from Bengal came down to 8 lakhs from 1.5 crores per annum. On the other hand, the import of British goods leaped from 22 lakhs to 43 lakhs. The same figures obtained for thread as well: imports that were worth 1 lakh in 1824–25 stood at 33 lakhs in 1832–33. Bengal's silk industry revealed the same story. The Company's monopoly over the salt trade and the high tax on salt brought utter ruin to indigenous industries.

> Areas marked for salt production were the coastal regions of the Bay of Bengal, stretching between Hijli, Tamluk, 24 Parganas, Dhaka and Noakhali. In 1795, Bengal's total salt production was 30,28,342 maunds. At that time, on the average, 28 lakh maunds of salt were produced in Bengal, half of which came from Hijli and Tamluk. An imperialist economy – one would have thought – would augment salt production in Bengal, but to the contrary, Bengal had to import salt from the coastal regions of Vishakhapatnam, Rajamundhri, Nellore and other places.[28]

In 1814, the shipping industry of Bengal suffered a big blow when a ban was imposed on the use of Indian ships for British–Indian commerce. There were several Bengali owners of ships, such as Ramdulal Dey, Panchu Datta, Ramgopal Mullick and Madan Dutta, even in the year 1813, but within a short time they were all compelled to give up their business.[29] It is to be noted that while during the latter half of the nineteenth century, apart from rice, all other agricultural products were exported without any customs duties, some highly finished Indian industrial goods, like fine cotton cloth, were stopped from being exported due to fears of competition. Among the many causes for the lack of industrial development was the absence of demand. When the national per capita income was low, it was but natural that the people would have less purchasing power. Besides, the profit margins of industries in colonial India were bound to be much lower than in other areas or in other capitalist countries.[30] It is quite obvious that for Indians, investing money in industry was a lost endeavour because of simple self-preservation.

Quite contrary to all this, the Company was more than keen that the natives should pour their surplus wealth into land. Through regulatory measures that were imposed one after the other, the zamindars were given more power and, simultaneously, oppression of the ryots was facilitated by the Company. The fourth regulation, introduced in 1794, gave zamindars the absolute right to collect the total amount of tax with or without the consent of tenants. In 1799, during the war with Tipu Sultan, in a time of extreme economic stringency, the Company introduced *Haptam*, the infamous seventh regulation. According to this provision, the landlord had the right to confiscate the entire property of the ryot should the taxes remain uncollected – and in some cases even the right to personally arrest the unfortunate ryot – and he (the landlord) was not required to take recourse to legal institutions like courts of law in order to teach the ryot a lesson. According to the 1819 regulation related to land lease, the creation of a class of intermediary landlords was declared legal. In 1828, even fallow lands were brought under the jurisdiction of the Permanent Settlement by the third regulation.

The Directors of the Company were from the start extremely aware of the political implications of the Permanent Settlement alongside its economic ones. The main architect of the Permanent Settlement, Lord Cornwallis, had told the Directors: 'As soon as it is declared that the land lease is secure you will see that those in whose hands there is a huge capital would not look for investment elsewhere but in the purchase of more landed property.' And in 1829, the then Governor-General Lord William Bentinck had written:

> I must say that the Permanent Settlement has been really successful as a shield against mass agitation and people's revolution. And by its benevolence a really large number of rich landowners have been created, who are extremely keen in maintaining the British rule and they have succeeded in exerting their undisputed hold over the people.

In 1861, three years after Empress Victoria (1819–1901) took over the task of administering India, the Secretary to India in the British government, in a message sent to his representatives in India, said: 'That there are many benefits accruing from the Permanent Settlement, Empress Victoria's government does not entertain any doubt about. The landholders too cannot but entertain in their minds a fondness for and an allegiance to a land tenure system upon which their identity rests.'[31] And there is no controversy now about how the system had succeeded in neutralizing its competitors by skilfully transforming them into loyal inheritors. Between the years 1757 and 1785, the main group of businessmen in Calcutta had belonged to the upper-caste community; but by the early nineteenth century, they practically disappeared from the business scene. Moving away from commerce, they gradually became dependent on real estate in Calcutta or agricultural land in the countryside; some even entered the moneylending trade. In this way, the huge property of Ramdulal

Dey got trapped in the land tenure system; and the story behind the liquidation of the business concerns of Sir Dwarakanath Tagore in the course of a single generation is more or less the same.

Although it was legitimate that the entire population of the colonies should collectively bear the responsibility of improving the condition of their 'motherland', for some reason the question of an even distribution of that responsibility simply did not arise. The wise rulers of the land did not find it difficult to comprehend that like the equitable distribution of wealth, the equitable distribution of poverty spelled danger. As a result, even a fraction of the small amount of profit left behind in the colonies did not reach the population at large; so too, the distribution of income derived from non-capitalist ventures remained iniquitous. The existence of a subaltern class was deemed necessary in the interests of the colonial powers themselves: a quiet, obedient group of attendants. They would gain the warm association of the rulers, receive permission to hob-nob with them, and finally, as the acme of benefits received, they would earn the prestige and the status of deputy rulers. It would also be impossible for this class to extricate themselves from this psychological trap. The rulers knew only too well that it was well-nigh impossible for this tenant class to accept that it is better to have an empty farm than to breed a mad cow. And because of this, they would willingly take some burden off the shoulders of their masters. At the least, this intermediary class would manage the situation on behalf of their masters when peasant discontent showed its face.

The ryots now came under the pressure of not only the zamindars, but also the several strata of the intermediary classes of deputy zamindars, thanks to the Permanent Settlement. Although the revenue due to the Company from the zamindars was more or less constant, the revenue the ryots owed the zamindars was never fixed. Moreover the landlords now enjoyed huge powers. It was because of this, therefore, that the peasants were compelled to offer land lease to the newly arrived landowning class. In the words of Bankimchandra Chattopadhyay:

> Lord Cornwallis has done untold harm to the peasants – overcome by grand illusion. He has made the contractors for collection of rent the owners of the land – what is the result? The zamindars remain oppressors of the peasants, something they had been from time immemorial. The tenants have lost forever, whatever rights to the land they had enjoyed. It is the peasants/ryots who are the real owners of the land and the zamindars not for a moment, ever; they are mere official collectors of revenue. Cornwallis has taken the land away from its real owners and given it to the revenue officers. This cannot benefit the peasants.[33]

According to the Census Commissioner Sir Thomas Munro, there was no landless peasantry in Bengal in 1842. But it took only thirty years for India to produce landless peasants to the tune of 75 lakhs. And according to the 1931

Census, of all men engaged in agriculture in Bengal, 30 per cent were landless. A large number among them also happened to be indentured labourers. Although there was a serious attempt made in 1823 to fix the rate of taxes of the peasants, because of the inherent suspicion of the bureaucracy and the severe opposition to the measure expressed by the 'British–India Association' of zamindars, all of this came to naught. In the meanwhile, Pabna had already witnessed a peasant uprising and mass discontent was evident in many places. Therefore, as a solution, a bill proposing the peasants' right to land was passed in 1885. According to its provisions, the zamindars could claim an additional 12.5 per cent tax over and above the existing rate, but could not increase the rate of taxation for fifteen years. Because of this law, and also the two amendments of 1928 and 1938, sublet tenants under tenants with rights did enjoy some limited rights, but the majority of the large number of tillers did not benefit even a jot. The main structure of the Permanent Settlement remained undisturbed with little difference to the tragic situation of the landless peasantry and the sharecroppers. Bankim wrote his 'Introduction' to the reprint of 'The Peasants of Bengal' keeping in mind the 1885 law on peasants' land rights. 'The description of the condition of the peasants I had given in "The Peasants of Bengal" no longer holds. The zamindars are no longer that cruel. The new law has clipped their wings, improved the lot of the peasants.'[34] But did this really happen? The ill fate of landless, destitute peasants was compounded by another factor: the ongoing famine in Bengal after the scarcity of 1867. Bengal became a land of everlasting famine caught in the coils of the Permanent Settlement.

In the land of Bengal that has been torn apart so many times and yet remained so colourful, another group made their appearance alongside the zamindars. Either directly or indirectly connected to British administration and commerce, they were either lawyers, clerks, solicitors, doctors, teachers or journalists. Their activities were more or less restricted to the arena of office-administrative centres, schools, law courts and hospitals – some of them comprised the bespectacled gentlemen that Bankim talks about. They were totally unconnected with the processes of production, completely detached from the means of production; these gentlemen depended on jobs or had to choose an income-generating profession for their livelihood. And along with this there was a special role reserved for them as intermediary landlords under the Permanent Settlement.

Economic theorists generally divide the national economy into three areas of income generation: the primary sector involving income derived from agriculture, animal husbandry, horticulture, fisheries, forestry, etc.; the secondary sector involving industry, mining, construction industry, irrigation and electrification; and the third sector involving income generated from transport, trade, and administrative and public services. One observes that in colonial India, the share of income generated from primary economic activities continually lagged behind; and while there was some improvement in the income coming from secondary sector activities, there was a non-stop increase in the income accruing from the third sector or the public services. One must not forget that 'this third kind of economic activity did not lead to the production of any goods or items of consumption. The income generated in this sector went to fill the coffers of the urban middle class to the impoverishment of those living in the villages'.[35] 'For whose welfare was all this?' In reply to Bankim's sharp query, one could have said that if there was anyone benefiting from the colonial rule, it had to be the zamindar class or the mixed bag of middle-class Bengalis. Most people of Bengal did not benefit even a fraction from the so-called progress or the schemes of improvement in society.

The colonial discourse engendered the two words 'Hindu' and 'Muslim' as a means to make legible the much divided network of Indian society; to make the tangled web that was the body-social more accessible. It is but obvious that regulation of the population becomes much easier if the populace across the country can be divided into distinct factions for the sake of knowledge. In colonial demography, such a broad division made it possible to evade the problems of dealing with a multiplicity of identities; the latter came to be subsumed within the division created by the two aforementioned words. In fact the two words became so regular in the language of the rulers that in the nineteenth century itself, at least among the upper class of those anointed 'Hindu', the compound 'Hindu–Muslim' came to be established as foundational to the realization and development of the self. In 'Letter on Hinduism' (written in the 1880s), Bankim had written:

> Search the massive vaults of the pre-Islamic age and, let alone Hinduism, you will not even find the word 'Hindu' anywhere . . . [now] one assumes not only that the whole Hindu race has a closed and complete religious doctrine but also that doctrine is what is, according to foreign thinkers, Hinduism.

The Permanent Settlement is as responsible for the establishment of 'Hindu' as an identifier as it is for laying the framework for Hindu–Muslim conflict.

It would be unreasonable to claim that the relationship between the two communities was easy or smooth in the period before the British rule when the dominant brahman ideology regarded the Muslims as lower caste, or that all the turmoil was a fall-out of the evil designs of the shrewd British. Just as there were many acts of give and take between the two communities, likewise, over a period of time, there was the creation of much difference and several impediments. In Bengali literature prior to the advent of the British, there are distinct traces of both unity and divisiveness among the two communities. The predominance of non-Muslims among the zamindar class was no less even during the Mughal period, but because of the way social relations were completely altered by the Permanent Settlement, that eminence acquired a different implication. In the new dispensation, Hindus were dominant among not only the zamindar class, but also among those employed in the third sector of economic activity – not just Hindus but those belonging to the upper castes. The currency of English in place of Farsi as the language of the court also aided the prosperity of the Hindus, at least initially. In fact the entire upper strata of society came under its hegemony. Is it any surprise, therefore, that a rigid, Hindu-centric mentality should pervade the social imagination? The absolute power of the non-Muslim zamindars opened the doors for dressing up the landlord–ryot conflict in the shape of a clash between the Hindu and Muslim communities. As it is, during colonial rule, the main ideologues among the Bengali intellectual class were people employed in the third sector of economic activity. It was an area of economic activity that had greatly expanded, but this did not mean there was no check to this inflationary trend – it would be unreasonable even to hope for such in the colonial economic system. Consequently, the competition between the communities grew fierce as the number of people who were claimants increased. Then, at a later stage in history when the Bengali Muslims stood up and demanded their share of the earnings of the third sector of economic activity, the Hindu–Muslim barrier became more complicated. Let me cite a brilliant example of this. The occasion: the pattern of voting in the Bengal Legislative Council on the 1928 Amendment to the Peasants' Rights Law of 1885. The members of the Swaraj Party (the Congress) refused to vote in order to safeguard the interests of the landlords. There was nothing in the provisions of the Amendment that could upset the applecart of the Permanent Settlement system, yet they saw to it that it was rejected. In this connection it is worthwhile to note that among those who were in favour of the Amendment, fifteen were Muslims and one a Hindu. And among those against the amendment were thirteen British, five Muslims and forty-three Hindus. Further, among the forty-three Hindus were much-honoured leaders of the nation. They may have had differences among themselves over many things, but that did not prevent them from extending their hands in unison to prevent the passing of the Amendment. Among them were: Saratchandra Bose, Jatindramohan Sengupta, Kumudshankar Roy, Kiranshankar Roy, Bijoyprasad Singha Roy, Bidhan Roy, Naliniranjan Sarkar. And in order that the Amendment did not get passed and the interests of the landlords remained intact, Subhas Chandra Bose extended active leadership to the Congressmen who opposed it.[36]

In the colonial age, because of the flurry caused by the presence of foreigners, the nature of the relationship between men and women underwent some changes too, especially among upper-caste Hindus. However, women were hardly visible even in the third economic sphere, despite the spread of education in their midst. On the whole, two kinds of economic roles were reserved for them: housework and reproduction of the labour force. But a kind of tension gradually arose between the home and the world in the upper-class, upper-caste society, altering the equation between the inner and outer worlds; the bonds of the joint family system came unstuck and various ideological positions regarding women began to circulate in society. All that anon.

Bankimchandra was not entirely wrong when he declared in the concluding portion of his essay on the 'Peasants of Bengal' that 'the modern Bengali society was founded upon the Permanent Settlement'.[37] His opinion was that it was founded upon a big mistake. But having said that – and as if to reassure his readers – he dismissed the whole idea, saying:

> Doing away with the Permanent Settlement will be tantamount to the possibility of Bengali society being reduced to total anarchy. We are not adherents of social revolutions and cannot ill-advise the English, especially, bringing ruin to an arrangement they had ensured permanency to under an oath to Truth, and show them up as liars in this world thereby earning eternal distrust of their tenants. I will only give such advice when I decide not to do good to the English and also when I would wish to bring harm to society.[38] .

At the beginning of the essay, Bankim had raised his voice in support of the peasants: 'Where they do not flourish, the country does not.' Had he forgotten what he had himself said earlier? On the one hand, there is compassion for the peasants, on the other for the English – and on top of that, an intense desire to win the favour of the zamindars. Does not all this make Bankim's essay self-contradictory? And was it only Bankim who was driven by such conflicting desires?

Ishwarchandra Vidyasagar (1820–1891), adopting Marshman's text, had written in his *History of Bengal* (Vol. 2): 'There is no doubt at all that Bengal has benefited enormously from the Permanent Settlement.' But in his view it had one fault: 'no measures have been introduced to protect those peasants who have eternally enjoyed revenue from land lease from the arbitrariness of the new class of landlords'. Nevertheless, 'Lord Cornwallis has strengthened the state administrative machinery, and has benefited the people through the introduction of the Permanent Settlement. The gratitude expressed by the countrymen for his generosity and sagaciousness is, therefore, not misplaced.'[39] And no less a person than Raja Rammohun Roy has actually written to the great ruler of England that by the help of the Almighty, merciful God, the English have saved the homeless inhabitants of Bengal from the tyranny and oppression of the Muslim rulers and have provided them with shelter.[40] So that England's commitment to altruism may be properly executed, he had advised that India would benefit enormously if the rich and forward-thinking European traders adopted to live in India permanently.

> In fact the relationship between Great Britain and India would have a strong and

long-lasting foundation if only India were ruled according to Utilitarian principles. In this way India could remain allied to Great Britain for an indefinite period and take advantage of its enlightened governance. In exchange India could become a partner and a beneficiary in the progress of that great country.[41]

According to him, even if India suffered some depreciation because of this, on balance there would be adequate gain. By getting rid of ancient prejudices and age-old superstitions through enlightened administration and scientific education, one day India would equal the Christian powers of the world.[42] But could what Rammohun had dreamt in the free air of an unrestricted open market ever become true in the structure of a colonial economy? And did this proneness to illusion lead him to completely evade any mention of the topic of the inhuman cruelty inflicted on indigo workers, and write instead that the condition of agricultural workers in places where the indigo leaf was cultivated was infinitely better than of those elsewhere?[43] He believed that there was nothing fundamentally wrong with the Permanent Settlement system and that everything would be in place if some minor repairs were made. Why only Rammohun, even the so-called angry Young Bengal advocates of those days also did not entertain any doubts about the fairness of the British administration.[44] So much so that when, during the age of nationalism, economists like Romesh Chandra Dutt began to construct a theory of increased capital flow in the country with the help of facts and statistics, they remained more or less silent about the internal social contradictions. In their theoretical thinking, the oppressions of the zamindars and the moneylenders would not acquire much importance. In the theories of the nationalist economists, it was 'race' that would gain preeminence and not 'class'. Just like by raising the single issue of 'race' it is possible to suppress all class-related questions, so too it is possible to construct the myth of cultural homogeneity.

And Rabindranath Tagore? Did he too not vacillate? In the Preface to Pramatha Chaudhuri's (1868–1941) *Talking about the Ryots*, he had written:

> I have no innate desire to cling to the zamindari land. I know that the zamindars are but leeches, parasites, creatures who are dependent on others. The tenants provide us with subsistence and the clerks bring all that to us – there is nothing in the system they could make us feel glorious about or fill us with manly pride.[45]

And in another place in the same essay, he had said:

> The problem is – the ryots lack intelligence – they are not educated and have little power and are struck with bad luck where money is concerned. They do not know how to protect themselves in any way. . . . It is neither nice to say nor hear that it is incumbent on us to prevent the peasants from acquiring independent land rights – but only those who do not have brains as small as peas are worthy of having such grand independence. From my small experience I can say that to transfer land

> rights to the stupid peasantry of our country would be tantamount to giving them the right to commit suicide.[46]

But why this fear? And why is it that the zamindars, talukdars and the numerous middlemen collectively have not allowed growth of the economy of the whole society for the sake of the Permanent Settlement?[47] Even after acknowledging such a situation, Saratchandra Chattopadhyay (1876–1938) made his mouthpiece Sabyasachi, in the novel *Pather Dabi* (*The Right of the Road*), declare: 'It is not for us to break our heads over the poor and harmless peasantry. . . . I do not have the energy or the time to waste in order to get them agitated. My business is with the middle-class, educated gentlemen.'[48] And the novel *Pather Dabi* is itself a manifesto of the ryot-hating middle-class gentlemen: 'The British have to be overthrown for the sake of the *bhadralok*, in order to extend and strengthen their interests.'[49]

Although the industrial workers were to be deployed in the struggle against imperialism, the peasants were to be kept totally out of the arena of conflict. The *bhadralok* had hardly any role to play in industrialization and it seems that there was no direct conflict between their class interest and that of the workers, but the situation was radically different in the sphere of agriculture. Did the prescriptive ruling of the Permanent Settlement reflect this difference? Why else would it be that despite numerous direct evidences of peasant revolt, such contempt was expressed towards them in the writings of the upper-caste intellectuals, freely adorning them with epithets such as dumb, stupid, tender-hearted, laid-back and helpless? Is not their class anxiety revealed in this continuous and relentless character assassination of the peasantry as a class? At least Bankim did not evade the problem of class neurosis. He pointed to this plain truth when he said: 'If the entire peasantry becomes angry, then where would we all be? What would be the prognosis?'[50]

Modern Bengali literature is but a narrative of the weaving and tearing down of the dreams of the *bhadralok*. The passage of time has wrought many changes in that tale of desire and anxiety. The promise of a destination with which the journey had begun was to a great extent fantastical. And modern Bengali literature written for and by the *bhadralok* therefore contains an account of that failure, with children's literature occupying an important place in the trajectory.

On the whole, children suffer most from the combined pressures of all kinds of oppression in the world. On top of this, those who veer away from custom-sanctioned conduct and observances, or those who are not able to adjust to the conditions and patterns of functioning of authority or adopt its prescribed policies – it has become a kind of general practice to bestow upon them appellations like 'immature mind', 'childish' or 'mentally retarded'. Thus, not just the individual but an entire community, class, race and even nation can be included in that category of the incompetent and irresponsible child.

In the perspective of colonial power, the backward inhabitants of the colonies are but 'children'. A majority of the world population entered the phase of their childhood anew in the age of colonialism. But, on the other hand, when these conquered people seek ways to free themselves from such humiliating circumstances, they express their dreams of patriotic uprising and the construction of nationhood with the help of the imaginings of a child. Children's literature is situated firmly in the interstices of these two opposing tendencies. There is no doubt at all that somehow or the other, the presence of elders lurk behind in their writings for children. But in the days of colonialism, especially in its nationalistic phase, this presence had to necessarily take a different configuration. In the colonial frame of reference, in a sense, even the elders were the children's kindred. Therefore, children's literature has come to bear conspicuous traces of the many-splendoured means and methods adopted for cultural domination and the construction of a distorted picture of childhood.[51] Children's literature belonging to such times becomes not only the elders' mode of self-expression, but also a mode of dialogue with the self – a biographical narrative of a community.

Notes and References

1 Rabindranath Tagore, 'Muktadhara', in *Rabindra Rachanabali,* Vol. 14, Visva Bharati, 1370 (Bengali calendar), p. 214.

2 V. Vološinov, *Marxism and the Philosophy of Language*, translated by Ladislav Satej and R. Titunik, London, 1986, p. 48.

3 Roland Barthes, 'Myth Today', in *Mythologies*, translated by Annette Levers, London, 1986, p. 114.

4 Ibid., p. 143.

5 Michel Foucault, 'The Order of Discourse', in *Untying the Text: A Post-Sructuralist Reader*, London, 1987, pp. 48–78.

6 Karl Marx, 'Letter' (written to Ludwig Kugelson, 11 July 1868), in *Marx–Engels: Selected Correspondence*, Moscow, 1982, p. 196.

7 Raymond Williams, 'Base and Superstructure in Marxist Cultural Theory', in *Marxism and Literature*, London, 1980, pp. 31–49.

8 Karl Marx, *The Eighteenth Brumaire of Louis Bonaparte*, in *Karl Marx: Selected Works*, Vol. 9, Moscow, 1977, p. 398.

9 Bankimchandra Chattopadhyay, 'Bangadesher Krishak', in *Bankim Rachanabali*, Calcutta: Sahitya Sansad, 1393 (Bengali calendar), p. 292.

10 Ibid., p. 288.

11 Ibid., p. 299.

12 Ibid., p. 292.

13 Ibid., p. 295.

14 Ibid., p. 298.

15 Ibid., p. 287.

16 Ibid., p. 292.

17 Ibid., p. 288.

18 Ibid., p. 305.

19 Rabindranath Tagore, 'Laraier Mul', in *Kalantar*, *Rabindra Rachanabali*, Vol. 24, Visva Bharati, 1371 (Bengali calendar), p. 271.

20 Karl Marx, *Capital*, Vol. 1, Penguin, 1979, pp. 931–40.

[21] Romesh Chandra Dutt, *The Economic History of India*, Vol. 1, New Delhi, 1970, p. 276.
[22] Sabyasachi Bhattacharya, *Upanibeshik Bharater Arthaniti: 1850–1947*, Calcutta, 1396 (Bengali calendar), p. 39.
[23] Sourin Bhattacharya, 'Rammohuner Arthanaitik Chinta', *Anuktta,* special twelfth edition, 1386 (Bengali calendar), p. 101.
[24] Badaruddin Umar, *Chirasthayi Bandobaste Bangadesher Krishak*, Calcutta, 1390 (Bengali calendar), p. 19.
[25] Sabyasachi Bhattacharya, *Upanibeshik Bharater Arthaniti*, p. 40.
[26] Ranajit Guha, *A Rule of Property for Bengal*, New Delhi, 1982.
[27] Ashok Sen, 'The Bengal Economy and Rammohun Roy', in P.C. Joshi (ed.), *Rammohun Roy and the Process of Modernization in India*, New Delhi, 1975, p. 113.
[28] Sourin Bhattacharya, 'Rammohuner Arthanaitik Chinta', p. 101.
[29] Ashok Sen, 'The Bengal Economy and Rammohun Roy', p. 116.
[30] Amiya Kumar Bagchi, *Private Investment in India 1900–1939*, New Delhi, 1989, p. 21.
[31] Badaruddin Umar, *Chirasthayi Bandobaste Bangadesher Krishak*, p. 29.
[32] Ibid., pp. 21–22.
[33] Bankimchandra Chattopadhyay, 'Bangadesher Krishak', p. 305.
[34] Ibid., p. 287.
[35] Sabyasachi Bhattacharya, *Upanibeshik Bharater Arthaniti*, p. 35.
[36] Bankimchandra Chattopadhyay, 'Letters on Hinduism', in *Bankim Rachanabali*, Vol. 3, Calcutta, 1378 (Bengali calendar), pp. 230–31.
[37] Pradyumna Bhattacharya, 'Samajer Matra ebong Tarashankarer Upanyas: Chaitali Ghurni', *Ekshon*, Vol. 11, nos. 5–6 (special issue), 1382 (Bengali calendar), p. 74.
[38] Bankimchandra Chattopadhyay, 'Bangadesher Krishak', p. 309.
[39] Ibid., pp. 309–10.
[40] Ishwarchandra Vidyasagar, *Banglar Itihas*, in *Bidyasagar Rachanasamagra*, Vol. 1, Calcutta, 1987, pp. 281–82.
[41] Rammohun Roy, 'An Appeal to the King in Council', in *Rammohun Rachanabali*, Calcutta, 1973, p. 508.
[42] Rammohun Roy, 'Dues on Settlement in India by Europeans', in *Rammohun Rachanabali*, Calcutta, 1973, p. 531.
[43] Sourin Bhattacharya, 'Ram Mohoner Arthanaitik Chinta', pp. 103–04.
[44] Ibid., pp. 530–31.
[45] Ibid., p. 529.
[46] Sumit Sarkar, 'The Complexities of Young Bengal', in *A Critique of Colonial India*, Calcutta: Papyrus, 1986, pp. 18–36.
[47] Rabindranath Tagore, 'Bhumika', 'Ryoter Katha', in *Kalantar*, *Rabindra Rachanabali*, Vol. 12, Visva Bharati, 1351 (Bengali calendar), p. 8.
[48] Ibid., pp. 10–12.
[49] Saratchandra Chattopadhyay, *Pather Dabi*, in *Sarat Sahitya Sangraha*, Vol. 13, Calcutta, p. 361.
[50] Ibid.
[51] Sirajul Islam Choudhuri, *Saratchandra o Samantabad*, Calcutta, 1983, p. 20.
[52] Bankimchandra Chattopadhyay, 'Bangadesher Krishak', p. 289.
[53] Ariel Dorfman, 'Childhood and Underdevelopment', in *The Empire's Old Clothes*, New York, 1983, p. 8.

2

The Fairytales of the Country and the Fairytale Country

When/Where?

Youthful Dakshinaranjan is making his way through the villages of Dhaka–Mymensingha. The time is the beginning of the twentieth century. He listens to popular legends recited to him by the village elders. He notes how the same tale can undergo a complete transformation in the hands of succeeding story-tellers; he observes how variegated the ingredients of the tales can be or how polygamous their mixture. He listens to them over and over again, at times taking their impressions on wax records with the help of an old-fashioned phonograph.[1] He tries hard to discover the latent strand of unity beneath all the swathes of the metaphorical cover; tries to make the tales more compact or bestow to them a more unified form by discarding either some of the raw material or their added refinements. As much as he knits the disparate details into the narrative structure, he omits almost the same amount for the sake of harmony and completeness of the tales. He is extra careful in his task of continually sorting, selecting and re-weaving the material; he keeps in mind that the natural felicity, the indigenous skill of the original teller are retained in the written text, and that both the rhythm of the original speech and its graceful, musical cadences remain intact. By such means, although Dakshinaranjan could not transmit into the written form an exact replica of its traditional model – the original oral composition – he saw to it that he preserved much of the feeling of the original.

Dakshinaranjan had arrived in Calcutta from Mymensingha in 1906, bringing along with him a few samples of this laborious work. He was able to establish contact with the publisher 'Bhattacharya & Sons' due to the help and encouragement of Sri Dineshchandra Sen. The manuscript travelled to the hands of Rabindranath Tagore, who enthusiastically wrote the Preface to the book. In 1907, *Thakurmar Jhuli* was published. The processes of transference from the oral tradition to its textual form being thus completed, the continually metamorphic tale of the teller became frozen in a pattern of immovable printed words.

Mymensingha–Calcutta: it is not as though the distance is merely geographical, or that the transformation ensuing the transmission of the material from the storyteller to the writer, from the listener to the reader, is all there is to it. From one atmosphere to another, the particular orbit the stories landed themselves in, the time and the specific society they were hospitably received in – all of these facts are as relevant as the actual processes of transference. The singular acquaintanceship between the sender and the receiver of the tale affected by the mediation of Dakshinaranjan has a definite context – a marked conjuncture of time and place. And to comprehend the significance of that fellowship, one would have to refer to those very parameters of time/place whence it was actually accomplished. For that, we are required to revisit those tumultuous days of the Swadeshi movement in the wake of the 1905 partition of Bengal. In order to properly acknowledge and come up with a substantive explanation of the extraordinary interest surrounding *Thakurmar Jhuli* witnessed among the *bhadralok*, we cannot but direct our attention to the context of the movement for national independence. If one delved deeper into Rabindranath's Preface to *Thakurmar Jhuli*, one would see that such an argument is also latent therein.

Rabindranath's 'Preface'

'Is anything more *swadeshi* than *Thakurmar Jhuli* in our country?'[2] Rabindranath Tagore's Preface to the book has this opening sentence. That he was not making use of the word '*swadeshi*' in the limited sense of its dictionary meaning but in the larger metaphorical sense of secondary meanings, becomes clear in the succeeding phrases: 'But alas, even this "pleasure bundle" is coming to us as a product of the factories of Manchester. Nowadays the Fairytales of England have become staple – the last resort for our children. Our Grandmother's Company has gone totally bankrupt.'[3] It is not only that the conjugation of opposing ideas, such as the factories of Manchester and '*swadeshi*' are there, but also that the entire text displays a proliferation of contesting binaries – at times explicitly, at others by throwing broad hints. We can, with ease, fill up the blanks: indigenous fairytales – European fairytales; the goods produced by agriculture – Manchester factory-produced goods; 'princes and the sons of other dignitaries', stories of Bangama–Bangami – ethics by Martin and made-easy editions of Burke's history of the French Revolution; 'mother's milk' – 'chickpea flour'; 'rituals, festivals, yatra, music, storytelling sessions' – 'horrors of English spelling books'; 'everyday utterances' – 'bookish language'; 'the magic of indigenous speech' – 'the magic of the English pen'; 'untutored women –

tutored women'. These binaries contain seeds of conflict and even hints of a bigger clash. And if one is not able to decipher the contours of that conflict, the special language of the fairytales, its particular diction, its old-fashioned naivete and folksy style – over which Rabindranath gushed – the significance of all that would remain forever undiscovered. And one would never understand why Rabindranath referred to the bankruptcy of the Grandmother's Company when dealing with the specific context of Bengal's own oral tradition.

But it is easy to guess, once we have glanced through the Preface, that Rabindranath was negotiating with the subject of folktales from the perspective of the Bengali *bhadralok* society. The lives of people which had fed into the narrative and the source of which stream had not totally dried up – 'those lives' were not the topic of his discussion. His sight was fixed on men of the educated class, those who had been estranged from the country's tradition owing to foreign learning, those who were separated from the life-stream of the nation, who had practically forgotten national art and culture, and who could not respond like those before to old-fashioned simplicities. A crippling sickness involving the lapse of memory (amnesia) had taken hold of such people. There are, in the essay, hints of changes in taste, alterations in mental attitude and thinking, and the metamorphosis that had overtaken the point of view and the 'sense of life' in Bengal. Rabindranath discussed this problem in greater detail in his lecture titled 'Swadeshi Samaj', delivered in the year 1904:

> Our hearts have become enslaved to the Whites, our tastes captive to foreign merchandise . . .[4] we complain about the various ways and the different means by which our national wealth has made a beeline for the foreign soil. But if our hearts were also to decamp there, and, one by one, all the things that are connected to the welfare of our nation were acquired by foreign power and nothing remained left behind, then, would that be a lesser cause of sorrow than the mere flow of cash?[5]

To Rabindranath, financial disaster is the same as the loss of subjecthood – equally important; he is also significantly aware of the link between the two. He knows that the fight with the British, besides being one of the political and economic kind, is also ideological. Therefore, along with the urgency to retrieve the nation from the clutches of foreign rule lay the equally important task of recouping the consciousness of the nation. Rabindranath believed that if our countrymen took over foreign manners and morals wholesale, became sahibs par excellence, aligning themselves with foreign interest, and in the process themselves became meaningless and inconsequential, then, it would not matter one bit even if the country were to gain political freedom. Freedom would not be complete and must remain fractured so long as we are not free of the shackles that have tied us to the all-powerful foreign capital, so long as independence is not worked out on every level of our existence.

But how are we to prepare ourselves for this total freedom? How can we embark on a project of '*atma-shakti*' (self-assertion) while simultaneously removing the ignominy of foreign rule? On one hand, Rabindranath was advising people about ways to strengthen the organization of the weak rural society through rural upliftment programmes; on the other, he was enthusing people to retrieve their lost or neglected tradition. He was encouraging a gathering enthusiasm for the collection of different cultural artefacts bearing the signature of the creative imagination of the rural folk. He was of the firm belief that if one wanted to discover one's true national identity, there was no way out but to discard all that was spurious and distorted, descend lower in the social strata, so that one could become initiated into what was an authentic 'sense of life'. Like many nationalist intellectuals of his time, Rabindranath found in rural life an adequate alternative to the otherwise oscillating, restless and disjointed lives of the Bengali *bhadralok* class. And he believed that no matter how much poverty, deprivation or delusion there was in the villages, or how much of its past glory was dimmed, it still retained its pristine social character[6] and was an example par excellence of 'ideal harmony'. According to Rabindranath, it was necessary for the self-forgetting nation to take recourse to those eternal social verities encapsulated in village society, take the lead from nation's ancient forms, in order to illumine nation's spiritual inheritance, instal its new apotheosis in its proper place and in its proper form.[7] To his synthesizing view, India's inherent dharma was the experience of sameness in difference, of unity among diversity. Which means that coexistence was his last word, the ultimate truth. Today, we may have doubts about the way in which nationalists like Rabindranath viewed and measured the lives of the lower strata of society, whence it was never possible for their true plight to be revealed. And if the consciousness of the lower strata became a mere replica of upper-class consciousness, then wouldn't it become quite valueless – not deserving of consideration? Could that kind of historical research which is based on the premise that the lower classes were mere objects of research, and not its investigating subject, ever attempt to discover – either as hints or as sign – its complex mental history?

In his nationalist phase, like his many other writings, the Preface to *Thakurmar Jhuli* also carried the anti-imperialist import of Rabindranath's thinking. But a strong indication that his thinking was circumscribed by upper-class sensibilities was already in evidence in those writings. It is no surprise, therefore, that Rabindranath should be captivated by the simplicity and felicity of *Thakurmar Jhuli*, but when he takes those old-fashioned simplicities as not just something beyond compare but as eternal verities – an example of something pure preserved in Bengali hearts from time immemorial, that act like an antidote/talisman to the devastations suffered from the vagaries of fortune by the gentlemanly class – then the political nuances of that fascination become quite plain. And it is not difficult for us to gauge that. Clearly, the tales had become linked with a very different kind of discourse and a radically new significance had been attributed to them; as an act of appropriation, a divergent context had extended its claim over them. It was not just Rabindranath but others like Aurobindo Ghosh, Haraprasad Shastri, Jyotindranath Thakur, Dwijendralal Roy, Ramendra Sundar Trivedi, Girishchandra Ghosh, Chittaranjan Das, Dineshchandra Sen, Swarnakumari Deb and Romesh Chandra Dutt[8] who praised both *Thakurmar Jhuli* and *Thakurdadar Jhuli* (1909) in similar terms.

In his book *Bangabhasha o Sahitya* (*Bengali Language and Literature* [1896], fifth edition 1926), Dineshchandra Sen reminds us that the language of the later edition of *Thakurmar Jhuli* is in no way the same as Dakshinaranjan Mitra Majumdar's original, or even its first published version. 'Hounded by the critics' and for the benefit of 'the barely educated clamouring readers', the compiler of the tales had himself made certain amendments – decreasing the volume of 'incomprehensible', 'provincial expressions' in the second edition, – for the benefit of the market. This is the version we get today. One cannot minimize the import of Dineshchandra Sen's observations about *Thakurdadar Jhuli*, that it is 'not a reed mat bought off the streets but as precious as a Persian rug', or 'a source of joy for children, an elixir of love for the youth and a moral text for the aged', or 'equally enjoyable to the ignorant and the wise alike'. The question remains: what eternal verities did the intellectuals of those days discover in such narratives that attracted them so much? We must adopt a very careful approach in our new reading of those texts; comprehend them in the context of their time and place, so that our understanding is not clouded by any predetermined notions. If we cannot advance with an open and a curious mind, if we do not scrutinize our decisions at every step, we would perforce become entangled in a new predicament and succeed in creating a new mesh of confusion.

Doing It with Stories

'Tell me a story': so many tales – involving prince and princess, heroes, foes and friends – are devised to satisfy such a demand made daily by children. It is entirely possible that the listeners of the stories are girls or boys belonging to peasant families, but nothing prevents them from imagining themselves as princes or princesses. Over and above this, there is no paucity of new inventions or range of creativity. If on one day we have Buddhu–Bhutum, on another it is Lalkamal–Neelkamal; if at one time it is Kanchanmala, at another time it is Pushpamala. But who are these characters – Buddhu/Bhutum or Kanchanmala/Pushpamala? Are they sheer products of the writer's creative imagination that exist only beyond the realm of actuality? Are the citizens of that never-never (fairy) land not connected in any way with our world of material reality? Or, to put it differently, do those sparkling characters have no relationship of intimacy with the listeners of the tales?

Buddhu and Bhutum – the two characters belonging to 'Kalabati Rajkanya', the first story in *Thakurmar Jhuli* – do not possess either attractive names or a pleasant appearance. Although they move about like human beings, they are not fully human. Yet they have similarities in appearance with two beings belonging to the human universe: Buddhu resembles the monkey, Bhutum the owl. Bhutum's *Ma* is a handmaid in the zoo; Buddhu's *Ma* is a female scavenger and collector of cowdung. They both live in shanties and somehow manage to eke out their living.

The story also has five princes. They carry attractive names, are dressed in a way that draws attention to themselves and command much authority. They are named after rare and highly priced objects. If one of them is called Hira (or diamond), the other is Manik (ruby or a precious jewel); if one of them is named Mukto (pearl), the other is known as Sankha (conch-shell) or even Kanchan (gold). The five princes own five flying horses, and a battalion of sepoys and sailors. Their mothers live in the interiors of the palace, resting their feet and whiling away their days happily.

Buddhu and Bhutum, and the five princes live respectively in worlds that are polar opposites. And the distance and difference between the ordinary and the mundane, and their opposite – the resplendent world – is but huge. Generally speaking, one complements the other; yet it is but natural that there exists no relationship of equality between these two distinct examples of self-contained heterogeneity. It would be also reasonable to consider that the five princes could, if they wished, cross the zealously drawn boundary posts or the limits of the Buddhu–Bhutum world as well as possess the passport for such an entry, whereas the latter has neither the right nor the ability to do the same.

But it is the powerful and unchallenged presence of one who is actually responsible for bringing both the worlds under a single design, and the source of all the might of the five princes as also the misery of Buddhu–Bhutum. He is the paternal figure of all seven – the king himself. It is not as if the king had abandoned Buddhu–Bhutum, or their mothers, out of a whim; the childless king, having acquired a magical root from a sadhu, had asked his eldest queen to grind it into a paste and give it to all the other queens so that they also could bear sons. But spurred by greed, the five elder queens made full use of the root acquired from the sadhu and the last two queens were left with nothing but the dregs. As a consequence, the first five queens were blessed with moon-faced male offsprings, whereas the remaining two had to stay content with an owl and a monkey as children. Thereafter Buddhu–Bhutum and their mothers had to leave the palace walls, and were deprived of royal comfort and pleasure. Although the king did not discriminate between Buddhu–Bhutum and his princely sons with respect to fatherly affection, he did not give the former the recognition they deserved as sons of a king.

While Buddhu–Bhutum were friendly with everyone and provided their mothers with whatever help they could, the five princes beat up one person or another and created a nuisance amongst all. In order to aggressively project their own power, these five princes tormented whosoever they came across. The people of the kingdom were fed up of their antics and irritated beyond measure.

A maiden with cheeks red as apples, and hair dark and wavy like clouds, initiated a conflict between Buddhu–Bhutum and the five princes. Like a bird of paradise floating on a silver barge with diamond oars in the sky, the maiden relayed the message: 'I am Princess Kalabati with hair dark and wavy as the clouds / Send your son to the land of Kalabati / Let him come laden with pearl-like flowers and drums and trumpets / I will come to your house as a slave to your son.'[9] Thus a competition began between the five princes and Buddhu–Bhutum, centering on who would acquire the right to her (Kalabati's) personhood. The five princes plotted to entangle Buddhu–Bhutum in an impossible situation; yet when some difficulty arose or a problem occurred, they had no other recourse but to seek the help of Buddhu–Bhutum. Buddhu–Bhutum – especially Buddhu – no matter how much injustice was done to him, was always ready to come forward and rescue the princes. When they are amidst some natural disaster or in the throes of misfortune, like being imprisoned in the abdomen of the 'three old hags', Buddhu–Bhutum – or more often just Buddhu – make their appearance as a 'dispenser of difficulties' and save the five princes from being humiliated. Buddhu wins Princess Kalabati's hand after having overcome many impediments; Bhutum gets married to Princess Hirabati. By the end of the narrative, we find that the five princes and their mothers are reduced to becoming objects of the king's displeasure, Buddhu–Bhutum and their mothers having interchanged positions with the princes and their mothers. The king seals the doors and windows of the rooms where the five queens live with their five princely sons. Those who had been deprived and humiliated now have newly acquired power.

On one hand, Buddhu–Bhutum are rewarded and established at the centre of power; on the other, the five princess are removed from the arena of operation and are compelled to stay out of all kinds of social competition forever. But at the end of the tale, a rather astonishing and significant change takes place. We come to know that Buddhu–Bhutum are not actually a monkey and an owl; these forms (their external appearances) are but camouflage. They had thus far deliberately dissembled themselves when actually they are as handsome as the gods. When Buddhu's wife Kalabati and Bhutum's wife Hirabati burn their disguises, everyone comes to know their real forms. And they receive honour surpassing humans from all the human beings around them. But this is not the end of the story. Following their release from all the confusion, their names also undergo a change. Buddhu–Bhutum come to be known by names which are more civilized and becoming: Budhkumar and Roopkumar.

The narrative can of course be read differently, interpreted from many angles. The reader can dress up the tale according to his taste and ideology, keeping intact its textual meaning. The reader can, in places, either through his/her unified vision or rather haphazardly, alter the significance of different sections of the tale, its characters, even events. The text's prospective readers can increase in number, its substantive political analyses undergo modifications, consequent upon any alteration of its import or change in its overall pattern. The shape the text takes on, the structure of meaning enfolded in it – more specifically, the way in which we regard the process of its structuration – all this cannot be detached from history or be regarded as neutral.

Let us establish the premises of our argument with a query: is there anyone in the narrative of Kalabati we may identify as its central (nodal) character? The question is rather a simple one – innocent, perhaps; and yet if one is deceived by its assumed guise of naturalness, many complexities of the text will simply go unnoticed. Our first job, then, is to determine which *a priori* truth/assumptions the question is founded upon. For we know that the nature of the query, its likely answer and the field of investigation are all tied up, and have definite boundaries. As some topics are marked as its legitimate subjects, so too there are others existing beyond its jurisdiction. Therefore, if one has to bestow adequate importance to the query, one will have to investigate/determine the theoretical world contingent to it. We will have to have a clear understanding of its problematic field or the exact design of that problematic field.

When we want to know if the text has a central character or not, we are actually trying to find out whether the text has any central significance, whether its structure is flawless and well-shaped. We regard that text as well-shaped in which each part is not only related to all other parts of the whole, but is also both symmetrically and decorously related to the whole; in which there is no conflict or discrepancy between parts and the whole, and each detail, every ingredient, is not in the least at variance with the total design; in which there is no slippage of part from the whole and also each part resonates the whole. There may be several layers of meaning in a well-shaped text, nevertheless each level is conditioned/controlled by the text's total structure of meaning. And it is this centrality of vision that renders the text well-shaped and carries the entire weight of its meaning; by whose grace its diverse ingredients are firmly tied together into a single meaningful narrative unit. It is a vision that occupies the central position in the narrative that is its main character. Instead of assuming that texts are by nature symmetrical, instead of taking the harmonious nature of the text as given, we would like to scrutinize the problematic field and ascertain whether, because of this capitulation to a given truth, we have not suppressed the question of the multivocality of the text.

There is no dearth of claimants to the position of the central character of the narrative of Kalabati Rajkanya. The king (Raja), Buddhu, Bhutum or the person after whom the narrative has been named – any of them can assume this position. Some have opined that the narrative has not one (single) but two complementary central characters or heroes: Buddhu and Bhutum. But let us see, by taking each of these characters separately and analysing them, what kind of conclusions we may arrive at.

The King

There is a structural similarity among most of the stories belonging to *Thakurmar Jhuli*, a common general design, despite their obvious differences. This design is easier to identify if one reads the narrative from its opposite end. Fairytales have an inevitable ending, predetermined and replete with moral lessons. The narrative has to reach a comfortable conclusion weathering many ups and downs of fortune, negotiating countless strange and wonderful events. It has to arrive at a predictable conclusion with an unquestioning regularity. The narrator or the teller of the tale may suspend his telling along the gaps of the stories or the numerous turns these take, in order to test whether the listener was asleep or awake, or in order to simply arouse his curiosity, but the narration does not come to an end so long as there is an answer to the all-too-familiar 'And then what happened next?' The question becomes irrelevant only when the tale comes to a full stop after contending with several pauses en route to 'what happened next'. And the concluding sentence, whether it be 'And the king lived happily',[10] or 'The king, Rakhal and Kanchanmala all continued to live their days happily',[11] or 'And afterwards, the king, queen, Arun, Barun and Kiranmala together with their progeny continued to rule throughout the ages',[12] always has the past continuous as its verb. The teller obdurately refuses to give in even if the listener's curiosity remains unfulfilled (after the pronouncement of such a final sentence) or the unsatisfied listener continues to hanker for more instalments of 'what happened next', harassing the teller no end. All destinations of 'what happened next' invariably turn on the last sentence – return again and again to what would appear as a rehearsed theme. Or else the teller folds up her tale with an oft-repeated two liner: 'My story has come to an end / and the *notey* tree has folded in.'

At the end of a fairytale these are words of consolation: all danger is past, there is no need to fear any more and usually there is no necessity for any change to take place. Everybody has been given what was her/his due, there is no room for any regret or complaint. Therefore, it is but natural that time will appear as if it has come to a stop. Any qualitative change of that ideal condition or an ascent towards a higher state is unimaginable. This reassurance about the possibility of a kingdom of happiness or an abode of eternal pleasure with which the telling of the tale concludes has space as its measure, not time. It is immune to temporality, existing as it does beyond the parameters of history and its processes.

One can easily take the fairytale apart, break the narrative into three phases or periods. Its beginning, middle and end are both distinct and yet interconnected. On the surface at least, none works against the logic of the other, as if the story has an element of inevitability that inexorably draws all its ingredients to a prescribed end. The tale moves infallibly from its beginning to its middle, from its middle to its close. If one looks deeper, one can find that although the teller enjoys certain privileges as to how to start the story, she has absolutely none in relation to its ending. How a story ought to end is sanctioned by tradition. When telling a fairytale, the teller has to observe certain narrative conditions; she has to weave her story keeping it within the confines of the prescribed limits. As a result, it is only in the 'middle' that the teller can reveal the power of her creativity and her artistic acumen. If entreated, she can add events to events in order to inject complexity to the tale, continually defer the narrative closure – that moment of absolute resolution – by complicating the stories from within. Like the episode 'Princess Kalabati', or the one in which the five princes remain captive inside the stomachs of three old hags, or in which their peacock boat loses its way and is cut adrift in the rainbow-coloured waters of the river, the teller can go on and on – increase the number of such exotic details and introduce all kinds of improbable situations which can cause harassment to the princes, and, in the same way, create impediments in the trajectory of the lives of Buddhu–Bhutum or make the testing of their mettle difficult and stretched. Thus the narrative becomes unquestioningly attractive and is able to arouse the curiosity of its child-listeners by such interjection of exciting conflicts, and descriptions that are sparse yet swift-moving, restrained yet wondrous. But no matter how much the narrator displays her artistic skill and expertise in introducing such danger-filled situations, her role in the narrative remains at best ancillary and minor. As if these trifle episodic moments are encircled by a narrative of crisis of a more primary nature: a kind of story that begins with a movement towards a conflict/complication only to end in an ultimate resolution to that conflict. The situations of minor conflict/complication have their own logic and are of independent volition; they can be subject to alteration or numerical variations. Also they are able to withstand much intense scrutiny, though outside the parameters of the primary and fundamental conflict, these would have no meaning or worth. Unless one is aware of the difference that exists between the significations of the minor and primary crisis situations as well as the relative importance of their various functions in the narrative, one would not be able to discover its inherent logic.

We have seen that it is not possible to introduce any qualitative change at the point where the narrative ends. But before we reach that still moment, the middle of the tale is full of ups and downs, and several constructions and deconstructions take place continually. Something untoward can happen for which stability can no longer be maintained, and a complete state of disorder can take over. The stories of *Thakurmar Jhuli* and *Thakurdadar Jhuli* mostly begin with a picture of perfect stability; in the middle we get the narrative of the fight against disorder, and at the end the old order is restored in all its glory. In the second (middle) section, therefore, we have a reversal of the first section, and in the third section (the conclusion), a return to the original state by inversing the reversed condition. We can arrange the three phases with the help of symbolical signs thus: A, –A, –(–A) = A; the middle section contains descriptions of many minor crises and their resolutions, and some among them may not reach any conclusion – which is to say that a, b, c, etc., such minor crises may be matched by the same and yet no fruitful conclusion reached. Rather, we notice that only they successfully conclude who can ultimately corner or confront 'A', the primary crisis. In the narrative of Pincess Kalabati, the five princes encounter many dangers and misfortunes but are unable to deal with any. At each point it is Buddhu–Bhutum who come to their rescue if not Buddhu alone, and it is they who eventually restore stability and peace in the country. And that means that the main argument of the story never departs from its major premise of crisis and resolution. At times the story may begin with a period of intense disorder, but it does not take one long to realize that there is an ever-present absent ideal that provides the measuring rod for evaluating the lapses and confusions of this period. Now the question arises as to what is this absolute ideal and who are they who uphold them?

'Kalabati Rajkanya' begins with the sentence, 'Once there was a king.' And after a long description of the prosperity of the ruler, it says: 'But the king was not happy, there were seven queens, not one bore a child. The king and all the people in his kingdom spent their days in sadness.'[13] However the story ends with: 'And then the king lived happily ever after together with his two youngest queens, Budhkumar, Roopkumar, and both the princesses Kalabati and Hirabati.' Clearly, according to the rules of grammar, the king occupies the place of the subject of the sentence. And it is equally clear that the tenants are unhappy when the king is unhappy and happy when the king is. But we see that by the middle of the story, the same king becomes inactive and, despite all good intentions, is unable to turn around the trail of events. Literally, it is a period of deep unrest in the kingdom. The five princes, unbridled, are devastating the kingdom and robbing the tenants of peace, yet the king remains totally inert as if he no longer has the power to prevent these unholy happenings. When Buddhu–Bhutum appear on the scene the king embraces them affectionately – weeping copiously while recounting his own sorry state, no doubt.

He has no means at hand to set right the wrongs that have been done to them and their mothers, mortally afraid that he is of his five elder queens. The queens on their part make a lot of noise upon seeing Buddhu–Bhutum with the king: 'The queens strike at the cheeks of Bhutum and throw him down on the floor;

slap Buddhu hard and throw him out. All the while the king stays immobile, not uttering a word. The queens blowing hot and cold in temper take the king inside the palace.'[14] It seems as if the pattern of relationship between husband and wife or father and sons has reversed, and social ties have become unstuck. Instead of the king remaining at the centre of power and in charge of social administration and governance, he has become an object of pity and humiliation. As if an extraordinary calamity has overtaken the country, divided and stratified, the entire hierarchical structure of society has become endangered. This calamity is the real crisis of the story and the king's loss of manliness, his paralysis, is an index of its signification. So long as the king is unable to take on the reins of governance of his kingdom, punishing those who have crossed the limits of decency, or is able to a make a vow to protect the meek and crush the wicked, there can be no respite from the crisis and no end to the misery of the ryots. Which is to say that there cannot be any end or resolution to the crisis until the king rises again, refilled with a new energy, revitalized and aware of his might and responsibilities. Buddhu–Bhutum come forward to restore the king's lost glory or eminence. It is to be noted that they harbour no grievances against the king. They do not speak a word against him despite all the neglect and humiliation. Their mothers who have spent their days and nights in utter misery – the two abandoned wives – do not have an ill word against the king, their husband; they do not demand that the wrongs done to them be redressed. Their devotion and regard for the king are not decreased an iota despite suffering extreme humiliation. On the other hand, the five queens dominate the king, keep him under their spell, in spite of all the love and attention they are given. If the two younger queens are ugly and disproportionate, and Buddhu–Bhutum neither human nor animal, the five elder queens are resplendent and to all appearances accomplished, with their aristocratic five sons functioning as Buddhu–Bhutum's opposites. But they are interconnected with the king who, by occupying the central position himself, brings them together, and their conflict becomes one between good and evil – demonstrating in one instance open defiance and in the other, a quiet submission.

The narrative of 'Kalabati Rajkanya' without exception, at least on the surface, holds forth that particular ethical observation which indicates that the king's ideas about happiness and sorrow, his moral consciousness, are of ultimate value. In the final analysis or reckoning, everything is subject to his approval. Those who ignore or disregard this injunction not only lose the comfort accorded by such ethical values, but also whatever guidance they may require in life. Such ethical principles are invariable and exceptional. If one strays from it or slips under, then there is no forgiveness or redress awaiting him. Which means that no matter how restricted a space the narrative involving the king occupies in the entire tale, it is impossible to deny his omnipresence throughout. When the crisis becomes deeper, its resolution is affected within the ethical parameters set up by the king himself. The king is not only a special person; placed in the highest echelon of a stratified social system, his presence has a certain meaning. He is the configuration of a social relation that informs the entire society and an image of an abstract power relation.

Buddhu–Bhutum have common sense, are circumspect, and therefore are worthy and humble. Because they possess these virtues, they are able to bring back justice, order and morality to the kingdom. They do everything in lieu of the king or on his behalf as his representatives, and as upholders of the virtues of kingship. We see that the rivalry between Buddhu–Bhutum and the five princes is never direct or open; it never takes the form of a clash or conflict. And it is not as if Buddhu–Bhutum are able to overcome all adverse circumstances by sheer physical strength or intelligence; all their successes indicate, unfailingly, that their moral/ethical consciousness are many times richer as compared to the five princes. Buddhu especially cannot even dream of putting the princes through any kind of scrape; there is no urge in him to take revenge. In the ultimate analysis, disregarding or being indifferent to personal loss and dangers, helping and protecting even those who are sworn enemies and refraining from sitting in judgment over them become, for Buddhu, the standard of morality and the true measure of ultimate goodness.

Now let us regard the picture/illustration that appears at the end of the printed text of 'Kalabati Rajkanya'.[15] On closer scrutiny, it would seem that the picture and the story have no apparent discrepancy so far as intention goes, nor is there any discordance in the narrative voice or stance. In fact we may easily accept the picture as a visual representation of the writerly text itself. The picture is thus: the king is seated on the throne with an umbrella overhead studded with precious stones. The two handsome, aristocratic princes, darlings of the throne, are seated on his either side; they are Budhkumar and Roopkumar. The king is not only seated in the middle, he also occupies a much larger space than the two princes; but like them, two greatly ornamented pillars are introduced into the picture so as to provide some kind of proportion to the composition. Decorative floor space and a picturesque ceiling are also there to add to the splendour of the king's chamber. The picture is oblong in shape and is bounded on three sides by three straight lines with a curved line, resembling a cupola, on the top. If one were to connect the apex of the king's umbrella and the two pillars by drawing a straight line, it would divide the king into two equal parts and similarly it would equalize the positioning of the two princes, put the ceiling and the floor space in a situation of complementary parallels; the pillars, the umbrella, the king, the throne and the floor space can be left out and yet one would have a sense of a complete surface from whichever angle one looks. By placing the monarch at centrestage, the picture acquires a wonderful symmetry. The formal and structural means by which the monarch is brought to the foreground render it expressive of the power and glory of

The king in his chamber, flanked by the two princes: 'Kalabati Rajkanya', *Thakurmar Jhuli*

monarchy. The picture is totally without any movement – not the slightest trace of any motion is registered therein. As a result, on regarding the picture one can easily presume that the power the monarch represents is eternal – it does not brook any alteration or decline.

Buddhu–Bhutum

But it is not sufficient to state only this. The surface meaning of the text is not all there is to it; many levels of meaning subsist both below and behind the apparent one. And if one leaves out or obliterates those explanations (meanings) that do not fit in or cohere with the main import of the work as extraneous, then, interpretation is bound to be prejudiced or one-sided. It is also feasible that all the ingredients that go to make up the text may not be amenable to a single explanatory grid; rather, the text may have a voice, however weak and muted, that could upturn the dominance of a single argument or the possibility of its fixed and indisputable meaning. Can not a sudden comment or an unplanned event create a tremor, howsoever slight? Rock the boat of a homologous text? And, in that context, make the text work against itself?

One could as well presume that the main object of the comparison between Buddhu–Bhutum and the five princes in 'Kalabati Rajkanya' is to show that the many-splendoured earth is false, and that the external pomp and glory-covered life is commensurately hollow and without any substance. It is a situation where the hot-headed, arrogant but in effect cowardly princes demand allegiance on moral grounds, demolishing all claims of the nimble, capable and ready-witted Buddhu–Bhutum. A debate is seen as being conducted among the shining representatives of the world of power, from the perspective of those living on the margins of society. And it is absolutely feasible that one would consider the assigned arena of functioning of Buddhu–Bhutum as a limited one, and that they are situated outside the domain of power; nevertheless, we cannot dismiss out of hand or deny the moral force behind their demands. Although Buddhu–Bhutum are 'princes' in actuality, they are spokespersons for all homeless, impoverished and lower-caste people. The tale is not a pure figment of imagination or a mere expression of wish fulfilment. At its bottom it is a gloss on life, no matter how partial or inarticulate. On one hand, the story throws light upon the chronicle of helpless, pitiful humans caught in the net of various direct and indirect oppressions of a feudal society; on the other, it gives you a picture of their overcoming. Thus the dream of countless humiliated human beings is captured in the fantastic image of the fairytale. One can easily surmise that this kind of tale, predicated upon a denouement ushering in a bright future, is a way of mitigating the intolerable burden of the present times; a kind of device, so to speak, to allow misery-stricken people to live.

That Buddhu–Bhutum are imagined as monkey or owl is not an attempt to interject novelty into the tale. It is a means to demarcate their distance from respectable society, and a way of holding up the difference between the two polar worlds more sharply and more visibly – for which reason they (Buddhu–Bhutum) are created as odd and as misfits, revealing signs that they are made of a distinctly different mould or cast. The tale demonstrates that no matter how resplendent the five princes blessed by kingship may appear from the outside, they are empty within; and 'they are counted more on account of weight than on account of merit', as the saying goes. On the other hand, no matter how poor and degraded Buddhu–Bhutum seem to appear on the worldly stage and not deemed to carry much weight, they are rich in their possession of treasures of the heart.

Despite all this, Buddhu–Bhutum have limited moral intelligence. That they cannot contradict the established rules and prescriptions or venture beyond their perimeter is amply demonstrated at the end of the narrative when, on discarding their guises, they are required to wipe away all differential criteria in order to deserve being installed at the centre of power. Borrowing a term from the Italian Marxist theorist Antonio Gramsci (1891–1939), we can say that the ethical consciousness by which the subordinate classes can identify their opponents (or the opposite party), but are unable to fathom the reach of their strength or understand wherein lies the limitation of its power, is primarily a 'negative consciousness'.[16] There may reside in this mentality some hints of a mature class consciousness, but these remain on the level of mere hints. The subordinate classes are not able to measure completely their historical destiny at the level of such consciousness. As a result, they desire to represent themselves in terms of their opposite, imagine themselves as a mirror image of the 'other'. Bespattered with conflicts, this mental image is not at this stage either self-dependent or sufficient-unto-itself. We may note that there is much to be desired in the realm of such self-sufficiency in the narrative under discussion. And, in the final analysis, the fact that our perception of order does not undergo an alteration merely reaffirms what is natural and eternal. In which context, it would seem that the mental image of the relation between the moral ideal connected with social structure is both prescriptive and historically validated. All dreams of progress, expectations of justice and yearnings for freedom that underlie the narrative ultimately fortify such an impression; strengthen the fetters of the power relations that bind the subordinate class. Instead of striking at the roots of domination, Buddhu–Bhutum allow themselves to be absorbed within it, effacing their own distinctiveness and difference.

Nevertheless, is it also not true that there is, in the narrative, some sign of that which is not a compromise, tolerance or subservience – rather a totally different level of subaltern class consciousness? Is there not some evidence in the text which may suggest that protest, as much as compromise, is true of subaltern class consciousness, no matter how weak the assertion or confusing the sentiment? Is there not some indication which makes us realize that the inhabitants of the 'lower depths' can ignore to a certain extent the rules and regulations imposed by the upper classes; that they can, if they choose to, cross over the set up boundaries and voice their opposition, albeit partially?

In the story, though Bhutum is older, he is thoroughly obedient to Buddhu and does what he tells him. He refutes him only once. That is when the five princes drown along with their boats and boatmen, and the bark which carries the two appears near the scene of the drowning. Buddhu says, 'My mind is troubled – something untoward has happened here. Come, let us dive and see what has gone wrong.'[17] In reply, Bhutum lets out: 'Let that be – I will heave a sigh of relief if they are dead. I can't dive for nuts.'[18] This harsh comment pierces Buddhu's tender heart like a sharp spear. He reprimands his brother severely. Finally, a compromise is reached wherein Buddhu dives into the sea tying a rope around his waist, and Bhutum stays on the surface holding on to the rope. Then onwards, they go different ways: Buddhu makes individual, independent decisions whenever the occasion rises, and, compared to Buddhu, Bhutum's role becomes relatively unimportant. Although Bhutum had uttered

'I will heave a sigh of relief if they are dead' in a fit of anger and because he wanted to punish the five princes himself, his revolutionary potential is nipped in the bud. Nevertheless, the value of his sharp personal utterance is manifold and one can in no way ignore his explosive exclamations. That sudden alteration of voice turns the narrative against itself, bringing about a slight shift in the tale's moral stance.

Buddhu–Bhutum make visible the dubiety of popular imagination and the irresolution internal to it. On one side there is obedience, on the other resistance; on one hand submission, on the other opposition. Buddhu is on the side of forgiveness and friendship. He would like to show that society may be full of oppression and suppression, it may also contain too many impediments, nonetheless it is possible to keep alive the spirit of peaceful cohabitation; this is not only possible but also desirable. For only those who accept everything without hesitation and without discrimination can overcome all trials and tribulations in life, endurance being the ultimate refuge for the helpless and the oppressed. Through the example of Buddhu, the narrative supplies us with a child-friendly ideal of endurance. There is nothing surprising about this, for within the narrative frame it is Buddhu and not Bhutum who wins the hand of Princess Kalabati – the princess is the reward for his unflinching devotion. Buddhu has little doubt about the moral regime he touts; he does not harbour any suspicion or queries regarding its justifiability. Therefore, regardless of the enormous skill and enthusiasm he manifests and the active role he takes in crisis resolution, he is not, in actuality, the protagonist of the narrative plot. The king holds the key to all the happenings in the tale.

At the opposite end, it is not Bhutum who comes forward to provide a radical solution to the discrepancies, obliterating all doubts and disputes. Nevertheless, in the story it is he who creates, in a real sense, the moment of crisis, suggesting an imaginary alternative, and hinting at another and different possibility. In the story, Bhutum is totally overshadowed by Buddhu; his faint oppositional voice gets completely muffled next to Buddhu's loud ringing tones.

The structure of the tale 'Der Angule' ('One-and-a-Half Thumb') may not match most stories belonging to *Thakurmar Jhuli*, but it easily bears similarity to 'Kalabati Rajkanya'. In this story, the familiar pattern of order–disorder–order is almost totally abandoned. 'One-and-a-half thumb' is no prince but the son of an ordinary woodcutter. *Ma Shashthi* ('Granter of Wishes') had given a piece of cucumber to the childless woodcutter and said: 'Take this to your wife, do not allow her to throw it away but eat the whole thing and after a week, a moonfaced, chubby, elephantine little baby boy will radiate in her lap and brighten up your house.'[19] But the wife had no patience and hardly had she received the cucumber than she ate it up, cutting off its top. As a consequence, she delivered a son who measured just one-and-a-half thumbs. But despite his dimensions, he was a remarkable boy. He began to pronounce words when barely out of the mother's womb, walked about everywhere, danced with a spring and ran as swiftly as a river downstream. No one could match his wits. The logic behind staging Buddhu–Bhutum as mere creatures – owl and monkey – also prevails in the presentation of the sharp-witted boy as only one-and-a-half thumbs in height. His diminutive height is but an index of the social degradation of the poor in society.

Compared to the tight structure of the Buddhu–Bhutum story, the narrative in this case is rather loosely structured; and its subject matter is not the restoration of a destroyed order. As a result, the telling of the story is light-hearted and smooth, its rhythm free and fleeting and, compared to Buddhu–Bhutum, a great deal more spontaneous. The language of its dialogues is not one bit stiff or lacking in genuine feeling. Even so, if 'one-and-a-half thumb' ascends the throne of the country, brightens its horizon by becoming one of its distinguished nobility, and is given a becoming name like Pippalkumar, the differentials that distinguish him from the others do not completely disappear. He is king for half of the day; during the other half he saws wood with his woodcutter father, making a sound like: *khut, khut, khut*.[20] The self-contradiction we had noticed in Buddhu–Bhutum, the pull in opposite directions, is made manifest through the vehicle of the combined personae of 'One-and-a-half thumb' and Pippalkumar. It is worth noting that the new name given to 'One-and-a-half thumb' is Pippal the oak, in other words, whose height becomes the signifier of his newly acquired power and glory. In every folk narrative, the idea of a continual ascendance in a stratified society finds various and varied expression. Different signs in the narrative, time and again, direct our attention to this continuing process of social uplift.

If we regard a tale as complete and whole in itself, we are less likely to notice anything beneath or beyond what is on its surface – and thus get entangled in the integrationalist outlook championed by either the traditionalists or the liberals, its implication being that society need not be completely transformed for the resolution of even the primary contradictions. They are forever ready to ceremoniously present before us the theory of social harmony, making the excuse of an inalienable, unchanging nature of society as eternal to it. People at the top take full advantage of sowing the seeds of this ideality, of harmonious coexistence. Because, the more the notion of reconciliation is diffused over the collective mind, the more firmly established is the culture of cohabitation – and all possibilities for resistance gradually fade away, the discordant voices being either appropriated or repressed. Reading the story of Princess Kalabati through the prism of upper-class proponents of social equality, we may conclude that the narrative does not display any gaps or fissures, and that a flawless imagination has patterned decorously all the components of the story; that nowhere does there exist a trace of complex awareness of any self-division.

Princess Kalabati

Now let us take up the topic of Kalabati Rajkanya, or Princess Kalabati. Kalabati had herself declared that she would become a handmaiden to whoever succeeded in the tests. When Buddhu appears in her palace and takes hold of the flowers of pearl, traversing the kingdom of the 'three old maids', wading through the waters of the red river, and escaping the notice of both '*kantha buri*' and the blind woodcutter, Princess Kalabati becomes aghast at the sight of his monkey-like image. But she is helpless and she can in no way disregard Buddhu's ownership rights. He asks her, 'Princess, to whom do you now belong?' The princess replies, 'I had belonged to my parents earlier. Then I became my own person. Now I am yours, I'll do whatever you say.'[21] Kalabati accepts Buddhu despite her many reservations; she submits to his exclusive rights over herself and without a murmur, gives up her freedom. Hit by the truth, a worried Kalabati at first throws away her bangles, loosens her hair as dark as clouds and falls to the ground. But almost as soon she takes control of her feelings and one cannot make out whether there is any regret in her mind. One does not find her behaviour to be in any way odd or come across any example of an unseemly remark. She is measured in her speech, treads with caution, does not do anything that may appear ill-fitting or uncouth, once she accepts Buddhu as her husband. She abides by the rules of an invisible yet inflexible system. Her gestures, both verbal and non-verbal, are rule-bound. Yet who can say that behind all these soulless gestures there do not reside deep sighs of regret? One has to remember that when Princess Kalabati first came across Buddhu, she had no inkling that he was a prince in disguise. Nevertheless, if she had not overcome her initial hesitation and accepted him as a husband in all humility, she could not have had the good luck to become a party to the glorious image of harmony and order with which the story ends. She could not have received an entry permit to that kingdom of happiness, had she not, at least in appearance, unhesitatingly accepted the supremacy of her husband and successfully passed the test.

In the story, the monkey appearance of Buddhu has two very different meanings, serving two very different functions. On one hand, it is a manifestation of the contrast between the marginalized people and the residents of places of power. On the other, (for the ideal wife) the husband's merits or good looks are least important, and the woman's existence is blessed and her desires are best fulfilled if she submits herself completely to her husband, totally surrendering her personhood. Although the story begins with skirmishes surrounding Kalabati involving the five princes and Buddhu–Bhutum, and she becomes the reason for their conflict, in the final analysis her role in the narrative is but slight. She merely brings to the surface the inner contradictions immanent in the two groups. She is a pretext or the sign of a link that exists between the two opposing groups of males.

Like 'Kalabati Rajkanya', many stories of *Thakurmar Jhuli* and *Thakurdadar Jhuli* begin with the lament of an heirless king.[22] If one scrutinizes the situation further, one discovers that the absence of a son is even more regrettable than the absence of a daughter to both the country and the countrymen. In the story 'Madhumala' of *Thakurdadar Jhuli*, it is directly stated: 'The king has both everything and nothing since he is without a son.' In the story 'Pushpamala', the queen and the wife of the constable, both childless, bathe in a pond named 'the pond of sons' so that their desire may be fulfilled. In 'Kalabati Rajkanya', the *sanyasi* (holy man) gives a root sanctified by prayer to the elder queen, saying: 'Mash the root and feed the young queens with this so that moonfaced sons are born to them.'[23] The son becomes the object of ultimate desire, as without a male progeny the dynasty comes to an end and the continuity is broken. Only a son can become the inheritor of his father; only he can become the legitimate bearer of his father's wealth. A worthy son is not only his father's representative, he is also his reflected image. Therefore, the entire people of a country become partners in the sorrow that digs deep into the heirless monarch's heart. And there is a deep anxiety lying at the root of all the sorrow: 'Would not the ties that cement a society and keep it whole become loose if the basic foundation of a social order – the devolution of power from father to son – collapses?' The origin of this collective fear is patriarchy, which permeates the entire social consciousness. This long-established tradition which has equated patriarchy with some kind of power makes one assume that the nature of power itself is patriarchal. The prime embodiment of patriarchy is the family; thus the spread of patriarchy entails an increase in the power of the institution known as family. It is therefore that familial relations cannot remain confined or limited to the family; it must spill over into other power relations, and, acting as a paradigm for all power relations, it must operate deeply and invisibly in the conscious mind of the society.

The young are always given the example of their elders: the family is but one of the many institutions of a political system such as the state. Nevertheless the family becomes a miniature world, the state's minutest indivisible unit. If one accepts the morality of family rule, one would have to acknowledge the legitimacy of all power relations associated with it. The state makes possible the existence of the family; and again, it is the family that ensures the continuation of the state. Compared to other state institutions, it is perhaps the family more than any other that plays the pivotal role in its perpetuation.

The picture of the ideal society we get at the end of a fairytale is actually an unqualified version of an ideal family. In this connection, the head of a country assumes the role of a father figure; the tenants are akin to children. Compared to the father, the knowledge of the children is perforce limited, their experience wanting. Just as the father has to, out of necessity, control the children, the king rules the state. The king is clearly the image of order whose standard-bearers are princes like Budhkumar and Roopkumar, whose class character is complemented by the requisite gender identity. If those two characteristics are not regarded as interconnected, the analysis would suffer – and our understanding of 'order' would likewise remain incomplete and lacking in clarity.

We have already gleaned from the narrative some signs of resistance among the lower orders. Now we would like to know how the female characters are drawn in the narrative, or from which perspective they are regarded. Are there any indications of self-awareness among the women in the narrative, or is it that we see them only through the male perspective and that the male gaze is all there is when we speak of women?

We have heard Kalabati telling Buddhu that she may have been beholden to her parents earlier but now she is his slave, and that there was no way for her to be totally free of 'familial bondage'. In this sense, she was not self-dependent even in the intervening period. She herself had openly declared to the whole country that she would become a slave of whichever person brings her pearl flowers and musical instruments; all arrangements for the conjugal union being already in place, all that was required was for her to bide time before the appearance of a suitable groom. As in her own country, Kalabati has no role to play even in Buddhu's realm. There she, along with Hirabati, wife of Bhutum, burn the monkey and owl disguises of their husbands without taking their permission. However, the world does not turn upside down as there is nothing to prevent Buddhu–Bhutum from appearing as their true selves. Further, Kalabati–Hirabati's existence serves no other purpose but to add glory to the power and prosperity of Buddhu–Bhutum. In fact, unless Buddhu–Bhutum enter the folds of matrimony, this purpose cannot be served: the assurance of peace and stability with which the tale ends cannot be fully and splendidly realized. Holy matrimony is an institution that acts as preparatory for the advent of princely progeny. It is hoped that Kalabati and Hirabati will not disappoint Buddhu–Bhutum, and, by giving birth to a male child at the right moment, they will ensure the maintenance of order and harmony in society.

The real origin of the crisis in the narrative is the presence of the five elderly queens who, out of greed, disregard the injunction of the holy man. Because of their waywardness, undeserving sons are born unto them who too have to pay the price for their mothers' wilful neglect. Ultimately, the five queens and their children are killed by the order of the king. By making the sinners pay as penance for the sins incurred, the country rids itself of the dangers that have beset it. Thus, without this narrative of restoration of hope and happiness the tale could not have ended; and the moral message the story conveys could not have been accomplished without demonstration of the punishment accorded to the five queens responsible for all the turmoil and unhappiness.

The Rules Governing Woman and Man Are Different

We can see with reference to the story of 'Kakanmala–Kanchanmala' in *Thakurmar Jhuli*, that there are different sets of rules governing man and woman in society. The narrative therefore raises the question of not one but two main points of crisis. These are not related by reason or operation; they take off from premises that are totally dissimilar. Nevertheless, until the two crises are resolved in unison, the story cannot have a satisfactory moral ending. Using the language of signs, one may say if *a* and *b* are the two main crises, then $-a, -b = -(a.b)$; *a* and *b* are tied together by some invisible thread and by some secret logic, and to bring them together can be said to be the aim of our investigation.

In 'Kakanmala–Kanchanmala', the first crisis has its origin in the king himself. Before he became a ruler, Rakhal, a cowherd, was his dear friend. The two were inseparable: the cowherd would lead the cows to graze in the meadow and the two friends would sit below a shady tree; the cowherd would play on the flute and the prince would listen to the melody. And in the illustration reproduced in the book we can see the fair prince, clothed in dazzling attire, listening rapt to the music of the flute with his arms entwined endearingly around the neck of the dark cowherd. The picture points to the difference in their positions in the social structure by highlighting the differences in the colour of their skins and in the style of their clothing. And it is this difference that is made manifest through the medium of language in the story. For example: 'the cowherd plays the flute, the prince listens to the melody' – in the Bengali language, the verb 'play' is deployed in the middle register and the

The prince and the cowherd: 'Kakanmala–Kanchanmala', *Thakurmar Jhuli*

verb 'listen' in the higher register. The world of difference between the two is brought home thus by means of grammar. And despite this wide gap, out of excessive affection for his friend, the generous prince gives his word to the cowherd that he will make him his prime minister when he becomes the king. But all this comes to naught.

The prince becomes the king and in due course there comes a queen; the treasury too spills over with riches – but Rakhal is consigned to oblivion. He is turned out of the door by guards at the gate when he turns up to catch a glimpse of his dear friend's queen. Suffering the pain of humiliation, he loses all interest in life and goes away, lord knows where. The king, however, cannot escape the sin of a promise broken or the wrongdoings he is responsible for. So one day it is seen that for no reason at all, his face, his body and his head are all covered with fine needles. Faced with such a crisis, the king breaks down completely and the queen, Kanchanmala, somehow manages the estate, hiding her grief.

At this point, a further complication is created by a parallel narrative. An astonishingly beautiful girl, Kakanmala, suddenly appears from nowhere and tells Kanchanmala that she would work as her maid if she was looking for one.[24] The queen purchases her in lieu of her bangle, on the agreement that the maid would pluck off the needles stuck in the king's visage. One day, on Kakanmala's advice, Kanchanmala goes to bathe in the pond. She has hardly entered the water when, in the twinkle of an eye, the maid adorns herself with the queen's clothes and jewels, commensurately alters the pitch of her voice, and commands the queen to come ashore. The queen comes out of the water after one last dip and discovers to her horror that the maid has turned into the queen, and that the queen is now her maid. There seems no possibility of any redress: all the tokens of rights and privileges belonging to the queen are now within the maid's grasp. Therefore Kanchanmala has to accept the privations befitting a maidservant. On the other hand, the maid Kakanmala's flamboyance has to be seen to be believed. Everybody is kept on their toes by her aggressive behaviour and show of unbridled power. Equally, everybody is amazed at the sudden transformation of the queen. But nobody dares utter a word. As for the king, he is helpless as the needles have blinded his eyes. An immense darkness obliterating all seeing has overcome him; he is hardly able to comprehend anything. But he has an inkling that his queen's intentions and actions have undergone a radical alteration, and his unhappiness crosses all limits. Flies hover over his body; pricked by countless needles, his face and limbs are taut with pain. But who is there to fan him, easing all such discomfort? And who is there to administer him medicines?

This extreme situation would have continued if not for a certain remover of difficulties who makes his appearance and redeems the situation. One day, the new queen along with the new maid meet a strange man at the *ghat* – steps that lead down to the waters of the pond. The man indicates that he is in need of a million needles. Kanchanmala brings him home, revealing her misfortune to him on the way. In order to test whether Kanchanmala is speaking the truth, the stranger goes to Kakanmala and says, 'Dear queen, today is the day for distribution of the sweet *pithe* [pancake] all over the estate.'[25] Both Kanchanmala and Kakanmala sit down to make the *pithe*. Soon it is discovered that all the sweets made by Kakanmala have no shape or taste and are indifferently produced, whereas Kanchanmala produces sophisticated versions of the *pithe* such as *chandrapuli*, *mohanbanshi*, *khirpuli* and *chandanpata*. It does not take the stranger long to realize that the maid is the actual queen; he wonders how she has come to occupy such a place. When it comes to decorating the floor with *alpana*, it is the same story all over again; it is proved that Kakanmala has no artistic sense, no aesthetic taste. It is then that the man dares to challenge her. He says: 'O you charwoman! Being what you are, how dare you assume the role of a queen?'[26] Kakanmala is furious at this act of defiance coming from a person who is of no consequence in her eyes. She orders the state executioner to see that the heads of the two offenders – the impudent man and Kanchanmala – are off. As the hangman goes after them, he is caught by the very man, who binds him hand and feet through the chanting of some mantras.

Then he plays his ultimate trick – as he chants some phrases one after another, millions of pieces of fine thread find their way into the needles stuck all over the king's body, and one by one they start to sew up Kakanmala's eyes and face. The king finds relief from the excessive agony he has been suffering, and Kakanmala dies after a few days of intense torment inflicted by the piercing needles. The king's eyes are opened, literally. And as soon as he opens his eyes, who does he see standing in front of him but Rakhal! The king expresses regret for all his wrongdoings, asks the forgiveness of his friend, appoints him as his prime minister and presents him with a golden flute. Thereafter, the king, the queen and Rakhal spend their days happily.

When one comes to the end of the text, one finds a picture showing the two friends dressed in elegant aristocratic garb and sitting side by side, with Rakhal the prime minister playing the flute and the king listening raptly. Rakhal is now a respectable member of society and class difference no longer comes in the way of their being seen together – all marks of class differentiation have been erased. The king had been guilty of breaking his promise and he had to suffer untold miseries for this; there was no end to the misfortunes that beset him. But finally, chastened by sorrow, he was able to liberate himself. He was able to emerge purified and blameless by correcting his errors of judgment. But Kakanmala was not allowed to undergo such self-correction; her heart did not experience any change as she was not given a chance for this to happen. Though the king was given an opportunity to do penance for the sins he had committed, the maid had only the ultimate punishment in store – death. On the one hand, the king had broken his word and failed in his duty to protect the royal office; on the other, although a maidservant, Kakanmala had aspired to become the queen. She had thus erred against the very injunctions of a divisive, hierarchically structured society. Both were examples of moral dereliction and waywardness. Both, in different ways, spelled disaster to the social order and violated the ethical ideals governing the mind of society.

We have seen how Rakhal, despite his lowly birth, by taking one big stride, was able to catapult to a higher order and become the prime minister. Where, then, does the difference between Rakhal and Kakanmala lie? Undoubtedly, Rakhal never hankered after the prime minister's post; he had no illegitimate desires; and he did not take advantage of his friendship with the prince in order to serve his own selfish interests. On the contrary, Kakanmala confounded the simpleminded Kanchanmala by devious means and robbed her of her rightful position. Which is to say that Rakhal was rewarded for his compliance with the established social order, whereas Kakanmala had to pay a price for her hubris. Not only that, Rakhal was the reason for Kakanmala's downfall despite the fact that they were both of the same social class.

Just as in society there are gestures and signs by which to distinguish between the good woman and the bad woman, so also in literature. Soft-spoken, modest women, as well as those who do not hesitate to submit that modesty is a feminine virtue, are good. Those women are bad who are inclined to ignore civilized behaviour befitting a woman, who disregard invisible yet actual courtesies, and are undignified and discourteous. We can easily identify the above-mentioned signs in the narrative under discussion. Rakhal had put both Kanchanmala and Kakanmala to test. What he saw was that in spite of being a queen, Kanchanmala was skilled in domestic chores, her work was orderly and aesthetically pleasing. And Kakanmala, despite being a maid, had no idea how to look after the house and was untidy from the start. It did not take long for Rakhal to determine who between the two was the queen. Moreover, we must not forget that it was the queen who was ruling the kingdom because of the king's illness. And we should have no hesitation in admitting that Kanchanmala was carrying on her royal duties reasonably well, having the right frame of mind to do so. At the opposite pole, the sudden acquisition of power had gone to Kakanmala's head and she ruffled everyone by ruling with an iron hand. The wide gap between the two women did not become a matter of concern for Rakhal all at once and it was not till Kanchanmala showed her expertise in the domestic field that he had reason to be suspicious. If Kakanmala had taken over Kanchanmala's role, the king's distress would have increased and he would not have been looked after properly. Kanchanmala was a good and devoted wife; Kakanmala bore neither of these qualities. She had not learnt the first thing about the fact that a dutiful wife is but another name for a happy home. Therefore, she did not earn the right to become the queen. It is not important that a woman demonstrates her expertise in affairs outside the domestic sphere. She has to prove herself in the interior world of her home.

The Good and the Bad in the Woman's World

There are two ways of coming to terms with those who unsettle the social order and are transmitters of disaster: one is to cure them; the other is to get rid of them. In the first instance, there can be a restoration of the social outcasts: by making them fit for a place in society through penance and ablution of sins. If the object of reform dispassionately and unhesitatingly admits to himself the sins leading to his fall, and there is a commensurate change of heart, the seeds of sin are automatically removed. In the second case, there is a deployment of strategies of demolition in order to control or come to terms with those professors of the language of alternate reality. In fact, so that the legitimacy of the established moral ideal is never put to question or never appears as odd, what is put in place is a system of character assassination. By trivializing or making short shrift of the spokesmen of the alternate ideology, by demolishing their arguments, we exempt ourselves of the responsibility of giving them due importance or of examining our own established moral order by their yardstick. If the male protagonist of the fairytale faces a crisis, the path for reformation and restoration remains forever open to him. Not so for the woman. In her case there is no respite till she is shown as unfit for society and turned out of its bounds completely. The only exception to this rule is perhaps the story 'One-and-a-Half Thumb' in *Thakurmar Jhuli* – for by the end of the story, the mother's sorrow comes to an end and she does not have to pay a price for her wrongdoings.

There are many tales in *Thakurmar Jhuli* where the exploits of she-devils loom large. Like seasonal diseases, they enter the inner world and make themselves at home; but in the end they cannot save themselves and they lose their lives at the hands of one or other prince. They are not comparable to ordinary women. It is possible that in the beginning the king loses his head over their assumed appearance or disguise, but when at last they reveal themselves, their ugly aspect does not remain hidden even to the king himself. But then why are the queens portrayed as she-devils time and again, or as outsiders to the realm of prince and princess? Is it not feasible to regard them as giving vent to a desire to stretch the limits of the prohibitions in place in society, in order to reject what has become the norm in man–woman relationships? Who are these outsiders – these she-devils – but an extreme version of those who would like to upturn age-old customs? We have seen how there were many reasons behind turning Buddhu–Bhutum into an owl and a monkey – an obvious one was to demonstrate that despite all the humiliation endured, it was they who represented and brought about good rule in the kingdom. In the case of the she-devil–queen syndrome, the same method is deployed for a very different reason. Buddhu–Bhutum may appear as owl and monkey but in actuality they are divinely handsome princes, whereas the she-devil–queens, no matter how beautiful they look, are ugly and haughty in real life. In the case of Buddhu–Bhutum, the distinction between them disappears at the end of the narrative, whereas in the case of the she-devils, the hidden signs of their difference, hitherto safeguarded, are made public at the end. Although these she-devils in the guise of queens have no legitimate expectations to become acceptable in society, they take on the role of good human beings having internalized all the signs of goodness, and choose to appear thus as long as they deem it necessary. For example, in another story belonging to *Thakurmar Jhuli*, titled 'Dalim Kumar', the she-devil eats up the queen and takes on her appearance in public. The king, however, never gets to know this. He does not find anything odd about the queen, who takes care of him in the same way she had previously been doing. It is not that the ill-natured, selfish women in the stories are always portrayed as she-devils; the *suorani*s or the king's second and younger wives are veritable she-devils in the way that, indulged by their kings, they completely control them – to the extent of even leading them astray.

The story of Neelkamal and Lalkamal in *Thakurmar Jhuli* is similar to the narrative of Buddhu–Bhutum. In this story, two brothers, Neel and Lal, like Buddhu and Bhutum, fight for their country, help the poor and the distressed, and restore the bewildered king to his former grace and glory. The king has two wives: one an epitome of gentility, the other a veritable she-devil and a figure of misfortune. The gentle queen's son is the golden-hearted Kusum. The she-devil queen's son is the iron-souled Ajit. The she-devil vampire sucks the blood of her husband's co-wife in the dark of the night till the gentle queen expires. But the devil-woman cannot control her anger, not being able to accept the friendship between Kusum and Ajit. The king's stables are emptied of his horses and elephants, and yet the she-devil's hunger is not satiated. One day she eats up her stepson Kusum right in front of the king. The king rushes out to save his son, but struck by the hair that the she-devil tears from her head, his limbs become senseless and he stands immobile like a fool. Tears flow down his cheeks but he has no recourse to remedy the situation, making his she-devil wife burst into gleeful laughter. Ajit, however, moved by the plight of Kusum, prepares to strike out at the queen. At this the she-devil, consumed by rage, loses all sense of proportion and even swallows up the child she had held in her womb! The towers of the palace begin to crumble and kin of the she-devils, wherever they are, begin to descend on the kingdom in hordes, wading through waters, stomping over trees and treading stony pathways. The ordinary folk are held in ransom by the devils; they leave the kingdom in desolation. It is a time of utter chaos and disorder. The king is reduced to a fool in captivity; the kingdom is totally taken over by devils.[27]

One can see that the king has surrendered all his power and dignity to the she-devil. It is she who is the root of the crisis. It is she who has reduced the king to a state of stupefaction. Ajit and Kusum, however, are not dead. A peasant venturing into the woods to look for bamboo-stalks discovers two eggs. The moment he throws the eggs to the ground to find out if they are serpent's eggs, two princes come out of the shells: Kusum and Ajit are thus reborn. They bear new names: Neelkamal, Lalkamal. They move on; there is no respite from their journey for them till the country is freed of all the ills that beset it, and the king is cured of his stupidity.

At long last, Lal and Neel arrive at what can be rightly called the devils' kingdom. They are able to subdue the devils and uncover their hidden secrets, taking hold of the wands of death and life. When they fling the wand of death, the entire clan of devils is destroyed and deprived of progeny. The two brothers are able to step into their kingdom and their own country after an interval of two months and thirteen days. The severed head of a devil is sent to the she-devil queen who hurries out of the palace at the sight. At this point Lalkamal displays the wand of death, making the she-devil collapse and die. The stupid king regains his wits the moment she dies.[28]

The story 'Golden Wand Silver Wand', belonging to the same collection, has a similar trajectory. A king finds a dazzling beauty in the forest and brings her home, not suspecting that she, far from being a human being, is a devil. A prince from another realm tries in vain to make the king aware of this but the besotted king is unable to free himself of his delusions. Finally the prince descends on the palace armed with the wand of death. He wrings the neck of the parrot who holds the secret to the life of the she-devil, saying, 'Now you devil, go to hell!' Almost at once the she-devil falls to the ground making a croaking sound and dies – but not before she attempts one last deathly pull at the throne of the monarch.[29] In truth, the queen had ventured beyond the parameters of her jurisdiction and even the realm of the throne had come within her grasp. As for the king, he had totally surrendered his dignity to the woman and lost his manhood as a henpecked husband enamoured of his wife. Instead of taking the reins of power into his hands, he had allowed himself to be humiliated and become foolish. In the face of demonstration of extreme power by the queen, he was left completely without energy and debilitated. At the subterranean level of such narratives lies the fear of female sexuality and misogyny. The king's loss of manhood and the erosion of his power are, in this context, complementary: one a transposition of the other. And it is possible for those who have no misgiving about the patriarchal nature of power to build upon this structure of similarities.

Even so, is there any indication that such structured assumptions always hold good and that somewhere something may not take place which, though trifling, might be at odds with it? In the story of Neelkamal–Lalkamal, Neelkamal, the son of the she-devil, is many times bolder and more sharp-witted than Lalkamal, the offspring of the good queen. Lalkamal has a heart of gold, Neelkamal is iron-hearted. Their previous names too demonstrate this truth: Lalkamal was known as Kusum and Neelkamal as Ajit. Although the she-devil ultimately fails and has to accept defeat at the hands of the good queen, does she not, in some sense, triumph through her son? Although she gains respect from society or succeeds in establishing herself on the social scene, at least the recognition that her son is 'the brave one' is partly hers. And in the context of narratives where no importance is given to questions of woman's selfhood or to the exercise of their rights – portrayed often as unlawful intrusions – does not this slight alteration in the relation of power presage something bigger?

The good queen, *duorani*, and such unhappy lots exist at opposite poles to the she-devil queen *suorani*, the 'happy ones'. The ambitious, power-hungry Kakanmala and the peaceful, subservient Kanchanmala also exist at opposite poles to each other. The consecutive stories declare that a woman's destiny is blind worship of the husband. And the several episodes of *Thakurdar Jhuli* repeat the adage *ad nauseam*.

In the story 'Madhumala', whether it be Champakala, Panchakala or Chandrakala, all ask the same question of the prince Madankumar: 'Husband, swear that you will keep me!' Madankumar hastens to assure them that he would indeed 'keep' them. And as he journeys home with Madhumala, with whom he is madly in love and for whom he had ventured beyond the seven seas, he lifts all three into his boat one after the other as something acquired gratis. The co-wives do not harbour any ill-feeling towards each other, nor is there any feeling of jealousy among them; their happiness lies in making their husband (in-common) happy. Therefore, bonds of affection begin to flourish between them. In the story, Champakala is shown to possess all kinds of skills: she is both very beautiful and learned in the sciences; no one can beat her in an argument. Yet without a husband her life is incomplete, almost without meaning. In spite of being so accomplished, she is not one bit egotistical and has no sense of self-pride. The moral of the story is that, on the one hand, a devoted and chaste wife has to accept the right of the husband to go to other women; on the other, she has to submit herself totally to him. Which is to say that the man feels honoured by accepting gifts from women; and the woman feels gratified by giving over everything to the man.

The compiler of the stories of *Thakurdadar Jhuli*, Dakshinaranjan, tells us that the tales in the volume were recited during intervals between ceremonial family affairs. Generally, elderly women would crowd the gathering, although some men and children would also be present. What purpose did the telling of these rather monotonous stories serve? Why indeed did they become a necessary part of the rituals? Why was it necessary for the woman to be time and again reminded of her sacred duties towards the family? Was the logic behind it all that unless the theory of male domination was eternally rehearsed by women, society may face total disaster?

In a society where woman is under the guardianship of man since birth and is obliged to be beholden to him, she does not have the wherewithal to ignore or evade the demands he makes on her. As a result, she is habituated to regarding herself as if through the eyes of man, and she is constantly engaged in evaluating herself in accordance with male expectations. Thus a section of the divided female consciousness becomes the bearer of the rules and edicts of a male-dominated social system. The many tales of *Thakurdadar Jhuli* aim to demonstrate, on one hand, how woman's ultimate identity, her final truth, is revealed in the way female consciousness has eternalized the notion of patriarchy, as a consequence of which there is an acceptance of the legitimacy of the authority of the family; while on the other, if by chance the woman's selfhood becomes assertive and she desires to become free of the ignominy of slavery and the humiliation of submission, then this is something wrong, immoral and worthy of blame. The difficulty of this proposition, however, is that almost without exception this division between self and other is bound to exist in a man–woman relationship, and that no matter how much the man would like it, it is not possible for the woman to remain totally without a sense of self. A woman can never be completely moulded in the way a man would like to see her. And therefore the conflict, which is forever on the verge of a conflagration, has to be kept suppressed with the help of an ideological arrangement or understanding. That is, if the woman calmly and without a murmur accepts all the dictums, memorizes the oft-repeated rules and regulations, and fulfils her duties without fail, then social harmony is assured.

Why should there be any surprise when the king tells Malanchamala, in the story 'Malanchmala' in *Thakurdadar Jhuli*: 'Mother, whoever you are, brighten up the house of your in-laws. And attain peace within yourself in the manner by which you calmed me down with your offer of water'?[31] And Malanchamala – what of her? The dead bodies of her child and husband lie on her lap, but her mind is not perturbed. Neither fear nor temptation can unsettle her calm. She brings her husband back to life by the sheer strength of her devotion. All the torture, misfortunes and her father-in-law's ill-treatment do not succeed in reducing her faith in the ritualistic devotion a wife bears towards her husband, and she does not fail in her deep conjugal fidelity. She repeats these few words *ad infinitum*:

> I touch my husband and say I am the faithful wife / What faults does he have / He is after all my husband / Husband's house, wife's grace / I'll sweep the path to it with my hair / my father-in-law will be taking that road / I will be the maid, the slave / feed myself by taking care of the cows but / nevertheless remain in this condition forever and ever . . .

Malanchamala has no point of view of her own. The husband laughs and Malancha laughs / she cries when he does / speaks when her husband opens his mouth.[32]

Malancha states the adage 'the devoted wife is bereft of sight and sound' through her life – it literally comes true word for word. Like the legendary Sabitri and Behula, she injects life into the dead body of her husband and nurses him back to health like a mother does to her child. Not only in this story but in several others, women bring men back to life again and again – literally snatching their husbands, at times their brothers, back from the doorsteps of Yama, the God of Death. Men carry the burden of living in this world on their shoulders; when they die, their women, by the sheer power of their virtue, raise them from the dead and bring them back to their place of work. Undiluted devotion and unquestioning belief in marital fidelity cover the women like an armour, making them mentally strong enough to overcome all obstacles. To bear children is the final goal of a woman's life, motherhood is her ultimate identity, women want to become like their own mothers – this myth is time and again demonstrated through the characters of patient and caring women. The myth obfuscates the pernicious truth that women are valued in society only as machines for the reproduction of labour power. A woman's power of endurance is glorified. Her masochistic tendency is constantly fuelled, leading to the strengthening of an almost suicidal inferiority complex that is inherent in her. Society not only stops at suppressing/oppressing woman, it makes her the vehicle for glorification of the same oppression. But no matter how much abstract myth tries to tie down dynamic organic life to a semblance of the unchanging historicity of society, or tries to approximate the density of truth, it fails to completely control or suppress reality and is not able to remove all traces of real life. As a result, the stories of women's plight get revealed in the interstices of the narrative, and only through hints do the intolerable conditions in which women spend their lives come to us.

There is a direct relation between *Thakurdadar Jhuli* and the lore surrounding the rituals. Dakshinaranjan Mitra Majumdar had compiled and published the ritual lore of Bengal under the title *Thandidir Thole* (*Grandmother's Bag*). These reflect the kind of desire instilled in the minds of the women of Bengal through the ages, the kind of belief sowed in their hearts – so that it is possible to recover a picture of how women could bear the strict edicts of Manu or Raghunandan through the ages by reference to the lores surrounding the rituals. It is possible by citing the example of some of these lores to indicate how small and restricted was the woman's desired world.

To the query, 'What happens if one worships the husband?', one is offered a handful of hopefuls, such as: 'The poor become rich / the woman attains the stature of Sabitri, the epitome of marital fidelity / becomes the adored object of the husband / gives birth to a son for adorning the husband's lap /

ends her life in the holy waters of the Ganges' ('Puniya Pukur').[33] Again, in 'Dashputul', she says:

> If I die now I'll be born as a human being again – will have a husband like Rama and become suttee like Sita, will have a father-in-law like Dasharath . . . and again will be an excellent cook like Draupadi, a bearer of sons like Kunti, will affect calm on others like the holy water.[34]

And yet again:

> I want a king of kings for a husband / a son-in-law who can brighten up the household / a brother who can astound the assembly with his wit / a son who can enlighten the court / a maid that is as precious as the silver box / sindur on the hair parting that will appear like a flame / iron bangles on my arms that will glisten like gold / clothes on the clothes rack that are overflowing / utensils that glitter like gold. ('Tush Tulsi')[35]

In the narratives of *Thakurdadar Jhuli*, the vermilion on the hair parting and conch-shell bangle on the arm are two powerful signifiers, evident in the following expressions:

> Pray that I keep polishing my conch shell bangle for ages to come.
>
> Let the sindur on my hair parting remain unfaded.
>
> You are my conch-shell / husband, take your maid along.
>
> She stooped at her husband's feet and let them touch the sindur at the parting on her head three times. ('Kanchanmala')

The Home and the World

If one thoroughly scrutinizes the various narratives of *Thakurdadar Jhuli*, one would discover that it is improper, even unlawful, for women to step outside the house. Men, however, can go out into the world for various reasons; for them to be housebound is most unbecoming. The extended outside world, an expansive arena, is there only for men – for only they have the right to enjoy the romance of the unknown. At times with or without reason – for the sheer pleasure of promenading or going on a hunt or even more, for being driven out by the machinations of a stepmother, or else for the purposes of trade or for conquering kingdoms or for winning the hands of princesses – men go out into the world. They face difficulties at every step – with their eyes and ears fully alert. As if there exists an open invitation to taste the wide earth with all their sensibilities. Whether or not their ultimate goal is winning the hands of princesses, they generally return home bringing more than a princess or two.

There is always someone across the seven seas and thirteen rivers who eagerly awaits them or remains dormant in order to be woken up.

Virtuous women have their rightful place inside the house; they do not cross the threshold even by mistake. It is to be seen that only an impostor, the enchanting sorceress who likes to entangle witless men in the net of deception by her beauty, roams the woods and the ends of the earth. On the other hand, those luckless women who lose the security of their hearth and home for venturing into the workaday world – they cannot return to their homes till their ill luck runs its course. Where men extend their experience by their involvement in and connection with the greater world outside, virtuous women continuously curtail their existence and avoid like poison any contamination of the external world. The husband's house is the primary goal of all their journeying – all their movements aim at reaching that place of holy pilgrimage. These narratives reinforce the myth that men are outward-looking – women, out of necessity, are inwardly inclined.

It is because the outside world is so overwhelmingly male-dominated that, although not lacking in power, Pushpamala, the eponymous heroine of the story, has to don a man's garb and keep her real nature hidden from public view. There are, however, two exceptions to this rule: the stories of Kiranmala, and Sukhu and Dukhu. Kiranmala appears as she is, a woman, when she undertakes the journey to rescue her brothers. And ultimately, when the millions of princes who had been turned into stone are restored to animate beings due to her benefices, they offer their thanks to her, touch her feet and say, 'You are blessed seven times over for your heroism.' In the story Kiranmala's courage, her prowess and her greatness are unhesitatingly acknowledged. Nevertheless, we must remember that Kiranmala did not come out of the house to go in search of her husband but with the sole purpose of bringing her brothers to life. In the story Sukhu and Dukhu, of course, Dukhu manages to carry back a prince as part of his load. But the real purport of the tale is that good girls are easily pleased and only bad girls make endless demands. In such stories, somehow, poverty becomes a special virtue.

Even when the social status of women is high due to reasons of birth, that their position is subordinate in the context of a husband–wife relationship is glaringly revealed in the Pushpamala story of *Thakurdadar Jhuli*. Princess Pushpamala and Chandan, the son of a constable, go to the same school. There the princess sits on a throne, while the son of the constable sits and writes at her feet on the ground.[37] But the day Pushpamala comes to learn that her parents had betrothed her to the son of the constable, she sits below and makes the son of the constable occupy the throne, in the realization that 'her husband's home is now her home'. Although her parents want to go back on their word, Pushpamala accepts Chandan as her husband, defying societal injunctions against inter-caste marriage. Not lacking in wit, learning, honour and bravery, she accepts her husband's domination without the slightest hesitation. When, in the story 'Kanchanmala', the heroine discovers that her husband is prostrate at the foot of a tree while she is aloft on the tree, she immediately comes down, abandoning her seat. She says: 'My lord, I have committed a grievous sin, I was sitting on the tree above not knowing you were below, please forgive me.'[38] In the stories mentioned above, we see that the difference in social status of men and women is but natural and proper. We can say without erring that the low-caste woman not only belongs to a lower social order, as a woman she occupies an even lower social position in that lower order.

Now the question remains, can one dismiss all fairytales in one word, saying they are not progressive? Also, can one proclaim that those who desire and seek social progress need not take these into account? The pattern of society that emerges in fairytales is without doubt backward, unevolved, full of self-contradictions and extremely divisive. A patch-up of century-old beliefs and superstition has produced this special likeness of the popular imagination, its underlying consciousness being made up of a complex of conflicting notions. That is why we find Bhutum or 'One-and-a-half thumb' besides Buddhu, or Kiranmala and Pushpamala besides Kanchanmala. In fairytales we have tortuous images of self-deception and self-flagellation, as well as marks of an attempt to comprehend complex and complicated situations, an endeavour to free our insights of all holistic perceptions. It would not be possible for the social imaginary to identify the various complications that prevail unless we give due weight to the many hesitations and indecisions that obtain at the moment of crisis, as well as the potentially explosive situation which awaits the crossing of boundaries of rules and restrictions. If that were so, we would impose the beliefs and opinions of those belonging to the upper class upon those standing below in the social hierarchy, and not begin from their end and give due importance to the wisdom that underlies their way of life. The folktales reveal values that are inseparably linked with the lives of the ordinary people. If we evade the truth of this organic relationship, no matter how good the intentions may be, all attempts to do good are bound to fail. Did this not happen in our society during its nationalistic phase?

Let us now return to the problem we raised at the very beginning of this chapter: did our nationalist intelligentsia discover any mark of authenticity in the folk narratives? What were the *swadeshi* elements that charmed them? As evidence of the upper-class way of thinking, let us return to Rabindranath's 'Preface' to *Thakurdadar Jhuli*. Rabindranath tells us that he was rather hesitant to open the book upon receiving it.

> I fear that its melody might get lost when faced with the hard, sharp as steel, modern Bengali prose. I had tried to make some girl adept in storytelling and yet educated

> try her hand at writing fairytales, but realized that the magic of the western style might have given her the language of the folktale, but not its essence.[39]

His main argument was that 'The elegance, charm and delicacy that obtains in the weaving of the tales in a folk narrative are extremely feminine and suited to women. The fount and origin of the tales being the maternal love of the entire Bengal.' That is why,

> when the youth of Bengal hears the tales he is not only happy to listen to the stories related – the melody of Bengal's eternal love for the young enters his imagination, enriching him with appropriate emotion.[40] That original and pristine emotion of eternal Bengal is now hard to find. Even the girls have forgotten their natural language, thanks to so-called education. And we would lose all (the Company would go bankrupt) if we do not without delay open a school for our modern grandmas and if we do not make them renew their connection with ancient language and thought.

According to Rabindranath, because of the loss of the flow of inspiration, human beings are gradually getting uprooted in Bengal; and along with this there is a hardening of their souls, their attitudes becoming selfish and distorted. The women of Bengal have a special duty as well as a responsibility to arrest this social degeneration, to revive the society anew, to make it inspirational again.

Is there a particular reason why women occupy such a large and important place in Rabindranath's 'Preface'? Is there any connection between this and the structure/pattern and values of upper-class Hindu families during colonial times? We shall take up this subject in chapter 4 of this book. But before that, we must comprehend the import of the pain of alienation whose undeniable traces we find in Rabindranath's thinking and in his consciousness. And we must try to understand the ideology whose impact created this new kind of division between people belonging to the higher and the lower strata in the society of the times, which led also to the erection of walls of unfamiliarity between them. In other words, what we would like to know is why or what was the urge behind our nationalist intelligentsia's search for 'authentic origins', which made them create a special image of the nation that they found in the fairytales of the nation?

Notes and References

1 Barid Baran Ghosh, 'Dakshinaranjan Mitra Majumdarer Jibanalekshya', in *Dakshinaranjan Sahityasamagra*, Vol. 2, Calcutta: Mitra & Ghosh Publishers, 1388 (Bengali calendar).

2 Rabindranath Tagore, 'Thakurmar Jhulir Prasangey', in *Dakshinaranjan Sahityasamagra*, Vol. 1, Calcutta, 1388 (Bengali calendar), p. 4.

3 Ibid.

4 Rabindranath Tagore, 'Swadeshi Samaj' and 'Atmashakti', in *Rabindra Rachanabali*, Vol. 3, Visva Bharati, 1371 (Bengali calendar), p. 530.

5 Rabindranath Tagore, 'Swadeshi Samaj', in *Rabindra Rachanabali*, Vol. 3, p. 539.

6 Ibid., p. 545.

[7] Ibid.
[8] Barid Baran Ghosh, 'Dakshinaranjan Mitra Mazaumdarer Jibanalekshya'.
[9] Dakshinaranjan Mitra Majumdar, 'Kalabati Rajkanya', *Thakurmar Jhuli*, in *Dakshinaranjan Sahityasamagra*, Vol. 1, Calcutta, 1388 (Bengali calendar), p. 9.
[10] Ibid., p. 22.
[11] Dakshinaranjan Mitra Majumdar, 'Kakanmala Kanchanmala', *Thakurmar Jhuli*, in *Dakshinaranjan Sahityasamagra*, Vol. 1, Calcutta, 1388 (Bengali calendar), p. 33.
[12] Dakshinaranjan Mitra Majumdar, 'Kiranmala', *Thakurmar Jhuli*, in *Dakshinaranjan Sahityasamagra*, Vol. 1, Calcutta, 1388 (Bengali calendar), p. 68.
[13] Dakshinaranjan Mitra Majumdar, 'Kalabati Rajkanya', *Thakurmar Jhuli*, in *Dakshinaranjan Sahityasamagra*, Vol. 1, p. 3.
[14] Ibid., p. 11.
[15] Ibid., p. 21.
[16] Antonio Gramsci, 'State and Civil Society', in Quentin Hoare and Geoffrey Nowell Smith, eds, *Selections from Prison Notebooks*, New York: International Publishers, 1971, p. 273.
[17] Dakshinaranjan Mitra Majumdar, 'Kalabati Rajkanya', *Thakurmar Jhuli*, in *Dakshinaranjan Sahityasamagra*, Vol. 1, p. 14.
[18] Ibid.
[19] Dakshinaranjan Mitra Majumdar, 'Der Angule', *Thakurmar Jhuli*, in *Dakshinaranjan Sahityasamagra*, Vol. 1, Calcutta, 1388 (Bengali calendar), p. 141.
[20] Ibid., p. 152.
[21] Dakshinaranjan Mitra Majumdar, 'Kalabati Rajkanya', *Thakurmar Jhuli*, in *Dakshinaranjan Sahityasamagra*, Vol. 1, p. 16.
[22] Dakshinaranjan Mitra Majumdar, 'Madhumala', *Thakurdadar Jhuli*, in *Dakshinaranjan Sahityasamagra*, Vol. 2, Calcutta: Mitra & Ghosh Publishers, 1388 (Bengali calendar), p. 383.
[23] Dakshinaranjan Mitra Majumdar, 'Kalabati Rajkanya', *Thakurmar Jhuli*, in *Dakshinaranjan Sahityasamagra*, Vol. 1, p. 3.
[24] Dakshinaranjan Mitra Majumdar, 'Kakanmala Kanchanmala', *Thakurmar Jhuli*, in *Dakshinaranjan Sahityasamagra*, Vol. 1, p. 28.
[25] Ibid., p. 30.
[26] Ibid., p. 31.
[27] Dakshinaranjan Mitra Majumdar, 'Neelkamal and Lalkamal', *Thakurmar Jhuli*, in *Dakshinaranjan Sahityasamagra*, Vol. 1, Calcutta, 1388 (Bengali calendar), p. 73.
[28] Ibid., p. 84.
[29] Dakshinaranjan Mitra Majumdar, 'Sonar Kathi Rupar Kathi' ('Golden Wand Silver Wand'), *Thakurmar Jhuli*, in *Dakshinaranjan Sahityasamagra*, Vol. 1, Calcutta, 1388 (Bengali calendar), p. 114.
[30] Dakshinaranjan Mitra Majumdar, 'Madhumala', *Thakurdadar Jhuli*, in *Dakshinaranjan Sahityasamagra*, Vol. 2, p. 404.
[31] Dakshinaranjan Mitra Majumdar, 'Malanchamala', *Thakurdar Jhuli*, in *Dakshinaranjan Sahityasamagra*, Vol. 2, Calcutta: Mitra & Ghosh Publishers, 1388 (Bengali calendar), p. 479.
[32] Ibid., p. 467.
[33] Kaliprasanna Vidyaratna, ed., *Meyeder Bratakatha*, Calcutta.
[34] Ibid.
[35] Ibid.
[36] Dakshinaranjan Mitra Majumdar, 'Kanchanmala', *Thakurdar Jhuli*, in *Dakshinaranjan Sahityasamagra*, Vol. 2, Calcutta: Mitra & Ghosh Publishers, 1388 (Bengali calendar), p. 421.
[37] Ibid., p. 427.
[38] Ibid., p. 509.
[39] Rabindranath Tagore, 'Thakurmar Jhuli Prasangey', in Dakshinaranjan Mitra Majumdar, *Dakshinaranjan Sahityasamagra*, Vol. 1, p. 5.
[40] Ibid.

3

Education and Lessons in Modernity

I

> In the city of Kolikata, on the tree-adorned banks of Goldighi, alone stands a frail dark doe bearing the name of the abode of Sanskrit learning. At present, the great hunter named Macaulay, wielding a pointed arrow, is all set to slaughter that faint-hearted doe. Observing this, the deer pleads with tearful eyes – 'Oh noble-minded Wilson, please protect me – save me.'[1]

Premchandra Tarkabagish, a professor of rhetoric at Sanskrit College, had composed the above prose passage in verse and sent it to the renowned England-returned orientalist Horace Hayman Wilson (1786–1860), author of the first complete English translation of the *Rig Veda*. But it was already too late by then; no matter how much the fear-ridden, frail doe appealed with tearful eyes, it was impossible for Premchandra, and even for the noble Wilson, to thwart the agenda of the hunter-king Thomas Babington Macaulay (1800–1859). Consequently, Wilson had no option but to write another passage in verse with appropriate embellishments and send it in reply to Premchandra, the scholar of rhetoric, advising him to depend on the endless mercy of a just God:

> Despite being endlessly trampled by the feet of many beings, despite being afflicted by beams that resemble the sparks emitted by the sun, despite being devoured by the likes of goats and turned over by a shovel, the slender weed is not destroyed because God showers his mercy on the weak.[2]

Notwithstanding Wilson's reassurances and the promise of divine compassion, it had not been possible to resist the decline of the Sanskrit College and thereby that of oriental education. The frail doe was never able to regain its robustness. During the tenure of Warren Hastings (1732–1818), the first Governor-General of India, the Calcutta Madrasa was founded in 1780, long before the Sanskrit College was established in Calcutta, in 1824. Profusely applauding Hastings' role in the spread of education, Ishwarchandra Vidyasagar had written:

> Before the rule of Lord Hastings, there was no attempt to educate the subjects. If the subjects remained sunk in the well of ignorance, there would not be any fear of the empire breaking up. Because of this, imparting education to these subjects had been considered as going against the politics of the rulers. But Lord Hastings, ignoring this policy, said that the English had taken over the rule of Bharatvarsha for the welfare of its citizens; therefore, it was the expedient duty of the English race to accomplish civilizing its subjects in every way. Owing to this command, schools began to be established in places immediately.[3]

There was no break in the practice of promoting the welfare of the natives even after Hastings left India. The endeavour to civilize the natives continued as before. The Benaras Sanskrit College was founded in 1792.

The two centres of oriental education, the Calcutta Madrasa and the Benaras Sanskrit College, were built and developed in keeping with the policy adopted by the Company of not interfering unnecessarily with the religious beliefs and practices of the natives. Moreover, the missionaries had been prevented from the sacred duty of planting Christianity on the soil of 'Bharatvarsha' before 1813. There was a fear then that because of missionary interference, the inhabitants of the colony might turn against the foreign rulers; there was also some disquiet among the natives about the unsolicited infiltration of the missionaries. The Directors of the Company assumed that if they posed no hindrances to the religious practices of the local residents, if their customary rituals and ceremonies, annual events and festivals went on as before, it would not only enable the rulers to win the faith of the natives in return for their goodwill, but also make it possible for the Company to carry on trade without any impediment.

On 1 January 1792, Jonathan Duncan, a resident of Benaras, wrote in a letter to Governor-General Lord Cornwallis (1738–1805):

> The establishment of the Sanskrit College will predominantly benefit the British. The image of the British will become more radiant in the eyes of the Hindus when they observe that far from being indifferent or contemptuous about their philosophy and scriptures, the government's enthusiasm about these is more than that of the local princely classes. The respect and amity of the Hindus towards the foreign government will then naturally become even greater.[4]

It is very clear from the letter that the Benaras Sanskrit College was not established with the dispassionate agenda of welfare of the Hindus. In fact, the Company wanted to uphold the College before the people as an exemplar of British nobility and magnanimity. Under the patronage of the government and camouflaged as pure and selfless pursuit of knowledge, the intention was to build a new kind of bonding between the ruler and the ruled – the structure of a new relationship. Further, Jonathan Duncan had informed Lord Cornwallis that through this institution, it would be possible to groom many able assistants who were experts in Hindu law.[5] It meant that because the rulers did not have adequate proficiency in the complex grammar of Hindu rituals and their violation, they specially turned their attention to scholars of Sanskrit – so that the administrative machinery did not become dysfunctional and so that there was no harassment due to partiality in the workings of the judiciary. But the bearers of Hindu scholarship were brahmans. Consequently, it was quite reasonable for the ruling class to assume that if they could exploit the clout the brahmans enjoyed in all strata of society, they would gain rather than lose.

One can find evidence of privileging brahmanical arrogance and culture even in the composition of the code of rules for the Benaras Sanskrit College. According to the code of rules proposed in the draft, non-brahmans would not have the opportunity to teach anything except medicine. Although the students had to appear for examinations in the presence of the Resident four times a year, the examination of principles regarded sacred by the Hindus could only be taken by brahmans. A special committee of brahmans approved by the Resident was responsible for the examination of a multitude of obscure subjects. The disciplinary rules of the college were required to be in accordance with the purport of the holy scriptures. The various rules and commands related to education that are discussed in the second chapter of the *Manu Samhita* were required to be observed verbatim.[6] This was why it was the duty of every college student to follow, with singlemindedness, each of the five kinds of *dharma* (religious practice) according to Manu's code – *barna dharma, ashrama dharma, barnashrama dharma, guna dharma, naimittika dharma.*[7] Clearly, the officials of the Company did not want to raise any questions about the notion of relative rights at that time. In the Calcutta Madrasa, too, there was a provision for education according to ancient Arabic and Persian conventions of learning, under the supervision of maulavis.

Signs of Switching Loyalties

Signs that the arrangement was not at all a permanent one became evident within a short time. 1793 was the East India Company's year for renewal of grants. At the same time, there was a premonition of the turnabout in the policy of the government apropos the religious beliefs and education system of Indians. William Wilberforce (1759–1833) placed a new proposal in the British Parliament during the discussion on grant-related matters, suggesting that the prohibition on missionary activities in India be lifted and schoolteachers be sent from England forthwith. But the proposal was rejected owing to strong opposition from one section of the Company's Directors. The argument of the opposing faction was that as in other cultures, the constitutive practices of the Hindu code were sufficiently effective; and that it was madness to catch hold of Hindus in order to convert them or to teach them anything more than the knowledge they already had within their grasp.[8] A Director of the Company recalled that England had had to bear the repercussions of this kind of madness earlier too, when America had slipped from England's grasp due to the establishment of schools and colleges. If the same mistake was repeated in India, the matter would conclude similarly. If the natives were enthusiastic about education, they would have to go to England; it was not necessary for England to go forward proactively to rescue the Indians. [9]

Although Wilberforce was dissuaded at that time, he broached the proposal again exactly twenty years later, in 1813, when discussion on the Company's grant was resumed. By that time a lot of water had flowed under the bridge and most parliamentarians had become inclined towards Wilberforce's position. Despite obstructions, his proposal was finally adopted. In the interim period of twenty years, the social standing of Wilberforce's collaborators had been enhanced in exact proportion to the increase in their numbers. One of Wilberforce's advisers was Charles Grant (1746–1823). From the brief outline of Grant's gradual ascendancy in the world, one can get an idea of the increased stature of Wilberforce's collaborators.

Charles Grant first came to India in 1767 with a job in the Military Department. Although he returned to England in 1770, he came back again in 1773 as the Company's representative. Within a short span of time he amassed huge wealth, before he left India for the last time in 1790. Among those who contributed actively towards the implementation of Lord Cornwallis' Permanent Settlement were Sir John Shore and Charles Grant. Grant joined the British Parliament in 1802 and was instated as Chairman of the East India Company in 1805. After returning to England, he started living as Wilberforce's neighbour in Clapham, and, in keeping with the name of the locality, the Clapham community grew progressively. Along with others, John Shore and Jacquary Macaulay were members of that community.

After the Industrial Revolution, it was not just the economic structure of England that continually underwent changes; simultaneously, many transformations took place in the ideologies pertaining to the ethical domain of society. The education of the Wellesley brothers and Whitfield and the propaganda of the Methodist church helped to instil new ethical principles in the social imaginary. In the next phase, in the last decade of the eighteenth century, a new edition of the Methodist compendium appeared under the title *The Resurrection of the Evangelicals*. Among the various, in some cases mutually contradictory, trends through which the mixed reactions of England's chief ideologies were being restructured at that time, this pure Christian principle was extremely crucial. And the spokespersons for the new sense of values were the pioneering theorists of the Clapham community. In due course, John Shore and Charles Grant began to be counted as 'Evangelical fathers', along with others.

On returning from India, Grant wrote a booklet titled *On the State of Society among the Asiatic Subjects of Great Britain, Particularly with Respect to Morals, and on the Means of Improving It.* The booklet had almost been completed in 1792, but Grant got it printed through personal enterprise and presented it to the Company's Directors in 1797. Despite its initial lack of impact, it was published as a deed of the Parliament in 1818, and eventually, his views were accepted lawfully. Wilberforce, the mouthpiece of the Evangelicals, fashioned his argument along the lines of Grant's reasoning. Before trying to uncover its rationale, it is necessary to have a clear idea about the theoretical framework of Evangelicalism.

Piety and Impiety, Education and the Lack of it

Among the principal strands upon which this theory was predicated was that of conversion. The Evangelicals believed that in man's life, there comes an unexpected but intense moment when his former identity gets totally obliterated. At that critical moment of transition, man gets both physically and mentally devastated; and he simultaneously experiences the pangs of sinning and the benediction of deliverance. This spiritual experience takes him to the threshold between life and death. And then, the dangerous stupidity that had engulfed him all this while – under the grip of his habitual inertia and enslavement to his propensities – disappears, and all his bonds snap instantaneously. Just as, on the one hand, a sudden flash of light dispels all camouflages and illuminates the reality of truth, and on the other, brings about a transformation of personality, that critical moment is the pious moment of a renaissance, a harbinger of a new promise. When man realizes that he is not free at all but a mere slave to blind instincts and social prejudices, and a mere flotsam in the current of everyday life, it is then that he comes out of his stupor and embarks on a new journey. If one wants to escape self-humiliation and the agony of suffering to attain absolution from burdensome sin, one would have to come to one's individual equation with God and singly bear the responsibility of that negotiation. Neither the mediation of the clergy nor perfect observance of the scriptures is a substitute for this solitary dialogue. After heartfelt penitence the consciousness of the man immersed in sin undergoes a real transformation, and he earns the right of self-governance. His enlightened mind is able to elude the falsity and temptations of the outside world, and unmistakably recognize the signs of the righteous path. If man does not keep his inner soul pure and untarnished even after that, and if he does not constantly carry on with battling anti-Christ/anti-God (*Ishwarbirodhi*) forces through toil and prayer, then the intense experience of attaining enlightenment and the memory of that resplendent upheaval gradually fade from his mind, and he loses the prop of that divine mercy which is so difficult to attain.

The person whose desired end is God's perpetual clemency, therefore, cannot selfishly keep others deprived of the benediction received by the enlightened soul. It becomes his essential duty to carry the message of this divine perception to innumerable ignorant people in the world. Evangelical theory was not a mere experience of taking refuge in inwardness or one of intense emotion; it laid equal emphasis on work and sermonizing. According to this view, work was the greatest antidote to indolence and *karma* (work ethic) was valuable in itself. But, on the other hand, the resources of hard-working people who were the producers of wealth were necessary to establish God's righteous kingdom. Consequently, in order to liberate sinful people from the veil of ignorance, the pious preachers have to be restrained, prudent and dedicated. The Evangelicals were not at all God-crazed mystics; they had sharp worldly wisdom. They believed that one cannot comprehend the significance or greatness of God's message by mere mental reflection or power of reasoning; one cannot render one's solitary, introspective experience through the sequence of logic. But if one is not directly acquainted with the Bible, the search for authentic knowledge is bound to fail. The Evangelicals were not partial to excessive disputation as they considered subtle philosophizing to be a conspiracy of the Devil. Even so, they acknowledged that people who were fuddled by stupidity needed a minimal education and at least some mental growth. In the opinion of the Methodists and Evangelists, unless one had proficiency in the Bible, one was not worthy of religious conversion. If the heart and soul were not receptive enough, indiscriminate sowing of the seeds of religion would fail to bear any fruit.[10]

The Evangelists believed that God's silent command and his obscure intent are expressed through history. One glorious example of that divine injunction was British rule in India. It was as though God was proclaiming that there ought to be a combination of ability and responsibility: one had to save innumerable sinful souls in India from the wickedness of praying to pagan gods and goddesses. The father of the Evangelicals, Charles Grant, spelt out this very message in an exaggerated fashion. A detailed description of the nemesis awaiting the Indian people, essentially the Hindus, spans a major portion of his book.

Grant's observations were as follows:

- According to the colonial census, the group of people who have been labelled as 'Hindu' have very little or no concern about ethics.
- The Hindu society is so uncouth because of this absolute absence of a moral conscience – nothing else can be found there except boundless greed and uncontrolled excesses.
- All spheres of Hindu society are replete with immoral perversities and shame-

ful superstitions, be it law and administration, culture, industry, agriculture, customs or rituals.

- The country has no dearth of natural resources; yet the Hindu quality of life is dangerously low, almost bestial, due to the lack of moral injunctions and rules.
- The primary source of all the troubles of Hindus is their religion.
- The greatest impediment to the development of the Hindu self-identity is the dictatorial rule of the brahmans, the race of priests who are the chief ideologues of the Hindu religion.
- The Hindus are consequently lifeless and ineffectual because of their unquestioning allegiance to the tyrannical brahman.
- Such is the iron-bound nature of the brahmans' hold on society that it is impossible to alter it even with the creation of new rules.
- There is no use in changing rules either – as long as the character of the Hindu does not undergo a sea-change, the abject, self-destructive Hindu masses will rot in their own, sinful quagmires; until there is an awakening of the intellect, an overall realization, there is no hope for betterment.
- The chief tool for extracting the Hindu mind from centuries of brahman autocracy and ages of superstitious beliefs is *education*.
- As soon as the Hindu mind is able to rectify its own errors and follies because of the benefits of education, the dark, prison-like edifice of the Hindu religion will fall apart – hence the erstwhile prisoners themselves will voluntarily choose the great ideals of Christian morality.
- And the aim of the Evangelicals is to facilitate such a revolutionary development of the mind.
- So perfect and so smooth is the Evangelical method of spreading Christianity through the benefits of education that there is no possibility of it causing any political unrest or turmoil, any riots or such clashes.
- The ultimate goal of the Evangelicals is the abolition of the massive gap, the obvious inequality, that is present between the English and the Indians; to abolish all differences in every sphere of life, be it religion, faith, customs or language, and mould Indians on the lines of the English.
- In order to achieve this goal, the Evangelical way would be to change the medium of education of India in order to show the right and true path to those who have strayed; to provide proper education to the unfortunate, the barbaric mother language has to be replaced with English.
- In place of the native alphabet, with the help of English, from just basic 'a–b–c's to far more difficult and nuanced propositions, all would become easily accessible to the Indians. Gradually, they will become acquainted with European aesthetics and Christian theology; they will even get the opportunity to explore English literature; as the boundaries of knowledge spread wider, the minds of the Indians will become purer.

- If they follow this circuitous path of gradual development, one day, even the naturally irrational Hindu will become a creature of reason. The light of reason will expunge any doubts they may have about the validity of Christian ethics and morality.
- The moment the Hindus ascertain that there is no longer any hindrance to anything physical or metaphysical – that is, neither on the pursuit of material happiness and security, nor on the pursuit of spiritual advancement – they will immediately eradicate all sorts of hatred from within themselves, and gladly and completely accept the orderly social system brought about by the British.
- Overall, wherever the English language and theological doctrines gain hold, the British trade will flourish – only in the dominance of a single language can the profits gained from colonies become stable and safe.

The lecture that Wilberforce delivered in Parliament in 1813 – 'The Enhancement of the Spiritual Knowledge and Moral Sense of the Indian Subjects' – was, from beginning to end, almost a reiteration of Grant's views. The fundamental logic of the Evangelicals was: if the Company had to maintain a monopolistic authority over India, it would not be enough to depend on regulating raw materials and labour; in the second phase of the colonial journey, human consciousness should be the main target and mainstay of the development of abilities.

As a result of the intense pleadings of Grant and Wilberforce, the British Parliament accepted the problem of education in India as one of its responsibilities. In order to keep that promise, the prohibition on missionary propagation was repealed and the 43rd Section of the 1813 law of the East India Company was compiled. According to that Section, a lakh of rupees were granted annually with the objective of 'the revival and enhancement of literature, of giving encouragement to learned Indians and the establishment and progress of science'.[11] The sentence generated complicated responses and led to the construction of several counter-discourses. The question arose as to whether there was a common thread that could provide a link between 'the rebirth of literature' and 'the inauguration of science'. If 'literary renaissance' comes to mean expansion of the Arabic–Persian–Sanskrit languages and if the meaning of 'the inauguration of science' is the spread of European knowledge, would it have been possible to fix a clear-cut policy about the medium of instruction? Did there remain an unbridgeable gap between the objective and its attainment, unbeknown to the makers of the law? Moreover, what could have been the meaning of the appellation 'learned Indians'? Which section of society would they have represented – eastern or western, and what kind of pursuit of learning were they the upholders of?

Of course, it did not take long to settle this debate. In 1835, the ultimate settlement regarding this uncertainty was concluded through the mediation of Lord Macaulay. In order to know what logical basis Macaulay's resolution was predicated upon, we have to take into account England's internal reforms between 1813 and 1835, because, right from the start, England's domestic and colonial policy had got inextricably intertwined. Macaulay's proposal for education was no exception to that common rule. The new educational policy in India and its modern system of instruction were composed in keeping with the reconfigurations of the chief ideologies of contemporary England.

Monopoly versus Free Trade

Whoever else might have had objections on the matter, the spokespersons of free trade had no reason for hesitation about the noble proposals that the enlightened Evangelicals had made to appropriate all that is Indian. Of course, despite similarity in their theories and knowledge, there were ample differences of opinion between the two sides. This was because even after progressing quite far, Evangelicals like Charles Grant took a stand against their own logic after a point. The decision that the Evangelicals had taken to wipe out ideological differences between the conqueror and the conquered, and the method that they wanted to deploy to assimilate and establish kinship with the 'other', made the claims of the supporters of free trade, the liberals, more compelling. It was the assertion of the liberals that in order to reach that desired target, there was no way except to open up the road to unrestrained trade in India. All efforts would be unsuccessful till such time as East India Company's monopoly over trade did not end in India.

As a high-ranking official of the East India Company, it was not at all possible for Charles Grant to accept this fact. In 1822, he and his sons carried on a strong battle in Parliament against the demand of abolishing the special opportunities and privileges of the Company. Despite their strong objection and eloquent protests, the pace of the Company's influence could not be slowed down. The flag-holders of free trade themselves carried forward the logic of the Evangelicals to its inevitable conclusion. Within a short span there was evidence that, as the balance tilted in favour of the former, a split had occurred among the Evangelicals. Charles Grant's son, another Charles Grant, who was unwavering in his support of the East India Company as late as 1823, changed his mind and swerved towards the Whig Party. He came to design the law of 1833, through the strength of which the term of the Company's trade-related hereditary lease in India wound up and the phase of its business operations ended. And in this matter his principal collaborator was Lord Thomas Babington Macaulay, son of Zachary Macaulay, one of the leading figures in the first generation of Evangelicals.

Many other people contributed to this changed outlook towards trade. The long list of names of the great heroes of that period is radiant even today, and the names of people like Jeremy Bentham (1748–1873), James Mill (1773–1835) and John Stuart Mill (1806–1873) have remained pertinent for various reasons. All three were priests of progress and authors of the new dispensation. Bentham, the proponent of the slogan 'the greatest good of the greatest number', fashioned a unique theoretical edifice: Utilitarianism. The intention of the benevolent and prudent Bentham was a numerical evaluation of man's labour and leisure.[12] According to him, if one could once uncover the means of measuring clusters of feelings like happiness and sorrow, pleasure and pain, etc., there would be nothing left to worry about. Testing that certain knowledge by the touchstone of Utilitarianism, one could ascertain all truth and falsehood. The inscrutability of the inanimate world then need not remain a mystery to logical-minded individuals any more. They could seek refuge in a stable and ordered policy that is freed of the dilemma between virtue and desire. Perhaps the key to Bentham's thoughts lay concealed in the ideal prison he conceptualized, called 'Panopticon'. Perhaps there remains a deep-seated connection between the architectural layout of a prison and the strategies of structuring the edifice of Utilitarianism.

Command and Punishment

The first booklet containing a proposal for the Panopticon was published by Bentham in 1791, and the second in 1822. The proposal got the sanction of the British Parliament in 1794. A suitable place for the prison, in keeping with Bentham's preference, was located in 1799. Even after all this, because of the indifference of short-sighted parliamentarians, Bentham's precious blueprint was sabotaged. Despite being rejected, and although the Panopticon never saw the light of day, that dream of the ideal prison-house has left as indelible an imprint on the modern social imaginary as in Bentham's theoretical reflections.

Simplicity of layout is a unique feature of the Panopticon. There is none of the superfluity of the ordinary prison in it, and no unnecessary doors, gates, bolts, chains and locks. The prisoners are not tied from top to bottom inside dark chambers; even if they are exiled from the outside world, they are not deprived of contact with light. In the centre of the prison, there is a tower that is inlaid with windows. These windows open to the interior of a quadrangle. Around the tower are the cells of the prisoners. The habitation of the prisoners is divided into cubicles; each prisoner is entitled to one cubby-hole. Each slot has two windows – one faces the tower while the other faces the outside. As a result, there is no lack of light in any of the compartments. Even so, all avenues of interaction between the residents of the lit yet shut compartments are completely blocked. They are simultaneously segregated and deprived of communication. Each of them is condemned to an unrelenting loneliness; there is no respite from or end to the torment of that solitude. Whatever be the crime, hardly any punishment can be more brutal than this. Bentham, of course, did not stop at that. He was not satisfied merely with the offenders being temporarily incarcerated within walls in the peripheries of the prison. According to Bentham's decree, it would also not do to get away with so little. It was not his only desire to withhold from them the pleasure of company. It can easily be guessed, speaking psychologically, that there was nothing 'medieval' about the Benthamite prescription of punishment. But of course, it was only natural that during the 'enlightened' period of the eighteenth–nineteenth centuries there would be no trace of the 'medieval' irrational, and that the patterns of behaviour of the so-called dark ages would have become obsolete.

In the bygone era, a convicted person had to bear the signature of submission to the sovereign; his entire body would bear the inscription of royal authority. At that time, an offender would be paraded before all and chastised publicly. A veritable carnival would erupt around the place of public execution. The royal decree would be proclaimed by the beating of drums, and pronouncement of the penalty would be spread by word of mouth. No discrimination would be made in the invitation to witness the spectacle; the poor, the newborn, the lame, the blind, the respectable – nobody would be left out. On a specified day, at a specific time, the offender would be brought to the slaughter-house. He was the main attraction of that festivity and the chief protagonist of the display. In order to arouse the curiosity of the crowd that was present, the moment of entrance would be delayed as much as possible. It was as though one could stretch the prologue till such time as the main actor appeared on the stage to put an end to the restless wait of the audience. As soon as the role of the prologue was over, the real drama would begin.

This event of punishment in the middle ages had certain unique features. The ambience of a holiday and an atmosphere of celebration were created by configuring the act of retribution in the form of a popular ritual. The condemned individual was displayed as a manifest example of the power of the ruler so that the very foundation of the ruler's influence got reinforced in the minds of the populace. The real purpose of all that fanfare and elaborate display was a garish exhibition of royal authority and an unabashed self-advertisement of state power. The gathering seemed to be split along hidden yet definite lines. On one side of the line were the offenders and the employees, and on the other were assembled the general populace. On the one hand, there was a manifest executionary power; on the other, it was implicit. It was as if the body of the condemned man was an exhibit; on it was being crafted the template of power. In fact so much ceremony and such ostentatious arrangements were made so that the workmanship of power could remain imprinted on the audience's minds forever. The introduction of this spectacle was not as much to punish the offender as to caution potential offenders. It was to remind them that if they deviated by a hair's breadth from the officially endorsed code of conduct, if they got indicted for 'anti-social' activities, they must lose the right to participate in the collective life of society. The person who had the evil intent of violating rules should be aware of the right consequences of transgression and the misfortune of being unprotected. Man's body was used as an apparatus to give a vivid example of that heartbreaking consequence. The severed parts of the body and the scattered remnants of the person carrying the mark of authority of the sovereign were used to impart a lesson in ethics to those who were to witness the rites of punishment. A lot of thought and reflection and adequate scholarship contributed to that lesson in morality. Experienced employees knew very well that if they did not have an approximate idea of the condemned man's bodily strength and his threshold of tolerance, his end might come without any warning – before the conclusion of his tenure and the destined final moment. The torture was varied by intensifying and weakening it, and its measure was kept in control so that there was no break in rhythm and the audience did not become exhausted or restless due to witnessing monotonous scenes. A lesson in ethics becomes fruitless if the spectacle of brutal mayhem cannot be relished. This was the foremost notion of the discourse of punishment in the past era.

There is a gaping difference between the Benthamite and the medieval punitive codes. According to the former, one could deter people by intimidation apropos the apposite retribution of misdeeds, and thereby maintain the stability and discipline of society. According to the second view, even if one's objectives were fulfilled temporarily by deploying medieval barbarism, it did not resolve the basic problem. In his book *Discipline and Punish* (1975), Michel Foucault (1926–1984) demonstrated that during the passage from feudalism to capitalism in Europe, along with a lot of other things, ancient beliefs about crime and punishment were gradually altered and eventually augmented. A new kind of penal theory was compiled that was commensurate with the requirements of the new age. The inner world of human beings acquired a greater respect and importance among the compositors of law.[13] An important signpost and a significant indicator in the making of that trajectory was Bentham's Panopticon. In Bentham's imagination, the citizens of his ideal state were so liberal-minded that they would not even by mistake imagine the violation of the regulations and proscriptions of society. Each dutiful and responsible citizen stood safe and secure in his fixed place, united in a relationship of bonhomie with others. Nobody had any regret or complaint; there was therefore no possibility of open rebellion or hidden sabotage. No one ever deviated from his own creed, or encouraged any kind of indiscretion that could create any fissure in the permanent arrangement of mutual goodwill or overlook any strand of the inviolable social contract. There was no scope for crime in Bentham's world view; consequently, there was no need to punish anyone. Abolition of punishment was the real objective of Bentham's penal code. The Panopticon was conceptualized to remove corruption and to eradicate misconduct from society.

Panopticon or Trap of Light

The prisoners of the Panopticon were separated from one another. But one could view each of them individually from the tower situated at the centre of the quadrangle. Moreover, it was not possible for any prisoner to know who or who all were observing him. As a result, each prisoner imprisoned inside a solitary cell knew that even if the sentinel was out of sight, he would still continue to remain under the surveillance of a pair of eyes. The work of patrolling became easier and much more effective because the sentinel always remained hidden from human sight. There was no botheration with locks and chains or the hassle of inflicting bodily torture; everyone was under surveillance.

The inmates of the Panopticon were each separately marked, labelled and identified – snared by the light trap. In Bentham's dictionary, an 'individual' did not simply mean a flesh-and-blood human being but was a measurable unit. That abstract unit was indeed the ultimate measuring stick with the help of which one could compare one with the other and faultlessly calculate the coordinates of each individual's ethical position. Bentham's 'science' spelt out the rules of drawing the outline of man's ethical growth and decline. For him, the prisoners of the Panopticon or 'surveillance' were just real matter. They were visible and one saw them, yet they could not see; they provided facts but they had no control over them. The prisoners, circumscribed by an invisible and unblinking gaze, experienced with all their heart the all-devouring presence of a one-sided power, but the *fons et origo* of that power stayed beyond their reach. Bentham had wanted that power should be established over the entire universe, and that its manifestation should be simultaneously perceptible and imperceptible. A relentless vigilance is exercised over the inmates of Panopticon; the more they internalize that perpetual monitoring, the deeper its influence seeps in, the more unbounded and subtle is the expression of that power. The exhibition of power becomes redundant, then, because in the new arrangement, there is no difference between the prisoner and the sentinel; the convict is his own invigilator there and engaged in his own surveillance. As a result of the decentralization of power, there is no definite centre of power as such; a Panopticon gets constructed in the mind of each individual.

Bentham hoped that any rational man in possession of good sense would understand the value of his ideal or model prison. He was at least certain that all the needs of the state machine could be met through the use of the master key named Panopticon. In the Preface to his booklet called *Panoptics*, Bentham gave a catalogue of the many ways in which society would benefit if the Panopticon became functional. 'So much – the sacraments of ethics, health care, the development of arts, the spread of education, the reduction in the responsibilities of the people, a strong and powerful economy – could be achieved through this simple scheme of architecture.' Any kind of man could easily be kept in that ideal prison; patients, criminals, workers, children – its door was open for all of them. There is no reason to get disturbed by the variety of symptoms in Bentham's analysis; whatever the disease, there is just a single medicine. By matching the signs of various social ailments, one can see that concealed behind the apparent variety is a structural similarity, and a secret link among separately visible misdeeds. Whatever the differences on the surface, all diseases are actually the same. If one can discern the line of their similarity, the diagnosis becomes very easy. In Bentham's opinion, the Panopticon was not what is normally meant by a prison. Its appellation was appropriate – it was a reformatory or nursing home. There was so much caution and so many hard and fast rules so that national integration would not be threatened, and so that nobody could cause any opposition owing to differences of opinion. Along with others, if children and workers could be fitted to the cycle of some daily habits, there would be no anxiety on that score. The easy and exact reproduction of social relationships would follow in the measured steps of the regularity of a machine, *à la* the immovable, in Bentham. It is not for nothing that Marx equated 'freedom', 'equality', 'property' and Bentham in one bracket while giving an account of the rules and ethics of capitalism.[14] Before making an entry into Bentham's golden bower of bourgeois promise, one has to acquire ability, become pliable and worthy. According to Michel Foucault's definition, discipline stands for the method through which one can control the mind of society, and impose the combination of pliability and worthiness on one's body.[15] It was Bentham's belief that the more one perfected the rules of discipline through practice and training, one's need to be driven by power would become redundant. The more firmly ingrained power took root within man's sense, the more awareness of its actions and reactions was benumbed. Bentham had dreamt of bringing under control man's consciousness in every sense of the term. The more absolute that dependence, the better; the more mysterious and covert it was, the more permanent and hurtful its impact. Earlier, many people had spelt out the ways and means of making effective the aspirations of the ruling class, but Bentham surpassed and overstepped everybody to reach the highest pinnacle of achievement.

Panopticon and Colonial Subjects

One can raise a related question here: was there no place for colonial subjects in Bentham's hairsplitting arguments? Were they such objects of apathy that they could be left out of even the triumph of power? In the catalogue of the prisoners of the Panopticon there was no mention of colonial subjects, but can one not detect their presence even in that elision? If one were to imperceptibly bypass the context of imperialism, could one do justice to the chronicles of the chief ideologies of contemporary England? During the colonial era, the economies of England and India were interrelated. If one were to discuss one without the other, one would necessarily get trapped in a variety of theoretical loopholes. Does this rule not apply to ideology too? Is the ideological connection between the colonial nation and the dependent state indeed so smooth that from beginning to end every statement is a reiteration, every sound an echo? In a world that is colonially inhabited, if one kept no track of where what happened and what might happen, and did not take the necessary measures, would it be possible for a few nations to maintain their colonial dominance for so long? Whatever difference of ability there might be, was there not a musical duet between the 'mother nation' and the chief and other ideologies of the colony? Perhaps the rhythm got broken intermittently; perhaps there was no harmony between the beat, measure and tempo, and camouflaged behind the duet, a surreptitious aggression went on. Perhaps excessive use of the impure, jarring note of colonial grammar had ruined the structure of the cohesive musical composition; it had not been possible to reach the determined musical note of accord. Yet the relevance of one to the other has never been lost. In the world of colonialism, there was not and could not be anything that was 'pure'. Therefore, if the colonial subjects were left out of the discussion of the progress of the bourgeoisie in Western Europe and in the account of the formation of its chief ideologies, a lacuna of large measure – in fact a very fundamental loophole – would remain.

The same has occurred in Michel Foucault's writings. Foucault has given a minute description of how, from the end of the seventeenth century, the canvas of Western Europe started shifting and the outlook of its chief ideologies began undergoing a change; different stratagems of success were being devised one after the other. But barring a few instances, and those too rather superficial ones, he never mentions the colonial subjects. On the other hand, mechanically connecting the colonial subject with the other would not have solved the problem. For that, the blueprint would have to include a new problematic that would simultaneously unravel the dialogue between the two sides. That mutual dialogue cannot remain in the same place forever; it too has different phases. The voice of one party or the other has been sharp at different times. At times the balance has tilted to this side, at other times to the other side. But if one does not have the ear to listen to both sides together, the discussion would inevitably be partial and oversimplified.

Utilitarian Benevolence and India

About the subject of imperialism, however, Bentham has not kept us mystified; he did not nurture any secrets about it. 'British India's living executor will be Mill, and I will be the deceased legislator' was a statement made by Bentham. Which meant that James Mill would be in the forefront while Jeremy Bentham pulled the reins from the wings; and the wonderful arena for this performance would be the Indian soil, as though the huge earthen mass called India was a laboratory of experiments in Utilitarian theory.

James Mill joined the East India Company in 1819; within a short while, he was joined by his son, John Stuart Mill. James Mill started his career as an Assistant Inspector and worked his way up to the position of Inspector in 1830. For a few continuous years, the Company entrusted to him the total responsibility of directing the fate of Indians as one of the Company's chief administrators. He fulfilled that responsibility with competence. It was but natural that Bentham's able student and collaborator would not encourage any laxity or weakness of nerves. Mill himself made it known that however distressing it was for a single person to manage six crore people, there was adequate pleasure in it, and fulfilment too.

Mill did not harbour any infatuation for India. In his writings, there is not the slightest trace of enthusiasm about this country. There is not a hint of orientalist attraction. The unique outline of India's history fashioned by the chief orientalists of the first generation, like William Jones and Colebrook, was the original basis of Mill's reflections on India and the character-building of Indians, especially the Hindus. But he did not have an iota of confidence in or respect for the methods of analysis and the various inferences of the orientalists. He wrote *The History of British India* (1818) from a new perspective, following a scientific method. Whatever else there may be in that source-book of India's history, there is no stamp of orientalist gentleness. Written in matter-of-fact language and rather tersely worded sentences, it spared nobody; none of those who had sung praises of the Hindus so far under the influence of wrong notions were spared.

Although the deductions of Charles Grant and James Mill about the character of Hindus were virtually the same, their methods of analysis were different. The amusing fact is that whatever subtle differences there may have been between the views of different groups of the Clapham community, the Whig liberals and Utilitarian theoreticians, in the sphere of colonial India, their conclusions amounted to the same. The Indian mentality got perpetually entangled within one theory after another.[16]

The main argument of Mill's *History of British India* was as follows: the Hindus are stuck at a primitive stage of civilization; their stories and legends, festivals and celebrations, rites and rituals, art and architecture, literature and culture, and entire range of activities bespeak their primitiveness. The changeless Hindu society had been stagnant at one place through the ages; as soon as the Hindus crossed a few levels of the lower registers of civilization, the resources of their enterprise got depleted. Mentally, they are immature and close-minded; there is neither any sophistication nor order in their thinking.

Men who are slaves of blind superstition think whatever their minds want to think and say whatever comes to their minds; on the strength of an unfettered imagination, they invent all sorts of bizarre stories – distasteful and supernatural narratives of ghosts, spirits, monsters and devils, gods and goddesses. The Hindus are devoid of sense and intelligence, and do not have knowledge of the material world or a sense of history. In their ancient literature, there is not a single example of a historical character; the affairs of gods and mortals get mixed up and confounded there. History and myth, reality and hearsay constantly get intertwined, and produce all kinds of weird matter. But not having the records and papers of Hindu history has not caused great damage either. The sooner the history of ruthless, barbaric people gets obliterated and sinks way down into the depths of oblivion, the more propitious it would be. It is our responsibility to uproot whatever remains.

It is as if a procession of 'no's runs through Mill's book. The Hindus have nothing – they never had. In his well thought-out opinion, the Hindus are the most inferior of the immoderate and ignorant people of the world. They have nothing called ethics, their nature and character is not good, they are cheats and traitors from their very birth. There is no indication of any thought or imagination regarding creation and the world in Hindu literature that demonstrates even an iota of familiarity with beauty and the divine. There is only 'indiscipline, restlessness, the stimulation of sex, conflict, supernatural signs, gigantic gods and devils, ferociousness and perversion'.[17] Mill was not the kind of person to spare anybody, not even Kalidas. In a few words, he dismissed the opinion of William Jones (1746–1798), the translator of *Abhijnana Shakuntalam* who had designated Kalidas as India's Shakespeare. In his opinion, the civility befitting citizens, love of poetry and eloquence – all these do not prove the existence of a developed civilization but, in fact, the very opposite. Excessive ornamentation of language and extravagance of words make man's consciousness polluted, and distracts his vision from the problems of society. A frivolous love legend like that of Shakuntala is required only in a country that is bound tightly by a despotic regime. The childishness of playing with words only befits the introductory phase or childhood of civilization. Besides, in layer after layer of *Abhijnana Shakuntalam* are all kinds of contemptible values. In it Kalidas has sung the anthem of all sorts of frivolities like licentiousness, superstition, weird beliefs and intemperate powers. The description of the rage of the sage Durbasa proves how widespread the nets of cunning brahmans are in Hindu society. The obscene influence of brahmans shows that there is no rejoinder to the stupidity of Hindus; if one wanders through the universe, one would not find a race as lazy and inactive as them. The long and short of it was that the Hindus have contributed nothing excellent in any sphere of life – be it religion, work or culture.

Utilitarian 'Science'

One need not state that behind Mill's incisive critique lies an imperialist arrogance. The self-centredness of that arrogance is imprinted in every line of whatever that piece of writing states and proposes. Moreover, Mill had the pride of a scientist; he could pronounce the ultimate judgment on every matter on the strength of 'science', and he did not stumble even for a moment. At the root of Mill's scientific vision was a profound message of empiricism. A common link emerges if Mill's objections about Hindu society are juxtaposed side by side. The Hindus have no sense of moderation; exaggerated statements and overdoing are a part of their 'racial character'. The Hindus do not keep track of the inner details of the material world, and this is why they cannot draw an exact replica of the manifest world. According to this positivist observation, if one climbs down the ladder of deductive logic from the phenomenal world and from the acknowledged heap of visible, material things, one can definitely arrive at scientific principles and incontrovertible truth. Even if the sphere of requirement is varied, 'science' is singular and unique. Through this internal unity, in the name of that unique and unparalleled science, the world can be divided into two clear spheres. One side of it is lit; the other is in the dark. On one side is scientific knowledge, on the other metaphysics. On one side are unadulterated facts, on the other supernatural imagination. There is no way of deviating from the course of history and the predetermined narrative of progress. One day, in the encounter between good and evil, good will triumph. The just kingdom of light, truth and science will be established after destroying darkness, falsehood and metaphysics.[18]

The conjunction of imperialism with this ideology that wears the garb of science is as clear as the light of day. Has the lasting impact of the *entente* that happened then through the agency or onslaught of the ideologies of Bentham and Mill been erased yet, and have we broken free of that bond? Or are we still returning the loan after they have extracted their dues, and, under the pressure of scientific historicist ideology, are we constantly surrendering more and more of ourselves?

The Dilemma of Sameness and Difference and the Paradox of Power

Mill's vision was as sharp as it was penetrating. In his analysis, the Hindus had no ability to keep anything hidden; and the Muslims were a little more advanced than the Hindus but that was about all. There was a distance of miles between them and the Europeans. All in all, there was no reason to be euphoric about India. There was such a lack of essential substance among Indians that it would not be going against logic to assume that they were like a container without contents or like floating signs. Mill's injunction was: if one wants to replenish that empty container, one has to procure its contents from outside; if one wants its floating signs to stabilize or give it some definite designation, one has to acquire a new system of signs. Because Indians do not have the resources of a spiritual capital, the poor people do not have any hope of deliverance except through the benevolence of the British.

Having reached thus far, one can easily suspect that there is a serious sort of fallacy in Mill's proposal of assimilation. This is so because on the one hand, he demonstrates that there is an unbridgeable gap between the English and the Indians, that their mental make-up and psychological propensity are totally unalike. On the other hand, he says that the gap can be bridged; that although difficult, it is not impossible. Is the difference between the English and the Indians, therefore, indeed external – and, cloaked by the apparent difference, is there a hidden link? In order to resolve the dilemma of sameness and difference, Mill had to take recourse to an abstract notion: that of the 'human condition'. He had to accept that whatever the differences between the two sides, the irony of fate was such that they were included in the same family of humans and bound by ties of kinship. When there was no way of correcting the mistake after obtaining the sanction and support of that ultimate state of existence and reposing one's trust in that exclusive sameness, one could embark on the holy task of assimilation. But even so, Mill could not manage all fronts because the idea that he called the condition of being, although useless as a theory, was very capable in the practical sphere. The pure, vacant unit was replete with all kinds of signs.

Like other idealist thinkers, Mill believed that there is no wearing away or destruction of the 'genuine' 'human condition' of that 'unfathomable' 'substance'. It is untouched by time and it does not alter by relocation. This universally valid human condition, unconnected with its functions in society or the reactions thereof, familiarizes us with man's essential nature.[19] But the deception is caught out as soon as one takes stock of the special features of man as demonstrated by Mill. Can one really save this mythic construction that transcends history from the contagion of history?

Mill's treatise on education, probably written in 1818, came out in the appendix section of the fifth edition of *Encyclopedia Britannica*. In that essay, he has written that the object of education is man's prescription for happiness. Education is a means by which man creates and attains happiness. Education is that medium by which man can be inspired and human consciousness regulated.[20] According to Mill, man's mind is divided into two large divisions: the physical and the moral. Health, labour, etc., come under the first part. Falling under the second part would be domestic education, practical and theoretical education, social and political education. The chief pillar of education is political education; the mind does not develop fully if that is shaky. There are many people in the world who have not evolved beyond the phase of animality; at some places they are a fraction of society, at others they are an entire community. It is because they have not received appropriate education that they are still groping in the dark and have been unable to unearth happiness. In one word, in the absence of Utilitarian knowledge, man cannot be free.

Candidly, Mill had further written in that treatise: we try with all our body, mind and speech so that the ideals of a sense of justice, good breeding and the pursuit of truth are equally established among all – the rich and the poor. Simultaneously, one should also pay attention that knowledge and intelligence are of equal measure – of course, if there is no hindrance or reason for objection.[21] In this statement is concealed the chief postulate of the Utilitarian compendium. In comparison to poor people, the moneyed are more intelligent. Lack of intelligence is the curse of the destitute; it is not because of their nature but due to poverty of resources that the majority of the people in the world are immersed in the darkness of ignorance. But what is the explanation for those adverse economic circumstances and do the rich have any role to play in the phenomenon?

Once they were confronted by this basic question, theorists like Bentham and Mill either bypassed it or got caught in a vicious circle: only those who are lazy and stupid are poor, and *vice versa*; on the other hand, those who are industrious and intelligent are wealthy, and *vice versa*. It is as though there is a natural connection, a causal relationship, and an infallible and self-evident link, like a natural law, between the earning of wealth and intelligence. We have been made to rehearse this unparalleled utterance, this resolution of sameness and difference, from the eighteenth century onwards in diverse ways and under various pretexts. The simple equating of hard work and success was the original slogan of the bourgeois march of victory, the basic formula of the bourgeois system. Bentham and Mill did not once deviate from their faith in this system, and unwaveringly observed the bourgeois doctrine. But they also had to take into account the price of singleminded observance of that dogged allegiance, both at the level of theory and practice. No matter how neat and tidy an ideology they wanted to formulate, their views were full of self-contradiction and their apparent appropriateness was sabotaged due to various contrary pulls, as happened in the sphere of Mill's notion of the human condition. No matter how much Mill wanted to liberate the meaning of the word 'human being' from all social paraphernalia and make it absolute and unconditional, the more particularized it became, the more it got enmeshed in a social context. One cannot avoid the tentativeness of meaning associated with the word 'human'. Along with it, the word 'bourgeois' that actually lies concealed behind the word 'human' is exposed repeatedly. Consequently, the notion of the human condition that Mill had to take recourse to when he got caught in the dilemma of sameness and difference does not get resolved; the effort to get the other to resemble the self and the dream of creating a semblance collapse.

Of course, for anything else to happen was also, in a way, impossible. However solid the structure of power may be, the expression of power is never one-sided. If there is no difference of signs between the ruler and the ruled, if the ruled become completely absorbed within the subject of signs, if the inequality of their relationship is wiped out completely, the basic premise of power becomes invalid. As a result, just as one has to draw the ruled closer towards oneself, one has to also keep them at arm's length. In this play of great contrary pulls, the equilibrium of the theory of signs gets destabilized. Because of the instability of the theory of signs, a secret view is formed along the lines of the meaning of power. However enormous the structures of power may be, there are many fissures and cracks within it. Those gaps are the entry-points for the opponents. Power cannot be impermeable or free of crevices. At the very base of power lies the weapon that can destroy it. This is what can be called a firm knot but a loose tie – a hostile intimation of power. Although Mill entered the fray after tightening his belt, he could not get away; a clear signature of this hostile intimation remains in his thoughts and his writings.

Did Mill not get despondent from time to time? Like other liberals, was he particularly optimistic about India's bright future? The 'social scientist' in him offered a judgment about India: that its art, literature and philosophy were absolutely hollow; that there was no logic in getting overwhelmed or wonder-struck upon seeing or reading about them. But as sociological documents, their value and importance was immeasurable. By deploying the infallible criterion of Utilitarianism, it was clearly proved that nothing is intelligible to Indians. They have neither knowledge nor curiosity whatsoever about the mystery of human existence and the goals of life. They feel blessed in merely gratifying their basic instincts. They are human beings with limited aspirations; they do not have the desire for pursuing happiness of great proportions. Moreover, Mill often thought that there was not much hope of redeeming Indians; no matter how much one attempted to enlighten them, they would remain in the darkness in which they already were. The irremediable ignorance of Indians would render all the efforts and systems of the Europeans futile at every step. The foul-mouthed Mill did not keep unexpressed his doubts about being able to change the minds and thinking of Indians. He had a lot of difference of opinion with other liberals on this matter.

Many believe that Mill was the author of the dispatch about the education of Indians that was sent from London to the Calcutta office of the East India Company in 1824. It was not possible for the conflicted Mill to accept that the manliness of Indians would be realized if they were educated in English. The same tone of dilemma is there in the proposal of 1824. In 1832, Mill communicated his disappointment when he testified before the select committee: it was not necessary and of no use for the natives to excessively emphasize the knowledge of English. What was predominantly necessary was to employ in government service such extremely submissive people with no views of their own – the question of whether they had mastery over English was therefore absolutely irrelevant. Mill's desire, thus, was not generous collaboration but complete control. Of course, the dividing line between assimilation and control was so blurred that it was impossible for those on whom the trials and experiments were being carried out to discern the difference. Did not Bentham, the person who dreamt of all-conquering power, also talk of total control under the pretext of assimilation? Does not the wondrous prison by the name of Panopticon serve as proof of the same idea?

Entry into a New Childhood

We have seen that the chief target of Bentham's discipline was a distinctive inmate of the Panopticon: the child. If one were to slightly extend the sphere of discipline, one could easily draw colonial subjects within its ambit. And if one connected the child and the colonial subject through a common link, one could produce a simple equation: child + colonial subject = colonial child. The dispatch of 18 February 1824 (probably composed by Mill) was an important directive on the desirable nature of the child's mind and how the colonial child ought to be reared.

Thirteen years earlier, on 6 March 1811, Governor-General Lord Minto (1751–1814) had regretfully written:

> There is no doubt in anybody's mind that the Indian system of education is undergoing a period of decline. The moral sense of the Hindus and Muslims has become lax; consequently, crimes like false undertakings and forging of documents are carried out all the time; they have both lost touch with their systems of education. If that connection is not restored, the country will be rampant with corruption.[22]

According to the calculation of the Christian missionary Alexander Duff (1806–1878), on the day that Minto documented the pathetic story of the spiritual nadir the Indians had reached – that is, 6 March 1811 – pure, unadulterated orientalism had reached the apex of its development. Subsequent to having reached the peak, it was not possible to prevent its descent. Orientalism was thereafter rejected by the infallibility of history.[23] On 2 October 1815, another proof became apparent: that the requirement of orientalism had worn itself thin for the administrative bosses, at least for the time being. Governor-General Lord Moira wrote: 'One would have to clear the mental barriers of the rising generation of boys and girls, and weave into their minds the fundamental concepts of Christian ideology in such a manner that their guardians do not get unduly agitated or alarmed.'[24]

Mill's dispatch arrived in 1824. As the spokesperson for the Committee of Directors of the Company, he wrote:

> There were two objectives behind the founding of the Sanskrit College and Calcutta Madrasa. One was to cultivate an aura of respect for the British among the Indians; the second was to awaken knowledge and intelligence in them. But the scientific thinking of the inhabitants of the Orient was so unformed that teaching these things would have entailed nothing but a waste of time. If one were to leave out abstract science and mechanical skills etc., what would remain is literature. In that sphere too, the retrogressive Orientals had not much to their advantage. They did not have anything more substantial than poetry. And who had ever heard that the cultivation of poetry requires institutions of learning like colleges? Moreover, those who take pleasure in poetry, in fact, do not benefit but are harmed by haunting the threshold of colleges.[25]

What, then, was the way out? Mill's advice was: as far as possible, the Hindus and the Muslims would have to be taught in their vernaculars, but they must remember to retain the essence and reject the chaff. It was the sacred duty of the British to make only 'essential learning' accessible to the Indians, weeding out whatever was corrupt.

Frankly discussing erstwhile principles, Mill wrote:

> It was a grave mistake to establish such centres of Oriental learning. As it is, in the bulk of Oriental texts, there is very little that is of worth. Besides, by not considering all its aspects, and by thoughtless indulgence, such learning has not curbed, but rather, provoked petty-mindedness and wicked intelligence among the Indians.[26]

The 'hard-hitting realist' Mill's antagonism to 'airy-fairy poetry', literature, etc., is well known. But by an irony of fate, through the mediation of Macaulay, literature would become the chief pillar of the colonial system of education. Eventually, it would not be the religion of the Evangelicals or the science of the Utilitarians but English literature that would emerge as victorious. But for whom was that literature – to which class of society would the various gems of English literature be made available?

One got a clue about which path to proceed along in order to procure a suitable answer to this question on 29 September 1830. On behalf of the Committee of Directors of the Company, the Madras government was informed that for the development of the intelligence and morals of Indians, one must, to begin with, closely observe the upper crust of society because they have leisure, and second, because they have a 'natural influence' on people of the lower strata. If one could initiate the rich to a higher kind of education, the views of people of all strata of society and the world of their perception would change some day, and the constitution of their collective mind-set would be totally transformed.[27]

Hereafter, Lord Thomas Babington Macaulay appeared on the stage. On 10 June 1834, his ship disembarked at the Madras port, and on that very day, this future controller of the fate of Indians made his first visual acquaintance with them. Macaulay could not suppress his laughter when he saw one of the people who he had come all the way to oblige, unasked. He has himself documented the experience of that first meeting. He felt that there seemed to be a deep incongruity between the complexion and nakedness of the virtually unclothed boatman wearing a triangular yellow cap, and his courteous manners and the tenor of his self-expression in his conversation.[28]

When a fiery debate was raging in the British Parliament about the Company's grants, Macaulay had delivered his life's most celebrated lecture about these famished, oppressed and ludicrous Indians. Proud of that lecture of 10 July 1833, he wrote to his sister the next day that, impressed by his eloquence, an elderly parliamentarian had compared him to the renowned orator Edmund Burke.[29] There is a close relation between Macaulay's statements on that day with the so-called modern educational policy. He had said in arrogant language opulent with figures of speech:

> A good administration in independent India is much more desirable than an India in a state of disorder that is subservient to Britain. Even if the Indians were to accept the subservience to their own Rajas instead of paying obeisance to British Collectors and Magistrates, there is no harm in that. One had only to ensure that they wore clothes marked with 'Made in Great Britain', and that being enamoured of British merchandise should be entrenched in their minds. But it was not sufficient to make Indians aware of the finery of goods produced in Britain. Their marketability would also have to be enhanced. It was much more gainful to conduct trade with civilized people rather than rule over barbarians.[30]

However, the same Mill on whose recommendation Macaulay had risen to the post of Legal Commissioner of India had never thought that the spread of capitalism could be ensured by just promoting the market. He was certainly a supporter of free trade as a policy. But he had enough theoretical objections in accepting the market as fulfilling all the requirements. For upholders of the theory of aggressive individualism,[31] the Utilitarian Mill and his close friend, the economist David Ricardo, it was much more important to increase the magnitude of capital than to extend the scope of the market. Behind the difference between Mill and Macaulay on the educational policy of India are two diverse schools of thought on the basic formula underlying the grammar of capitalism. Only he who did not have the slightest doubt about notions of boundless colonial expansion and the all-round assimilation of consciousness could have penned the educational proposals of 2 February 1835.

Macaulay's Proposals for Education: A Pamphlet of Modernity

No sooner than he had reached India than Macaulay was appointed as the president of the Committee of Public Instruction. The rest of the ten members were equally divided into two opposing camps apropos education. Five of them were in favour of indigenous education and five were for western education. The five supporters of eastern education were H. Shakespeare, H. Thoby Princep, James Princep, W.H. Macnaghten and the chairman of the Committee, T.C.C. Sutherland. On the other side, the five supporters of western education were W.W. Bird, Saunders, Bushby, Charles Trevelyan and J.R. Colvin. One must remember, Charles Trevelyan (1807–1886), a member of the second faction, was Macaulay's brother-in-law; and two members of the first faction, H.T. Princep (1792–1878) and James Princep (1799–1840), were brothers. Besides, while the intense debate on the issue of education of Indians was raging on, James Princep, who had deciphered the Brahmi script, was chairman of the Asiatic Society of Bengal. He had taken over the post in 1832, after Horace Hayman Wilson retired. With the eleven-member Committee of Public Instruction thus split into two groups of five, which way the balance would tilt depended entirely on the recently arrived progressive young man from Britain. During that historic moment of transition, the president of the Committee gave a verdict supporting the western system of education, ruthlessly demolishing one by one the rationale of the supporters of indigenous education. Macaulay's proposals worked out a synthesis of the Evangelical and the Utilitarian arguments.

In 1824, from the London-based headquarters of the Company had come the message (perhaps, again, at the behest of James Mill) that Indians should be instructed in their native language 'as far as possible'. The very words 'as far as possible' convey that he had sufficient doubts about whether it was possible to impart higher education in the Indian languages, implying once more that one would inevitably have to accept English as a medium only if they were incapable or if there was no substitute for it. Macaulay put an end to all the uncertainty and filled the void created by Mill's dispatch. Unwilling to get carried away by the orientalist sentimentalism or heed the opposite camp's pleas and objections, Macaulay pronounced his opinion in an unwavering voice: no, there was not even one language in India through whose medium one could disseminate 'useful' knowledge; the disbursal of education was possible only through the medium of English. In Macaulay's opinion, there was nothing special to say about the regional languages; and the languages used in quotidian life were indeed impoverished. There was no corpus of literature, not to talk of scientific thinking. Because of this unending indigence, it was not possible to translate any significant book into the regional languages. Unless one borrowed from some advanced language, this lack could never be overcome. If one left out the regional languages, what would be left were Sanskrit, Arabic and Persian.

Whatever else might have been his problem, Macaulay did not lack in honesty. He confessed openly that he did not know the basics of Sanskrit or Arabic. But that did not do much damage because even without knowing the classical languages of the eastern hemisphere, he understood clearly, after talking to the orientalists, that Sanskrit and Arabic were not comparable to the great languages of Europe. And, as in all other matters, as far as the wisdom, glory and heritage of the past were concerned, the orient paled by contrast.[32] Macaulay had no doubt that if one searched all of Sanskrit literature and assembled all its matter at one place, the volume and value would amount to even less than the primers for beginners in the English language. His mandate was radical demolition and not the nurturing of oriental studies. Otherwise, one would have to teach such medical science by the use of people's earned wealth and the support of the government that would shame even a quack doctor in England; one would have to teach such astronomy that reading it would make even an innocent-minded girl in a boarding school in England burst into laughter. The people living in the east understood by the term 'history', descriptions of thirty-feet-tall kings and emperors, their reigns being as long as their appearance was huge – not ten or twenty years but 30,000 years. The eastern people's knowledge of geography was similarly full of strange imaginings such as molasses-laden seas or cream-filled oceans. A single shelf of any good European library was enough to house all the knowledge of India and Arabia put together.

There was a unique combination of humongous ignorance and potent self-confidence in Macaulay – we have seen a shining example of that rare blend in James Mill earlier. Macaulay was Mill's able successor. Taking into 'consideration' all aspects, Macaulay's well thought-out opinion was that in order to be freed of the obligation of teaching an inert history–geography–science–philosophy, one would have to interpret Section 43 of the East India Company's laws of 1813 differently. The words 'rejuvenation of literature' complicated the explanation of that Section. It was Macaulay's opinion that it is not possible to resurrect a literature that does not have and never had a vibrant life of its own; intelligent law-makers could never have uttered such irrelevant nonsense. And what if they had said it? Learned and eminent men also make mistakes at times. But if such mistakes were not corrected in time, that itself would be a cause for regret. If one did not have timely knowledge of the transformed state of affairs, if one just followed the government's orders blindly, one could not keep the danger at bay. If it was settled, therefore, that the renaissance of literature meant stirring the soul of Indian literature through the mediation of English, the encouragement of educated Indians would mean arranging for the welfare of English-educated Indians. It meant that only those who were acquainted with Milton's poetry, Locke's philosophy and Newton's physics could be decorated with the appellation of 'an educated Indian'. Those who spend sleepless nights deliberating on the multifarious uses and benefits of various kinds of reeds or the profound mysteries of being immersed in the Supreme Being need not be considered.

Macaulay had communicated quite emphatically that despite the illusory ideas that orientalists nurtured, at least one section of Indians was fully aware of the spiritual and practical value of the knowledge of English. Where one could not get students unless one offered scholarships in the field of oriental studies, people begged and paid in order to try and learn English. Even here, the *market* identified the chief propensities of the social mind-set. The natives were eager to acquire English education but there was no suitable system; there was a demand and yet there was no provision. What stronger proof could there be of the futility of the policies of the government?

Like other liberals, Macaulay also fundamentally believed that on the matter of buying and selling, whether you went to Kanpur or Cheapside, human nature was one and the same.[33] In other words, he who did not have knowledge of worldly affairs was not fit to be designated with the title 'human'. Mill and Macaulay were both of the same opinion that it was not possible to analyse human nature except by original and genuine bourgeois analysts. But at least on the subject of the dilemma between unity and diversity, Mill had some disquiet. Macaulay, on the other hand, was a different breed of human being. He was not one to get confused by subtlety of analysis. Macaulay had fashioned his incontrovertible logic starting from the hypothesis that Indians were primitive versions of 'man' or 'bourgeois man'. If one took the hypothesis as a self-proven truth, one had to acknowledge that the adolescent Indians would not be able to take one step forward without the guardianship of the British, who were authenticated by the bourgeois ideology. Macaulay made it known in no uncertain terms that if people of the civilized races managed the education of barbarians, it was not only unnecessary but also reprehensible for the teachers to give importance to the views of the students. The orientalist instructors were vulnerable to this deadly flaw and the spokesmen of a self-destructive policy. The greatest impediment to the mental health of the subjects was their distorted sense of taste.[34] In Macaulay's eyes, Indians were the object of education and not its subject. It would be good for both sides – the teacher and the taught – if the latter accepted everything silently and with devotion.

Phrases like 'the purification of taste' and 'the blossoming of mental health' occur quite frequently in Macaulay's proposal. Similar similes and figurative expressions abound in Charles Grant's booklet; words like 'healing', 'repayment' and 'superstition' recur in a wearisome way in his writings. In his impeccable language, 'The true cure of darkness is the introduction of light.'[35] There are many such illustrations in Mill's writings. It is noteworthy that an unprecedented confluence of the three streams of medical science occurs in the similes and figures of speech used by Grant, who was involved in the life and after-life of Indians, and those used by Mill and Macaulay, who were engaged in 'scientific' solutions to the earthly problems of the Indians. The sum and substance was that the ideal of health was single and unique. Judged from that firm and impartial perspective, the signs of the ill-health of Indians are easily discernible. They should shed all uncertainties and reservations, and seek the protection of foreign doctors or psychiatrists. Without that, there is no hope of restoration of their health. There is an excellent example of how much the picture of an ailing society had got ingrained in Macaulay's mind. In order to explain that it is desirable for the government's policy to be altered with the passage of time, he wrote: Let us assume that a house is built according to the government's directions and it is realized later that the house no longer has any use; it would then be an act of prudence to demolish that building. Even in this account of the construction and deconstruction of a building, there is a simile of ill-health and its recuperation. This test of breaking and making can be applied to any institution; but Macaulay's exemplar of a 'sanatorium' or 'nursing home' was stunning and absolute.

Macaulay tabled quite a few illustrations to lucidly explain that the sincere effort to deliver Indians from being sucked into the vortex of failure has the sanction of history. By way of detailed explanation, he wrote: At the root of England's rapid progress are the achievements of the Greek and Roman civilization. Because the English had the adaptability and modesty to accept from others, their language gradually became the repository of universal knowledge and its medium of commerce. The English language was in the process of being exalted to the level of the chief language of Southern Africa and Australia. Why only in England, did that not happen in Russia also? Just two or three generations ago, the inhabitants of Russia were less developed than those living in the Punjab. Now, however, thanks to the generosity of the English, tasteful and educated Russians had become fit to participate in the assemblies and meetings of London and Paris. In order to get recognition in the world's hall of audience, therefore, it was the duty of Indians to follow the correct path of self-improvement, inspired by the examples of other races. The narrative of European history, therefore, is the original narrative. The blueprint of India's history must therefore be configured in the same pattern.

But was there any basic contradiction between the description of the historical trends as outlined by Macaulay and the orientalists' sense of history? Did not the orientalists also believe that India would regain its lost seat in the assembly of the world through the beneficial proximity of the English, and that the renaissance in India would happen on the basis of the ideal or the model of the European Renaissance?

H.T. Princep, an adherent of oriental education, documented his views against the proposals of Macaulay; the date of the note was 15 February 1835. And no matter what objection he might have had apropos Macaulay's statements, he too had no doubt about the greatness of Europe. On this basic question, the advocates of eastern and western education were of the same opinion. Princep reiterated the earlier logic about oriental studies. He had nothing new to say. First, if one enforced English, Indians who were blinded by religion might be incensed. Secondly, everybody in the country, especially the conservative Muslims, would not by any means accept English education. Princep of course said that no matter how immature or regressive Indian and Arabic philosophy might be, the ideas of Bacon, Locke or Newton originate therein. Next to this utterance of Princep, in one corner of the note, there is the sharp remark of John Drinkwater Bethune (Beaton), a member of the council, saying that it is a deadly statement.[36] The tone of the remark makes it clear that according to the opinion of the gender-sensitive Bethune, the greatest pioneer of modern women's education, the west is not indebted to the east in any matter and can never be.

In a sense, Princep had unnecessarily entered into a war of words with Macaulay because the answer to two of his objections, especially the second one, was there in Macaulay's proposal itself. He had given due respect to the view of the oriental educationists that the range of English education was bound to be narrow. The Machiavellian Macaulay had drafted his logic with extreme dexterity: on the one hand there was aggression; on the other there was a proposal for peace. It was because there was no doubt about the fundamental logic of the oriental educationists that Macaulay could write that proverbial sentence: 'We should now try in every way to create a bilingual class among the crores of Indians and us – a class which, despite being Indian by blood and birth, would be English by taste, views, moral principles and thought processes.'[37] It was his wish that the improvement of the regional languages should be entrusted to these Indians. The more words and definitions were borrowed from the different branches of western science and knowledge, the more loaded with meaning the regional languages would be. If these regional languages could become the vehicles of knowledge, one could, through these languages, educate even those who were ignorant of English in not too distant a future.

Lord Bentinck wholly approved of Macaulay's proposals. The new warrant was issued on 7 March 1835. No book related to oriental knowledge would henceforward be printed at the expense of the government. The net sum of money allotted for education would be spent for the spread of English literature and science through the medium of English.[38] Keeping in mind the possible reaction to this one-sided royal mandate and in order to reassure the natives after the Section of 1835 came into effect, it was said in the report of the first annual session of the Committee of Public Instruction: 'The provision for developing regional literatures was the basic goal of the Committee, but if the ability to impart education was not acquired, all organization would go to waste – before the natives could teach, they would have to be educated.'[39]

The more firmly established foreign rule became, there was a commensurate increase in the authority and prioritization of the English language. It displaced

Sanskrit/Arabic/Persian and gradually became the greatest prop of power. What was earlier an alternative medium of expressing one's thoughts rose to become, irreplaceably, the language of power. Macaulay took the process to its culmination. Along with that, he executed a transformation of great measure; the historical significance of that change is incalculable.

Eventually, with the mediation of Macaulay and through the shifting of priorities, it was established that it was not the Christian faith or western science but English literature that was the root of all knowledge, the elixir that cured all disease, as though all the values that the Evangelicals and the Utilitarians supported were embedded fully in English literature. Acquaintance with English literature, the compendium of eternal knowledge, automatically opened the doors of self-improvement. Transcending their limited association with their era and country, the works of Chaucer/Shakespeare/Milton had spread all over the world. In fact they reached even Indians with the message of salvation and the intimation of eternal truth. On 12 October 1835, the pioneer of the new education policy, Lord Macaulay, wrote in a letter to his father Zachary Macaulay (1768–1838), an Evangelist and a member of William Wilberforce's Clapham Association:

> That Hindu who has once got the taste of English education has inevitably slackened in his attachment to the Hindu religion. The quality of modern education is such that by virtue of spreading the Christian faith, one could transform the world view of upper class Bengalis within thirty years; perhaps no trace of idolatry might then be left in them.[40]

However, what if there were changes in the way of thinking of the Bengalis or Indians but the reflective ability of the English administrators did not improve correspondingly? Would that not create another crisis? If there were no new and blossoming talents, could the phase of assimilation be extended 'indefinitely'? If the distance between the aggressor and those who had been assaulted could not be maintained, would not the very process of collaboration come to an end? Macaulay understood well enough that if the English administrators did not have a mastery over the English language and literature that was worthy of reverence, the Indians could turn against the English rulers one day through the power of English education itself. Under Macaulay's advice, English literature was received as the ultimate measure of morality. Because of its acceptability as such, that literature became a new ground of conflict and got embroiled in the vortex of several opposing ideologies. It became extremely necessary, then, to keep an account of things like whether it was the ruler or the ruled who had greater control over the English language and literature, and which side was ahead of the other.

The Indian law of 1853 was regularized on Macaulay's advice. It was decided that candidates who wanted to join the civil service of the East India Company would have to sit for an examination in English language and literature. That compulsory paper's total marks would be 1000. Colonial pressure was added to internal pressure. English literature, hitherto considered an impure subject, attained a seat of honour and found a place in the curriculums of many universities in England. Modern English uprooted classical Greek and Latin; in the rise of the low-born, the aristocrats fell into ruin. The first teacher of English literature at Oxford University, Walter Raleigh (1861–1922), taught English in the Anglo-Oriental College in Aligarh before going to Oxford. The account of Walter Raleigh's appointment is witness to the deep links the educational policy of the colony had with the development of English in England itself.

In the matter of India, Macaulay had another contribution apart from educational policy. He was the compiler of the new penal code of Indian military law. The new law was introduced on 1 January 1862 on the basis of the proposed draft he had tabled and left behind in 1835. But why was there a gap of so many years between the conception and execution of the law? According to the commentary by Macaulay's successor and predominant devotee Fitz James Stevens, the Sepoy Mutiny of 1857 proved once and for all that there could not be any synchronization of opinion between the Europeans and the Asians. Despite the noble intentions of the British, it was not possible to work out an *entente* in the civil or military spheres with the Indians.[41] This meant that it was only after the 'troubled times' of 1857 that the British authorities became fully aware about the limits of the process of 'assimilation'. The far-sighted Macaulay, of course, had rightly grasped the key to the reciprocity between the two pillars of the mechanism of the nation – through the means of ideology and oppression. He had given suggestions about how to use one's abilities through both methods – perceptible and imperceptible.

The book titled *On the Education of the People of India* by Lord Macaulay's brother-in-law and associate, Trevelyan, was a supreme and famous example of liberal thought about 'assimilation'. Trevelyan's practical and worldly wisdom was sharp; he was not a person to be enchanted by or to indulge in the fantastic belief that India would eternally be ruled by England. Because he thought otherwise, he was able to write in the book, published in 1835, that the modern educational policy had been framed taking into account a prospective future when the bond of the current relationship between two distant countries that were situated at two extreme ends of the earth would snap. Two ways of gaining independence were open to India – either a bloody revolution or peaceful reforms. The upshot of revolution would be discord. At the cessation of all its ties with England, India would sink into the barbaric state of pre-British days. And if they proceeded slowly and gradually towards reform, the friendship between the two countries and their inner bonding would remain intact.[42] There would certainly be an unbreakable link between India's spiritual evolution and England's economic advancement.

In his book, *The Expansion of England* (1888) – which Queen Victoria's (1819–1901) daughter, the crown princess of Germany, had requested her mother to read; which the royal poet Lord Tennyson (1809–1892) had recommended to Prime Minister Gladstone (1809–1898); and which had impressed the supreme trader Cecil Rhodes (1853–1902) – the 'historian' J.R. Seeley (1834–1895), the chief founder of the Imperial Expansion League, and the author of *Ecce Homo* that had found an ardent admirer in Bankimchandra, had expressed his misgiving that if India sank into chaos again, if its government closed the ports there to English businessmen, England's annual loss would amount to 60 million pounds.[43] In order to ward off this alarming future, reform was as necessary as was the reconstitution of the Indian mind-set. In Macaulay's and Trevelyan's thinking, one can get an unexpressed suggestion of not just colonialism but the introduction of the rules and practices of neo-colonialism. The first step towards this agenda of restructuring would be to initiate people of upper-middle-class and middle-class communities to the ways of Europe through English education, and provide the key to a new perception of the world. In the words of Trevelyan: 'The natives will not rise against us because we shall stoop to raise them: there will be no reaction because there will be no pressure.'[44] Not only that, through the good offices of upper-class people, that wondrous education would gradually seep into and spread within all strata of society to reach its core. Trevelyan believed in his heart of hearts that although knowledge would advance, the insights of wisdom would not surface, because 'Those highly educated people would be their schoolteachers, translators, writers . . . those very people would be the leaders of the masses.'[45]

Did our native leaders shoulder that responsibility and proceed on the jagged path shown by Grant–Bentham–Mill–Macaulay–Trevelyan with an unshaken confidence?

II

The Native Leader Class and Determination Befitting Students

> Some Hindu young man belonging to a well-known family living in Paris who is devoted to scholarship and teaching has recently written a letter to the president of the Adi Brahmo Samaj and has dispatched an excellent, logically worked out essay connected with that letter about political independence and a special method to ensure immense success for Indians. We are making public the aforesaid letter and essay below with immense appreciation.

That 'excellent, logically worked out' and lengthy essay in English written in 1878 was 'made public' with 'immense appreciation' in the 421st issue of the *Tattwabodhini Patrika* in Bhadra 1800.[46] At the end of the essay, 'Young Hindu' was printed instead of the name of the writer.

The central argument of the writer was as follows. If Indians did not accept wholeheartedly the justified claim of England over India, a great split would appear in the communal life of the nation. If the verbose Bengali *babus* deluded their countrymen by raising the chant of freedom, it would not be possible to prevent the fissure. If they did not become cautious in time, the volubility and madness of these shortsighted *babus* would push India towards a colossal disaster because there was a limit even to the patience of merciful England. There are a lot of illustrations in history of how fatal it is for the weak to insult the powerful. In America, the 'Red Indian' natives and the ancient inhabitants of Peru and Mexico have had to pay the price of such arrogance. If Indians lose their sense of proportion, and a huge gap forms between their aspiration and achievement, it will not take them long to be slotted among the species of extinct beings such as the Dodo bird. To lament the lack of freedom without acquiring the ability to gain freedom is a kind of indulgence that the new *babus* give in to. Doing away with that stupidity and indolence, they should imbibe a lesson in modernity from liberal-minded England.

The author spelled out clearly that the independence that Indians had become so eager about was thanks to being under the spell of the Europeans, especially the Teutonic races. Citing the orientalist scholar Max Mueller, he said:

> Max Mueller himself has said that one does not get any sign or evidence of this mentality, even in the days of India's glorious past. Absorbed in thoughts of the other world, engrossed in the pursuit of abundance, the people of that era never bothered themselves with political questions or problems.[47]

In the opinion of the writer, Charles Darwin's theory of evolution has proved to the hilt that according to the law of nature, only the strong have the right to survive; brutal nature has no compassion for the weak. Those whose consciousness has got enmeshed in the fine web of metaphysical argument or spiritual theory should learn from nature. Nature is not at all gentle-natured and tender-hearted like affectionate Bengali mothers. She has a different sort of method for disciplining unruly children.

History evolves by being driven and persecuted by the impatience endemic to human nature. Pressing ahead through many uprisings and revolutions, brave men like Caesar, Cromwell, Napoleon and Bismarck emerged in Rome, England, France and Germany respectively. The rule of such extraordinary men is legitimized not through the strength of their policies but through the might of physical force. This theory of bodily strength is as applicable to races as human beings. Only powerful races can be leaders of the world. No matter how the feeble might resist them, no matter how much they might curse them like ignorant people, no change is possible in the rule. Instead, if the vanquished accept the victorious with their heart and soul, it ultimately stands to their gain. In fact, even if the victorious are inferior to the vanquished in the matter of civilization, it does not matter. Based on the opinions of thinkers like Maumsen, Carlyle, David Hume and others, the author has expressed his opinion that this is the all-pervasive theory of history, the sacrosanct law of nature. Subsequently, instead of resisting or wasting time on what is inevitable, the Hindus should become devotees of the mighty. They should acquire the outlook of 'wise teachableness'.

It is the unending good fortune of Hindus that the rule of no other country but England has been established in India. Having been able to come in contact with England, all four segments of India – art, trade, political consciousness and science – would benefit some day. It was the author's sincere conviction that through the enlightenment of western science, all superstitions would be eradicated. The Hindus, who did not have any knowledge of reality, would become aware of the material world, and India would gradually become a modern nation. If India wanted to be in the same league as Europe, it would first have to voluntarily accept the domination of the English. In the absence of self-knowledge, the Hindus think they have come of age and have mature minds, but they are actually 'rather childish'. Therefore, if they do not proceed cautiously but go overboard, they would themselves invite their own doom. On the one hand, they would be considered inferior to the whole world and victims of their own mockery. On the other, they would get whipped harshly. And that would be the appropriate punishment for their immaturity and political treason. Therefore, it is useless to blame those wise men who have reared and nurtured the Hindus with the intention of promoting their happiness.

In this essay, next to several orientalists like Darwin and Hume, the names of many other western thinkers have been mentioned: Socrates, Bacon, Newton, Sydney, Milton, Goethe, Schlegel, etc. Along with them were mentioned Ram, Vikramaditya, Chandragupta, Babur, Akbar, Shahjahan, Panini and the Hindi poet Chand. In the opinion of the 'Young Hindu', one can get an idea of India's ethical degradation by comparing its proud past with its ruined present. To get over this lamentably sorry state, in order to establish itself once again in the assembly of the world, one needs 'wise teachableness' – the subservience and determination befitting a student.

There is a small editorial note at the end of the essay:

> This proposal is excellent but we cannot agree with one of the positions taken – the one where the writer has supported Darwin Saheb's opinion. Compared to Darwin's decree, there is a stronger moral law, in support of which the Society for Preservation of the Native Inhabitants of England has been established.[48]

This anonymous letter by a 'Young Hindu' is an exemplar of the terrific speed with which English education was being disseminated. Whatever its organization of language, the letter had no suggestion of independent thought; there is only reiteration of the set jargon of English ruling men along with imperialist theorists. The Hindu youth was an immigrant not just in the literal sense, but in heart and soul. But does the immigrant not have to think of constructing his own habitation one day? Is it possible to eternally wander through sundry lands, carrying tents? And if one has to build one's own abode, is it possible to be in accord with the master at every step? If one were to view it from this perspective, is the history of upper-class Bengalis of the colonial era not a serialized history of agreement and breaking away?

Education and Student Discontent

Just eight years before the letter of this Hindu youth was published along with the editor's eulogy, an essay with an opposite point of view had been printed in the *Tattwabodhini Patrika* (issue no. 400, Shaka 1798). The essayist's query there was: 'Why does education in our country not reap results?' Like the question, the answer too was sharp: English education is entangled at every turn with the power of England; as a result, learning itself gets increasingly cancelled out. In incensed language, he wrote:

> You are thinking that your superstitions have been demolished, but no! When I see that the western power of subjugation has swallowed all your education and intelligence, how can I say that you do not currently worship power more than you did in the past? 'Hold an umbrella over wherever a group forms' – this is what is called a prayer to power.[49]

The result of the above-mentioned subordination has been deadly.

> Ask them to dance like dolls, dress as jesters, ask them to drift with the multitude, ask them to repeat rote words like a parrot, and I will give your words a place of reverence. But if you ask them to exercise their intelligence independently, if you ask them to go ahead by keeping a connection with the past and present of one's own country, if you ask them to put their education to practical use by considering person, place and time, if you ask them to be live people, it transpires in brief that it is disaster! Is this the result of education and learning?[50]

What, in fact, is the benefit of acquiring such learning?

> If an individual's process of education is completed in this instant, immediately he is attacked by the three professions of law from one side, medicine from another and engineering from a third.[51] Getting absorbed by the enchantment of western education produces a great disrespect to one's own country and its history. . . . Our perennial knowledge becomes that only England's history is a history and the history of all other races is worthless. It is a deed of terrible audacity to consecrate

> England's heritage instead of the legacy of the common human race. To ascribe the greatness of human nature as the attribute of England is the same as to take it as an attribute of the ruler of Delhi or of God.[52]

In the opinion of the author, we are so overwhelmed by foreigners that there is in us neither the determination nor the ability to invent or unravel any new thought. What remains to be done now is just 'to eulogize England, to proclaim its glory, and declare subservience to the mighty'. What else? Or is it oppression and domination of the weak and infirm, or denial of all their virtues! Is this what is called the pursuit of learning?[53]

An amazing introduction to the strange method of pursuing learning that was being followed in India at the time was published in the *Tattwabodhini Patrika* (no. 402, Magh 1798). In the essay 'The Current State of Education in Bengal', observing the excessive eagerness of a teacher of literature towards independent thought, the student community of the college feels oppressed and conveys their complaint to the principal. The displeased principal communicates clearly to the teacher: 'Our duty is to follow the method of teaching literature that is followed in other colleges. You are not a teacher, just an interpreter. The students are not students but only an audience.'[54]

These writings in the *Tattwabodhini Patrika* were published after the first struggle for independence, or the Sepoy Mutiny of 1857. After this national uprising, the image of British magnanimity underwent quite a change. One could spot the claws and the teeth of a lion-like Britain. The authorities themselves became sceptical about the feasibility of English education. Perhaps many people remembered the warning message of 1793, what a spokesperson of the Directors of the Company had said against the proposal of Wilberforce and Grant. In 1848, after becoming Governor-General, when Lord Dalhousie was thinking of establishing a university in India in the mould of British universities, the president of the Board of Control, Sir Charles Wood, had counselled that wherever else it might be, the university should not be established in Calcutta; it was not possible for the government to give jobs to all highly educated people – and if they did not get jobs, their sense of disquiet would rise, not decrease. It meant that one should become cautious before great trouble took place; there was no use providing fuel needlessly.[55] After the 1857 Mutiny, many among the bosses were in support of annulling the plan for the university. But eventually it was considered preferable to follow the path shown by Macaulay. It was decided again that English education was the great tonic for lack of peace.

On 6 March 1860, in his convocational address, the Pro Vice Chancellor of the university, Ritchie, said: 'Of the different working stratagems of self-defence of the nation, the most certain, vital and inexpensive is education. . . . Educate your people from Cape Comorin to the Himalayas, the 1857 mutiny will not be repeated a second time then.'[56] But in spite of creating such a no-holds-barred system of education, the dilemmas of the authorities regarding the intentions and movements of the natives were not removed. A news item published in the *Education Gazette* was a fall-out of this:

> In a well-known newspaper in English, it has been printed: 'The Indian government, in a move to oppose English education, has committed an act of indiscretion. No Indian person trained in the English language joined the Sepoy Mutiny. This itself is evidence that a strong devotion to the English Government is born out of learning English.'[57]

Or in *The Hindu Patriot* of 31 December 1857, where Harish Chand Mukherjee (1824–1861) wrote in a regretful tone: 'The educated will have to pay considerable damages without even being linked with this atrocious episode – the impression of the 'civilized world' regarding Indians would get overturned, and for the next many years, all paths leading to society's progress would get blocked.'[58]

On the one hand, there was no end of inertia and blind emulation; on the other, there was a desire to be proactive and an effort to exercise one's intelligence. The intelligentsia of those days was situated between these two poles. The distance between the two poles was also subject to expansion and erosion, growth and contraction; and it was possible to choose various kinds of views and paths even within that. But did we too not play an active role in the building of this inertia that was a result of this educational practice? If there has been a history of this sharing, haven't we turned our back to ourselves in the phase of that deconstruction? Or is it that construction and reconstruction went on, and has been going on, simultaneously – and that too partially?

The Lesson of Modernity: The Dilemma of Acceptance and Rejection

In order to demolish Macaulay's logic, H.T. Princep had written in a note dated 15 February 1835: 'Everybody does not have a clear idea about how profound the Hindus' reverence and love for Sanskrit is.' Macaulay wrote his reply on the margins of Princep's note: 'Just because people have a respect for and devotion towards one language does not mean that they would want to learn it.' In this context, he acknowledged the arbitration of a celebrated Bengali scholar: Rajabahadur Radhakanta Deb (1783–1867), a great scholar of Sanskrit and Persian, author of the immensely popular *Shabdakalpadrum*. Radhakanta had conveyed to Macaulay that there was no person in this country – not even in Benaras – who would study Sanskrit without any remuneration and just to satisfy one's thirst for knowledge.[59]

A few years before this dialogue between Macaulay and Radhakanta Deb on 20 February 1817, the Hindu College was established – primarily through the eagerness and enterprise of the natives. The name of Henry Vivian Derozio was linked organically to the initial chapter of Hindu College. A new group, Young Bengal, was formed through the influence of an encounter with this young professor. Derozio's students were irate and obstinate, sharp critics of the orthodoxy and irrationality of the bankrupt Hindu society. The unrest of Young Bengal, however, did not last for long. Many students of Derozio lost their lustre as they advanced in age. Suppressing the vibrancy and eternally restless nature befitting youth, they became servants of the conservative Hindu society. Among Derozio's followers, except for Dakshinaranjan Mukhopadhyay, none were scions of wealthy families. Moreover, before Macaulay's proposals got accepted, there were hardly any opportunities and facilities for earning money open to English-educated youth. From the end of the 1830s, there were premonitions of improvement of life of those who belonged to the third estate. According to many historians, there was a close link between the belligerent attitude of Young Bengal and the lack of economic independence of their early phase. The more unrestrained the doors of the third estate was for those who were English-educated, the more utterly the tone of many of them changed – and came down from the treble to the bass.[60]

In an essay titled 'On the Colonization of India by Europeans', published in the magazine *Kaleidoscope* (issue no. 2, September 1929) edited by Derozio, there is a desperate appeal to open this closed door. Where would the English-educated youth stand, how would their knowledge and sciences develop, and how could the mutinous steam that had grown within them be thwarted, if they did not get the enthusiastic patronage of the Europeans?[61] A long essay that had been sent from England was published in March 1830 in Derozio's magazine; the name of the essayist was cloaked within the letter 'F'. The sum and substance of the essay was that there could be no two opinions about the imitative propensities of the inhabitants of Calcutta. The inhabitants of the east are also human beings; therefore, the desire for worldly progress is also present in them. A government running on the principle of good sense should not let go this golden opportunity. If the imitative Bengalis were given opportunities and facilities, and if they were drawn closer, they would not become hostile to the whites like the African natives. And if one were to advance skilfully like this, one could reverse completely the thought–awareness–intuition–perception of the entire race.[62] Of course, a great enthusiasm for English education was awakened among a fraction of the natives long before the founding of the Hindu College.

Sibnath Sastri (1847–1919) wrote in his book, *Ramtanu Lahiri o Tatkalin Bangasamaj* (1904):

> The venerable David Hare had got vexed by the requests and recommendations of

> those who sought admission in his school. Such an anxiety was born among people to teach their respective sons English that it became difficult for Hare to step out of his house. If he stepped out, groups of boys would run after the palanquin, saying 'me poor boy, have pity on me, me take in your school'.[63]

In sacred remembrance of David Hare, the foremost hero of education and unparalleled pioneer of modernity, grateful Bengalis had been offering their homage on his death anniversary. Sibnath Sastri said in the context of 'Young Bengal':

> the student community newly graduated from Hindu College like Krishnamohan Bandyopadhyay, Rasik Krishna Mallick, Ramgopal Ghosh, Tarachand Chakrabarti, Shibchandra Deb, Pyarichand Mitra and Ramtanu Lahiri have accepted the discipleship of Macaulay with all their heart. . . . Their training has been in the hands of the three chief mentors of modern Bengal – the first is David Hare, the second Derozio, the third Macaulay.[64]

This opinion is equally applicable to many who were not as directly linked with the Young Bengal movement. On 2 June 1861, Kishorichand Mitra (1822–1873), a student of Hindu College and author of Dwarakanath Tagore's biography, *Memoir of Dwarakanath Tagore* (1870), delivered the 19th David Hare Memorial Lecture. The lecture had extensive evidence that Macaulay's dreams had been fulfilled to a great extent. Like Macaulay, Kishorichand Mitra also believed that those who had been considerably influenced by the thought and ideas of Shakespeare–Milton–Bacon–Newton–Johnson or Edison were bound to undergo moral improvement. There was therefore no reason for the nation to unnecessarily waste time over the ethical beliefs of the natives, which could, on the other hand, be counterproductive. The authorities should take a lesson from how the ethical sense of the working class of England was being shaken due to this shortsightedness.[65] It is noticeable that right from the start, the Bengali *bhadralok* as a subject was getting intertwined with the subject of the inhabitants of other colonies and the working class of England. The *bhadralok* were excessively conscious of the knowledge and respect they received by virtue of English education. In no way would they consent to identifying themselves with barbaric Africans, or workers without any ethical sense or conscience.

In 1878, Sir Surendranath Bandyopadhyay (1848–1925) delivered the Hare Memorial Lecture. The title of the lecture was 'Lord Macaulay and Higher Education in India'. Macaulay and Trevelyan would not have had any reservation about the subject or what it had to say, whoever else might. In the opinion of Surendranath, the close relationship that had grown between England and India had higher education at its root. Even if the political links between the two countries were severed one day – ('God forbid such a disastrous occurrence to ever happen') – England would forever be obliged and grateful to the Indians.[66] He believed that as a result of this interaction, western masculinity would blend with eastern femininity and a new kind of civilization would be constructed. It is noticeable that the inhabitants of the colony and the colonial power were linked apropos traditional, male-centred notions of the 'temperament' and 'nature' of men and women – as if England were the 'natural' protector of India like men are of women. The metaphor seemed to indicate that the eulogy of England by Indians should be compared to the wifely service of devoted young women to their husbands.

But was not the appeal for identification between the English and Bengali *bhadralok* hindered right from the start? On 11 December 1823, the pioneer of Bengali ritual reforms and initiator of the new dispensation, Rammohun Roy (1774–1833), wrote that 'famous' letter to Lord Amherst. He had sent the letter to Bishop Heber and wanted him to forward it to Lord Amherst. One can gauge from Heber's daily jottings that he was simultaneously delighted and amazed to read what Rammohun had written. He could not believe that an illustration of such wonderful English, such a sense of discernment and such forceful utterances could come from an Asian.[67] One knows from Trevelyan's statements that Lord Amherst sent that letter to the Education Committee. Perhaps the members of the Committee had praised Rammohun's draft and been overwhelmed by his expressive skill. Rammohun had not received a reply to his letter – nevertheless there is no doubt that it had been carefully preserved in the files of the Education Committee. In fact the entire letter was published in 1838 in Charles Trevelyan's book, *On the Education of the People of India*. In it Rammohun had appealed to Lord Amherst that the Rs 1 one lakh allotted on account of the education of Indians should not be spent in the sphere of oriental education. Indians would not benefit one bit by reading the Vedanta: they would only learn about the absolute truth, the illusory nature of the world, impossible strategies of achieving complete immersion in God – all worthless things, like the *mantra*s one has to recite to get deliverance from deplorably sinful deeds such as the killing of goats. Instead mathematics, natural science, chemistry, physiology and other beneficial subjects should be arranged to be taught.[68] It is rather difficult to reconcile with the fact that this letter of 1823, in which Rammohun Roy was so utterly dismissive of the Vedanta, was written by the same man who was a follower of the thought of Acharya Sankara (780–812) – the ideologue of Advaita Vedanta who himself had translated five Upanishads into Bengali (1816, 1817, 1819) and four into English (1816, 1819); and who wrote a new commentary titled 'The Most Celebrated and Revered Work of Brahmanical Theology establishing the Unity of The Supreme Being' (1815) on the *Brahma Sutra*, the pendant text for all streams of the Vedanta – Advaita, Vishishtadvaita, Dvaitadvaita and Dvaita. However, whatever be the complex psychology behind his disavowal of the

Vedanta in front of the sahibs, there is one common powerful word that is common to both Macaulay's proposal and Rammohun's letter: 'utility'. And, even more surprisingly, Macaulay's minutes also contain flippant jokes about losing oneself in the formless, shapeless *Brahma*![69]

Despite this, there is still a wide gap between Macaulay's precepts and Rammohun's hopes. Macaulay would give to that very literature the honour due to the chief subject, of which there is no reference in Rammohun's letter. There would always remain a gap between the Indian's prayer for blessing and the granting of the boon by the English. Subsequently, even the Rammohun who was so devoted to European science had to say that he did not admit being obliged to England in any sphere except technology; the life-giver of science, literature and religion was the oriental soil.[70]

Ishwarchandra Vidyasagar (1820–1891) had opposed J.R. Ballantyne's textbook-related proposals by using the very logic of Rammohun. Ballantyne had wanted that the students of Sanskrit College be taught Bishop Barclay's *Inquiry*. In protest, Vidyasagar wrote to the secretary of the Education Committee, F.J. Mowatt, on 7 September 1853, that if Barclay's *Inquiry* was included as a textbook, it would cause harm rather than any benefit. He wrote: Because of some special reasons, mentioning which is unnecessary here, we have had to continue the imparting of education of the Vedanta and Samkhya in our Sanskrit College. There are no two views any more about the erroneous ideas on which the Vedanta and Samkhya are based. Although erroneous, this philosophy has been occupying a seat of boundless reverence in the minds of the Hindus. Aiming to lessen the influence of teaching these in the Sanskrit curriculum, one would have to introduce thoughts countering such ideology with the help of some strong philosophy in the English curriculum. Bishop Barclay's book, *Inquiry*, has been presented almost along identical principles as those of Vedanta and Samkhya philosophy, and is not currently considered as powerful philosophy even in Europe. The object, therefore, will not be realized with its help. On the other hand, by reflecting on this text with concentration, when Hindu students studying Sanskrit will know that the cluster of theories in Samkhya and Vedanta philosophy are being supported by the theories of European philosophers, their respect for these two branches would increase instead of waning.[71]

Clearly, Vidyasagar had a profound distrust of the merging of eastern and western learning. He was at least not a candidate for lending his ear to the incantation of '*melaben Tini melaben*' ('blend us He will'). But did he or anybody like him say anything regarding the subject of imperialism being at the root of all bonding and merging? In this country, the logic of liberal trade was first attacked by Michael Madhusudan Dutt's (1824–1873) classmate, Bholanath Chandra (1822–1910). In an essay published in *Mukherjee's Magazine* from 1873 to 1875, Bholanath said clearly: 'The English actually want Indians to continue to live by farming. By holding aloft the flag of liberal trade, they want to camouflage that simple truth. If India becomes self-sufficient in the sphere of industry, then England's path to industry is bound to suffer an impediment.'[72] From his incisive deliberations, it is at least clear that foreign education could not fully overpower the natives' awareness of reality.

Rabindranath Tagore's book of essays on education is proof of that consciousness of reality. In 1299 (Bengali calendar), 'Shikshar Herpher' was read in the Rajshahi Association. There was quite a similarity between Rabindranath's point of view and that of the proposal of the second essay in the aforementioned *Tattwabodhini Patrika*. In Rabindranath's opinion too, as a result of English education, boys did not gain any 'nourishment of the mind, expansion of heart and strength of character', but merely learnt imitation by rote and servility.[73] We 'only act as labourers in the province of Saraswati. Our backbones become crooked with labour but our human qualities do not develop in a comprehensive manner'.[74] The use of the words 'province' and 'labour' in the context of education is notable.

In his desire to attain self-reliance and effort to awaken inner strength, on 12 December 1901, Rabindranath established the Brahmacharya Vidyalaya in Santiniketan. But centering on which ideal did he desire to attain self-reliance? In the essay 'Tapoban' (1909), written during the era of the Swadeshi movement in Bengal, his opinion on the subject of the 'main source' of the 'Indian civilization' was: 'The energy that civilization attained by the constant endeavour of forest dwellers did not awaken due to the competition of different kinds, that is why that "power" was not chiefly outward-looking.'[75] Can one claim, following this line of argument, that the competitive spirit had been recently exported from Europe to not just India but to *all* colonized countries? But no; at least at that time, Rabindranath firmly clung to the view that the Indian civilization was unique as far as transcending antagonisms born of competition is concerned. As a result, the preacher–principal of the newly established Brahmacharya Vidyalaya had no hesitation in writing: 'If the jungles of Africa were India's hermitage, I could say that to live in conjunction with nature was just imaginary.'[76]

In his effort towards self-sufficiency, therefore, did Rabindranath become hostile to the occident and take an extreme fanatical pride in his own race, wanting to erase the history in between? In 1902, he wrote in a letter to Professor Manoranjan Bandyopadhay:

> It will not do to give place to anything that is opposed to Hindu society: according to the advice in the *Samhita*, students would touch the feet of their Brahman masters as a mark of respect and fold their hands in a *namaskar* to other teachers – practising such customs is in keeping with the rules.[77]

Was it Rabindranath's desire to compose another edition of the rule-book of

Benaras Sanskrit College? If one turns from education to orientalist education, is it not like evading the fundamental question? After going round in circles, is there no way but to come back to square one? Rabindranath's thought, however, did not remain static at one place forever; his opinions changed considerably with time. During the national movement phase of 1905, many enterprises for constructing an alternate education system were initiated. But the plan of 'eastern and/or western education' worked in most of these efforts. Its signature has remained in children's literature and in textbooks written for children. It was indeed difficult to be free of a plan that materialized out of the efforts of many days and the contribution of many people. What, therefore, was to be the fate of innocent children?

In the mind's eye of the opium addict Kamalakanta, a character created by Bankimchandra, the scene of a shop comes alive.

> Written over the room in big, brass letters was: MESSERS BROWN JONES AND ROBINSON – Nut suppliers – established 1757 – ON THE FIELD OF PLASSEY. Messers Brown Jones and Robinson, offer to the Indian public a large assortment of NUTS – Physical, metaphysical, logical, illogical, and sufficient to break the jaw and dislocate the teeth of ALL INDIAN YOUTHS who stand in need of having their dental superfluities curtailed. The shopkeepers called: 'Come, black boy, come and consume experimental science.'[78]

Did not at least one per cent of the white boys of England also get a taste of this shopkeeping along with the black boys?

III

Education and the White Boy

It cannot be fortuitous that during a phase of discontent, at the end of the eighteenth century, religious societies were born one after another in England: the London Missionary Society, the Church Missionary Society, the Religious Tract Society and the British and Foreign Bible Society. The Society for Promoting Christian Knowledge had been established a hundred years earlier. Within a few years of these religious societies, two education societies were established: the National Society for Promoting the Education of the Poor on the Principles of the Established Church throughout England and Wales, and the Nonconformist British and Foreign School Society. The objectives of the different societies were very clear. Even if they were undeterred in their original target, as and when new situations arose, their working strategy altered accordingly.

In 1819, the Anti-Infidel Committee was established with the support of the Society for Promoting Christian Knowledge. According to the Committee's own advertisement, its main objective was 'to thwart the dangerous workers' movement that had surfaced in London and various industrial towns of North England'. In 1823, the Committee announced that in the meanwhile six lakh, seventy-seven thousand, four hundred and ninety-one books had been sold, and the problem was not as grave. But after the people's agitation of 1832, they had to think anew. The General Literature Committee was established as a new step. Next to the titles of the many stories published by the efforts of the General Literature Committee would be printed the words: 'For Servants'. The same arrangement was apportioned both for controlling religious opposition at home and infidels abroad.

On 29 September 1857, a great debate took place regarding a serious subject during a session of the Church Missionary Society. An example of how the first independence struggle, which was purely a sepoys' mutiny according to the sahibs, had shaken the ruling community is available from the Society's work report. The topic of discussion that day was whether the common people of India would get infuriated and join the sepoys, or would they remain trustworthy or at least passive. From the records and papers of the Society, one can know the results of that discussion and the decision the members reached. They arrived at the judgment that if the various Protestant missionary committees and their supporters did not join hands, if they did not take the plunge as a group with the pledge to eradicate the widespread lack of education among the natives of the colony, the efforts and labour of so many days would get wasted, and their favourite *Bharatvarsha* would slip through their fingers. From this was born the Christian Vernacular Education Society. Other committees and societies also did not lag behind in the sacred mission of carving the lower classes of their own nation and of the colonies in moulds after their own taste.

Within seven years of being established, the Religious Tract Society printed thirty-five lakh booklets. By 1815, it had 124 branches spread all over England. In a list of books published for the young printed by the Society in 1820, one can find John Bunyan's (1628–1688) *The Pilgrim's Progress* (Part 1, 1678; Part 2, 1684). There is no doubt that the officials of the Society accorded a special importance to *The Pilgrim's Progress*, because the book was eventually translated into not one or two but a total of 147 languages. In the hand-outs of various religious societies, there would be tales of sacrifice and endurance, alongside counsels on respecting God and Caesar, and on repaying all debts up to the last penny. The Religious Tract Society took the holy pledge of spreading Christianity not only within its own country, but also in the colonies. In 1878, it proudly announced that its 'emissaries of truth had spread to all regions of the world'. Although this mission of proselytization did well for a long time, it became quite evident towards the end of the nineteenth century that the old presumptive truths would not work as well as before; the need was for other kinds of 'emissaries of truth'. Dangers at home and abroad, and falling prey to an all-pervasive anarchy might devastate everything.

In order to control the new situation, the imperialist policies were changed in the seventh decade of the nineteenth century. Commensurately, it was as if there was a makeover in England's educational policy and the literature composed for children. The new Education Act came into force in 1870; there was a craze about publishing books and magazines for children. The Religious Tract Committee started publishing the *Boys' Own Paper* (1879–1967) in 1879. By the middle of 1880, the sale of the paper exceeded ten lakh copies.[79] For a hundred years, the *Boys' Own Paper* eulogized British imperialism in various ways. It handed to children, in different packages, a potent concoction of imperialism and nationalism. A few years after its inception it organized a seminar on 'What is real imperialism?', at which a manager of the Religious Tract Committee delivered the plenary address. He said that it was the chief objective of imperialism to arrange for the 'deliverance of the souls of non-Christians'; the British empire was a successor of the ancient kingdom of Israel. The speaker appealed to the British government to spread 'the voice of freedom to all corners of the world'.

Under the pressure of the new requirements, a cosmetic change showed up in a large proportion of the English juvenile literature of that period. Although the sum and substance of what was said remained more or less the same, the bearers of the new message took the robes off the missionaries and changed their garb – as can be seen in the gradual evolution of the *Boys' Own Paper*. This does not mean that religious proselytization through the agency of literature ceased entirely. Even up to the fourth decade of the twentieth century, stories of the 'Jungle Doctor' series were being published. Their locale was Africa; their message was that without the limitless mercy of Christ, there was no hope of liberation for the degraded blacks. Not only the stories but also the author's name, Paul White, proclaimed the same 'noble' agenda.

Wise Teachableness and Children's Literature in Bengali

At least the missionary sahibs did not find it difficult to understand that children's literature had a special role in spreading the virtue of 'wise teachableness' in the childlike minds of the inhabitants of the colonies. At the beginning of the nineteenth century, in 1818, with the support of the Serampore Baptist Mission, the first paper for young adults in Bengali was published: *Digdarshan*. The editor of the paper was John Clark Marshman (1794–1877). Involved with the Serampore Mission was William Carey (1761–1834). Some idea of what Carey's moral instruction was can be located in the cautious utterance of his *Itihasamala*: 'Therefore, I say, pay heed, everybody! Even if some person born into an inferior caste becomes educated through the company of the best and the most erudite, his ability and excellence going beyond his lineage does not find expression.' On the title page of *Digdarshan* were written: 'Several lessons compiled for the youth'. Raja Rammohun Roy was also involved with this magazine – in an indirect if not direct manner.

The School Book Society was founded one year before the publication of *Digdarshan*, in the year of establishment of Hindu College. The resolve to form this Society was taken in a session at Fort William College, on 6 May 1817. Among its members were Ramkamal Sen (1783–1844) and Radhakanta Deb; Tarinicharan Mitra (1772[?]–1837) and Maulavi Karam Hussain were the 'native secretaries'. The work of the Society was the 'Preparation, publication and cheap or gratuitous supply of works useful in schools and seminaries of learning in English and Oriental languages, but not the furnishing of religious books'. A few months after the Calcutta School Book Society was established on 1 September 1818, the plan of its establishment was announced ceremoniously in an assembly organized in the Town Hall. David Hare (1775–1842) was directly involved with this Society. From 1 January 1823 to the last day of its functioning in 1835, he was the School Book Society's European secretary. In the language of the leader of the first ranks of the Young Bengal movement, Pyarichand Mitra (1814–1883) of *Alaler Ghare Dulal* fame, 'the School Book Society and the School Society were like twins'.[80] In 1822, through the efforts of the School Book Society, *Pashwabali*, a second periodical for adolescents in the Bengali language, was published.

According to government accounts, between 1813 and 1830, a total of Rs 2,65,847, Rs 18,400 and Rs 69,433 were spent in the Bengal, Madras and Bombay Presidencies respectively, on education.[81] In 1825, the sum of money increased abnormally in the case of Bengal Presidency, taking a huge leap to reach Rs 57,122. In the same year, Bombay Presidency got Rs 8,961 and Madras Presidency Rs 480 *in toto*. A reason for this unnatural increase in Bengal was that the appeal the School Book Society had made to the government for financial aid was granted on 9 March 1825, with the Company's Directors' Committee sanctioning Rs 6,000 annually.[82] It was therefore not surprising that the School Book Society announced in its seventh report, within a very few days: 'In this language [Bengali] the Society's labours have been most productive and it now possesses publications on almost every subject of elementary instruction.'[83] In 1830, Dwarakanath Tagore was appointed as a member of the Society. In that year's report, which was the eighth report, it was said about the Society's agenda: '[We] desire to afford books, the perusal of which may be the means of advance in the scale of civilization of all the inhabitants of the British territories in India.'[84] But through what method could they proceed in order to accomplish their mission? In reply to this grave question, it was declared 'that while the Society pursues a noble object, it pursues it by a method which is possible to all, whether English, Mussalmans, or Hindus. It insults no opinions, it attacks no religious prejudices, but seeks only to impart general knowledge leaving that to work its own way.'[85] Holt Mckenzie, who prepared the seventh resolution of the Permanent Settlement, the method of *haptam*, and left an immortal example of administrative skill,[86] stated in an annual convention of the School Book Society: 'The more people get familiar with European knowledge through the medium of Bengali, the more their curiosity will increase about the original language, English. The main aim of the committee is to use the regional language as an occasion to reach Indians to the brink of English.'[87]

In 1820, the School Book Society published the *Hitopadesha* for 'the Welfare and Solace of the people'. The book, compiled by Srijukta Babu Ramkamal Sen and the perseverance of the managers of the *pathshala* under the Serampore Mission, came out of the Serampore Press. In the introduction to the compilation, it was announced that the School Book Society had been appointed, and:

> The Head Officer and his wife and many fortunate English people of Calcutta and fortunate Bengali people have assisted this society. This community is patronizing the education of the Bengali people a great deal. When one thinks of the arrangements that the English and Bengalis have put together for assisting the cause of education in this country, it at least gives rise to amusement. The knowledge, counsel and enthusiasm of English and Bengali people have come together for this cause. One can sense what good fortune prevails in this country.[88]

Ramkamal Sen was the member of a government committee formed to assess the state of the country's medical system. Mentionable among other members were Trevelyan and Sutherland. The report signed by Ramkamal Sen ended with a fervent question: 'Is there any biological or ethical incompatibility in the inhabitants of this country because of which they would not be able to become proficient and fluent in English like the natives of Ireland, Scotland or Wales?'[89] But it was not enough to have the ability; one had to know how to use the ability well. One's brain would flourish and one's heart's desire would be fulfilled only if one paid heed to wise people's well-meaning words. For arousing the people about their welfare, here are some examples of good counselling compiled by Ramkamal Sen and the Serampore religious missionaries: 'It is man's duty not to exceed one's capability in performing a task'; 'If the king, in his own state, does not make his subjects obey him by his civil behaviour and love, and does not express philanthropy and mercy to them while he still has the ability to work for their welfare, then he loses that ability'; 'Let everybody remain as God made them'.[90] The manner and skill by which simple-minded boys could climb the ladder 'that would enable them to reach the peak of civilization' had been spelt out in *Nitikatha* (*Part 1*, 1818), published by the School Book Society. The book had been written by three people: Radhakanta Deb, Tarinicharan Mitra and Ramkamal Sen. One of the stories in *Part 3* of *Nitikatha* went:

> Education can be acquired with care and achieved with practice. A boy used to not take care over the practice of learning and waste his time whimsically; neglecting good teachings and good counselling, he would wander along bad ways. Later, in his youth, when he suffered from the lack of food and clothing, he started working for two rupees a month; but that led to a lot of unhappiness. Due to this, he asked one of his friends plaintively, 'Hey brother, how do you get more money than anybody gets in the country by working for the sahibs, while I who am immersed in work all day . . .'[91]

The name of the story is 'The Subject of the Learned and the Stupid'. The summary of the good counsel was: 'There is a mutual relation between being "well-educated" and getting jobs in the offices of the sahibs; the Bengalis achieve their highest object when they get this job; if they aspire for something more, if they have the desire to rise higher, their fall is inevitable.'

A fusion of English education and Christian good breeding left nothing else to attain. To express that ideal of good breeding, a Bengali translation of John Bunyan's *The Pilgrim's Progress*, *Jatrirader Agrasarena Bibaran*, came out in 1821; it was translated by Felix Carey (1786–1822). In 1836, the Christian Tract and Book Society published a book of ethics by the name of *Sadacharadipak* in order to spread the greatness of Christianity; the book became excessively popular. But the most important role in the gradual progress of English education and the spread of civilization was that of the School Book Society. If the first age of Bengali children's literature was to be entitled the 'School Book Society Age', it would not be too much of a misnomer.

Six years after the establishment of the School Book Society, in 1823, a society on a different model was founded in Calcutta: the Gaudiya Samaj. This establishment aimed to follow native culture, and the Sanskrit and Bengali languages. The synthesis that had developed between oriental and occidental knowledge right from the beginning is worth remembering. In the zealous endeavour to integrate the two, many bizarre situations had been created. One example was in the *Calcutta Gazette* of 13 June 1831: it was announced through a government advertisement that the recently deceased Colonel Joseph Boden of the East India Company had donated all his moveable and immoveable property to Oxford University towards the cause of cultivating Sanskrit literature; his aim was the refutation of Hindu philosophy and, connected to it, the spread of Christianity.[92] Alongside the establishment of the Gaudiya Samaj, the Tract Society, Christian Knowledge Society and Asiatic Society were founded. A few years after this was established the Society for Bangla Bhasha Translations, or the Vernacular Literature Committee. There were just three Bengali members in this Committee: Jaykrishna Mukhopadhyay (1808–1888), Rasamay Dutta (1779–1854) and Debendranath Thakur (1817–1905). The objectives of the Committee spelled out that it would produce high-quality books for the perusal of common people that the four committees – namely, the Tract Society, Christian Knowledge Society, School Book Society and Asiatic Society – would not be able to produce.[93] The Grahastya Bangla Pustak Sangraha (Bengali Family Library) was associated with the institution. The first published book of the Vernacular Literature Committee (*c.* 1852–53) was *The Adventures of Robinson Crusoe* (1719) – a definitive work of the multitalented and multifaceted Daniel Defoe (1660–1731) who was at once a trader, a journalist, a pamphleteer, a spy and a novelist.

One of the foundational texts of English literature, *Robinson Crusoe* posits a completely self-sufficient hero. In fact the novel is a successful embodiment of the ideal of self-sufficiency without which it is impossible to conceive of *homo economicus*, and the notion of self-development without which bourgeois hegemony is not valid. It is not surprising that Thomas Babington Macaulay had posited both the self-made man and the famous British Governor-General Warren Hastings on the lines of Defoe's hero. Macaulay's glorious account of Hastings' achievements, titled 'Warren Hastings – An Essay', was published in October 1841. In it Macaulay sought to prove why Warren Hastings was far more talented than some of the greatest minds of Europe in spite of being at the centre of myriad scandals; that any comparison of Hastings with any other officer of the Company would be akin to comparing the greatest baker in London with Robinson Crusoe, because the latter had had to first construct the yoke, the fence, the scarecrow, the tools, the machinery and the furnace before he could bake a loaf of bread.[94]

On the other hand, Karl Marx (1818–1883) has a series of jokes on Macaulay's proto-Hastings Crusoe. In fact Marx's *Grundrisse: Introduction to A Critique of Political Economy*, a collection of seven notebooks written in 1857–58, begins with a stringent critique of 'Robinsonade', the theoretical unit gleaned from Defoe's novel. According to Marx, 'Robinsonade' is a perfect example of the distinctive eighteenth-century imagination of self-conceit and vanity – it is the perfect myth propagated to obfuscate the notion of social duty that the achievement of a productive individual in society is in practice the socially dependent production of individuals.[95] The novel itself carries the suggestion that even Defoe could not avoid the topicality of this notion of social duty in the bourgeois eulogy of *Robinson Crusoe*. That is because the novel is not complete in just the narrative of the unique master who is segregated from everything and everyone immersed in his own grandeur; a second person enters its frame. No matter how much Crusoe, the stranded castaway in his will to survive, tries to create his own independent, solitary island, Man Friday inevitably finds his way to the waterlocked space. In the novel, Man Friday is the indelible trace of the so-called social duty. Of course, this signature is cleansed and made tolerable by Man Friday's unwavering devotion to Crusoe. Through the dyad of the independent Crusoe and the devoted Man Friday who is astonished by Crusoe's inventive powers, *Robinson Crusoe* becomes, perhaps even without Defoe's knowledge, a narrative of bourgeois assignation and the overwhelmed colonial servant, and, in turn, an indirect proof of the complex linkages between capitalism and colonial expansion.

Another Robinson, Reverend John Robinson, had translated the book – probably with Indian Man Fridays in mind. The first translated edition of *Robinson Crusoe*, of course, was not a pure translation. Lest the readers were unable to catch the connotations and tone of the original text due to the cultural distance, the period, setting and characters were changed and integrated within a familiar atmosphere; they were reconfigured under a native cover. Robinson Crusoe was transformed to an Armenian merchant living in Calcutta. After the shipwreck, he finds refuge in one of the islands of the eastern archipelago. Although this Robinson created by John Robinson was adequately popular, in the fourth edition, the translator retrieved his name and identity and reinstituted him in his own greatness.[96] Perhaps the directors of the Vernacular Literature Committee thought that by then the cultural distance between the British and the Bengalis had been reduced considerably through their active efforts, and a capacity to appreciate the original taste had been born in the Bengali reader.

Apart from books of translation, treatises meant for the use of domesticated Bengali girls, like Madhusudan Mukhopadhyay's *Sushilar Upakhyan*, were published. In 1858, the Calcutta Christian Book Society published *Bangiya Pathabali*. At the beginning of this book, readers were advised:

> Oh reader, you are sinful, and it is essential for you to be freed of whatever faults you might have by violating God's injunctions and all the mischief of the mind. In this book, much has been written about sin and liberation, especially that of the mercy of Jesus Christ, the redeemer of mankind.[97]

Shishushiksha and *Barna Parichay*

A new class of primers was published in 1849: *Shishushiksha* (*Part 1*) by Madanmohan Tarkalankar (1817–1858); the next year, in 1850, the next two parts of the primer were published. There can be no possible comparison between the lucid and accessible prose of *Shishushiksha* and the austere, uninteresting language of the books published by the missionaries or by the School Book Society. Madanmohan was a proponent of women's education; he was the patron of the girls' school conceived of by Drinkwater Bethune in 1849. Thus, at least officially, *Shishushiksha* was produced in the interest of providing education to women. In his dedication to Bethune on the title page of the primer, Madanmohan had written:

> A lot of people would be aware that the education of children in the native languages remains incomplete because of the absence of books that one can read at the

> primary level. I have set out to produce a set of books in the hopes of remedying this absence and *especially to aid the education of girls* and in these few words I introduce them.[98] (Emphasis added)

Madanmohan was not just a collaborator of Bethune, but a colleague and classmate of Ishwarchandra Vidyasagar (1820–1891). For more than four years they taught at the Sanskrit College together. The influential work *Sanskrit-Yantra* was published in 1847 due to their joint efforts. Their amity was however shortlived. From differences in opinion to changes in ideals and finally complete separation – eventually their relationship broke irrevocably. After Madanmohan's death, his son-in-law Jogendranath Bidyabhushan (1845–1904) brought allegations of plagiarism against Vidyasagar in the context of *Shishushiksha*. In retaliation, seventeen long years after the allegations were levied, Vidyasagar wrote the small but angry *Nishkritilabh Prayas* (1888). It is difficult to say how successful he was in his efforts at deliverance and countering the claims of the complainant. However, Madanmohan's *Shishushiksha* and Vidyasagar's *Barna Parichay* are too intricately connected for any critic or historian to extricate them from the nexus.[99] This much can be said without hesitation, that *Shishushiksha* made a huge contribution towards the unprecedented success of *Barna Parichay*.

For long afterwards, some sections of *Shishushiksha* (*Part 2*) found a place in *Barna Parichay* (*Part 2*). Vidyasagar announced in the advertisement to the 52nd edition of *Barna Parichay* (*Part 2*): 'In the last part of the book, the part that had been cited as belonging to *Shishushiksha* has been omitted.'[100] On the other hand, Vidyasagar constantly kept revising and streamlining *Shishushiksha*. In the advertisement to the 91st edition of *Shishushiksha* (*Part 3*), published quite some time after Madanmohan's death, he wrote:

> *Shishushiksha* (*Part 3*) has been amended from beginning to end with special care and effort. Editing with a view towards facilitating the understanding of young boys and girls, some parts of it have been expanded, some altered and some deleted. There is no doubt that in matters like interpreting meanings, it will now be far more convenient for boys and girls than earlier.[101]

Part 1 of *Barna Parichay* was published in April 1855, and *Part 2* in June the same year; 60 editions of *Part 1* were published in twenty years, and 62 editions of *Part 2* in eight years. *Shishushiksha*, especially *Part 1*, remained popular for many years, but in competition with *Barna Parichay* it lagged behind and ultimately got erased from memory. Accounts of the sales of *Barna Parichay* demonstrate that over long years, it enjoyed sole supremacy in the domain of children's minds. In Vidyasagar's lifetime itself, more than 35 lakh copies were printed in 152 editions. But that famous poem of *Shishushiksha* is still inscribed in people's memories: '*Pakhi shob kare rob raati pohailo*' ('The chirruping of birds signals the end of the night'). Many lines of this twelve-line poem in *Payar* metre have internal rhymes: *shob rob, koli shakoli, gan man, nishir shishir*, etc. Quite a few lines bear witness to the fact that Madanmohan had no mean talent for poetry: for example, '*Shital batash boy jurae shorir*' ('The body is refreshed as the cool breeze blows'). This is followed by the stanza that has '*Patae patae por-e nishir shishir*' ('The nocturnal dew falls on each leaf'). Two things – a plain thought and a line full of wonder – are intertwined with each other. Despite Vidyasagar's revision from beginning to end, signs of Madanmohan's poetic prowess were not expunged fully from the cleansed *Shishushiksha*. Moreover, there is no doubt that although the two friends shared many views, their aesthetic sensibilities were disparate. A major evidence of this is that whereas descriptions of nature were given adequate importance in *Shishushiksha*, there was no mention of scenes from nature in *Barna Parichay*. Perhaps many people will agree with this lament of Krishnakamal Bhattacharya: 'The distinctiveness that Madanmohan's unique talent bestowed on him was an invaluable asset of Bangla literature. That very uniqueness could have endowed Bangla literature with variety; Vidyasagar's language would not then have remained the inalienable feature of Bangla.'[102]

The style of Madanmohan's moral education can be estimated somewhat from a few sentences of *Shishushiksha, Part 2*: 'Dismiss inertia'; 'Let the affluent stay happy'; 'One should always speak the truth'; 'Do not be disobedient to your parents'; 'What is there to fear in speaking what is right?'; 'Childhood is the time for education'; 'It is extremely essential to be well-behaved'; 'Laziness is the source of endless faults'; 'It is essential to pay the royal revenue'; 'It is wrong to violate the guru's instructions'; 'Do not talk while the lesson is in progress'.[103] Vidyasagar also could write sentences like this. But it was not possible for him to write, 'Supernatural subjects are marvellous' or 'Everybody should meditate on God'. In both parts of *Barna Parichay*, there is no mention of God or religion. (However, in Vidyasagar's *Bodhodoy* [1851], there are the words 'God is formless, much like the consciousness'; the same Vidyasagar who had resigned from the Tattwabodhini Sabha in 1859 had himself chosen this sentence from a lecture delivered by Debendranath Thakur, the progenitor of Tattwabodhini, in 1841.[104])

The 91st edition of *Shishushiksha, Part 3*, which was modified from beginning to end by Vidyasagar, seems more or less like another version of *Barna Parichay*.

> It is as though the Gopals and Rakhals have returned here under other names. The heading of the first chapter of the book is, 'Everyone loves a well-behaved child'; it hardly needs to be told that the title of the second chapter is 'Nobody can stand an unruly boy'. The chief qualities of a 'well-behaved child' are: 'S/he does whatever the elders tell him to do, s/he is never disobedient to them. Whatever s/he is told once not to do, s/he never does.'[105]

On the other hand, unruly boys never heed anybody's prohibition or control. There is no way they can be tempered. A wonderful precept is elucidated in the chapter, 'Do not be greedy about other people's belongings'. Gopal, the boy with good sense, picks up a gold necklace he finds on the staircase and thinks: 'If I keep it with the gate-keeper – who knows, he is not a respectable fellow – he might steal it in his covetousness for gold.'[106] This means that it is not prudent for respectable *bhadralok* to trust lowly people. Who will be answerable if they acquire bad habits due to scarcity of resources? Whatever be the name of the boy – Beni–Madhab / Gopal–Rakhal / Ram–Shyam – there is no doubt that they are all children of respectable households. As examples in describing the good qualities of Ram–Shyams, it has been said that they are so good that 'they never say a bitter word, *even* to their servants and their maids';[107] the use of '*o*' (*even*) after 'servants and maids' is particularly noticeable.

In this edition of *Shishushiksha*, a novel method has been used with the aim of spreading the virtue of obedience in the mind of the child. An individual child is directly addressed, and described as possessing the virtues of the docile child or the vices of the wayward child. For instance: 'See Madhab! Beni will never be able to learn his lessons. He will always remain stupid and get hurt. Take care that you do not become like Beni.'[108] Or: 'Rakhal, have you met Ram and Shyam of the Ghoshal household? . . . What could I say about their virtues!'[109] Those who are being shown and held up as examples of good and bad are used purely as instances. The commentary of the storyteller is the chief subject to be considered here. But on whose behalf is the storyteller assuming guardianship of voiceless boys without any preamble, and reiterating injunctions one after another with carefree aplomb? In the lesson 'Unkind human beings are like beasts', on observing the cruel behaviour of a few wayward boys towards animals and birds, the 'soft-hearted' teller speaks up with a wounded heart: 'Well, do they not have parents or any guardians who could restrain them?'[110]

The all-knowing, omniscient teller of tales has taken on the responsibility of introducing the guardians to the stupid boys. In the lesson 'The many faults of false words', it is declared: 'Nobody loves a boy who is a liar. Teachers despise him. What more need I say? Even if he goes crying from door to door, nobody will feel any kindness towards him.'[111] The lesson at the end of *Barna Parichay, Part 2* ends thus: 'Not getting enough to eat, desperately burning with hunger, he would wander crying from door to door; even so nobody felt any affection or sympathy for him.'[112] The similarity between the choice of words and sentence construction of *Shishushiksha* (91st edition) and *Barna Parichay* is not just fortuitous. Why only in these two lessons – there is no real difference in subject matter, tone of voice or sense of values between the two books. It is easy to gauge why another edition of *Barna Parichay* by the name of *Shishushiksha, Part 3* could not be at par with Vidyasagar's *Barna Parichay*. In both the books, the teller's observation never changes. His unshakeable seriousness remains from beginning to end; every word of his has a tone of reprimand. At every step, he communicates that he does not believe that young people can have opinions of their own. In fact, childlike behaviour is an eyesore to him. It is the task of children to just learn – and learn with an absorbed mind. They can even garner the raw material for learning from birds and animals if they want to: 'Oh children, if you observe the behaviour of birds and beasts with concentration, you can get much good counsel from there' (*Shishushiksha*, *Part 3*).[113] The title of the composition of which this sentence is a part is: 'Dogs are very loyal to their masters.'

Prabhu bhakti (devotion to the master) is a favourite subject of Bengali writers of children's textbooks. In the fifth part of *Shishushiksha* published in 1851, that is, Rajkrishna Bandyopadhyay's *Nitibodh* written in emulation of William Chambers' *Moral Classbook*, some advice is given regarding 'Behaviour towards superiors and inferiors':

> Everybody's station in life is not the same; the difference of education, intelligence, heart, status etc. causes some to be considered great, some low down, some masters, some servants . . . the person . . . who works for another in a monthly or annual schedule before he gets a salary is known as a servant. The duty of the servant is to be forever attentive in the service of his master and to respect and honour him appropriately. . . . Servants who are dedicated to their masters could even accept giving up their lives for their masters.[114]

Apart from *prabhu bhakti*, subjects that occur over and over again, to a lesser or greater extent, in all treatises of ethics and textbooks are: 'The relationship between a king and his subjects'; 'Serving elders'; 'Studies and hard work'; 'Serving others'; and 'Judging the qualities and flaws of different castes'. These mutually related subjects are signifiers of the narrowness of the colonial gentleman's nature and range of inquiry about life. Through the medium of these, the five kinds of *dharma* as decreed by Manu – the duties of a particular caste, duties of each stage of life, duties of *varnashramadharma*, *gunadharma*, and daily rites and duties – seem to come back in a new shape in each changed situation. A new regimented and clear picture of social organization develops out of this.

In spite of being under English rule, it is rather obvious that the brahmanical dictums gleaned from the laws of Manu would still hold ground in the unconscious of the upper-class and upper-caste society of Bengal. However, no matter how deep the nexus was between the brahmanical and colonial grammars during British rule, there were instances when that understanding was flouted; examples of this abound in the modern primers *Shishushiksha* and *Barna Parichay*. The two categories where differences from Manu's axioms are most noted are that of caste and gender.

According to the brahmanical point of view, knowledge was not something to be disseminated freely – its spread needed to accompany the protection of the barriers of caste and religion. On the other hand, due to western influences, it was obvious that the education system in nineteenth-century Bengal would seek to loosen, at least a little, the erstwhile stranglehold of prevalent prescriptive measures. It was but to be expected, then, that this irrevocable loosening would leave its trace on the primers composed for children of the time. Let us examine how 'caste' and 'gender' were configured in *Shishushiksha* and *Barna Parichay*.

'Varna' (Caste)

We first meet the protagonist Gopal and his antagonist Rakhal of *Barna Parichay* in *Part 1* of the primer. However, at least till 1858, till the eleventh edition of *Barna Parichay*, they were situated in *Part 2*. By then the crowd of children in the primer had also thickened – it included Tarak, Ishan, Saday, Sashi, Abhay, Uday, Beni, Ram, Navin, Bhuvan, Girish, and of course Gopal and Rakhal. Surprisingly, except for Gopal and Rakhal, none of the other boys had been burdened with the weight of a surname; Gopal and Rakhal were the only ones clearly marked by a family name. In the second lesson of *Part 2* of *Barna Parichay* (eighth edition, 1858) we find: 'The Sarkars have a son. His name is Rakhal. . . . He is not as good a boy as the Ghosal boy Gopal.'[115] However, very soon (though it is difficult to ascertain exactly when), Rakhal Sarkar and Gopal Ghosal are seen to have lost their *varna* markers and join the congregation of the other boys. In no future editions of the primer do they earn back their familial contexts. The moment Gopal and Rakhal, the two prototypes of the modern ideal, become free of the limiting identifiers imposed on them at birth, they become representatives of the moral economy that is essential for the functioning of a social system based on ideal types.

On the other hand, in *Part 1* of Madanmohan Tarkalankar's *Shishushiksha*, we hear a boy declare: 'I am a brahman; my name is Ramnath.'[116] His open declaration of his *varna* identity (in spite of Vidyasagar's tampering, and a thousand corrections, improvements and rejections) remains strong as ever. Consequently, the brahman Ramnath never gets an opportunity to be a public representative figure on the lines of Gopal or Rakhal.

'Linga' (Gender)

It would be putting it rather mildly if we term the following incident as just 'surprising'. The same Vidyasagar who had dedicated his life to the betterment of the oppressive conditions plaguing the lives of women in Bengal, who had written 'Balyabibaher Dosh' ('The Evils of Child Marriage', 1850), 'Bidhaba Bibaha Chalu Houa Uchit ki Na Atodbishoyok Prastab' ('Treatise on Whether Widow Remarriage Should be Made Prevalent', 1855) and its second edition in the same year, 'Bahu Bibaha Rahit Houa Uchit ki Na Atodbishoyok Prastab' ('Treatise on Whether Polygamy Should Be Prohibited, 1871) and its second edition in 1873, as well as the obituary titled 'Prabhabati Sambhasan' (1892) in memory of a young girl he was extremely fond of – even he gave no place to the girl-child in his *Barna Parichay* (1855). In his primer, all the students are boys; parents and teachers are busy with the correction and improvement or necessary rejection of only boys.

One possible explanation for why *Barna Parichay* is devoid of girls could be that under the aegis of child marriage in mid-nineteenth-century Bengal, the actual possibility of education of girls was next to nothing. In the concluding paragraph of 'Balyabibaher Dosh' ('The Evils of Child Marriage') published in the *Sarbasubhakari Patrika* (instead of an expected vilification of the nay-sayers and valorization of the supporters of treatises on widow remarriage and polygamy), an emotional Vidyasagar had written: 'Whatever I have said thus far in this paper on child marriage is but a prelude. There are numerous reasons, arguments, instances in this regard that are left. I will not hesitate to gradually put those forward.'[117] In the same essay, he lamented: 'Girls are hardly acquainted with the alphabet when their wedding day arrives.'[118]

Yet, in spite of the excuse of the actual situation of education, one still fails to come to terms with the absence of women in *Barna Parichay*. That is because *Barna Parichay* is not a clerical account of the prevalent customs of the day; it is meant to be a historically minded tract for future generations. Its business is not with *what-is* but with *what-can-be*. Therefore the mystery remains as to why *Barna Parichay* speaks so much about Gopal and Rakhal, and stays absolutely silent about their sisters.

It is not as if there was anything lacking in Vidyasagar's efforts as to *what-can-be* in the sphere of women's education. He had opened the Narishiksha Pratishthan Bhandar (Institute of Women's Eduction) without waiting for government assistance. His constant appeals to the government resulted in him securing grants on 1 May 1862 for establishing girls' schools between 1858 and 1861 in seven suburban towns: Birsingha, Udayrajpur, Rasulpur, Govindpur, Rishra, Kuran and Udaygunge. Much before this, in December 1850, soon after the establishment of the Calcutta Female School by John Elliot Drinkwater Bethune on 7 May 1849, Vidyasagar accepted the position of honorary chairman of the school. Then, in 1856, when the government took over the expenses of the school, he became the chairman of the Board of Directors on Bethune's advice.[119] And Madanmohan Tarkalankar composed the three-part *Shishushiksha* with the express purpose of betterment of education of the students of the Bethune School.

Therefore, it is not too unjust to hope that (whatever may have happened in *Barna Parichay*) at least in *Shishushiksha*, one will get to meet girls. And the fact that it happened so has irrefutable proof, in lesson 4 of *Part 3* of the first edition of *Shishushiksha* (1850). Of course, it must be noted that during its inception there was a marked discrepancy between the ratio of men and women present in the text – in spite of its dictums like 'Education is necessary for women' (*Shishushiksha*, *Part* 2, lesson 12). Thus, considering that the book was written for the purpose of educating women, except for a fleeting presence in lesson 4, women are completely absent in it.

The title of lesson 4 in the 1850 edition was: 'Good boys and girls love everyone equally.' The instances of two girls serve as an example to be followed by a boy named Rakhal. The narrator of the lesson advises Rakhal that he has observed the two sisters, Sama Ghosal and Bama Ghosal, to be ideals in every respect. They are as beautiful without as they are within. No trace of malice mars their body or mind; they are so pure in every aspect that there is no possibility of any squabble between them regarding anything. Thus the narrator's honest advice to Rakhal, based on the examples of Sama and Bama, is: 'Good boys and girls love everyone equally.' It is really commendable that examples of two home-bound sisters is used in order to teach a boy a lesson on 'goodness'.

However, we will be not just surprised but stunned if we revisit lesson 4, *Part 3* of *Shishushiksha* in its fifteenth edition, published in 1860 – two years after the demise of Madanmohan Tarkalankar. The student named Rakhal is still there; so is the narrator–teacher. But the title of the lesson now reads 'Good boys love everyone equally', and the two examples now are Ram Ghosal and Shyam Ghosal! Thus girls vanish from the only lesson in *Shishushiksha* they had appeared in, ousted by the brothers Ram Ghosal and Shyam Ghosal who secure their position in the book. It is impossible to deduce who was responsible for this unforeseen, almost spectral change in gender. Was it Madanmohan, or Vidyasagar, or an unknown third person? One must accept that the sudden entry and equally sudden exit of girls from the Bengali primer at such a critical historical juncture is deeply symbolic. To go a little further, even if we consider the dictum 'Education is necessary for women' as sacrosanct, the mystery of Sama–Bama's disappearance makes it imperative that we recognize how the reconfiguration of women as always-already predicated upon the reconfiguration of men was a necessary feature of Bengali brahmanical modernity.[120]

But is it so easy to exorcise the spectres of those who were banished from the world of primers as soon as they made an entry? Can the woman or the shudra ever be completely suppressed, whether in the time of high brahmanism of Manu or in modernity? Especially in a moment of reformation, when the iron-bound dictums of Manu had become quite a source of discomfort for many well-educated Bengali young men?

At the end of the fifth lesson of Bankimchandra's *Sahaj Rachana Shiksha* (second, third and fourth editions, sequentially, in 1894, 1896 and 1898, respectively), with the intention of testing, the author had asked the question:

Using the following subjects and statements, construct sentences using adjectives, adjectives of adjectives, and adverbs:

Subject	*Statement*
Son	Serving one's parents
King	Rearing his subjects
Wife	Serving one's husband
Learning	Dependent on habit.[121]

From the nature of the question, it is not difficult to guess that according to Bankim, there is a 'natural' concurrence between 'subject' and 'statement/moral'. If one wants to, one could slightly extend the thread of connection and include shudra along with son, king and wife.

In the 'Letter Writing' chapter of *Sahaj Rachana Shiksha*, Bankim has written about the 'correct' or traditional mode of address: 'If a brahman were to write a letter to a shudra, he should write a text of his blessing. If a shudra were to write a letter to a brahman, he should write a text of his *pranam* (regards).'[122] But Bankim also knew that in the new arrangement, some old customs were getting rejected. That is why, immediately after giving this advice, he had to admit regretfully: 'But many shudras do not observe this any more.'[123] Bankimchandra's other instructions apropos greetings are also notable:

> One must remember that one cannot do away with the title 'Srijukta Babu'. . . . Those who have any title, like Raja, Maharaja, Rai Bahadur, Khan Bahadur etc. must write them in the superscription of letters. Like 'Maharajdhiraj Srisheeljukta Bardhamanadhipati Mahatapachandra Bahadur Prajapalak Bareshu', 'Mahamanya Srijukta Honourable Sir Ashley Eden, K.C.S.I. Barabareshu'.[124]

In a nutshell, one must have a clear idea about who belongs to which level in a hierarchical society, and it is a great wrong to contravene the rules of address. Bankim's opinion about what kind of use of language and sentence construction is appropriate for Bengalis is: 'The language of the capital is most familiar, more than that of other places. . . . The word *chhari* (stick) is used in Calcutta's *bhadra* society. It can be used . . . only whatever is used by lowly and rustic people cannot be used.'[125] There is no way that Bengali society can reject an iota of the all-consuming supremacy of the *bhadralok*. The language of urban 'educated' people is civilized and the language of the so-called lowly or rustic people is uncivilized – a medium for the *bhadralok*'s self-identification is the indication of this differentiation.

However, one cannot be a *bhadralok* unless one possesses quite a few good qualities. The identity attained by virtue of birth is not enough. In order to awaken senseless Bengalis, in page after page and book after book, there seem to be hymns in support of the greatness of hard work. A few sentences out of that very famous *First Book of Reading* by Pyaricharan Sarkar, published around 1850: 'A bad boy does not go to school or learn his tasks.

. . . How will he earn his bread? . . . take care of him and . . . teach him to work, then he would not beg from door to door.'[126] In *Shishushiksha, Part 3*, 91st edition: 'Oh children! If you saw the labour of ants and honey-bees, you would understand that one should not be lazy and waste time.'[127] There is no substitute for hard work, it is impossible to advance without diligent perseverance – these are precious gems in the collections of maxims of various writers of books on ethics. The capability for hard work is again the ultimate touchstone for judging different races; it is the only measure of assessing who are civilized and who are not. In *Shishushiksha, Part 5* ('Nitibodh'), Rajkrishna Bandyopadhyay writes:

> The people of those regions who are averse to hard work, making their living out of whatever they can get hunting and gathering fruit, are uncivilized. The natives of America and Australia and the negro race are still in this state today. . . . In the entire world, the Germans, Swiss, French, Dutch and English are the few races that are more industrious than all others; because of this, their situation is also superior to any other race.[128]

There is a deep bond between hard work and the acquiring of education. In *Part 1* of Akshay Kumar Dutta's (1820–1886) *Charupath*, spread over three parts (1853, 1854 and 1859, sequentially), there is a detailed description of that deep-seated bond:

> The reason for the condition of all the barbaric natives of hills and all the lowly people of all countries being so deplorable is that they do not pursue learning and education. . . . See, the beautifully civilized European races like the English have improved their condition so much with the power of their education.[129]

And those who have intelligence but no education can at least take their lessons from learned men. Did Bankimchandra, in his *Sahaj Shiksha Path*, write 'The Bengalis have intelligence: the English have education',[130] to explain that there is a relationship of giver and recipient, offering and acceptance between the educated and the intelligent? Was Vidyasagar motivated by this belief when he wrote in his *Charitabali* about enhancing devotion and enthusiasm for studies among boys?

> Some great men, in trying to fulfil their intended achievements, have exhibited such unquestioned hard work, unwavering enthusiasm, noble tolerance and even firmer perseverance, and some of them have not got dislodged from their business after intolerable oppression and restraints of poverty, having suffered limitless sorrow.[131]

Did he, in fact, write *Jibancharit* to explain all these and fill both these with the life-narratives of European scholars? To sum up, are the people of various races interconnected through the disparities in their abilities? Is there any link between the progress and wealth of one party, and the backwardness and poverty of the other side? These are not at all to be considered; as long as one is able to shake off inertia and get up, all problems would get solved almost magically. Did the authors of the new compilations and the makers of the new texts for the *bhadralok* not think even once that it is doubtful whether the majority of the people of this country can procure two fistfuls of rice after driving themselves to toil all day and night? And that behind that pitiable state is a considerable contribution of the industrious *bhadralok* endowed with physical prowess? At least Akshay Kumar Dutta was not able to evade this serious question; in *Charupath*, *Part 2*, he wrote:

> The simple-natured farmer who is a follower of law is a thousand times more admirable and venerable than the man who makes money by unjust means . . . is it the excessive unruliness of the inferior tendencies of the wealthy and respectable people that they do not work hard enough to amass wealth for the prosperity of society in accordance with their abilities by cutting down their own luxuries?[132]

The subject of wealth and philanthropy, in fact, is intertwined with hard work. Just as it is necessary to be aware of the value of wealth acquired by labour, just as it is one's duty to protect and augment one's wealth, so one should now and then help deprived people by means of that excess of wealth. This is what is called working for the welfare of the people and social service. That is why: 'Thieving is a great fault; everybody despises those who thieve' (*Barna Parichay, Part 1*); 'Do not eye other people's wealth with greed' (*Shishushiksha, Part 3*); 'To steal is a sin and a crime' – 'Seize the thief' (*First Book of Reading*); 'One becomes graceless if one wastes money' (*Shishushiksha*, Part 2); 'Sweet is the bread that one earns by one's sweat' – 'Thank God we are not in want' – 'We ought to be kind to those who are in want' – 'Deign to hear what the poor man says. Do not feign to be deaf. His tears are the sure signs of his grief' (*First Book of Reading*). At first sight, it might seem as if the same ideals have been upheld in the books of ethics written by Bengalis and Samuel Smiles' *Self-Help* (1859); but bound within the parameters of middle-class inferiority, the possibility for Bengalis to acquire their intrinsic power was indeed limited. What they wanted to say was: in spite of the miserable state of affairs in the colony, the social mobility that has been possible in the country will have to be put to some use even in a minimal or insignificant way. One would have to become an able worker; to ensure obedient submissiveness, there was no harm in confining youth in prisons akin to Bentham's Panopticon. One cannot expect much from faithful employees. In their eyes, reality was not a social application or process but just 'a thing out there'. They did not need or be obliged to know anything more than this; they would be grateful to move on unconsciously, obeying the dictates of fate.

The greatest medium for this brutal ideal, the introduction for entering the life of the worker, was Vidyasagar's *Barna Parichay*, written in direct and concise language. In every section of the book, there is evidence of unstinted consolation through the promises of colonialism. But it became clearer, compared to earlier, how false they were within six years of the publication of *Barna Parichay*. The situation changed quite a lot after the nationalist uprising of 1857, and a counter-incitement started.

The Sepoy Mutiny and Children's Literature

The Sepoy Mutiny shook the minds of the authorities of the religious associations of England. The Church Missionary Society formed the Christian Vernacular Education Society with the noble intention of expelling restlessness and lack of education from the minds of Indians. In 1850, this Society published a monthly magazine for children: *Satyapradip*. In 1869, the Calcutta Tract Society published a monthly periodical for women called *Streelok* and one for children called *Jyotiringan*. Kaliprasanna Ray's *Charitamanjari*, published ten years after the Sepoy Mutiny, is a sparkling example of the kind of truth that was being served and the enlightenment that was produced through the medium of children's literature. It was said at the beginning of the book: 'The great man who planted the foundations of the British empire in India is Robert Clive.' The author stated that the sepoys had mistakenly behaved cruelly with English men and women. The book, 'useful for all in Bengali schools', was replete with unashamed and undiluted eulogies of the British. Some parts of *Charitamanjari* were deleted summarily from the English version; in some places of the translation, the writer was assisted by Krishnakamal Bhattacharya (1843–1932), a writer for the magazine *Abodhbandhu* edited by Beharilal Chakrabarti (1835–1894).

At the end of the nineteenth century, Bireshwar Pandey (1842–1919) became especially popular as a children's writer; in 1888, one gets to know from the introduction to his published *Aryapath*:

> These days, there is a real lack of the sense of ethics among our little friends. . . . Frightened by observing this state, all guardians have become eager to unearth methods of redressing this. The news of this colossal damage has reached as far as remote England . . . an Education Commission was appointed for this. The commission advised the Sarkar Bahadur that it was indeed obligatory for them to impart the education of ethics to the community of Indian students. The Sarkar Bahadur has accepted the suggestion.

At the request or under the stewardship of the government, Bireshwar Pandey wrote character sketches of ideal men of the Indian Puranas in *Aryapath*. Krishnakumar Mitra, editor of the magazine *Sanjibani*, wielded his pen with the same intention. Khagendranath Mitra (1896–1978), historian of children's literature and an author himself, said: 'Contemporary children's literature in

Bangla is ordered within the restraints of rules that is in accordance with its conception, and like food and clothing, its production is also regulated by governmental counsel.'[133]

Attracting attention to the anarchy that had spread all around by trying to compete with gradually expanding education, the Swarashtra office sent a necessary statement to government administrators on 31 December 1889. On 17 August 1889, in the drawing room of the Internal Affairs Office (Education), some proposals were accepted about the kind of arrangements that should be made regarding 'disrespect towards the authorities' and 'defiance of the management'. Among them, some proposals that are worth mentioning are as follows. The punishment will have to be given in such a way that it can teach the offender an appropriate lesson. If someone is prosecuted for violating orders, his special advantages and privileges will have to be snatched away. A moderate amount of caning can be practised on young boys. But even after doing all this if it is noticed that it is not possible to reform the student, it is desirable that he be expelled from school or college. It is essential to keep a strict watch on the behaviour and conduct of the students. A report on the ethical conduct of every student must be sent to guardians with the considered views of the principal master. Along with this, annual prizes should be instituted for honest conduct. Responsibility could be assigned to students of higher grades for maintaining discipline in school and, to whatever extent possible, outside school. It is extremely necessary to organize moral education outside school and produce an effective book of ethics.[134]

Before accepting the proposals, the Internal Affairs Office had solicited the opinion of many government officers of high rank and revered people in the state. By way of reply, the Inspector of Schools, E. Masden, wrote to the Chief of Public Instruction in Madras: 'It is necessary to turn attention to lessons in manners for the students. Although Muslim and Hindu boys of the upper castes are of refined nature like the Europeans, the lower-caste Hindus lag behind. They must enforce strict regimens of uniform, especially in schools that taught English.'[135] The intention was clear: the uniform would draw the English-knowing boys within the purview of the same group; on the other hand, it would definitely place them outside the crowd of boys who are illiterate in English. The uniform was not just a garment that was fit for wearing but a marker of some distinct signs. It simultaneously unites and separates, is dependent and independent. This too displays the same play of similarity and difference.

The Secretary of the Bengal government, P. Nolan, expressed himself anxiously: 'It seems now that students can be kept under control only by the kind of discipline exercised by government schools and colleges. Even so, it will not be possible to entirely curb the delinquency of disobedience because students are being instigated from outside the school premises.'[136] The secretary of the British Indian Association, Babu Pyarimohan Mukhopadhyay, expressed doubts about whether there would be any special benefit in imparting ethical education to students.[137] The advice of the secretary of the Indian Association, Babu Surendranath Bandyopadhyay (1849–1928), was: 'With the noble intent of curbing student indiscipline, Samuel Smiles' *Character* and *Self-Help* should be incorporated within the college syllabus.'[138] At the recommendation of the Swarashtra office, although Sir Amir Ali (1849–1928) extended his complete support, Nawab Abdul Latif (1828–1893) was a little conflicted. On 28 June 1877, it was Abdul Latif who wrote a letter to the personal secretary of Lord Lytton:

> Let Walter Scott's novel, *The Talisman*, be expunged without further delay from the university curriculum; no pious Muslim will ever send his child to study a novel in which Muslims have been tarnished in a bizarre and unjust manner; there is no reason to do so either. As it is, western literature is adequately 'deorientalizing' and 'denationalizing'; over and above that, if books like that are taught, the gulf will increase, not be bridged. The attempt to acquaint Muslims with western knowledge will be unsuccessful.[139]

But Sir Alfred Croft, KCIE, Chief of Public Instruction in Bengal, surpassed everybody in the brilliance of his opinion. According to him, at the base of the disobedience and lack of discipline among students was the fatal hazard of translation. Ever since the word '*bhadralok*' had been used synonymously with 'gentleman', a wrong notion had gradually become embedded in the minds of the Bengalis. Despite having no talent, they have been trained to think of themselves as being the equals of the English. Consequently, the students belonging to the *bhadralok* community now want the respect and rights that English students get on the basis of their family honour and their self-acquired strengths. They do not understand that there is no congruence between their aspirations and their abilities. It is necessary to properly impress on the minds of Indian students that there is no humiliation in being submissive to legitimate mastery, and respectful towards the sense and discretion of elders.[140] Has the effort towards assimilation become successful to an excessive extent? In the path to progress, have the *bhadralok* come too close to the gentleman? Was it to evade this dangerous intimacy that the government and non-government officers became so anxious about 'ethical education' and 'discipline', and so keen to bring back a healthy educational atmosphere in Indian schools and colleges?

There is no doubt that many Bengalis felt a want of safety after the revolutionary moment of 1857. Not only Bireshwar Pandey but many others started relating the story of India's glorious past to children, either through direct government assistance or of their own accord. A supreme example of that is the extremely popular discourse on ethics, *Sunitisandarbha* (1891), compiled by Chandroday Bhattacharya Bidyabinod, Professor of Sanskrit at Bangabashi

College. Exuberant eulogies of the book were published in papers like *Hope*, *Hindu Patriot* and *Amrita Bazar*. In its advertisement, the compiler wrote: 'His honour Shri Babu Chandranath Basu, MABL, in a gesture of affection to me, has corrected the book from beginning to end.' What was surprising was that Krishnakamal Bhattacharya wrote about *Sunitisandarbha* that the book would certainly earn regard among orthodox revivalists.[141] Whether it received that or not, there is no doubt that those who were devotees of the English conveyed a lot of praise to the writer. Chandroday Bidyabinod's advice about one's duty towards the king was:

> After giving a special thought to the errors of the king, after ascertaining its truth or otherwise, it is one's duty to express it most cautiously. If the king is a tyrant by nature, remains preoccupied in indulging himself without looking at the joys and sorrows of his subjects, even then, instead of suddenly criticizing the king, or deciding to go on a counter-offensive, explain to him his faults hundreds and thousands of times like a friend. Treason and ingratitude is the same thing; nobody should allow themselves to get inculpated in this sin.[142]

Before this, in Rajanikanta Gupta's (1849–1900) *Aryakirti* (*c.* 1889) too, it was said about the Sepoy Mutiny: 'During the aforementioned terrible times', etc. Yet, the book has a special gravity. This was the first time that a full-bodied biography had been composed on the basis of Indian characters. At least the British model was rejected in the literal sense of the term. In the advertisement, the author wrote: 'Compared to the textual narratives of foreigners, in the textual narratives of native people . . . self-respect and an accompanying ethical knowledge is stronger.'[143] It was in *Aryakirti* that Lakshmibai, the Rani of Jhansi, got a place worth mentioning.

Before this, in some essays and books written for children, one could observe a minor though clear expression of pride in one's nation and nationalism. For example, in the essay 'Affection towards One's Own Nation', in the book *Gyanchandrika* (1838) by Gopal Lal Mitra: 'Even if the inhabitants of your nation are low and contemptible, honour them, and even if the nation is a desert, sing its praises.' After the Sepoy Mutiny, in the sixth issue of the magazine *Sakha*, established in 1883, an essay by the title of 'Surendrababu's Imprisonment' was published. The epilogue to this essay on Surendranath Bandyopadhyay's imprisonment said: 'Readers! Learn to shed a few tears for your wretched motherland. One day, India's prisons will be purified by you. One day, the misfortune of the country will be banished by your anguish. One day, the name of your country will shine due to your glories.'[144] The name of the essayist was Bipin Chandra Pal. On the other hand, in the magazine *Balak*, established in 1885 and edited by Gyanadanandini Debi, there was the hint of a turnabout in Bengali children's literature. Driven by the belief that there is, or at least should be, a world outside the ordered web of education and jobs, the effort to establish an alliance through goodwill was almost completely rejected. Quite a few poems and plays written for children by Rabindranath Tagore were published in the magazine *Balak*. As a witness to the fact that that there was a contrary inspiration in Bengali *bhadralok* life, let me mention a fragment of an article from *Balak* of Aswin–Kartik 1292 (*c.* 1885): 'This means the requirement of a fad. Ours is a phlegmatic temperament, so we do not have fads in our etiquette. We are very civilized, very intelligent, and not crazy about anything. We will pass exams, work for a living and eat.'[145] The author of this essay, written in the form of a letter, was the twenty-four-year-old Rabindranath. But will society acquit those who are full of fads, incompatible, uncivilized and not sharp-witted?

IV

'Once there lived a bird'

'Once there lived a bird.' As soon as one hears this, it seems as if a session on fairytales is about to start in full swing. A group of boys and girls are sitting in a circle surrounding the narrator. Incessantly talking, the narrator will run out of breath, his throat will become hoarse, but the audience will not give him any respite. They are not the kind to give up that easily. No matter how the exhausted narrator tries to find a means to put a full stop or wind up the thread of the narrative, his unrelenting audience will just not let him stop and will go on posing obstructions. Their questions are endless but the vocalized form of all the questions is just one: 'And then?' Till such time as their desires are satisfied, until their eyes shut in sleep, they will carry the story forward by the force of this unique question as their prop. They will not let the narrator utter the last sentence and breathe a sigh of relief.

'Once there lived a king.' In the opening sentence of Rabindranth's *Tota-kahini* (*Parrot's Tale*, Magh 1324), he has completely abided by the trend of the oft-heard beginning of a discourse, 'once there lived a bird'. But although there might have been some promise of narrating a fairytale, was it preserved till the end? Did Rabindranath literally follow the challenge of constructing a fairytale according to narratorial injunctions to satisfy the hopes of the readers? The story is of course replete with stock characters from fairytales. There is a king; along with him there are also minister–courtier–pandit–artisan–labourer–goldsmith–soldier–subaltern and many others. And there is a bird; it is hardly a bird but a nuisance incarnate. It is the bird that comes and causes all the hassle. If the wise and stable king did not get cautioned in time, his golden kingdom would have gone to the dogs. So what was the fault of the bird? 'It was stupid.' It sang songs but did not read the scriptures. It jumped and flew, but did not know what etiquette is.[146] But did that really cause such a cosmic turbulence? The king said: 'Such birds are of no use. Yet they eat wild fruit and cause losses in fruit stalls and the royal bazaar.'[147] It was no wonder that the king became red with fury at the audacity of this paltry bird from somewhere. It was his magnanimity that he did not immediately execute the bird. But the question is: was there any novelty in the way the king expressed his anger? Did he not utter phrases hackneyed by excessive use? If you juxtapose 'of no use' against 'bazaar', are you not reminded of those two definitive words – 'utility' and 'market'? This valuable pair of words has recurred like classical axioms in writings from Bentham to Macaulay, from Rammohun to that of several Indians. There is no doubt that the king of *Totakahini* has mouthed Macaulay's jargon. If one thinks that it is written in a light vein, that there is no logic in dragging heavy issues for discussion into a story of four pages, all doubts will be dispelled by the last sentence of the first part of *Totakahini* – at least they should. This is because it is not possible for someone who has understood the gist of 'utility' and 'market' to retrace his steps; surely he will be all in a flurry to get in motion an excellent 'educational' system. 'Utility', 'market' and 'education' get mixed up and become a compound substance. The king in *Totakahini*, anxious about losses, also roars like Macaulay: 'He called his minister and said, "Teach the bird a lesson."'[148] One can discern from the manner of the king's command how fatal, how double-edged an oft-used word like '*shiksha*' is. Written with an oblique irony, Rabindranath sometimes juxtaposes two contrary terms, and sometimes constructs the suggestion of a contrast by resorting to one word, in *Totakahini.* Crossing the limited range of denotation, he keeps enhancing the associations of words. On the one hand, there is a catalogue of 'versus': song versus scripture, jumping around versus etiquette, etc. Apart from this, if one proceeds along the logic of these 'versuses', one can find a trace of some concealed contrary terms: 'stupid'–'learned', 'impractical'–'practical', etc. One could extend the catalogue of 'versuses' as long as one desires. 'Who will stop the words once they run?' But whatever be the number, at the base of different contrary terms there are two sets of terms that control: spontaneity/repression and play/control. On the other hand, the word '*shiksha*' itself equals a hundred words; there has been no need to use a separate word opposite the word with multiple meanings. By its very openness, the word has not recoiled from drawing and incorporating contrary words into itself. Impressed by the exploitative ability of the word '*shiksha*', if it gives rise to a contrary mood in someone, if one wants to read 'punishment' in place of '*shiksha*', he cannot be blamed much. It does not contradict logic, yet maintains the applicability of the word.

The king is over and done with it after giving the command; who will bear the onerous task of teaching the bird a lesson? The nephews of the king are summoned; they search for the pandit. The pandit informs, after hair-splitting deliberation and analysis: 'The reason for the above-mentioned creature's lack of learning is . . . that the nests the birds build with ordinary hay and twigs cannot hold much learning.'[149] Therefore it was decided that 'it is essential, before all else, to build a proper nest'.[150] After the learned men of the king's court get their fees and depart, goldsmiths sit down to build a golden cage.

The subject of the golden cage has been mentioned previously also in Rabindranath's writings – for example, in his poem 'Dui Pakhi' ('Two Birds', 1299 / *c.* 1892) from the collection *Sonar Tori* (*The Golden Boat*): 'The caged bird was in the golden cage / The wild bird was in the woods.'[151] The example of the contrast between the free bird and the caged, fettered bird is ubiquitous in folktales and narratives.

> There are old similes in *Totakahini* and many components of the oral folk literature have been used. However, even if the sense of the idiom is the same, the central idea has changed. A new metaphor, a modern parable has been created in the same mould as and under the cover of fairytales.[152]

The account of the helpless bird placed in a golden cage has got intertwined with the story of the cruel structure of the modern system of education.

People from alien lands come in crowds to see that wondrous cage of Rabindranath's *Totakahini*. Some say, 'It is education at its best.' Some say, 'Even if education is not achieved, a cage has been built. How lucky the bird is!'[153] Did Bentham not name that delightful cage long ago? Are not the state of the prisoner of the Panopticon – that mouthful of a word for a prison, built along the lines of a lunatic asylum, hospital, school, factory, what not – and that of the caged bird of *Totakahini* the same? In the opinion of Michel Foucault, in order to reinforce discipline one sometimes has to chart the space within a determined periphery and make a closed though separate cordon.[154] One can slay the insensible only if the battle array is arranged properly. The cage in *Totakahini* is not just a symbol of the school building; Rabindranath tries to show through the narrative of the cage how children are trapped into being regimented in military array, subjected to the profound thinking, deliberation and counsel of so many eminent, learned people with creative minds!

The real work starts as soon as the exterior shape of the cage is built. Immediately after the goldsmith heads towards home after collecting his bag of tips, in accordance with the advice of the pandits, the nephews send out summons for writers of treatises. Therein starts an imitation of the treatise, an imitation thereof, and an imitation of that imitation. In the sequence of imitations, a mountain of treatises piles up. Has Rabindranath used the writers as a means to satirize the manufacturers of bitter concoctions – in other words, the creators of children's textbooks that were produced with the noble intention of augmenting the moral strength of children? In 'Shikshar Herpher', written many years before *Totakahini* and delivered at a gathering of the Rajshahi

Association in 1892, Rabindranath had said: 'All the common books of the world can be divided chiefly in two sections – textbooks and non-textbooks. It will not be unfair judgment to include the books that are selected by the Textbook Committee in the last-mentioned category.'[155] Alongside, he provided a short catalogue of unreadable books: 'There is no lack of primers of alphabets, textbooks for children's learning and books of ethics, but I don't term them as books for children.'[156] 'By concentrating excessively on protecting the moral health of children, what had to happen has happened. The world of the students' books was on one side and the world that they inhabit on the other; in the middle there was just the bridge of vocabulary and grammar.'[157] Would the prisoners of the cage ever be able to walk over this collapsing bridge?

The cage was built, the books were arranged; what was needed now was daily repair and vigorous surveillance. 'Many people got to work and in order to keep an eye on them, many other people got to work. . . . They and their numerous cousins on both sides sat happily, laying out cushions in a room in the upper storey of the brick house.'[158] Was there not an intimate connection of the spread of education in colonial times with the increase in income of the third estate, the sphere in which no material and consumer goods are produced? Is it very difficult to recognize the various cousins on both sides and their successors? At that time, a few years after the writing of *Totakahini,* by a certain kind of calculation, it was quite evident that the number of individuals who were engaged in 'learning for the sake of earning' was increasing by leaps – in fact Indians were exceeding in head-count the learners of 'civilized' and 'progressive' countries like France, Germany and England. In 1925–27, when the number of Indian students in colleges and universities was 94,000, it was 58,000 in France, 89,000 in Germany and 42,000 in England.[159] There is no doubt that due to not knowing the ratio between the total population and the number of students, the basis of the comparison is quite shaky. But from the census of 1955–58, one can get an idea of this ratio in the colonial times: 'In India, among every 10,000, the number of graduates in the university was 6.82, 4.37 in France, 6.21 in West Germany, 5.68 in England.'[160] Within this abundance of the third estate in India, there was no cause for the progeny of the *bhadralok*, the 'bespectacled babus', for regret or blame. They could have gone on earning their living and living their lives simultaneously with their eyes shut and with a cheerful mind. But the problem was that 'although the world is deficient on many counts, there are sufficient fault-finders'.[161] One of them comes and speaks thus into the king's ear: 'The cage is progressing but nobody keeps any track of the bird.'[162] Who is this fault-finder who complains about the workers at the king's court?

The king's perpetually devoted nephew dispels the king's confusion: 'The nephew said, ". . . These fault-finders malign people because they do not get enough to eat." Hearing the reply, the king understood the situation clearly, and immediately the nephew was adorned with a gold necklace.'[163] The king is knowledgeable in everything; if the sycophants give a little hint, everything becomes clear as crystal to him. But it is difficult for us to arrive at any clear theory about the character of the fault-finder. Is he a representative of the illiterate and the starving who are outside the *bhadralok* community? Or is he educated but unemployed, one of the distressed gentlemen? Or is he an agent of those drop-out malcontents for whom the absence of deprivation is itself a deprivation? Is the fault-finder a mouthpiece of the narrator, of not only the narrator but also the writer?

Whoever be the fault-finder, hearing the analysis of this critic, the king is a little shaken:

> The king desired to see at what terrific speed education was moving. One day, therefore, he himself turned up at the school with friends, councillors and ministers. Immediately, there was the resounding music of conch-shells, bells, drums, kettle-drums, bell-metal plates, flutes, tom-toms, cymbals, war-drums *et al.* near the doorway. The pandits concentrated on reciting their *mantras* in full-throated voices and with the tufts of their hair shaking. All the supervisors, mechanics, labourers, goldsmiths, writers, and all the various cousins sang the sound of victory.[164]

The king himself sees the state of affairs and is amazed: 'Strange! The sound is not insignificant', he says.[165] The nephew is right next to him: he is adept at placating the king and working towards his own weal. Moreover, being a near relative, he would certainly be the king's trusted person. Is the Latin word '*nepot*', meaning nephew, not hidden in the root of the word 'nepotism' – which is a synonym for the word *swajanposhan* (nurturing one's own)? The Indian nephew, of the same genre as the Latin *nepot*, explains to the virtually confounded king a cacophony of sounds: 'It is not just the sound. The meaning (*artha*) is also considerable.'[166] In this irrefutable sentence, both the everyday meanings of the word *artha* (meaning and money) are there. To keep a school running requires as much labour as funds. Also, the words that take the king by surprise have nothing to do with money. The onslaught of this meaningless assortment of sounds was causing yet another senseless injury; the poor bird is at the point of losing its life.

Seeing such fanfare and hearing the uproar, the king is going back fairly satisfied, but the fault-finder poses a hindrance again. He had hidden himself in the hedge so long; as soon as the king crosses the doorway and is about to climb on to his elephant, he utters: 'Maharaj, have you seen the bird?'[167] The king returns and says to the pandit: 'One must see the art by which you train the bird.'[168] The thing that the king, the director of the school, wants to know is not what was taught to the bird but how it was taught: the essence of the method of learning.

> The method was so much more overpowering than the bird that the bird could hardly be seen; it seemed as though it would do not to see the bird at all. . . . There was no food or drink inside the cage. Just innumerable pages from innumerable books were being torn and stuffed inside the bird's mouth with the nib of the pen. Singing was definitely obstructed; even the aperture through which the bird could scream was sealed.[169]

The bird that sang and did not read the scriptures was trained to master etiquette in such a way that it had no opportunity to protest, let alone sing. The teaching method was also simple and not particularly convoluted. The bird had nothing to do but silently accept it. Until it attained the difficult-to-acquire ability for silent and passive observance of the instructions of the wise and the learned who speak in one voice, there would be no respite from study, application and training.

In the essay 'Shiksha Sanskar' (1313, Bengali calendar), Rabindranath had written in a comparative analysis of the education system of India and Ireland:

> It was not just language but Irish history that was no longer taught. They would not even be properly taught the geographical details of Ireland. It was they who had had wanted that in learning the history and geography of foreign lands, the boys would remain ignorant about their own land. Consequently, what had to happen, happened. The whole country was permeated by mental sluggishness. Irish-speaking boys entered school with intelligence and curiosity and came out with impaired minds and a hatred for knowledge.[170]

Were the wishes of the Trevelyans and Ramkamal Sens thereby fulfilled after so long? It was they who had wanted that by combining intelligence with learning, Indians should become skilled in the English language like the natives of Ireland, Scotland, Wales. But although clever in their manners and speech, and polished on the outside, could those who were stuffed inside a grinding mill of words without sense between their entrance into and departure from school, be anything but sticks of sugarcane bereft of any juice? 'The reason for this was that this education system was a mechanical process, it did not engage minds and the boys became parrots.'[171] Despite some changes due to differences of locale and period, the methods of imperialist grammar remained more or less the same. And the methods and severity from which neither the blacks nor whites got any respite are evident from Rabindranath's awareness in his essay 'Shiksha Sanskar': 'It was the design of the National School System to construct the Irish in the mould of the Anglo-Saxons and make Englishmen out of them. . . . It is not difficult to understand that the authorities are trying to get their political agenda to penetrate our education.'[172] Was it to expose this 'political intent' that after inspecting the house of learning, the contented 'king commands the ear-pulling *sardar* to tweak the ears of the fault-finder when he gets on to the elephant'?[173] Was there just one strategy to chastise the impudent students? If the pandit could not do it, there were the ear-pulling *sardars*. If people did not want to get steeped in the illusion of ideology, repressive arrangements were ready at hand.

A proof of how successful the effort to implant education with a political agenda was: 'The bird slowly became thoroughly, respectably half-dead.'[174] Did this mean that the number of players who could participate in a 'charade of artificial skills',[175] who could act as suppliers to others' tasks, increased by one? In the opinion of the guardians, although the situation was quite hopeful, the stupid bird refused to cooperate occasionally and commited acts of insolence. 'But due to the fault of habit, the bird would look at the morning sunlight and flutter its wings improperly.'[176] There was no escaping this; moreover, what happened was that on some days the foolish bird became grossly insolent: 'It could be seen that with its slender beak, it was trying to break the bars of the cage.'[177] Infinitely bewildered and peeved by the uncivil behaviour of the bird that rebelled against education and the king's court, the police constable summons the potter. He turns up at the abode of learning with a hammer, furnace and fuel. 'What beating upon beating the bird got! Iron fetters were made and the bird's wings were cut.'[178] Would it not do to not cut the wings? At least it would slightly enhance its beauty if nothing else. But for those whose basic chant is 'utility', to bother their heads about beauty is as improper as unjustifiable. Moreover, to initiate and discipline ignorant people, it was necessary to bind their bodies within a disciplinary framework.

In the opinion of Michel Foucault, right control is not achieved simply by teaching human beings or imposing a series of particular gestures on them; one cannot deploy the body in a measured way unless one can bring some symmetry between the regulated movements of the body and the corporeal form. It is essential to teach everybody the correct and fine use of the body in a way that there is no impairment of skill and waste of time. The teaching of exercise is essential. One must be so heedful about the economy of gestures targeted towards the formation of an able and useful body that if one is not cautious from the beginning, the result of one's prodigality could be fatal. It is reasonable to cut down and remove whatever is extra, unnecessary and redundant so that one does not have to burn in repentance later.[179] On the strength of this very logic, the wings of the bird in *Totakahini* are cut and its feet are put in fetters. With a pen in one hand and a spear in the other, 'the pandit created such a to-do over it – that is called education'.[180] For so long the bird had been half-dead, but now it died once and for all – which means that it became a thorough gentleman. Instead of being happy at its good fortune, the bad-mouthed fellow who was deprived of the grace of Lakshmi, that wretched fault-finder, let it be known that the bird had been killed. The king comes to his senses again – he summons his favourite nephew. The nephew says, 'Maharaj, the bird's education is complete.'[181] What are the signs of accomplishing complete education? The bird does not jump, does not fly, does not sing, does not yell if it is not fed, does not utter a sound if pressed or squeezed. Only the dry leaves of books make a rustling sound in its stomach.[182] Certainly, all the qualities of an able bearer of orders are present in the erudite parrot who reproduces rote learning.

Initially it was stupid; it used to sing, it jumped and flew, and never read the scriptures. But by the end of the story it becomes proficient in etiquette and a unique pandit. In the course of the story, the bird moves from one pole to the opposite pole. Just after going beyond the first stage, Rabindranath draws up to a full stop. But no matter how unruly and restless the audience is, no matter how it bothers the narrator with 'What happened next?' or 'After that?' in the story that starts with the sentence 'Once there lived a bird', does the audience also not become all ears to hear its predetermined, concluding utterance: 'After that, the bird started passing its days happily' or some other variation of it? It seems that there is a gap midway through the story – instead of the mischievous king getting exhausted, the healthy bird becomes exhausted. In the sentence 'Once there was a bird', the word 'was', in the first person active voice of its verb in the past tense, indicative of its existence, does not change its tense. In the narrative written in the style of a fairytale, the bird does not cross the bounds of place and time, and does not find shelter in the dreamland of narratives of daily life. Consequently, the liberated bird becomes a memento of an obsolete past, the iconic memory of a ruined age.

Whether this narrative of the past has any grounding in reality or not, because Rabindranath does not cause the past to get re-established in any way, even though a trace of romantic nostalgia and remote causality remains in the story, he can directly link up the chaotic present with history. Because he has written the gist of modern history in the backdrop of ancient fairytales, the contradiction between hope and fulfilment manifests itself so conspicuously and the story strikes as that sharp. Through the force of an oblique, ironical modulation of voice, Rabindranath violates custom and brings in an entirely new subject in the guise of an old topic. His greatest support in this task is the character of the fault-finder who seems to be the secret assailant, goes about guardedly protecting himself, but turns up at the appropriate time and tries to deal a blow from behind the bush. The fault-finder constantly destabilizes the permanent system handcrafted by the king and his team of associates. He exposes the tumultuous business that goes on in the name of stability and education, and the cruel oppression that is unleashed on children. There is no envisioned image of a bright future in *Totakahini*, no promise of deliverance. The story ends on a note of lament: 'In the southern breeze of the new spring, the sigh of the young plants agitated the sky over the woods in full blossom.'[183] Spring arrives as usual, the southern breeze blows, but blended within it is the deep sigh of new leaves. It is as if these new leaves, or young ones, have realized that some day they will be removed from this celebration of greenery. Only the dry leaves of textbooks will then rustle within them.

Two writers of the 'motherland' and the colony had respectively dedicated themselves to plumb the depths of Utilitarian educational inquiry: Charles Dickens (1812–1870) in *Hard Times* (1854), and Rabindranath in *Totakahini*. Moreover, the child-audience of *Totakahini* is its very subject: in this story, they do not get the dishonour due to passive, doll-like subjects but the respect due to subjects who are active participants. In fact, Rabindranath wrote this protest song targeting those dacoits who have deprived children of ownership rights by constantly grinding the disciplinary mill:[184] 'Ha re re re re re, please let me be / Like the free birds in the jungle, let me be happy.'

But if Rabindranath did not write a fairytale despite abiding by the exterior of a fairytale, did others too not write and leave behind something like neo-fairytales, and deploy the pattern and flavour of folk texts to compose some *bhadralok* narratives for 'enlightened' and literate children?

'What follows inevitably . . .'

'What follows inevitably . . .' – a deep sigh lies concealed beneath the words spoken in such a casual tone. How little in life is within man's control! He has hardly any power to reverse the decree of fate. Everything is predestined. Creation is not without basis; there is a deep design behind it. Man cannot fathom the logic behind one event following another. Even so, it is not difficult for him to sense the gradual unfolding of the inescapable. If one does not accept with a happy heart and ready mind whatever is and continues to be, all that one gains in life are distress and disquiet.

But could the novel whose name is *Dukkhojayir Jayajatra (Victorious Journey of the Conqueror of Sorrow*, 1940) instruct one to appeal to fate with a feeble soul? Can one triumph over sorrow if one does not have the will to combat the power of the adversary? Yet at the very beginning of Dinesh Mukhopadhyay's novel, in fact on page 3, we come across a soliloquizing in a mild tone: 'Whatever followed inevitably . . .'.[185] Entangled in this utterance of the narrator is a description of the life struggle of the hero: fate at one end and heroism at the other. Is there a contradiction between the viewpoints of the deterministic narrator and the self-reliant hero, or does the writer try to demonstrate that there is no incompatibility between the two philosophical notions of determinism and free will? At the end of the novel, the narrator informs us: 'Perhaps the image of the divine finds its realization in human aspiration.'[186] It means that human desires flower while travelling on the path to spiritual fulfilment. An axiomatic truth like 'What followed inevitably . . .' easily finds a place in the hero Mintu's story of how he gained selfhood. But what does the writer mean by human will and God's image? To penetrate the deep mystery of manifested and formless, archetype and its representation, one must know what it is after which 'What followed inevitably . . .', and what it is that happened all the while.

Mintu's world gets transformed and turned around as soon as he steps from boyhood to youth; he sees that 'the entire world is standing on a mound of quick sand. His father's death had not only brought scarcity in their home but also disorder.'[187] What was the state like before the affectionate father's untimely death? 'The picture of their earlier aristocratic life floated before his eyes. The affluence of their business manifested itself in their home: What a huge granary they had for rice! . . . the whole house was alive with people.'[188] One can with aplomb match the first part of 'Kalabati Rajkanya' in *Thakurmar Jhuli* with the picture of this ruined aristocracy: 'The elephants in enclosures meant for them, the horses in their stables, the precious gems in their coffers, the chambers full of gold coins; the Raja had everything. Apart from this, the royal kingdom was replete with ministers, councillors, soldiers and sepoys.'[189] But how one thing leads to another! Many such kings' kingdoms get devastated – the whole country gets infested by monsters who take possession of the royal palace. Did the monsters not ambush Mintu's household too! 'Now all that remained was that enormous palace of the older days which was a wreck . . . but a few days later, the creditors would come to seize their house in place of what was owed to them. They have prepared the decree long ago.'[190] Mintu has to come out leaving his dear palace, with his mother and younger sister beside him. 'Ma stood far away, raised her hands towards the sky and said: God!'[191] In order to articulate all her regret, suffering and harassment, the helpless widow has just one word in her repertoire: 'God'. Immediately after this, the narrator tells us: 'What followed inevitably was that the mother who was radiant with beauty and grace and serene as a goddess . . . had to take up the profession of a maid.'[192] If one describes Mintu's mother's beauty and nature while composing the narrative of the reversal of her fate, the reader's mind inevitably imagines the sad *duorani*'s face. And, the commitment that remains implied at the end of the text, in the sentence 'What followed inevitably . . .', does not remain secret any more. After all the sun and moon are still there; will this grievous injustice not be avenged? Even if the hapless mother has nobody to protect her, is there no God to protect her and is Mintu not beside her? Mintu will go out on a conquering mission, he will remain undaunted by storm and tempest, he will not get flustered by hindrances and hazards. No matter how, he will reach his destination, he will wipe the tears off his mother's eyes and retrieve her lost elegance; the circle will be complete. Mintu is not the kind of boy who will go unnoticed amidst a crowd of average boys; his poor attire is his military disguise – he is actually a prince.

'Mintu also dreamt while sleeping; the group of the conquerors of sorrow was moving on by itself. There were dense woods all around. The intense dark nightmare had surrounded them from all four sides. Even so, instead of getting scared, they continued on their victorious journey with unwavering minds.'[193] From

> some secret core of his mind . . . somebody seemed to say: the conqueror of sorrow would now proceed to an unknown land to accomplish his victorious expedition. In the shady grove of the azure woods there, he would dive into the centre of the pond next to the temple and pick out the diamond case. That case would contain the souls of thousand ogresses. He would slay those and get back his proud trophy.[194]

But princes who are embroiled in difficult struggles have friends as well as enemies. Can one seek out the right path without the unsolicited help and unstinted generosity of friends? In the novel, it is as if the frog and the she-frog engaged in a dialogue atop the branch of a tree, an ancient crone sitting at the curve of the road, a proficient sanyasi, an owl who can prophesy up to three ages, the firm and stable banyan and peepul trees (all stock figures in Bengali fairytales) transformed their apparel, altered their appearance, changed their names and manifested themselves as Santosh Babu, Chatterjee Moshai, Mister Mukherjee and Soumya. In the list of Mintu's well-wishers, the person whose name is written in the boldest letters is not a character in the novel. Despite that, Mintu has been inspired by him to suffer the travails of rough times and be strong on the basis of his own self-confidence.

When Mintu goes out of the village on a pilgrimage and reaches Calcutta, he pays his respect towards his mentor: 'Before him was the image of Vidyasagar.'[195] The place for establishing Vidyasagar's statue had been selected with care: 'Here one could see the university building and Vidysagar's statue.'[196] Mintu goes to see it whenever he can. Seeing it over and over again, 'He felt tempted. This was the university where the repository of the world's knowledge eagerly awaited working for human welfare.'[197] Adjacent to the university is 'the most esteemed college in Bengal – Presidency College'.[198] Vidyasagar's idol, Presidency College and Calcutta University mingle in Mintu's mind and become one and the same. Does the prince of *Dukkhojayir Jayajatra* who is overwhelmed by the lure of education rise from the pages of *Barna Parichay*? Was it Gopal, the considerate and well-behaved boy, who played false with his name and entered Dinesh Mukhopadhyay's novel?

As in *Barna Parichay*, in *Dukkhojayir Jayajatra* too there is constant use of various verb forms for 'studying' one's lessons. Mintu's mother says to him constantly: 'Study. Study with concentration.'[199] Outwardly grave, imposing and ill-tempered but tender inside, made of conflicting gentle and harsh aspects, Santoshbabu, the schoolmaster with meagre wages, desires that 'Mintu should grow up and be educated.' Hearing that Mintu would stop studying and take up a downright clerical job, he 'does not feel happy from within'.[200] It is he who sends him to Calcutta. After Mintu grows up through his own efforts, Santoshbabu finds him a job in Mr Chatterjee's textile shop. It not only provides Mintu food and clothing, but he is also able to carry on with his studies. The more Mr Chatterjee, who appreciates merit in other people, sees of the honest, industrious and virtuous Mintu, the more pleased he is. Mr Chatterjee thinks once that he would have Mintu collaborate in his own business; but since he is not governed by a petty or selfish intelligence, he changes his opinion thinking of Mintu and the nation. He calls Mintu and says to him:

> My desire was to keep you within this trade and business . . . but I reflected on it and realized that if an able boy like you studies more, you could be engaged in something greater than business. Of course, the industry and commerce of the nation is not something to be trivialized – this is what brings the country wealth and enhances its prestige. But you need to study; there is a need for honest people in different sectors of the country.[201]

In Mr Chatterjee's shop, one day Mintu comes face to face with a distinguished customer. That he is distinguished is obvious from his very countenance – 'a fair form and proportionate build'. He is not just treated to a glimpse of him; in an unexpected way, he is also introduced to him. The distinguished person is 'a professor of English literature in Presidency College, member of the Imperial Service, IES'.[202] Through that very introduction, Mintu progresses one more step in his journey towards conquering sorrow. Of course he would; for one, Mr Mukherjee is a professor of English literature, that too in Presidency College. Over and above that, he is a member of the Imperial Education Service.

A universal feature of adolescent literature about education in Bengali is its reverence for teachers of English, and its contempt and neglect of the Sanskrit pandit. Bengali writers have constantly underscored the humiliation and distress experienced by those who are followers of eastern methods of education. Along with this, they have sung eulogies to the triumph of western education through which one can access that repository of universal knowledge for human well-being that was waiting to be tapped. Through this very education, another world opened out for the Bengali *bhadralok*; the landscape of their knowledge got altered. The wondrous significations of the western world that they gathered from history simultaneously inspired and moved them. The European Renaissance, the Reformation, the Enlightenment, the western practice of rationalism and democratic revolutions – all became sources of inspiration and examples eminently worthy of emulation. And have not many learned men lost their sense of direction in the futile hope of constructing their own reality and history according to the rationale of the European model – as if there was no alternative to the narrative of European history; as if all our endeavours would be futile if we did not match our native narratives step by step with that singular narrative; as if all problems would cease if one could 'emulate the call of the tempest'[203] of an alien land. Irrespective of whether one succeeds in laying the strong foundation stone of western capitalism, one can construct a monument to the many-splendoured western thought. Behind such heartrending anxiety is a deep sense of inferiority induced by discourses that in turn were products of the power–knowledge complex. But even though the Bengali *bhadralok* welcomed wholeheartedly the bourgeois class of England – the chief pioneers of socio-economic, political and cultural transformation of a new England – and desired to become their mirror image, it was not possible in reality. The reason was that where the engine that drove English society was the English bourgeois class, the *bhadralok* community of Bengal was completely dissociated from the means or constituents of production. Moreover, those were in the control of the English bourgeoisie, the ideal of the Bengali middle class. Was it not due to this ruler–ruled relationship that the Bengali *bhadralok* had to, perforce, choose the role of the follower? In the novel *Dukkhojayir Jayajatra*, Mintu thinks, 'The Bengali is so poor today because he has forgotten how to conduct business.'[204] Was it not the same Mintu who, responding to Mr Chatterjee's advice about leaving business and becoming a salaried person, stared 'with an admiring look' without blinking his eyes[205] at the celebrated and great man?

Mintu observes that in an uncanny sort of way, thanks to the mercy of Mr Mukherjee, member of the Imperial Education Service and professor of English Literature, the doors of Presidency College open to him one day; not only does he get a place in the college but also in the hostel. After getting admitted into the college Mintu discovers, thanks to the English education there, perhaps: 'No, there is no such pettiness here. Nobody desires to know who is poor and who is rich.'[206]

In the hostel, he gets acquainted with Binay and Soumya. Binay is *binay* (modest) only in name; nobody can match him in bragging. And Soumya is extremely modest and free of arrogance, 'although he is the only son of a Kumar Bahadur' and the owner of unlimited wealth. 'His [Mintu's] opinion regarding rich people changes instantly during his life at the hostel.'[207] What next? At the end of a phase of extreme rigour accompanying a difficult resolve, Mintu passes the IA examination attaining the first position. 'Even the sahib principal of the college' praises him.[208] The word 'even' above is full of signification. The sahibs occupy a place over and above that of everybody else in a stratified society. The next stratum is occupied by the Bengali *bhadralok*, but the *bhadralok* community is also divided in many ways. In order to differentiate between the social prestige of schoolmasters with meagre wages, shopkeepers and professors of English language, the titles 'Babu', 'Mashai' and 'Mister', respectively, are used. Simultaneously, the word 'even' in the sentence above suggests how far Mintu, the conqueror of sorrow, will go – and where his triumphal chariot will stop.

At the end of the story, the village boy comes back to his village in the guise of a conqueror. People come rushing to the bank of the Batashi river to greet him. Hiralalbabu, member of the Union Board, gets into a great flurry to entertain his guest. There is a great stir all over the village. The chief superintendent of the police station welcomes the prince with an obsequious gesture. But ignoring all, Mintu proceeds towards the ordinary cook at Hiralalbabu's house. Mintu's mother hugs her son. 'The captive prince has returned today.'[209] He has cast aside his camouflaged identity and manifested himself in his own person. Mintu is worthy of everybody's awe and respect; he is the absolute ordainer, a highly placed government employee – a magistrate. The story cannot proceed beyond this. In the account of Mintu's gradual improvement, there is an automatic full stop. Even if the curiosity of the audience or reader is not gratified, the narrator's mouth is sealed. He will have to repeatedly utter the same words: 'The magistrate then started governing happily.' Behind the narrator's inability lies not only the structure of the fairytale narrative, but also the limit of the *bhadralok*'s resolution of his own life. If one accepts the fairness of British rule and educational policy, the story has just enumerated 'What followed inevitably . . .'. If one is a follower of the royal will in the name of God's will, can one's dream of attaining one's inherent power be realized?

It is noticeable that the novel *Dukkhojayir Jayajatra* was published in 1940, yet there is no reference in it at all to the National Movement or the Second World War, as if there was nothing called a world outside. Instead of getting embroiled unnecessarily in riots and uprisings, the lives of Gopals are worthwhile if they can keep studying with concentration – as if just by persistent effort in one's studies one can reach the pinnacle of success. The novel is governed by a very simple, linear myth of progress. The *bhadralok* narrative composed in the camouflaged mould of the *lok kahini* (folktale) therefore documents no class distinction and has modulation of voice. The language of the single-dimensional novel is also commensurate: it is bloodless and static; it has neither radiance nor flavour. Due to its single dimension, there is no need for much invention in the skill of its composition or in the presentation of its subject. Story after story can be constructed in the same format and with the same appearance. Consequently, within two years of the publication of *Dukkhojayir Jayajatra*, Dinesh Mukhopadhyay was able to publish another children's novel along the same lines: *Tepantarer Math*.

Often, even the names of stories and novels have been virtually the same. For instance, let us take Sukumar De Sarkar's *Dukkhojayer Mantra* (1354, Bengali calendar). The narrator lets us know at the end of the story, on behalf of the protagonist Indrasen: 'Today, he has got the charm by which to overcome sorrow – hard work, contentment, love. He will spread these charms all over so many states and countries. Before him are his new inspiration and a new world.'[210] But long before Indrasen, another group of people have spread over many states and countries a new inspiration in search of a new world. If Indrasen speaks in unison with them, will it not be counterproductive? More importantly, even if they so desire, will they be able to sing in one voice? In the colonial period, quite a lot was written about gradual advancements in family life in the English language too. Even if there is not much provision for enjoyment there, there is no scarcity of spirit. Although the simple, linear myth of progress may seem the same in structure everywhere, its meaning is bound to change with differences in spatial and temporal location. Evidence of how much its import could change is provided by the classic English novel for adolescents of the colonial era, Thomas Hughes' (1822–1896) *Tom Brown's School Days* (1857).

Once there lived Brown

Tom Brown's School Days starts with a eulogy of the Brown clan. The Browns are people of a very simple and innocent nature – they are stubborn but hardworking. Yet they are the ones who have repressed the world. Whether in America's jungles or the mountainous regions of Australia, where is their authority not felt and where have they not left an imprint? Wherever the English army or navy has planted its flag of victory, the Browns have shown evidence of their valour. At the root of all of England's military achievements is their bravery and bodily strength. There may be differences in opinion about the scholarship, intelligence and good looks of the Browns, but nobody will deny that they are a belligerent race. Their house is in White Horse Vale – that sacred locale where, shattering the power of the Danes, the noble-minded Alfred had irrevocably established the bond between England and the Christian faith.

One of these Browns is Tom. Tom's father is an unadulterated Tory; he has an unwavering reverence for God and king. Tom's mother is a talented woman; many know her by her specific appellation. Madam Brown's reputation as a skilled 'teacher of servants' is quite widespread. One of the servants who receives such a suitable education is Benji. It is the same Benji who narrates legends of the Brown family to Tom; he recounts with relish tales of heroism of Tom's forefathers. The qualities of the Browns are elaborated not only by Benji but by the narrator himself, in the beginning of the novel, borrowing Benji's voice to express his own views. Using Benji, an 'able' representative of those who live by their labour, as a mouthpiece, the narrator embarks on a direct and dual conversation with a section of the community of readers: 'You people (intellectuals, parliamentarians, etc.) want to persuade us by writing reports in newspapers that you belong to the same category as us, that is the working class. God forbid! Please spare us! The cities are far too civilized, far too polished.'[211]

What is the objective of this verbal artistry? Does Thomas Hughes want to point a finger at the discrepancy between the upper and the lower classes, or does he want to camouflage the truth of disputes and clashes even as he foregrounds the subject of the hierarchy of classes? In reality, Thomas Hughes had an indefatigable eagerness and enthusiasm about working-class people. In his personal life, he had undertaken many ventures for the improvement and welfare of the working class. Was there some pressure of anxiety working beneath so much enterprise? Hughes was a 'Christian socialist'. He used to teach voluntarily and regularly in a night school in a slum of London. He was involved with the Cooperative Movement. And it was through his effort that the 'Working Men's College' was founded in London. Like the hero Tom of his novel *Tom Brown's School Days*, Thomas Hughes was born in White Horse Vale; and like Tom, he too went to study in the famous Warwickshire Rugby School. Was there any connection between Hughes' benevolence towards workers and his having received his education in Rugby School?

The reason for the fame of Rugby School was not just that a game was named and popularized courtesy its patronage. The chief reason was that the proverbial Dr Thomas Arnold held the post of principal of Rugby School for fifteen long years (1828–1842). Dr Arnold's theory and methodology of education not only changed the strategy of running schools, but brought honour and approbation to the institution called the 'public school'. At the time that he took charge at the helm of Rugby School, there were great transformations going on in England. After much debate, discussion and excitement, the Reform Act was accepted in 1832, by which the middle classes were able to appropriate quite a lot of land from the aristocratic community. Thanks to the Reform Act, behind which were the contributions of Bentham, Mill, Grant Jr., Macaulay and many others, the middle classes also got the right to vote. It was about this Reform Bill that Rammohun Roy wrote in a letter to William Rathbone on 31 July 1832, that he was extremely happy the Bill was entirely successful despite the aristocratic community's excessive opposition and pathetic dearth of political ethics. Conveying his hearty congratulations, he said: 'I thank God that I can now feel pride as a fellow subject of yours. I can express sincere joy that I had the unbounded good fortune to see the liberation of a nation – not only a nation, but of the entire world.'[212] Despite Rammohun's exhilaration, however, there is no way out but to acknowledge that the liberation of the world was a far cry – for, thanks to the Reform Act, the condition of the working classes of England became even more critical. In the Reform Act, the right to vote was linked with the subject of wealth, and because of that, the workers lost whatever little rights they had before – for instance, in Westminster or Preston. The middle classes got the political right to participate in parliamentary elections but the working classes were deprived. At the very moment of the success of the middle classes were sown the seeds of a future conflict.

It was Thomas Arnold's most sincere belief that this potential conflict could be avoided, and that although it is difficult to find an antidote to class struggle, it was not impossible. He wanted boys not just from families of aristocrats, noblemen or clergy, but also from families of the upwardly mobile and sons of industrialists, to get a place in public schools. Through education, they would all realize that if one was not a dutiful citizen, if one was not aware of one's responsibilities towards the 'public', social integration would be endangered, and the social system nurtured with care would be shattered.[213] The moment in which the Reform Act was activated was significant from many perspectives. It was the golden age of England's imperialist expansion. Is there any doubt, therefore, that colonial subjects also got a place in Arnold's list of the 'public'? He himself used to run the school along the lines of ruling an empire. Groups of British administrators would pass out of the public schools and get scattered, with the noble intention of maintaining 'peace' and 'stability', all across the different colonies of Great Britain. Through that relationship, all inner discontent would be kept at bay. Even in the administrative system of Rugby School, workers and colonial subjects were linked in an inextricable bond. Thomas Arnold was lucky not only in his students but also his children. One of his sons, Matthew Arnold (1822–1888), was the author of *Culture and Anarchy* (1869); another son, William Arnold, was the Chief of Public Instruction in Punjab. One gave some thought to his nation, the other to its colony.

The novel *Tom Brown's School Days* was what Thomas Hughes, Thomas Arnold's direct student, offered him as teacher's remuneration. In this novel full of autobiographical components, the same thing is said in many different and roundabout ways. The ideal students of public schools should engage themselves in service to the people of their country. By combining 'responsibility' with 'duty', they should observe civility and avoid mischief with their body, mind and soul. Encouraging softness and sentimentality is likely to lead to the end of all manliness, and to a waste of human effort. Of course, at the end of the novel, the author conveys that it is only through a combination of motherly–sisterly–wifely love, tenderness and chastity, and the strength, courage and wisdom of father–mother–teacher, that one can attain the all-virtuous God.[214] Even so, in the material world, it is desirable that at least the social roles of men and women should remain separate. In the novel, Thomas Hughes demonstrates that Dr Arnold had cultivated and honed the abilities that had been coursing through the aristocratic blood of the Browns through successive generations. The revered principal had instructed how to augment England's savings of several ages with interest.

A brilliant instance of this increase in interest can be cited from the cover of a compilation of government documents on education that included Macaulay's 1835 Minutes. This colonial compilation was published by the Baptist Mission Press in 1862, and the compiler was H. Woodrow, Inspector of Schools.

On the cover of the collection, a few lines of information about the compiler were offered: H. Woodrow was a student of Rugby School; he was a staunch devotee of Thomas Arnold. Thomas Hughes found in him the inspiration for one of the characters in *Tom Brown's School Days*; if that was so, that character must have been constructed by combining blazing masculinity and tremendous honesty.[215] Would the combined presence of Thomas Arnold and *Tom Brown's School Days* on the jacket of an entire compilation of colonial documents really be too bewildering?

The muscle-flexing Tom and Mintu humbled by diffidence are inhabitants of two opposite regions. The Toms say that they want to grab everything. The Mintus do not have such lofty aspirations; their aim is limited. The Toms know how to snatch by their skill, strength and strategy; the Mintus have not received such 'wicked education'. They just go on taking examinations – the cycle of their examinations never ends. Because they are stuck in the periphery defined by first-boy and last-boy, the value of prizes–scholarships–awards is a lot for the Mintus – implying the Gopals.

The Iron Fetters of First-Boy and Last-Boy

The revered Ganak Thakur (fortuneteller) knows everything. He does not have to read hands or frame horoscopes – by just looking at the face and demeanor of the questioners, he can tell who is good and who is bad, whose future is bright and whose dark. When someone says, 'Ganak Thakur, I greet thee / Please foretell my future / I fall at thy feet',[216] Ganak Thakur understands immediately that he is very polite and unassuming. On the other hand, when someone comes and calls out, 'Why, Thakur, are you silent with your face covered by your hand? / You have to read what is written about my future, it would not do to be clever',[217] there is no doubt that he will incur the displeasure of the fortuneteller. The indisputably successful picture of the first boy or the good boy floats in the inner eye of the fortuneteller: 'Day by day, he will become learned / His honour will be broadcast within the country and outside / All his life, he will live in health and happiness / He will bide his time, laughing and dancing with joy.'[218] The astrologer unhesitatingly tells the second boy or the bad boy of his inevitably pathetic end: 'I realized long ago, seeing your looks and trend, / That if you don't mend your ways, in misfortune you'll end / Like the oil mill all night you will snore / And spend your day begging from door to door.'[219] The 'bad boy' only likes to play and sleep; he does not bother with rules and regulations. And Ganak Thakur? He knows everything. He seems to have a third eye, and knowledge about the past, present and future. Not only is he Ganak Thakur in Jogindranath Sarkar's (1866–1937) book *Khelar Gaan* (*Playful Song*), but, under different names and in different ways, he pervades all of Bengali children's literature. The world of the child is clearly divided into black and white; on the line at the centre, guards stand watch continually. Their observation is always alert. These are the sentries who control and determine the past, the present and the future of these children.

The idea of good and bad in children is so rigid that in most cases the narratorial stance does not change with change in authorship. Everybody writes the same story tirelessly – a story that seems to have no beginning and no end. In a transient world, it is a perpetual play of pass and fail, reward and reprimand, welcome and farewell, blessing and curse. A few excerpts worth citing are as follows. 'The good boy struts / With joy in his heart / He has earned a reward / After his heart / The bad boy stands / Like a beast / With a dunce cap on his head / What a great prize!' (Jogindranath Sarkar, 'Bhalo Chhele Manda Chhele' ['The Good Boy and the Bad Boy'], in *Rangachhobi*, 1895).[220] 'The Inspector Mahashay blessed him. The Mahashays blessed him. Wearing a gold medal, Haru went to touch his father's feet. Charu went home alone with a tarnished face' (Dakshinaranjan Mitra Majumdar, *Charu o Haru*, 1912).[221]

> Mr Gupta had entered the police department as an ordinary sub-inspector, but he had become an employee in a high post through his own merit. . . . As a reward for his work, he has got the title 'Rai Saheb' from the government. And it has become almost public knowledge that soon, on the occasion of the birthday of the Raja, his name would be there in the list of the Rai Bahadurs in the ceremony for distribution of titles. (Nripendra Krishna Chattopadhyay, *Udashi Babar Akhra* [*Udashi Baba's Den*], 1942).[222]

'And in the annual examination, I stood first in Sanskrit and English; and in the overall I was first, equalling the exact marks that Jogesh got. Both of us got the same prize. In the prize meeting, we sat next to the Headmaster on the first bench'[223] (Dakshinaranjan Mitra Majumdar, 'Last Boy', 1927). 'You will be surprised to hear that in subsequent days, [Paramanand] passed his M.A. too. Now he does a wonderful clerk's job at fifty rupees salary in Macpherson and Macpherson' (Saroj Kumar Roy Choudhury, 'Paramanander Bipad' [Paramanand's Misfortune], in *Rangin Akash*, 1940).[224]

> The gentleman has returned to India after acquiring learning by wandering around in many famous European countries like England and Germany. This time the prize-giving was getting rather delayed in wavering over selecting the chairman. Around this time, reading about the England-returned gentleman, seeing his photographs and learning about his achievements, the Headmastermashai thought of getting the matter of prize-giving over and done with by making him the chairman. (Nikhilesh Sen, 'Paribartan' ['Transformation'], in *Romanchakar Kahini*, 1941)[225]

> If asked how far he had studied, Habul would say, 'Up to the pre-Matric class'. Whatever the word might mean, Habul used to believe that everything from class one to nine was all pre-Matric. By this reckoning, it was enough that he did not

introduce himself as an 'undergraduate'. (Nanigopal Chakrabarty, 'Bidyarthi Habul' ['Habul the Student'], in *Ramdhanu*, Kartik 1349)[226]

One can cite innumerable utterances like this. Many writers, both well known and relatively unknown, have reiterated this same point year after year, decade after decade. These perpetual exemplars have multiplied the incantatory powers and the enchanting illusion of the myth of 'first-boy–last-boy' several times over. No special transgression of the archetypes of Gopal and Rakhal, constructed in Vidyasagar's *Barna Parichay*, has taken place. Now the question is: what is the view of those who are circumscribed within the parameters of first-boy–last-boy about writers located outside its peripheries? In a story called 'Oder Bibek Buddhi' ('Their Sense and Conscience') by Ashalata Sinha, she says, addressing her readers: 'You people whose parental homes are in Ballygunje, whose Mama's house is in Bhabanipur and Mashi's house is in Bagbajar, will not understand anything. To understand this narrative, you also have to go to Palashpur with me – at least mentally, in sympathy and imagination.'[227] But what, after all, is the extent of that sympathy and imagination? It will be noticed that the mental attitude of children within the type of first-boy–last-boy towards these 'others' (people who work) is basically of two kinds: either contempt or compassion.

In Saroj Kumar Roy Choudhury's 'Paramanander Bipad', the narrator is able to inform us with aplomb: 'It is not necessary for the sons of *bhadralok* to keep in good health. They, after all, are not going to do farming, nor will they work as coolies at Howrah station.'[228] It implies that intellectual effort is a class apart from physical labour. By the power of the infallible rules of classifying labour, the former has gone to the share of *bhadralok*, the latter to *chhotolok*. Paramanand goes astray by keeping bad company. Who are his companions? 'Do the sons of *bhadralok* have time? They have studies and school. He has got into the company of the sons of *chhotolok*. They have nothing to do with studies or school. Some of them are cowherds, some fishermen and some farmers.'[229] Why do *chhotolok* not have lessons or school? The *bhadralok* narrator, of course, does not bother himself with this question. The source of the strengths and weaknesses of this kind of narrative is the homogeneity of the narratorial pose. Since there is no variety of expression, one single utterance occupies the entire space of the narrative. Due to the strength of that reiteration, the difference between the writer-narrator and reader gets erased. The predominance of one view or ideology gets established through the single pronouncement – that ideology overwhelms the reader's consciousness. On the other hand, a homogenous narratorial stance is monotonous and cannot be classified. Consequently, it never completely influences the mind of the reader; there remains a gap somewhere. A massive portion of Bengali children's literature provides evidence of how terrible the modest Gopals can become in order to fill that gap. Of course, there are many Gopals who are *bhadralok* through and through. Their sensibility prevents them from being contemptuous towards or dismissing the *chhotolok*. An endless compassion fills their heart about those who are starving and half-starved.

In Dakshinaranjan Mitra Majumdar's 'Charu o Haru', Charu, the son of the upstart zamindar of Roopnathpur, and the modest Haru, the son of a poor tenant, study in the same school. By his very nature, Haru, the conqueror of misery, leaves Charu, who is spoilt silly by pampering, far behind in studies. One can very well expect the story to pave the way for an exceedingly conflicting situation: that the rise of sons of tenants might cause the fall of princes. In fact one day it is about to happen likewise, but Haru's father, Paran, the eternally oppressed tenant, prevents it. When Charu crosses the limits of persecuting Haru, he explodes in a rage that he has nurtured for long: 'He leapt like a lion to seize Charu.' Seeing such a monstrous event about to take place, Paran comes running with a loud exclamation: 'Haru! Haru! Oh what are you doing? Disaster!' He explains to his son later:

> Khokonbabu has hit you – he is a zamindar, a Raja – is that how you are supposed to behave with him? . . . If Khokonbabu has done you any wrong, please forget about it. Greet him with folded hands when you meet him. He is greater than you – a zamindar – he is akin to God.[230]

Is this merely a statement of Paran, steeped in his servility? Or does this statement also demonstrate the endorsement of the narrator? The doubt is dispelled in the very next sentence. Haru feels ashamed and contrite about his momentary weakness: 'Haru heard everything that his father had to say. . . . He paid obeisance to Charu mentally. . . . He forgot how much Charu had tyrannized over him.'[231] The sooner and more easily the Harus forget the 'tyranny' inflicted by the Charus, the more propitious it bodes all around and the more permanent the age-old system will be. At the end of the story, although Haru gets a gold medal and Charu is made to wear a dunce-cap, the social structure remains undamaged and the status quo is not tampered with. There is no damage to the stable arrangement. Although Haru is the son of a tenant, he is well-behaved, considerate and like the son of a *bhadralok* should be. Although he was born into the household of a peasant, there is not the slightest doubt that in course of time, he will be counted among *bhadralok* society. Here too it is the same assimilation – the chief strategy by which potential rebellion or protest can be repressed.

Is this a consequence of Macaulay and Trevelyan's filtration theory? Could anything else have been possible? Was the flow of knowledge and the dissemination of power not contiguous from the very beginning? The greatness of this amazing flow of sensibility is described in many Bengali schoolboy stories. In order to appreciate this greatness fully, 'one has to see, to begin with, from where and how the sap collects at the root of this illusory universal tree'.[232]

In the story 'Charu o Haru', the *bhadralok*'s effort towards assimilation has been excessively exposed. Other Gopals have proceeded with much greater caution. They have come in the garb of well-wishers, for instance, in the novel *Dui Bhai* (*Two Brothers*) by Achintya Kumar Sengupta, written in the 1940s. Binay, the son of a zamindar, seethes in rage inwardly on seeing his father's oppression of the poor. He vows to redress the misfortunes of those who are mistreated. Binay explains to his father who is obsessed with power: 'Are the subjects not the children of the zamindar? We will rule them and exploit them, but will we not look after them or save them from distress?'[233] Dipak, the hero of Jogeshchandra Bandyopadhyay's play, *Bidrohi* (*Rebel*, 1926), says the same thing. He and his accomplices get together and put to shame Dashu Ray, the oppressive zamindar of Keshavpur. At the end of the play, the repentant zamindar appeals to the student Dipak: 'Now tell me Dipak, counsel me about how I could do penitence for my sins.' By way of reply, Dipak reiterates an oft-heard truism: 'All of us in Keshavpur – Hindus, Muslims, all – comprise but a large family! The guardian and leader of this family is you.' An eminent example of how to broach the subject of the custodianship of 'aristocrats' after mixing and blending both native and foreign narratives is Narendra Deb's *Parag o Renu* (1944). In the preface to a reprint of the book, Narendra Deb wrote:

> In my adolescent years, I was once impressed by a famous novel from a foreign land. When I sat down to narrate a long story to the children of the '*pathshaala*' at their request, this story that I had read as an adolescent crept into my mind again and again. In the narrative content of the novel, therefore, its influence has greatly expressed itself.

The famous foreign novel which the narrative content of *Parag o Renu* resembles almost *ad verbatim* is Frances Hodgson Burnett's *Little Lord Fontleroy*, published in 1886. In the original novel, Cedric Errol is a boy who belongs to New York city. Having lost his father very early in his life, he receives unstinted affection from his mother. Despite that, he is not spoilt; he is able to draw everyone towards him by virtue of his good behaviour. He does not look at anybody in a demeaning manner. His best friend is the owner of a grocery store. That person, a hardcore Republican, is his ideal. One fine day he gets to know that his father was the grandchild of an English lord who had been disinherited by his grandfather because he had married an American woman. At the command of his grandfather, Cedric undertakes a voyage to England. Although his mother is with him, once they reach England he and his mother are housed in different places. The old man is not willing to accept an American woman as his daughter-in-law. She is therefore housed at some distance from Cedric. But under the influence of Cedric's gentle nature, his irascible, uncivil and perverse grandfather undergoes a change of heart. Thanks to the grandson, prosperity returns to the landlord; all the subjects acclaim this in one voice. Subsequently, when Cedric gets embroiled in a conspiracy involving property, his Republican friend comes forward to rescue him. When all the turmoil comes to an end, Cedric's grandfather accepts his daughter-in-law with welcoming words. After so long, his mind's eye is opened. He is able to perceive the nobility of character of Cedric's mother's. And Cedric's Republican friend too changes his views and gets converted to be a supporter of the English aristocratic class.

The outline of *Parag o Renu* is very like the original story. The arrogant Raja Mahendra Ray has disinherited his eldest son Ranendra Ray for marrying Uma, the poor daughter of a commoner's household. The son of Ranendra, who had an untimely demise, is the tender-hearted, undefiled-by-sin Parag, who grows up in Calcutta. There, he develops a close friendship with the owner of a stationery shop, Kalibabu. Almost every day, Kalibabu gives Parag lectures about how worthless the parasitical zamindars are, and how hollow their pride of status, wealth and false aristocracy has made them. The later events in the Bengali novel are also akin to the English original.

Our subject of discussion here, however, is the ideological agreement or disagreement between *Parag o Renu* and *Little Lord Fontleroy*, rather than the similarities in their narratives. At the beginning of the Bengali novel, Kalibabu is an uncompromising critic of the zamindar Ranendra. Being able to gauge his views to a certain extent, the Diwanji of Lakshmipur suspects that the man must be a devotee of the ideals of Soviet Russia. At the polar opposite end of Kalibabu's ideals is Raja Bahadur Mahendra Ray. An extravagant and oppressive zamindar, he takes an exaggerated pride in his lineage. In between these two extreme ends is Parag, brought up by the education of Uma who functions from behind the wings. Parag is just a necessary agent who uncompromisingly resolves the opposition between these two contradictory ideologies; he is just an instrument to bring about the rule of symmetry. On the one hand, his unlimited innocence and compassion assists Kalibabu to mellow the high-pitched tone of his extreme viewpoints. On the other hand, he converts the formidable zamindar, insolent in his pride, into a kindly man who wishes everybody well. Eventually, the novel distances itself from being a critique of the cult of aristocracy and situates itself at a middle point; a 'bad' and a 'good' zamindar are both equally feasible there. If the large wealth that the zamindar controls is used in an honest and unselfish manner for the welfare of the subjects, if the zamindar becomes an executor devoted to justice, there is no need to make additions or alterations to the basic system. Kalibabu, however, is not satisfied by these benevolent acts. He wants that the wealth should be converted to capital, that many factories should be established in the country, that many industrial endeavours should become visible, and that the zamindar should change his mask and become a capitalist. The grandson of Diwanji, Nitai, a representative of the new age, says to the face of the powerful and majestic zamindar: 'The wealthy, the worker, the zamindar and his subjects – none is lesser than the other.' Nitai talks about their dignity, but he has no objection to the unequal distribution of wealth. The Parags of the new age will give voice to the stupid, pallid and dumb lower classes, and the people in the lower rungs will always be overwhelmed with gratitude by the immense magnanimity of the upper classes. This deeprooted belief will be found in many nationalist writers of children's literature. Therefore, when Kalibabu, who has always sharply critiqued all ideas of discrimination in *Parag o Renu*, says to Makhan the sweet-maker, 'What if you are the son of a confectioner? There is not an honest fellow like you in all of *bhadralok* society', it does not seem like a purely unpremeditated utterance. Are there no people in Bengali children's literature who have wanted to come out after breaking the iron fetters of first-boy–last-boy?

Crossing the Threshold of First-Boy and Last-Boy

Many have wanted to, but how many have eventually been able to do it? This torment of failure is there in Rabindranath Tagore's 'Chhuti' just as it is there in *Totakahini*. Phatik in 'Chhuti' too initially jumps around, takes wing, does not read the classics and does not know etiquette, like the bird in *Totakahini*. Everybody got hold of this totally 'stupid' boy and tried to make a pandit out of him. Yet right next to him is Makhan – his 'quiet, well-behaved brother who was dedicated to learning'. One should oil heads that are already oily, that is what makes those heads blossom – at least the Rakhals believe that. Phatik has neither ever been able to express these words frankly, nor does he ever get an occasion to do so. Letting Makhan remain with his mother, Bishambharbabu brings the unruly, disobedient Phatik, inattentive to his lessons, to Calcutta. Phatik's chapter of reformation starts under the guardianship of his *mama* Bishambharbabu and his *mami*. But in a city made of suffocating bricks-and-stones, he feels cooped up and asphyxiated. Greatly distanced from the plenitude of nature and far away from his mother, he cannot get himself to adjust within this life. Neither is he able to become a self-confident student. Ultimately, thwarting all attempts to convert him to a Gopal, the 'useless, eccentric, stupid' boy takes his 'leave' from this world. In Rabindranath's story, the word '*chhuti*' is a pun. Both connotations – 'freedom to function without any constraints' as well as 'death' – are suggested through the word. Phatik has to take leave ('*chhuti*') because he has no freedom ('*chhuti*').

In the two ironical uses of the word '*chhuti*', there is the hint of the two-fold strategy of violating the paradigm of first-boy–last-boy. Those who want by no means to be Gopals have two roads open before them: either to remove themselves from the world, or to create for themselves an ambience for entertaining themselves replete with humour, colour and amusement. Their repudiation takes one of two forms: either a sad departure or an incisive, sometimes bitter, sarcasm. Of course, there is an underlying path that traverses back and forth between departure and sarcasm, sadness and bitterness.

In the compilation of stories titled *Boarding School* (1932) by Mohanlal Gangopadhyay, there is the sadness of bidding farewell. Although the stories are somewhat unconnected, they are loosely and mutually related through the link of the same narrator. The narrator, Bahadur, suffers many bereavements one after another. Two close friends of his die in separate and unnatural accidents. The innocuous simpleton of the class, Narayan, stands first in his Matriculate examination but goes insane before the result is out. Bahadur's pubescent curiosity is aroused and centred around a girl called Gangamani, but that too ends in separation. The stories in the book, written in a light and gentle tone, are very different from most schoolboy stories.

An example of a second form of repudiation is Abanindranath Tagore's play, *Shib Saudagar* (1325, Bengali calendar), about a village school. The names of the students of the school are Tota, Bhnota, Iching, Biching, Chnachi, Muchi, Shib Saudagar and Bhaluk. Of these, two names are especially suggestive – Tota and Bhnota. Tota is a quiet and well-behaved boy, and a 'pandit', while Bhnota is mischievous, defiant and, literally, 'stupid'. Whereas Tota chews a pencil and says, 'The guru hasn't come, what can one do about the lesson now?' – Bhnota says, 'Anyway, I threw the book into the flood water; all that needs to be done now is to drown the gurumashai.'[234] Bhnota looks askance at Tota: 'There is a kind of bird in our country. It studies whatever you teach it.'[235] Bhnota converts his knowledge gained through education into a weapon. Sensing that the Panditmashai is coming, he says: 'No delay now – sit down with your books – the A for *ajagar aashchhe tere* (*ajagar* [the python] is coming).'[236] Not only that; he and his companions keep disrupting Tota's studies. Tota has nothing to say of his own; he just keeps spewing all the tortuous words he has been taught. And the others comment obliquely and keep providing contorted words. They correlate Tota's lifeless words with their context and invest them with life. For instance, when Tota says, as though reciting a multiplication table, 'cage, hammer, school', Iching suddenly pipes in with a quip: 'castigation'. This fourth word unites the three earlier disparate words. It converts into sentence form, the insufferable experience of student life: in the cage called school, students are castigated with hammers. Whatever else the Rakhals can or cannot do, they experience a different kind of joy in harassing the good boys or seeing them getting harassed.

The hero of Lila Majumdar's 'Bodyinather Bori' ('Quack Doctor's Pill', 1940), Kolu, hearing the Mastermoshai continuously praise his son Bidhushekhar, thinks: 'What a boy indeed this Bidhushekhar was!'[237] Kolu is tired hearing about him but he certainly does not express his state of mind in such language;

when he opens his mouth, he has to be polite and well-mannered. However, this is how a secret weapon is constructed: an uncivil, vulgar tongue to counter civil and genteel language. To get some respite from the Mastermoshai, Kolu feeds him a *bodyinather bori* which he stuffs into his *paan*. He believes that anybody who eats this *bori* does not remain human any more but becomes a monkey. Kolu wants to take revenge on those who brand youngsters with the appellation of 'monkey' day in and day out. And how strange! Mastermoshai disappears on the very day he swallows the *bori*. His father announces, 'Oh Kolu! Your Mastermoshai has become a headmaster and has gone to Bishtupur.' Kolu thinks to himself: 'Why Bishtupur? I would have understood if it was Kishkindha [the legendary kingdom of monkeys].'[238] Although he cannot see the Mastermoshai who gloriously wallows in his fatherly pride in his human form any more, Kolu intermittently visualizes: 'Would those be two long-tailed creatures sitting in the dark on the ledge of that house? One seems familiar; the other one must be Bidhushekhar.'[239]

It is not as if being a Rakhal necessarily entails being reckless. Rakhals too have the fear of losing their security and the apprehension of becoming or producing Gopals. In Lila Majumdar's 'Ganshar Chithi' ('Gansha's Letter', 1940), Gansha pens his anxiety on that score: 'There are a lot of children in the school at the beginning of the year, but at the end, there are only a pathetic few left. Yet Mastermashai's business of goats is flourishing more by the day.'[240] It is Gansha's deepseated belief that Mastermashai's goat business is thriving by grazing students. Lila Majumdar's diminutive Rakhals can really sting, camouflaged behind apparently innocuous postures. But why just Lila Majumdar? Manoranjan Bhattacharya, Sibram Chakraborty, Premendra Mitra, Narayan Gangopadhyay and many others are veterans in this skill. But it is Sukumar Roy who deserves the honour that is due to the pioneer who invented this artistry.

Most of the characters in Sukumar Roy's 'schoolboy' stories and the students in his plays are not at all courteous, gentle or well-behaved. They are inhabitants of the domain of Rakhals. At every step, they confront the hard and fast, finely measured and pre-designed principles and practices of Gopals; they render the socially acceptable appellation of 'good boy' worthy of ridicule. Sukumar Roy made audible the voice of Rakhals that could barely be heard earlier, thanks to the construction and the influence of miniature versions of *bhadralok* (Gopals). It is perhaps not entirely fortuitous that one out of the two stories in *Pagla Dashu* that are obviously didactic is called 'Gopaler Pora' ('Gopal's Studies'). In this story, however, Gopal is a shirker of his studies and, like Vidyasagar's disobedient children, gets his just retribution from mentors. Apart from these two stories, in the others, it is the Rakhals who shame the Gopals. The most shining representative of those Rakhals is Pagla Dashu; he is virtually unparalleled in snubbing the boastful and bragging boys. From the very name Dashu has been given, it can be gauged how extended and how organized the world of Gopals has become, how the Gopals have marginalized the Rakhals, and how firm the foundation of the ideological agency called 'school' has become. The Rakhals are now either rendered mad or assume the posture of madness as a strategy. One cannot resolve whether Dashu is really mad or 'just plays the fool'.[241] Pagla Dashu has been absorbed into a grinding mill of a system that is classified into levels and sub-levels. In that suffocating ambience, Dashu's maverick nature or eccentricity is a proven strategy to alleviate the pressure of unbearable tyranny and devise an open space for himself. How successful he is in this matter, we get to know from what the narrator of 'Pagla Dashu' says: 'If any of us had done such a thing on that day, we would have been punished, but because Dashu is "crazy", he was not punished.'[242] The narrator of 'Chinepatka' ('Fire Crackers') also informs us: 'All the masters went back to their respective classes after some amount of scolding and telling us off. He was not punished because he was "crazy".'[243] His classmates' suspicion about his madness, however, is not removed in any way. If the others make fun of him, he does not get annoyed. In fact he exaggerates over and above their opinion and engages in relating various strange anecdotes about himself. He entraps the so-called good boys who are the epitome of good behaviour and converts them into objects of ridicule. Over and above that, if they are braggarts, they are laughed at even more. Dashu is especially 'generous' to those who are arrogant about their affluence. 'There was no end to Shyamchand's stylishness about his clothes and in his etiquette' because his father used to 'hold a big job in the office of a sahib'.[244] He impresses everybody by displaying his English watch and fountain pen. And the pride of possessing these few English objects changes even the language that he speaks; in every other sentence he intermittently uses English words and phrases like 'slow', 'fast', 'main', 'spring', 'regulate', 'iridium' and 'American Stylo and Fountain Pen Co., Philadelphia'. In the world surrounding Dashu and his friends, the master and those who are mastered keep constantly changing places. It is no wonder that if his classmates ask him why he is wearing pantaloons, Dashu replies, 'In order to learn English properly.'[245]

Sukumar Roy's *Pagla Dashu* is an aberration in every sense of the term of the paradigm of schoolboy stories that was fashioned by Vidyasagar and Dakshinaranjan Mitra Majumdar. His stories overstep the threshold of the 'first-boy'/'last-boy' story. In 'Nandalaler Manda Kapal' ('Nandalal's Bad Luck'), therefore, he can write with great ease: '[Nandalal's] entire mind was focused on studying Sanskrit – that is, on the Sanskrit prize.'[246] He does not study for the sake of studying; he studies with the hope of getting this prize, which is the first-boy's stamp of pedigree. It is because the Pagla Dashus who are the Rakhals of society do not hope to get that prize that they make us alert to the colossal farce that colonial education is. Time and again, they subvert the

Illustration by Abanindranath Tagore in Rabindranath Tagore's *Totakahini*

accepted social codes and systems. In 'Dashur Khyapami' ('Dashu's Whimsy'), in the scene of the play enacted by the boys, Dashu disregards with aplomb the sequence of entrances and exits. Without any reserve, he violates the constraint of fixed dialogues. No one can guess at which instant he will appear saying 'here he comes back again', and muddle up the beginning, middle and end of the play. Not only in this play but Pagla Dashu confounds the determined before-and-after of the farce of *bhadralok* life compiled by the joint contribution of Grant–Bentham–Mill–Macaulay–Rammohun–Vidyasagar and several others. But how much can he achieve all alone! After all, the Gopals stand against him in a single file.

In Vidyasagar's *Barna Parichay*, of the two chief controllers, one is the teacher and the other is the father. The space of the teacher is the school and that of the father is the family. If one divides their domains like this, could one be liable for oversimplification? Would it be a gross error to interchange the names of teacher and father, school and family?

Notes and References

[1] Brajendranath Bandyopadhyay, *Kolikata Sanskrit Colleger Itihas* (*The History of Kolikata Sanskrit College*), Vol. 1: 1824–1858, p. 20.

[2] Ibid., p. 21.

[3] Ishwarchandra Vidyasagar, *Banglar Itihas*, in *Bidyasagar Rachanasamagra*, Vol. 1, Calcutta, 1987, p. 288.

[4] H. Sharp, ed., *Selections from Education Records*, Vol. 1: 1781–1839, Calcutta, 1920, p. 10.

[5] Ibid., p. 11.

[6] Ibid., pp. 11–12.

[7] *Manusamhita*, Shloka 25, translated by Bharatchandra Shiromani and Jadunath Nyaypanchanan, Calcutta, 1336 (Bengali calendar), p. 77.

[8] H. Sharp, ed., *Selections from Education Records*, Vol. 1, p. 79.

[9] Ibid.

[10] Eric Stokes, *The English Utilitarians and India,* Delhi, 1989, pp. 29–30.

[11] H. Sharp, ed., *Selections from Education Records*, Vol. 1, p. 22.

[12] Jeremy Bentham, *Introduction to the Principles of Morals and Legislations*, London.

[13] Michel Foucault, *Discipline and Punish: The Birth of the Prison*, Harmondsworth: Penguin, 1982, pp. 104–31.

[14] Karl Marx, *Das Kapital*, Vol. 1, London, 1979, p. 280.

[15] Foucault, *Discipline and Punish*, p. 137.

[16] Jashodhara Bagchi, 'Review of *The English Utilitarians and India*', *Nineteenth Century Studies* (editor: Alok Ray), No. 11, July 1975, p. 383.

[17] James Mill, *The History of British India*, Vol. 1, London, 1848, p. 385.

[18] Bhaskar Roy, *Scientific Realism and Indian Emancipation*, London, 1986, p. 226.

[19] James Mill, 'On Education', in *James and Stuart Mill on Education*, Cambridge, 1931, p. 11.

[20] Ibid., p. 1.

[21] Ibid., p. 61.

[22] H. Sharp, ed., *Selections from Education Records*, Vol. 1, p. 19.

[23] Alexander Duff, 'The Early or Exclusively Oriental Period of Government Education in Bengal', *Calcutta Review*, Vol. 3, No. 4, 1845; reprinted in *Nineteenth Century Studies* (editor: Alok Ray), No. 9, January 1975, p. 29.

[24] H. Sharp, ed., *Selections from Education Records*, Vol. 1, p. 25.

[25] Ibid., p. 91.

[26] Ibid., p. 92.

[27] Ibid., p. 179.

[28] George Otto Trevelyan, *The Life and Letters of Lord Macaulay*, Vol. 1, Oxford, 1978, p. 334.

[29] Ibid., p. 287.

[30] Stokes, *The English Utilitarians and India*, pp. 43–44.
[31] C.B. Macpherson, *The Political Theory of Possessive Individualism: Hobbes to Locke*, Oxford, 1972, pp. 263–71.
[32] Thomas Babington Maculay, *Minutes on Education*, Calcutta, 1835.
[33] Stokes, *The English Utilitarians and India*, p. 39.
[34] Thomas Babington Macaulay, *Minutes on Education.*
[35] H. Sharp, ed., *Selections from Education Records*, Vol. 1, p. 80.
[36] Ibid., p. 126.
[37] Thomas Babington Macaulay, *Minutes on Education.*
[38] H. Sharp, ed., *Selections from Education Records,* Vol. 1, pp. 130–31.
[39] Charles Edward Trevelyan, *On the Education of the People of India*, London, 1838, p. 23.
[40] George Otto Trevelyan, *The Life and Letters of Lord Macaulay*, Vol. 1, p. 421.
[41] Ibid., p. 386.
[42] Charles Edward Trevelyan, *On the Education of the People of India*, p. 193.
[43] John Robert Seeley, *The Expansion of England*, Chicago, 1971, p. 152.
[44] Charles Edward Trevelyan, *On the Education of the People of India*, p. 193.
[45] Ibid., pp. 48–49.
[46] Benoy Ghosh, ed., *Shamayikpatre Banglar Samajchitra* (*The Image of Bengali Society in Contemporary Papers*), Vol. 4, Calcutta, 1980, pp. 309–23.
[47] Ibid., p. 311.
[48] Ibid., p. 323.
[49] Benoy Ghosh, ed., *Shamayikpatre Banglar Samajchitra* (*The Image of Bengali Society in Contemporary Papers*), Vol. 5, Calcutta, 1981, p. 53.
[50] Ibid., p. 54.
[51] Ibid.
[52] Ibid., p. 56.
[53] Ibid., p. 57.
[54] Ibid., p. 26.
[55] Nihar Ranjan Ray and Pratul Chandra Gupta, eds, *Hundred Years of the University of Calcutta*, Calcutta, 1957, p. 34.
[56] Ibid., p. 72.
[57] Benoy Ghosh, ed., *Shamayikpatre Banglar Samajchitra* (*The Image of Bengali Society in Contemporary Papers*), Vol. 3, Calcutta, 1980, p. 199.
[58] Harishchandra Mukherjee, 'Eighteen Fifty Seven', *The Hindu Patriot*, 31 December 1857; reprinted in *Nineteenth Century Studies* (editor: Alok Ray), No. 12, October 1975, p. 451.
[59] H. Sharp, ed., *Selections from Education Records*, Vol. 1, p. 122.
[60] Sumit Sarkar, 'The Complexities of Young Bengal', in *A Critique of Colonial India*, Calcutta, 1985, p. 23.
[61] Gautam Chattopadhyay, ed., *Bengal: Early Nineteenth Century (Selected Documents)*, Calcutta, 1978, pp. 34–35.
[62] Ibid., p. 58.
[63] Sibnath Sastri, *Ramtanu Lahiri o Tatkalin Bangasamaj*, Calcutta, 1977, pp. 46–47.
[64] Ibid., p. 141.
[65] Kishorichand Mitra, 'The Hindu College and Its Founder', in Pyarichand Mitra and Gouranga Gopal Sengupta, eds, *A Biographical Sketch of David Hare*, Appendix B, Calcutta, 1979, p. 154.
[66] Surendranath Bandyopadhyay, 'Lord Macaulay and High Education in India', reprinted in *Nineteenth Century Studies* (editor: Alok Ray), No. 9, July 1979, p. 94.
[67] Charles Edward Trevelyan, *On the Education of the People of India*, pp. 59–60.
[68] Rammohun Roy, *Patrabali*, in Ajit Kumar Ghosh, ed., *Rammohun Rachanabali*, Calcutta, 1973, pp. 433–36.
[69] For a detailed discussion on this subject, see Sibaji Bandyopadhyay, 'Macaulay and Rammohun', in Sayantan Dasgupta, ed., *A South Asian Nationalist Reader*, Delhi, 2007, pp. 135–59.

[70] Michael Edwards, *Bitish India 1772–1949*, London, 1969, p. 142.

[71] Ishwarchandra Vidyasagar, Letter written to F.J. Mowatt, Secretary of the Education Council, translated by Satyabrata Chaudhury, in Santosh Kumar Adhikari, ed., *Bidyasagarer Nirbachita Patrabali (Selected Letters of Vidyasagar)*, Calcutta, 1392 (Bengali calendar), pp. 22–23.

[72] Manmathanath Ghosh, *Manishi Bholanath Chandra*, Calcutta, 1946, p. 142.

[73] Rabindranath Tagore, 'Shikshar Herpher', in *Shiksha*, *Rabindra Rachanabali*, Vol. 12, Calcutta, 1960, p. 281.

[74] Ibid., p. 283.

[75] Rabindranath Tagore, 'Tapoban (1)', in *Shiksha*, *Rabindra Rachanabali*, Vol. 12, pp. 78–101.

[76] Ibid.

[77] Satyendranath Roy, 'Introduction', in Satyendranath Roy, ed., *Rabindranather Chintajagat: Shikshachinta*, Calcutta, 1988, p. 19.

[78] Bankimchandra Chattopadhyay, 'Baro Bajar', *Kamalakanta*, in Gopal Haldar, ed., *Bankim Rachanasamagra*, Calcutta, 1973, pp. 145–46.

[79] Bob Dixon, 'Empire: Fiction Follows the Flag', in *Catching 'Em Young*, Vol. 2, London: 1978, pp. 75–119.

[80] Pyarichand Mitra and Gouranga Gopal Sengupta, eds, *A Biographical Sketch of David Hare*, Calcutta, 1979, pp. 44 and 54.

[81] H. Sharp, ed., *Selections from Education Records*, Vol. 1, p. 29.

[82] Ibid., p. 185.

[83] Khagendranath Mitra, *Shatabdir Shishu Sahitya: 1818–1960*, Calcutta, 1969, p. 77.

[84] Ibid., p. 53.

[85] Pyarichand Mitra and Gouranga Gopal Sengupta, eds, *A Biographical Sketch of David Hare*, p. 54.

[86] C.E. Buckland, *Dictionary of Indian Biography*, Benaras, 1971, p. 263.

[87] Pyarichand Mitra and Gouranga Gopal Sengupta, eds, *A Biographical Sketch of David Hare*, p. 66.

[88] Ramkamal Sen and Officers of the Pathshala of Serampore, 'Introduction', *Hitopadesha*, Calcutta, 1820.

[89] Charles Edward Trevelyan, 'On the Education of the People of India'; Khagendranath Mitra, *Shatabdir Shishu Sahitya: 1818–1960*, p. 34.

[90] Ramkamal Sen and Officers of the Pathshala of Serampore, 'Introduction', *Hitopadesha*.

[91] Khagendranath Mitra, *Shatabdir Shishu Sahitya: 1818–1960*, p. 64.

[92] Anilchandra Das Gupta, ed., 'The Days of John Company', *Selections from Calcutta Gazette, 1824–1832*, Calcutta, 1959, pp. 615–16.

[93] Khagendranath Mitra, *Shatabdir Shishu Sahitya: 1818–1960*, p. 64.

[94] Thomas Babington Macaulay, 'Warren Hastings: An Essay', in *Critical and Historical Essays*, Part 1, London, 1907, pp. 160–200.

[95] Karl Marx, *Grundrisse: Introduction to the Critique of Political Economy*, Harmondsworth: Penguin, 1973, p. 83.

[96] Asha Gangopadhyay, *Bangla Shishusahityer Kramabikash*, Calcutta, 1368 (Bengali calendar), pp. 76–77.

[97] Khagendranath Mitra, *Shatabdir Shishu Sahitya: 1818–1960*, p. 77.

[98] Madanmohan Tarkalankar, *Shishushiksha*, *Part 1*, compiled by Ashish Khastagir, Kolkata, 2003, p. 32.

[99] For a detailed discussion on this subject, see Sibaji Bandyopadhyay, *Abar Shishushiksha*, Kolkata, 2010, pp. 19–26.

[100] Ishwarchandra Vidyasagar, Advertisement for *Barna Parichay*, *Part 2*, 62nd edition, in *Bidyasagar Rachanabali*, Calcutta, 406 (Bengali calendar), p. 1021.

[101] Ishwarchandra Vidyasagar, Advertisement for *Shishushiksha*, *Part 3*, 91st edition, Calcutta, 1900.

[102] Bipin Behari Gupta, 'Puratan Prashanga', Section 1, Calcutta, pp. 53–54.

[103] Madanmohan Tarkalankar, *Shishushiksha*, *Part 3*, revised by Ishwarchandra Vidyasagar, Calcutta, 1900, pp. 6–15.

[104] Satishchandra Chakrabarti, 'Post Script 11', *Devendranath Tagore's Autobiography*, Section 6, Calcutta, 1962, p. 29.
[105] Madanmohan Tarkalankar, *Shishushiksha, Part 3*, revised by Ishwarchandra Vidyasagar, p. 5.
[106] Ibid., p. 7.
[107] Ibid., p. 10.
[108] Ibid., p. 7.
[109] Ibid., p. 9.
[110] Ibid., p. 13.
[111] Ibid., p. 14.
[112] Ishwarchandra Vidyasagar, *Barna Parichay, Part 2*, in *Bidyasagar Rachanasamagra*, Vol. 1, p. 34.
[113] Madanmohan Tarkalankar, *Shishushiksha, Part 3*, revised by Ishwarchandra Vidyasagar, p. 22.
[114] Rajkrishna Bandyopadhyay, *Shishushiksha, Part 5* (*Nitibodh*), Calcutta, 1851, p. 11.
[115] Ishwarchandra Vidyasagar, *Barna Parichay, Part 2*, eighth edition, 1858, in Ashish Khastagir, ed., *Bangla Primer Sangraha (1816–1855)*, Kolkata, 2003, p. 40.
[116] Madanmohan Tarkalankar, *Shishushiksha, Part 1*, compiled by Ashish Khastagir, p. 3.
[117] Ishwarchandra Vidyasagar, 'Balyabibaher Dosh', in *Bidyasagar Rachanabali*, Calcutta, 1999, p. 560.
[118] Ibid., p. 558.
[119] Indra Mitra, *Karunasagar Bidyasagar*, Kolkata, 2001, pp. 47–54.
[120] For a discussion on this subject, see Sibaji Bandyopadhyay, *Abar Shishushiksha*, pp. 47–54.
[121] Bankimchandra Chattopadhyay, *Sahaj Rachana Shiksha*, in Gopal Haldar, ed., *Bankim Rachanasamagra*, Part 1, Calcutta, 1973, p. 1188.
[122] Ibid., p. 1199.
[123] Ibid.
[124] Ibid., pp. 1198–99.
[125] Ibid., p. 1199.
[126] Gouranga Prasad Basu, ed., *Pyaricharan Sarkar: The First Book of Reading*, Calcutta, 1985, pp. 56 and 57.
[127] Madanmohan Tarkalankar, *Shishushiksha, Part 3*, revised by Ishwarchandra Vidyasagar, p. 21.
[128] Rajkrishna Bandyopadhyay, *Shishushiksha, Part 5* (*Nitibodh*), p. 16.
[129] Akshay Kumar Dutta, *Charupath, Part 1*, Calcutta, 1876, p. 1.
[130] Bankimchandra Chattopadhyay, *Sahaj Rachana Shiksha*, in Gopal Haldar, ed., *Bankim Rachanasamagra*, Part 1, p. 1187.
[131] Ishwarchandra Vidyasagar, *Jibancharit*, in *Bidyasagar Rachanasamagra*, Vol. 1, p.129.
[132] Akshay Kumar Dutta, *Charupath, Part 2*, Calcutta, 1898, pp. 39 and 43.
[133] Khagendranath Mitra, *Shatabdir Shishu Sahitya: 1818–1960*, p. 115.
[134] *Papers relating to Discipline and Moral Training in Schools and Colleges in India*, *Selections from the Records of the Government of India – Home Department*, CCLXV, Number 8, Calcutta, 1890, pp. 1–2.
[135] Ibid., pp. 57–58.
[136] Ibid., p. 122.
[137] Ibid., p. 125.
[138] Ibid., p. 131.
[139] Ibid., p. 137.
[140] Ibid., p. 144.
[141] Chandroday Bhattacharya Bidyabinod, *Sunitisandarbha*, Calcutta, 1893. (The argument of Krishnakamal Bhattacharya is printed at the beginning of the book.)
[142] Ibid., p. 91.
[143] Rajanikanta Gupta, Advertisement for *Aryakirti*, Calcutta, 1889.
[144] Cited in Khagendranath Mitra, *Shatabdir Shishu Sahitya: 1818–1960*, p. 116.

[145] Rabindranath Tagore, 'Letter 5', *Chithipatra*, in *Rabindra Rachanabali*, Vol. 1, Calcutta, 1995, p. 871.
[146] Rabindranath Tagore, *Totakahini*, *Lipika*, in *Rabindra Rachanabali*, Vol. 26, Calcutta, 1970, p. 132.
[147] Ibid.
[148] Ibid.
[149] Ibid.
[150] Ibid.
[151] Rabindranath Tagore, 'Dui Pakhi', *Sonar Tori*, in *Rabindra Rachanabali*, Vol. 3, Calcutta, 1969, p. 43.
[152] Discussed in Manabendra Bandyopadhyay, ed., *Adhunik Bharatiyo Golpo*, Kolkata, 2000, p. 195.
[153] Rabindranath Tagore, *Totakahini*, *Lipika*, *Rabindra Rachanabali*, Vol. 26, p. 132.
[154] Foucault, *Discipline and Punish*, p. 141.
[155] Rabindranath Tagore, 'Shikshar Herpher', *Shiksha*, *Rabindra Rachanabali*, Vol. 12, p. 227.
[156] Ibid., p. 277.
[157] Ibid., p. 285.
[158] Rabindranath Tagore, *Totakahini*, *Lipika*, *Rabindra Rachanabali*, Vol. 26, p. 133.
[159] Sabyasachi Bhattacharya, *Aupanibeshik Bharater Arthaniti: 1850–1947*, Calcutta, 1989, p. 126.
[160] Ibid.
[161] Rabindranath Tagore, *Totakahini*, *Lipika*, *Rabindra Rachanabali*, Vol. 26, p. 133.
[162] Ibid.
[163] Ibid.
[164] Ibid.
[165] Ibid., p. 134.
[166] Ibid.
[167] Ibid.
[168] Ibid.
[169] Ibid.
[170] Rabindranath Tagore, 'Shiksha Sanskar', *Shiksha*, *Rabindra Rachanabali*, Vol. 12, p. 291.
[171] Ibid.
[172] Ibid., p. 293.
[173] Rabindranath Tagore, *Totakahini*, *Lipika*, *Rabindra Rachanabali*, Vol. 26, p. 134.
[174] Ibid.
[175] Rabindranath Tagore, 'Rayater Katha', 'Kalantar', *Rabindra Rachanabali*, Vol. 24. Calcutta, 1970, p. 426.
[176] Rabindranath Tagore, *Totakahini*, *Lipika*, *Rabindra Rachanabali*, Vol. 26, p. 134.
[177] Ibid.
[178] Ibid.
[179] Foucault, *Discipline and Punish*, p. 152.
[180] Rabindranath Tagore, *Totakahini*, *Lipika*, *Rabindra Rachanabali*, Vol. 26, p. 134.
[181] Ibid., p. 135.
[182] Ibid.
[183] Ibid.
[184] Rabindranath Tagore, 'Shiksha Sanskar', *Shiksha*, *Rabindra Rachanabali*, Vol. 12, p. 293.
[185] Dinesh Mukhopadhyay, *Dukkhojayir Jayajatra*, Calcutta, 1981, p. 7.
[186] Ibid., p. 53.
[187] Ibid., p. 5.
[188] Ibid., p. 6.
[189] Dakshinaranjan Mitra Majumdar, 'Kalabati Rajkanya', *Thakurmar Jhuli*, *Dakshinaranjan Rachanasamagra*, Vol. 1, p. 3.
[190] Dinesh Mukhopadhyay, *Dukkhojayir Jayajatra*, p. 6.
[191] Ibid., p. 7.

[192] Ibid.
[193] Ibid., p. 13.
[194] Ibid., pp. 25–26.
[195] Ibid., p. 42.
[196] Ibid., p. 23.
[197] Ibid., p. 32.
[198] Ibid., p. 41.
[199] Ibid., p. 6.
[200] Ibid., p. 18.
[201] Ibid., pp. 43–44.
[202] Ibid., p. 35.
[203] Rabindranath Tagore, *Jibansmriti*, *Rabindra Rachanabali*, Vol. 17, Calcutta, 1965, p. 375.
[204] Dinesh Mukhopadhyay, *Dukkhojayir Jayajatra*, p. 42.
[205] Ibid., p. 44
[206] Ibid., p. 50.
[207] Ibid., pp. 55–56.
[208] Ibid.
[209] Ibid., p. 71.
[210] Sukumar De Sarkar, 'Dukkhojayer Mantra', in Kshitindranarayan Bhattacharya, ed., *Ramdhanu*, Baisakh 1354 (October 1942), p. 17.
[211] Thomas Hughes, *Tom Brown's School Days*, Bombay, 1958, p. 11.
[212] Rammohun Roy, *Patrabali*, in Ajit Kumar Ghosh, ed., *Rammohun Rachanabali*, Calcutta, 1973, pp. 457–58.
[213] Brian Simon, *Studies in the History of Education: 1710–1770*, London: Lawrence and Wishart, 1960, p. 214.
[214] Hughes, *Tom Brown's School Days*, p. 347.
[215] H. Woodrow, 'Blurb of Macaulay's Minutes on Education', in *India Retain the Years 1835, 1836 and 1837*, Calcutta, 1862.
[216] Jogindranath Sarkar, 'Ganak Thakur', 'Khelar Gaan', in *Shishupathya Granthabali*, Calcutta, 1988, p. 118.
[217] Ibid.
[218] Ibid.
[219] Ibid., p. 117.
[220] Jogindranath Sarkar, 'Bhalo Chhele o Manda Chhele', *Ranga Chhobi*, in *Shishupathya Granthabali*, p. 87.
[221] Dakshinaranjan Mitra Majumdar, 'Charu o Haru', in *Dakshinaranjan Rachanasamagra*, Vol. 2, Calcutta: Mitra and Ghosh, 1981, p. 272.
[222] Nripendra Krishna Chattopadhyay, *Udashi Babar Akhra*, Calcutta, 1985, p. 33.
[223] Dakshinaranjan Mitra Majumdar, 'Last Boy', in *Dakshinaranjan Rachanasamagra*, Vol. 1, p. 256.
[224] Saroj Kumar Roy Choudhury, 'Paramanander Bipad', in *Rangin Akash*, Calcutta, 1985, p. 24.
[225] Nikhilesh Sen, 'Paribartan', in *Romanchakar Kahini*, Calcutta, 1980, p. 21.
[226] Nanigopal Chakrabarty, 'Bidyarthi Habul', in Kshitindranarayan Bhattacharya, ed., *Ramdhanu*, p. 372.
[227] Ashalata Sinha, 'Oder Bibek Buddhi', in *Rangin Akash*, p. 12.
[228] Saroj Kumar Roy Choudhury, 'Paramanander Bipad', in Rangin Akash, p. 16.
[229] Ibid., p. 17.
[230] Dakshinaranjan Mitra Majumdar, 'Charu o Haru', in *Dakshinaranjan Rachanasamagra*, Vol. 2, pp. 254–55.
[231] Ibid., p. 55.
[232] Sukumar Roy, 'Bujhiye Bola', *Abol Tabol*, in Satya Chakrabarti, ed., *Upendra Kishore – Sukumar Rachanasamagra*, Calcutta, 1983, p. 427.
[233] Achintya Kumar Sengupta, *Dui Bhai*, Calcutta, 1981, p. 45.

[234] Abanindranath Tagore, *Shib Saudagar*, in *Abanindra Rachanabali*, Vol. 5, Calcutta, 1983, p. 346.
[235] Ibid., p. 349.
[236] Ibid., p. 348.
[237] Lila Majumdar, 'Badyinather Bori', in *Lila Majumdar Rachanabali*, Vol. 1, Calcutta, 1984, p. 202.
[238] Ibid., p. 205.
[239] Lila Majumdar, 'Ganshar Chithi', 'Badyinather Bori', in *Lila Majumdar Rachanabali*, Vol. 1, p.177.
[240] Sukumar Roy, 'Dashur Kirti', *Pagla Dashu*, in Satya Chakrabarti, ed., *Upendra Kishore – Sukumar Rachanasamagra*, p. 459.
[241] Sukumar Roy, 'Pagla Dashu', *Pagla Dashu*, in Satya Chakrabarti, ed., *Upendra Kishore – Sukumar Rachanasamagra*, p. 456.
[242] Ibid.
[243] Sukumar Roy, 'Chinepatka', *Pagla Dashu*, in Satya Chakrabarti, ed., *Upendra Kishore – Sukumar Rachanasamagra*, p. 457.
[244] Sukumar Roy, 'Chaliyat', *Pagla Dashu*, in Satya Chakrabarti, ed., *Upendra Kishore – Sukumar Rachanasamagra*, p. 458.
[245] Sukumar Roy, 'Pagla Dashu', *Pagla Dashu*, in Satya Chakrabarti, ed., *Upendra Kishore – Sukumar Rachanasamagra*, p. 455.
[246] Sukumar Roy, 'Nandalaler Mandakapal', *Pagla Dashu*, in Satya Chakrabarti, ed., *Upendra Kishore – Sukumar Rachanasamagra*, p. 462.

4

Travelling Between the Home and the World

> For stealing in this manner, repeatedly, the reverend master expelled him [Madhab] from the school. On hearing this account in detail, his father abused and punished him adequately. After some days, he sent him to another school. He started stealing there once again. The reverend master rebuked and punished him extensively and turned him out. Seeing and hearing all this, his father developed great contempt for him. Enraged, he turned him out of home.[1]

> Once upon a time, there was a boy who brought back from school another boy's book that he had stolen. This boy's parents had died while he was very young. His aunt had brought him up. She saw the book in his hand and said, 'Bhuban! Where did you get this book?' He said it was the book of a boy in school. She understood that Bhuban had stolen this book from the school. But she did not ask him to return the book. Neither did she castigate him or forbid him to steal. Bhuban's bravado got aggravated by this. . . . In this manner, he gradually became an experienced thief. . . . After some days, Bhuban got caught as a thief. . . . The judge ordered Bhuban to be hanged. At that time, Bhuban came to his senses. When he was taken to the place where criminals are hanged, he requested the government officers to kindly let him meet his aunt once and for all. Bhuban's aunt was brought there, and on seeing him, went towards him weeping loudly. 'Mashi, what is the use of weeping now?' Bhuban said. 'Come close to me, I will say something in your ear.' When Mashi went close to him, Bhuban put his mouth close to her ear and forcibly bit her ear off with his teeth. After that, he rebuked her and said, 'Mashi! You are the reason for this hanging. When I first started stealing, you had known. At that time, if you had imposed your authority and prohibited me, I would not have been in this state today. You have not done that – that is why this is your reward.'[2]

If one places these two parts of *Barna Parichay* side by side, the fundamental argument behind Ishwarchandra Vidyasagar's theory of children's education manifests itself. It is inadequate to call it the fundamental argument. It is the essential substance of his enquiry on children. Vidyasagar's text of injunctions on how to raise boys and make 'men' out of them gets circulated in a deep and grave voice. In order to tame boys, one needs manly firmness and uprightness. This work cannot be accomplished by the womanly attributes of delicacy, modesty and gentleness. Severe, harsh, grave and solemn fathers or father-like individuals are the only able figures of authority. Boys get ruined by tearful, gushing mothers or mother surrogates. There is a need, not for the inconstancy or sentimentality of passion, but for unaltered steadiness and resolute firmness. Otherwise, one gets overwhelmed by the blind attachment of parental affection.

Behind Vidyasagar's injunction, there are a few current, commonsensical views about the identity and behaviour of the adult male and female, and the immature child. Girls are by nature ignorant, effusive and straightforward. Due to excessive heartfelt passion, they lose their sense of understanding and discernment. The specialities of masculinity are just the contrary: men possess intellect and a sense of logic. It is not as if they do not transgress once in a while, but through introspection and intuition, and by being alert to the dangers they are surrounded by, men find their way back. And what about the child? All the difficulty is concerning him. His intellect has not matured and his 'character' has been not been 'formed', so the 'normal mental' differences of boys and girls often get blurred. The jeopardy is due to their not being differentiated adequately by the specifics of gender. How fatal this blurred interface is for the code of social symmetry can be understood by the extent of various child-related bans and taboos. In the nineteenth and twentieth centuries, many books were written in Bengali examining the objectionable inclinations of the child. One of them is Satishchandra Chakrabarti's *Santaner Charitragathan* (first published in 1912). Ironically enough, the book was reprinted for the third time in 1978, which happened to be the 'International Year of the Child'.

The 'Character' of the Child

The book *Santaner Charitragathan* (*Moulding the Character of the Child*) had raised quite a hue and cry in that age. Magazines like *Prabashi*, *Nabyabharat*, *Udbodhan*, etc., praised the book in glowing terms. Ashwini Kumar Dutta (1856–1923) wrote:

> I do not think this class of books is there in the Bengali language. If there is a copy of your book in the hands of all fathers and mothers living in Bengal, and if each child or boy's character is shaped in accordance with it, the nation will progress.[3]

Not just Ashwini Kumar Dutta but many other preeminent individuals of the nation declared their applause for Satishchandra: the first Indian vice-chancellor of a university in India, Gurudas Bandyopadhyay (1844–1918); chemist Prafulla

Chandra Ray; lawyer Saradacharan Mitra (1848–1917); founder-editor of newspapers like *Dashi*, *Mukul*, *Prabashi* and *Modern Review*, Ramananda Chattopadhyay (1865–1943); Satishchandra Bidyabhushan; headmaster of Barishal Brajamohan Vidyalaya, Jagadish Mukhopadhyay (1861–1932); editor of *Bharat Stree Mahamandal*, Krishnabhamini Dasi (1864–1919).

'Oh reader, please trust in this prognostication of mine. Any person with a heart who will demonstrate negligence towards all these pure duties will never get any commiseration for his wrongdoing even if he sheds tears over it for a long period.'[4] *Santaner Charitragathan* begins with these words of caution from Jean-Jacques Rousseau (1712–1778), author of the modern encyclopaedia on the rearing of children, *Emile: Or, On Education* (1762). Not only at the beginning but through the entire book are strewn such valuable words of wisdom and references as well as quotations from several chief thinkers of Europe, such as the great soul Arnold who was the famous teacher of Rugby School, Locke, Spencer, Bentham, James Mill, John Stuart Mill, D. Payne, Samuel Smiles, Froebel, Victoria the Queen-Goddess of England, David Hare, the friend of India, Kipling and Joseph Mazzini. The writer, of course, did not leave out Bengali thinkers. Along with the Europeans, he included the supreme ideal men of India, the memorable forefathers of new Bengal – mainly Raja Rammohun Roy, Devendranath Thakur, Bhudeb Mukhopadhyay and Chandranath Basu. Pleased no end by the abundance of these references, Ashwini Kumar Dutta wrote in a congratulatory vein to Satishchandra Chakrabarti: 'Your advice has been excellent and extremely practicable. And it has become all the more valuable due to being corroborated by scholars of pedagogical theory.'[5]

Replete with the support of native and foreign specialists of child education, in the chapter 'Kanna' of this book, Satishchandra gives a description of the character of the child. Encouragement of crying, which is indicative of 'the child's extension of his intrinsic authority', 'his unruliness and mulishness', encourages the intractable features of children. If the child can gain what he wishes for or accomplishes what he wants to do simply by crying, where lies the hope for his good education?[6] What is the method of developing the 'normal' creature called a child who is 'driven by an indomitable inclination' into becoming a 'well-educated', 'social' being? In Satishchandra's opinion:

> The natural objective of disciplining is to tame the rebellious mind of the child . . . obedience is one of the principal supports of that good disciplining . . . the immediate and cheerful observance of injunctions is a sign of natural obedience . . . it is desirable that his head bow to your authority. Guardians of children should always have such a mastery over their children that even if their children cannot understand the fairness of it, they can be compelled to do such and such work without any further delay.[7]

Offering solace to the guardians, Satishchandra writes that if one keeps perpetually at it, the quality called obedience will definitely be sown in the child's heart. 'Gradually, many trees producing elixir with their profusion of branches will be seen in homes all over because if we can train dogs to be obedient, there is no reason not to be able to impart the precept of obedience to children. Children are certainly not inferior to dogs.'[8] One is reminded that even *Shishushiksha, Part 3* (91st edition), which was revised by Vidyasagar and edited by Madanmohan Tarkalankar, advised that children should have submissiveness and loyalty to the master comparable to dogs.

The principal method of awakening that deep devotion was the control of sexual desire and consciousness in children, suppression of their senses and the teaching of restraint. Satishchandra's counsel about a wicked affliction of puberty such as masturbation was: 'The primary duty of parents who seek good for their children . . . is to specially alert their children well in time about control of a similar precociousness of their sexual abilities and against the untimely and unnatural use of their reproductive organs.'[9] But the difficulty was that even the ever-faithful dog goes hopping mad against the indulgence of its master's rearing, shakes itself and stands up. If children too, in imitation of them, turn against the healthy – although with a flavour of bitterness – affection due to the excesses of the elders, and suddenly turn wild without any rhyme or reason, what needs to be done? Accepting Locke to be the arbitrator, Satishchandra's frank reply is:

> When children demonstrate such a subversive attitude against the authority and injunction of parents, it is one's duty to tame them by using any method. Like the rebellion of the state, all kinds of severity are to be followed while repressing rebellion within the family . . . whether it is ruling the family or the state, if all other methods fail at all times, the punitive code should be followed.[10]

Here too we see that the 'family' is linked to the 'nation', and just as it is for the uneducated lower classes, even for the upper classes, the 'family' is the microcosm of the national organization – the smallest and most indivisible unit of the collectivity of society. In the kingdom of the family, fathers and mothers are the guardians, and the subjects of the kingdom are children. In Satishchandra's book, seeing the reiterative use of 'father–mother' / '*janak–janani*', one might think that we have advanced beyond the age of *Barna Parichay*. The father no longer has all-pervasive authority; the mother is co-sharer of authority within the family. The mother and the father are collaboratively employed in the noble task of formation of the child's character. In his Afterword, the writer reminds us:

> Please remember that the mother and the father's responsibility will not end with burdening the innocuous child's frail head with a pile of books, subjecting him to irresponsible caning and handing him over to a master whose be all and end all is

> his wages. Remember that the pile of ingredients that are useful in the fashioning of Bharat Mata are within your control in the shape of children. Whatever mould you pour this soft, moist clay of the child in, Bharat Mata will be formed likewise.[11]

It implies that there is no peace to be gained by pushing the innocuous child into the cage of the school; one has to convert the home into a school too.

In the magazine *Udbodhan*, views regarding the formation of the child's character were expressed in a joint appeal about the family and the school: 'The foremost and predominant incantation of human life is the great maxim "Victory must begin at home" . . . we request everybody to read this book . . . it is desirable that such books are selected as textbooks for school.'[12] In his book, Satishchandra has referred to a statement akin to that of Chandranath Basu: 'If we do the initial spadework silently inside the home for some years now, we will be able to earn the right and be eligible to step outside.'[13] How will that 'initial work' be achieved? The writer calls upon educators at school and at home: 'O fathers all! Please arrange for the good moral education of your children, even after overcoming a hundred hurdles and accepting a hundred inconveniences.'[14]

In Satishchandra's powerful summons, why has the pair of father–mother suddenly got severed? Are the familial spheres of the father and the mother different from each other? The writer does not keep us in any doubt for he writes in the very next sentence: 'Oh mothers all! Please help with your body, heart and soul.'[15] Do mothers have to silently support and assist the organizer of moral education, the father, in that very work that needs to be rooted inside the home, and without which one is unable to step outside? According to Satishchandra, mothers are a little extra vocal. Due to a lack of sense of proportion, they keep causing fissures in the paternal system:

> If the child is a little unruly, mothers resort to hobgoblins, tigers, foxes, ghosts and the like . . . in this manner, our well-wisher mothers make us so phobic about ghosts from early infancy that our entire life gets spent in trembling like this . . . beware! Don't arrange to dig live graves for your children by instilling the unfounded fear of hobgoblins *et al.* or telling stories about ghosts and spirits . . . we need men in this nation. Cowards are the fallen lepers of society.[16]

If mothers do not heed this appeal of Satishchandra, will these coward sons, the lepers of society who are buried alive, return to punish them for their lack of discernment? Will they, like Bhuban, bite their ears off forcibly?

Satishchandra's objection is not only apropos ghosts and spirits. He is equally belligerent about fairytales:

> Whatever stories there are for children here, most of them are full of ghosts and spirits . . . the ones that have not been possessed by ghosts have been replete with the obsessive love of princes and princesses. In the child's heart, in his very infancy,

> the seeds of a certain passion are sown with the help of describing the marriage of the ruddy-cheeked girl and the fair-skinned boy . . . by their influence, many genuine Gobindalals become bad and Shaibalinis go mad.[17]

On the other hand, just five years before the publication of *Santaner Charitragathan*, in his Foreword to *Thakurmar Jhuli* (written in 1907), Rabindranath Tagore had said with a tone of regret: 'Where did they go – the prince, the mythical avian-consorts *Byangoma–Byangomi*, where are the wealth and treasures of the seven kings that you can only get after crossing seven seas and thirteen rivers . . . the company of Swadeshi grandmothers has become totally bankrupt.'[18] Satishchandra's threat and Rabindranath's regret, the story of the affluence of the team of grandmothers enabled by the investment of new capital and the narrative of their subsequent impoverishment – are not the two descriptions of prosperity and utter ruin mutually linked?

If one wants to understand the meaning of Rabindranath's lamentation that is overwhelmed by the spirit of *swadeshi*, one will first have to take into account the woman's gaining of new rights. One gets an abstract image of the new ideal woman of the nineteenth century in the much-read and revered *Sushilar Upakhyan* (*Story of the Well-Behaved Woman*) by Madhusudan Mukhopadhyay (Parts 1 and 2, 1859; Part 3, 1860), composed for Bengal's home-bound middle-class girls, and published a few years after *Barna Parichay* with the support of the *Bangabhashanubadak Samaj* (Bengali Language Translation Committee).

The Narrative of Sushila's Birth

The account of Sushila's birth in *Sushilar Upakhyan* starts with the prayer of the zamindar, Babu Jayachandra Bandyopadhyay. The village of Bijaynagar in Dharampur district is a part of Jayachandra's special taluk. He lives there. It is self-evident from the name and address of the esteemed landlord that he not only hails from a good family and is an affluent man, but he is also 'excessively pious'. Moreover, he has received his education from a 'public school in Calcutta'.[19] Who dares obstruct his victory?

But first, is there any link between the greatness of Jayachandra Bandyopadhyay's name with the writer of the Foreword to *Sushilar Upakhyan*? The Bangabhashanubadak Samaj did not just stop at translating books from English – they even took decisions about publishing original books as a means aimed at enhancing the knowledge and uplifting the minds of Bengalis. That is why the authorities of the committee organized a literature competition in 1850. It was decided that each author would be given a one-time payment of Rs 250 more if 2,000 copies got sold. That year, out of ten applicants, two were selected by the jury: Rangalal Bandyopadhyay's (1827–1887) *Padminir Upakhyan* (*Padmini's Story*, 1858) and Madhusudan Mukhopadhyay's *Sushilar Upakhyan*.[20] Was the similarity of names between the unique patron of the Bangabhashanubadak

Samaj, Jayakrishna Mukhopadhyay, zamindar of Uttarpara, and Jayachandra Bandyopadhyay, zamindar of Bijaynagar, indeed coincidental?

Jayachandra Bandyopadhyay is not like numerous other zamindars – can all ten fingers of our hands be the same? He is an extremely good man. His craving for philanthropy is irresistible. His subjects are so 'overwhelmed' by his behaviour that they 'deem him a father figure'. 'Be it during prosperity or calamity, they are forever'[21] at his door. Because there are a lot of *bhadralok* living in Bijaynagar and its neighbourhood, at the request of the magistrates and judge sahibs of Dharampur district, the Company Bahadur opened a school. All the three languages – English, Bengali and Sanskrit – are taught there. But Jayachandra is not content with just this; the theory of filtration of Macaulay and Trevelyan has taught him that one has to constantly enlarge one's circle of education. It is not an act of good sense to limit the light of knowledge within the narrow bounds of the *bhadralok* community. Bound by the promise of other people's welfare, Jayachandra voluntarily opened a free school for the cause of the lower-caste boys. He commanded that a *pandit* and a *gurumahashay* be employed at a salary of ten rupees and six rupees, respectively, in that school. They would concentrate especially on the agenda of making the boys well-behaved, teach them the religious scriptures and the creed of ethics, and impart such education that they can read easy primers, take lessons in handwriting and keep basic accounts. There was no need to go beyond these and teach them difficult subjects. The children of lowly people were to study here from the fifth to the tenth year and then move on to educate themselves through scholarships.[22] Although there were different curriculums for the sons of *bhadralok* and *chhotolok*, although much was omitted from the latter due to perceptions of excess, because of the magnanimity of Jayachandra, 'The disqualification of ignorance was removed from the children of lowly people. Gradually, they pursued learning and became passionate devotees of learning.'[23]

Jayachandra's desire did not get fulfilled simply by piercing lowly boys with the arrows of learning. He also turned his attention to girls. Whether genteel or lowly, the problem of the ignorance of girls belonging to either sphere who were so far untouched by the panacea of education was resolved, and their illiteracy was eradicated by Jayachandra's zealousness. But even in this matter, his class consciousness was sharp. Lest the girls of respectable homes get contaminated by coming into contact with girls from lower classes, he founded two women's schools in Bijaynagar. One was dedicated to the cause of girls from the lower classes and the other to girls from respectable clans. He set up whatever codes he had set up for boys from the lower classes for girls belonging to the same order. But for the maidens of respectable families, it was necessary to follow codes that were more refined and an education that was superior. Realizing this, he appealed to the European ladies of Calcutta that they should kindly send two learned schoolmistresses to the girls' school in Bijaynagar – one a

European lady and the other a native gentlewoman. These two schoolmistresses should be highly proficient in the Bengali language, because the girls would have to be taught all subjects in the native language.[24] It did not take long for the European wives to respond to Jayachandra's appeal. Promptly, there appeared a foreign lady from the Female Normal School at Calcutta and a Bengali lady from the Central School connected to the Normal School. The Bibi's monthly salary was fixed at Rs 50 and that of the native woman at Rs 25. At last, Jayachandra, the man with a passion for education, was successful. Through his active dedication, Bijaynagar accomplished four tiers of education: boys and girls hailing from high and low families got divided into not one but four slots.

In the first part of *Sushilar Upakhyan*, published in 1859, Jayachandra attains easy success in the spread of female education. There is nobody in Bijaynagar who wants or is able to obstruct him. The composer of the *Upakhyan* could accomplish the impossible by perceiving the greatness of his imagined character, the godlike Jayachandra, in as hyperbolic terms as possible. As a result, he did not have the time or the need to turn to those kinds of nitty-gritties. Although the intensity of the opposition to women's education of 1859 had abated to a certain extent, a debate regarding female education went on in the Hindu community for a long time. In reality, although many industrious men demonstrated greater courage and affluence than Jayachandra, there could be no comparison between them and him when it came to the assessment of success.

A debate went on for long about whether girls have the ability to imbibe learning. God had created men and women in two different moulds. Irrespective of how mutually attractive the two may be to each other, the differences between them are greater – for instance, women by nature are deficient in intelligence. The education of girls in the same manner as boys, therefore, is not only useless, but contrary to established principles in every sense. It is preferable that the path to the chambers of women and men be separate. If not, it would cause damage and there would be impediments to the smooth functioning of the home. In the booklet *Prabartak o Nibartak-er Dwitiyo Sambad* (*Second Dialogue between the Proponent and the Opponent*), published in November 1819, Rammohun Roy wrote through his mouthpiece, the opponent:

> . . . on the subject of intelligence, when did you ever test women's intelligence that you designate them to be less intelligent so easily? Because if the individual cannot experience and absorb the education and learning that is imparted to them, it is possible to term them as endowed with little intelligence. You have almost not imparted any education and learning to women. Then how do you determine that they are without any intelligence?[25]

No matter what reservation the natives had, the Christian missionaries were sufficiently enthused about women's intelligence. In order to test the intelligence of women, in 1819 itself, the Female Juvenile Society for the Establishment and Support of Bengali Female Schools was founded with the support of the Baptist Mission. On 25 March 1824, the Ladies' Society for Native Female Education in Calcutta and its Vicinity was established by the enterprise of the Church Missionary Society. Before that, in November 1821, Miss Cook (later Mrs Wilson), the first lady teacher appointed by the British and Foreign School Society, reached Calcutta. She opened quite a few free girls' schools with the assistance of the Society for Native Female Education. After the renewal of the charter in 1813, when certain restrictions were curbed in the functioning of the missionaries, they turned their attention to girls alongside boys. The missionaries rightly understood that if one had to enlighten the 'uncivilized' Indians about Christianity, it was necessary to make inroads from the front as well as from the rear. If the foundations of the inner quarters were shaken, the map of the entire Indian social structure would get overhauled. In the words of an authority of the Society for Native Female Education, 'it is impossible to work towards civilizing and undertaking the moral education of a country whose girls are ignorant and downtrodden'.[26]

The missionaries reasoned that with the burning example of an evil custom like *sati*, there was no doubt about the poor condition of Hindu women and the primitivity of the Hindu religion. It was only the conservative, deluded and simpleton orientalists who did not refrain from singing praises of Hindu society. Of course, the missionaries' intention was not fulfilled – there was no flaw in their sincerity or effort, but one could not free the Hindu Bengali from the prejudice of dreading other religions and believing that it was preferable to die clinging to one's own religion. Even if one was partially successful, one could not draw the entire society within the purview of Christianity. In order to stop the missionary onslaught, in order to keep the 'purity' of the inner quarters intact, all those who believed in the harmony between the west and the east had joined hands. Although there were scores of disagreements about their views and methods, although the customs and codes of their pledge to salvage women were different, there was a profound agreement somewhere. Rammohun Roy had taken part in female education, so had Radhakanta Deb (1783–1867) – this was one matter in which all differences predicated on kinship or religion got virtually erased.

On 20 March 1851, Radhakanta Deb wrote in a letter to Drinkwater Bethune:

> It was in the age of Hastings that open schools were attempted to be established for girls. But up to that time, those who were considered genteel folk thought that sending girls to these kinds of schools was detrimental to their dignity. . . . When in 1821, the British and Foreign Society sent Miss Cooke (later Mrs Wilson) to this

> country with the plan of educating Hindu women, there was a special objection to sending Hindu girls to these open schools. At that point, expressing the viewpoint of the Hindu community, I wrote to Reverend W.H. Pearce, the gist of which communication is: There is no need to summon a session of the society to discuss the imparting of education of girls in the public school by Miss Cooke. If necessary, Miss Cooke may be involved in the imparting of education in the newly established missionary schools for destitute girls . . . the Hindus would remain specially grateful to her if along with common learning, girls who were poor and yet hailed from respectable clans could learn some handicraft and lessons on technology from her. The young women who were thus educated could be appointed as the mistresses of the women who were part of the Hindu elite. Through this, there would be no interference in the customs and codes practised by Hindus from time immemorial, yet education would circulate among women.[27]

It is very clear from the letter that by using the word 'women', Radhakanta Deb wanted to talk about the Hindu women of respectable families. His chief anxiety was how to maintain the 'sanctity of Hindu customs and codes' while simultaneously deploying the services of Miss Cooke, and despite circulating education among respectable Hindu women, how to save them from the defiled touch of Christianity. Right from the beginning, female education was inextricably intertwined with the question of Hinduism. The notion of Hinduism, of course, did not remain stagnant. It evolved in keeping with the times, and the ideals and context of women's education got transformed along with it.

With the help of Radhakanta Deb, Gourmohan Vidyalankar, the head pandit of the School Society who became the *munsif* of Sukhsagar later, wrote *Stree Shiksha Vidhayak* (*A Guide to Women's Education*). Through the efforts of the Female Juvenile Society, the first edition of the book came out in March 1822. The second edition, in support of Miss Cooke, was published in August of the same year; the responsibility for the reprint was undertaken by the School Book Society. In his booklet, Gourmohan tried to refute the allegation of women being endowed with a lesser intelligence, in the same vein as Rammohun's reasoning. As soon as they get a little respite from household work, using their own intelligence and without any guidance, girls draw patterns on the floor with rice flour (*alpana*), make sweetmeats and do so much more – all these are signifiers of their natural creative skills. Secondly, there is no link between education and widowhood – it is indeed an imagined notion. There are references to several learned women in the Puranas. The female education that 'sahibs' have undertaken as an enterprise, therefore, would heal the fractured fate of women and they too would get a taste of classical learning. But the question is: what would girls gain by reading the classics? Gourmohan did not bypass the question in the least. He said openly that women do not study, and if women who are 'ignorant like beasts' had

Woman, a sketch by Jamini Roy.

> classical knowledge, by knowing how to serve the husband and the father in law, by knowing what fruit they could reap by serving them and being obedient to them, they would serve and obey the instructions of their husbands in keeping with the dictates of the classics. Women these days are almost ignorant – due to this reason, they are vulnerable to many flaws. If they were knowledgeable in reading and writing, they would have been able to take time off from their own housework and serving their husbands to read books and apply themselves to the execution of their duties with a stable mind.[28]

Does this mean that 'modern' education is needed to repress and subdue the fundamentally passionate and perpetually restless nature of the woman? Thanks to the mediation of the sahibs, would the codes of the *Manu Samhita* become even stronger and the duties of women more firmly encoded? But Gourmohan himself explained in one place in his book that if girls got education, they would also be able to take stock of their dues. If girls broadened their notion of what is due to them – if, after gaining classical learning, they became averse towards classical injunctions and did not want to remain satisfied in the gratification of their husbands, would a terrible social crisis not manifest itself? A perfectly clear imprint of this doubt has remained in the thought and discourses on women's education, in literature written for adults and children, and in debates around suitable curriculums for women.

The Hindu Balika Vidyalaya was established on 7 May 1847. The founder of the school was the legal secretary of the Government of India and the president of the Educational Committee, Drinkwater Bethune. In his inaugural lecture, Bethune said:

> It is imperative to open the doors and expedite the trend of the new educational scheme that was inaugurated thirty years ago, and is benefiting young men endlessly, to young ladies also. As a result of the establishment of the girls' school, Hindu girls from respectable families can get the advantage of studying 'openly'.[29]

Many people stood by Bethune on that day – among them Dakshinaranjan Mukhopadhyay (1814–1878), Ishwarchandra Vidyasagar and Madanmohan Tarkalankar. The author of *Shishushiksha*, a one-time master of Sanskrit College, a learned judge and a deputy magistrate, Madanmohan wrote an article called 'Stree Shiksha' in the second issue of the magazine *Sarbashubhakari* (Ashwin, Shakabda 1772). Much of it was taken up with a lot of exuberance over Bethune.

> We feel that by observing the plight of the wretched women of this country, some compassion has coursed through the veins of merciful God . . . for the purpose of . . . executing this good deed, he has brought from a far off land a liberal-minded, magnanimous man . . . at this moment, he is the principal director of our educational society. His name is Honourable Drinkwater Bethune.[30]

To prove that girls were capable of imbibing education, Madanmohan wrote exceedingly compellingly in 'Stree Shiksha':

> Are they not human beings? Are they not to be counted among animate creatures? Do they not have the faculty of intelligence? Do they not have retentive power? No ability to debate? And no perception of similitude? . . . The father of the world has only instituted some minimal differences in appearance between men and women. He has not created any disparity in mental abilities.[31]

Did Madanmohan want to strike at the base of the ingrained prejudice about the radical distinction between men and women? Since time immemorial, patriarchal control has fashioned a notion around female identity as though it arises from some divine agency. If one were to extricate women from the complications of various social signs, if one were only to filter the sap, one would see that their 'pure' 'identity' has no link with time and place. There is no alternative trajectory for women except to bear the liability of the perpetually stable mark of a time-honoured sign. There was never any other way, nor will there ever be. Did Madanmohan himself become doubtful about his own utterance? Otherwise, in that same essay, why did he have to retract, and reacquaint his readers with the signs of female identity that are beyond time and space: 'By nature, the species of women is well behaved, modest and bashful'?[32] Ultimately, even 'Stree Shiksha' cannot overstep the threshold of phallocentric discourse. The question as to whether Madanmohan's advancement and retreat occurred while he was in his senses is irrelevant. In a patriarchal society, everybody has to be a victim of this dilemma to a lesser or greater extent. The extent of Madanmohan's withdrawal, of course, had crossed limits in places. He squandered quite a few sentences to explain how the burden of men would be lightened if women were given a proper education:

> If the people of our country get tempted about earning wealth, it is just not possible that women would disappoint them if they became learned . . . they would sit in the inner quarters and innovate many kinds of arts and crafts, and through those the aspired wealth could easily be generated.[33]

In *Shishushiksha* (*The Education of the Child*), *Part 2*, the sentence he constructed in order to give an example of a word with the consonant–vowel combination of '*shya*' is memorable in this instance: '*Streeloker bidyashiksha kora abashyak*', i.e. 'It is essential (*abashyak*) for women to gain learning and education.'[34] Now the question is: for whose self-interest and wherefore was this essential?

Five years after Bethune's death, in 1856, his school was upgraded to a government school aided by government expenditure. Vidyasagar became the secretary of the committee constituted to supervise the school. On behalf of the committee, the Lieutenant-Governor of Bengal, Cecil Beadon, and Vidyasagar sent a letter to the masters of distinctive Hindu households in Calcutta. In order to reassure them, it was said in the letter: 'This school is only for aristocratic Hindu girls.'[35] Vidyasagar, of course, reposed no trust in government aid and founded thirty-five schools for girls in the four districts of Hooghly, Burdwan, Midnapore and Nadia on his own enterprise between November 1827 and May 1858. In reality, modern female education developed and spread in Bengal due to combined contributions from various quarters – the Christian Missionary Society and their schools, the School Book Society, the Brahmo Samaj, religious organizations, intrepid individuals like Vidyasagar who followed their own views and methods, and British government officers. If all this had not happened, it would not have been possible for Babu Jayachandra, revered by Madhusudan Mukhopadhyay, to establish two schools for girls in Bijaynagar village, Dharampur district without any opposition, and neither would Sushila have been born there.

The Growing Up and Blossoming of Sushila

It is not likely that Madhusudan Mukhopadhyay reposed a lot of trust in the learning and intelligence of female students. It was, in fact, because he did not, that he not only completed his business with signs and gestures in *Sushilar Upakhyan*, which was composed 'for the use of girls from middle class households in Bengal', but he was not satisfied till he underlined everything in bold letters. The name of the district was Dharampur ('the abode of *dharma*'), the name of the village was Bijaynagar ('the city of victory'), the name of the zamindar was Jayachandra ('the victorious') and the name of the heroine was Sushila ('the good-natured'). The names of the characters in the narrative were crystal-clear; there was no need to let any time elapse in order to judge their character. By looking inside the crystal-glass once, one could clearly understand whether the male and female characters were unblemished or flawed. The author especially left no loophole in Sushila's clean interior. He wrote in vivid letters: 'I pray to god that by reading this, young girls take care to become industrious, dutiful and honest like this girl.'[36]

Sushilar Upakhyan is an unadulterated moral tale in which, through the ploy of metaphor, the author presents simple-minded girls with a few valuable ethical principles. Consequently, there is no trace of complexity in the organization or expression of the narrative – there is not the slightest inconvenience in reading the prosaic verse narrative strung in a single harmony. No matter how monotonous or tedious Madhusudan Mukhopadhyay's writing might seem today, through the simplicity of his writing style in *Sushilar Upakhyan* there remains a frank deposition of the mid-nineteenth century *bhadralok*. Was that deposition solely that of Madhusudan Mukhopadhyay?

Although Sushila's father is not rich, he is a merchant – he, therefore, sends

Sushila to the *bhadralok* girls' school in Bijaynagar in order to get educated. Immediately, Sushila becomes a favourite pupil of her teachers. Why not? The maternal teachers in the school would teach a few *shloka*s of the *Dharmashastras* before all else. Sushila would learn these verses daily; who could beat her when examined on rote learning? Although the History of Bengal, Ancient Archaeology, Grammar, Geography, Arithmetic and Art were taught in the school, Sushila's spiritual investment is the *shloka*s of the *Dharmashastras*, the supreme asset of her life. For Sushila, work is like play. She loves the game of

> cooking – the way girls like to play at cooking and feed their dolls who they imagined to be their children. She loved this game but other games were not that palatable to her. Her mother had once told her that many subjects regarding household duties could be learnt through this game.[37]

Just as her mother had taught her that play is not unadulterated play – that there are many profound theories in play, Sushila's father had similarly reiterated a wise message about the noble objective of studies: 'Sushila! I am educating you so that you can be a supreme housewife. Take care, my dear, that you are never irreverent towards such a serious subject.'[38] This implies that in the case of girls, both study and play are means and equipment for becoming well-versed in household chores. Nothing has been created in the world for their unnecessary entertainment. Not just Sushila's parents but even Mary Carpenter – founder of the Central British Women's Committee (1871) of the National Indian Association, with which was linked the committee of the progressive Brahmo Bangamahila Samaj, the opposing faction of the conservative Keshabites – had said the same kind of thing in 1866 while giving counsel on the subject of a curriculum that is appropriate for Hindu girls: 'In order to make the core of girls more tender and governed by taste, there should be adequate provision for flower arrangement and the practice of music. Along with that, it is necessary to teach Art, a light exercise unaided by machine and "Natural Philosophy".'[39]

Sushila is not selfish; she is not ungenerous about distributing among friends whatever advice she gets from her father, mother or pedagogical mothers. Wasting time is anathema to her; therefore, 'whenever she saw that many women were sitting together and talking idly, she would entertain them by taking up a pleasant book from the household Bengali book collection like *Shishupalan* [*Rearing the Child*] or *Nar–Nari* [*Man–Woman*] and start reading to them.'[40] It is difficult to say whether it provided entertainment to them, but thanks to the example that Sushila set, it did not take long to cure the disease of gossiping and maligning others in Bijaynagar. Whoever sees Sushila, a manifestation of the goddess Lakshmi, with her capability of supervising household artefacts and the care she takes over house work, understands that 'A woman can never be a supreme housewife without being well educated. It is, therefore, extremely necessary for parents to get young women to undergo an excellent course of studies in their childhood.'[41] Did Gourmohan Vidyalankar not say the same thing in his book *Stree Shiksha Vidhayak*?

Was there any doubt that by the decree of Prajapati, the god of marriage, the learned Sushila would get married to an ill-tempered and pious individual? Her husband Chandrakumar is an ordinary, salary-minded clerk. But it is not possible to measure a man by his salary; there are few unsullied and industrious people like him in all of India. Sushila passes with honours in a difficult cookery test before Chandrakumar's father, whose firm belief is that 'It is exceedingly necessary for every woman to be a supreme cook.' Her parents-in-law are extremely pleased with her modest behaviour and sweet words. And the husband? Well, what can one say about him! Could such a good man and noble individual like Chandrakumar be indifferent towards a wife who, at every turn of phrase, declares herself as subservient, and lets her husband know with great humility, 'Lord, I believe that the be all and end all of our species is to serve one's husband and give happiness to one's husband'?[42] There is no way but to praise the extraordinary discretion, intelligence and sense of proportion of the learned Sushila. She gifts Chandrakumar with three sons, and does not unnecessarily burden her pious husband by giving birth to the liability called a daughter. Since such propitious things happen, there is no doubt that a benediction like 'May your husband live long and let your *sankha* [conch-shell bangles] and vermillion be indestructible' will also find realization in Sushila's life. Madhusudan Mukhopadhyay left no loophole unplugged in fulfilling the wishes of his male and female readers. At the end of the narrative, Sushila drifts to her eternal sleep after placing her son in her husband's lap. As the manifestation of a reward subsequent to the deeds befitting a devoted wife, she prostrates herself at the desired abode of chaste women whose husbands will be alive forever.

It may be perceived from the substance and summary of the division of the narrative that there is nothing new in *Sushilar Upakhyan*. This tale of a woman's life has been taught in various ways through the ages to girls. It has been narrated during female rituals of *bratakatha* (tales told as part of fasting rites for women) and fairytales, with the limits of women's aspirations circumscribed within the paradigm of stories about wish fulfilment. But although he maintained the exterior structure of the *panchali* (verse fables recited at rituals) or fairytale, Madhusudan Mukhopadhyay did not want to merely pour old wine in new bottles. He was equally conscious that in keeping with the changed circumstances, the views on the idealistic connotations of female social roles had also undergone a change – or at least that they should undergo a change. The Sushila of *Sushilar Upakhyan* was simultaneously perennial and modern. The author's objective was to demonstrate that there is no disharmony between the two.

What are the signs that identify Sushila's modernity? She names her first son Priyambad ('the sweet-tongued one'). The book *Shishupalan* is her all-time companion; she therefore knows

> The things that puny lads crave for are not good things to crave for . . . Their fantasy is that they will do their own thing in the way that they wish to . . . Boys and girls of a tender age are given to self will. . . To the end of their childhood, if one could instil and firm up the notion within the gentle core of boys that it is harmful to be self-willed, I cannot tell how beneficial it would be to them in the future.[43]

Writing many years after *Sushilar Upakhyan*, even after the end of the nineteenth century, Satishchandra Chakrabarti had written the same thing about child psychology in his book *Santaner Charitragathan*. Like him, Sushila also believes that 'If parents want their sons and daughters, indeed, to be obedient and under their control, it is the duty of both of them to be in accord.'[44] The 'intelligent and learned' Sushila knows in which book there is the fundamental key to the magic of taming one's progeny. When Priyambad is four years old, she hands him *Barna Parichay*. Needless to say, after this, it is not possible to retard Priyambad's growth; the indomitable tendencies befitting boys in him automatically get subdued, and Sushila's able son gets transformed into a well-behaved boy. It is not only on Priyambad but also on the other two boys that the same method is deployed. They all become gems among boys. The fame of Sushila who has given birth to such gems spreads far and wide. The name of her second son, Bashambad ('the submissive one'), is testimony to the skill and success Sushila attains by way of rearing children – or, as some may say, in slaughtering children.

But would Madhusudan Mukhopadhyay stop at just weaving long narratives out of the stories of Priyambad–Bashambad–Satyambad ('the truthful one')? Can any moral tale be complete if one does not connect the 'good' and the 'bad' by cause and effect? Hence, an 'ignorant, stupid, restless' boy inevitably presents himself in the novel – Sushila's neighbour Manorama's son, Jadab. But the saving grace is that in the village in which an ideal mother like Sushila lives, disruptions by Jadabs cannot become established practice over a prolonged period. Endlessly hearing words of reproach apropos the bad nature and unruliness of her son from her neighbours, the exasperated Manorama seeks refuge in Sushila. Her firm opinion is that only Sushila can suggest remedies for 'properly rearing' her son. Manorama becomes aware of the duty of a mother towards her child by hearing the elegant words of the dedicated Sushila. Goaded by Manorama whose conscience is newly awakened, the stupid boy turns over a new leaf. There is no further anxiety about Jadab who is now akin to Priyambad. Sushila has no sense of discrimination – she assists not just the Manoramas who hail from aristocratic families, but also those who are born in humbler families. Once the fisherman Duliya's wife had said a few sharp words about her alcoholic husband before Sushila. Hearing criticism of her husband from the lower-caste woman Duliyani, Sushila, who is devoted to her husband, stares at her in stunned amazement; 'for a little while, her tongue betrays no words or expression'. When the temporary stupefaction passes, her tongue, of course, becomes excessively active. By relentlessly uttering maxims from sacred texts, Sushila transforms the lower-caste woman's way of thinking. Within moments, Duliya's wife becomes devoted to her husband. Duliya also overcomes his craving for alcohol and puts his mind to earning a living.

Sushila also teaches Malabi, the daughter of a rich household:

> Whether the husband is sympathetic or unkind, pious or impious, whether he fulfils his responsibilities towards his wedded wife, it is not at all seemly for women to be disrespectful to their husbands. A chaste wife ought not to be irreverent towards her husband even if he is enamoured of prostitutes.[45]

Sushila is learned in the classics and a *pandita*, a female pundit; while giving advice to Malabi, she narrates many ancient tales from bygone eras like 'Bhaktamal'. She even recites to her the 154th *shloka* of the fifth chapter of the *Manu Samhita*: 'Even if the husband is devoid of good conduct, infatuated with other women or without any credentials of learning and the like, the pious wife will always serve the husband like a god.'[46] Sushila is not just learned in the classics – her worldly wisdom is always vigilant. She knows that one must not let money rot. That is why she turns to the business of moneylending, and the family's wealth and affluence increase day by day. Was Madanmohan Tarkalankar thinking of Sushila when he wrote in his essay, 'Streeshiksha', that if women are educated, they will be capable of earning even while staying at home?

Sushila's eldest son Priyambad, a student of the government school, learns in the 'very difficult language Sanskrit'; habituated to reading the very greatly useful English textbooks too, he does not lag behind in philanthropy. He regularly goes to the school for the low-caste boys and girls of Bijaynagar. He conducts exams for the learners and counsels the *guru mahashay*s about what and how to teach the boys and girls from lower castes. It is almost inevitable that he will receive scholarships from class one onwards for two to three years, get the position of a master when in the third grade, and that his salary will be fixed at fifty rupees. By virtue of this, he also gains a gem of a wife. Thanks to the training of her mother-in-law, 'within the course of a very few days, Priyambad's wife became as well mannered as Sushila'.[47] Did Sushila not narrate historical legends in the manner of storytelling in his childhood so that Priyambad would become an able government employee, so that he would be counted as a respectable member of the third sphere of income generation? Did she not tell him 'how the English had come here, how much trouble Siraj-ud-Daulah had caused for them, and which British ruler had benefited our country in a special way'?[48] The wife of the judge sahib of Dharampur district, the headmistress of the Female Normal School, gets amazed when, during a conversation with Sushila, she hears about Mrs Wilson's sacrifice and greatness apropos the eradication of the 'lack of education' among Indian women! It is not just that she is amazed but the memsahib, who is impressed by Sushila's talents, appeals to the judge sahib that Sushila's husband Chandrakumar must be made a deputy magistrate. The sahib is pleased to hear the loyal and pious Chandrakumar's 'softspoken' English, and the petition of the headmistress of the Female Normal School is granted.

That Chandrakumar becomes a magistrate from a clerk in one leap has at its base not just the recommendation of the judge's wife – there is another, hidden reason. Of course, it is evident in the words of the judge sahib: after coming to Bengal, 'the chief officer of the intelligent government' 'had not heard of another pious, talented woman like Sushila'. 'It has been a great duty that we have accomplished by having honoured and promoted to a high position the husband of a woman like this.'[49] Does that mean that there remains no special reason for anxiety if one were to entrust the responsibility of maintaining 'discipline' in the country to the husbands of the rigid and dispassionate Sushilas around whom blows such a cold wave? And that the foundation of the British empire would get a little firmer if educated men and women maintain peace and stability in the home and outside, within and beyond, simultaneously?

One could draw a table to explain the web of connections between the chief characters, both male and female, of *Sushilar Upakhyan*:

Judge The Headmistress of the Female Normal School			
Jayachandra			
Chandrakumar (Deputy Magistrate) Priyambad (Master)	Jadab	Sushila Priyambad's wife	Manorama Malabi
Duliya		Duliya's wife	

By changing the names of the individuals, if one were to replace them with some appellations that would include all, the outline of Madhusudan Mukhopadhyay's fantasized social collective becomes clear:

The British Ruler Zamindar			
Gopal	Rakhal	Gopal's mother/wife	Rakhal's mother/wife
Lower-class man		Lower-class woman	

If the Gopals and Rakhals were born in *Shishushiksha* and *Barna Parichay*, their mothers and wives – the able wives and companions of *bhadralok* in service, the *bhadramahilas* – manifest themselves in *Sushilar Upakhyan.*

When Pyarichand Mitra's *Etaddeshiya Streelokder Purbabastha* (*The Former Condition of Women in This State*, 1880) was considered to be excessively serious for inclusion in the curriculum of the girls' school, he found out that *Kathamala*, *Bastubichar*, *Sitar Banabash*, *Nar–Nari*, *Barnabodh*, *Nitibodh*, *Charitabali*, *Akhyanmanjari* and *Sushilar Upakhyan* were the books that girls had as texts for the lessons in their curriculum. It was in planning the deletion of the last-mentioned book from the curriculum, perhaps, that Pyarichand composed *Bamatoshini* (1881) – 'for the use of girls'. But even if there was a difference of structure between *Sushilar Upakhyan* and *Bamatoshini* (1881), there was no difference of statement. And, what a surprise – the name of the hero, the ideal householder, is Gopalchandra Deb! The names of Babu Gopalchandra's wife–daughter–son are also similar: Shantidayini (peacegiver), Bhaktibhabini (pious in spirit) and Kulapaban (pedigreed or of a pure clan), respectively. Another name for Sushila, in fact, is Shantidayini: 'What tolerance, what sweet words, what dutifulness, what devotion to god! If one sits next to such a woman for a few moments, it acts as a balm to one's soul.'[50] Shantidayini rears Bhaktibhabini and Kulapaban, and makes 'human beings' of them in the same manner as Sushila does; she brings peace, not only to Gopalbabu's family but to the world outside too.

The long and the short of both Madhusudan Mukhopadhyay's and Pyarichand Mitra's message is: a necessary condition for reformation of the child's character is reconstruction of the mother's character. There is an inkling of this requirement in Vidyasagar's *Barna Parichay*; in the transformed social circumstances, there will be no use for old-fashioned women like Bhuban's *mashi* whose heart is their be-all and end-all. One now needs able assistants for the father and the teacher – like the competent, clever yet patient Sushila – in order to maintain a balance of priority between feeling and thinking. If one is unable to replace the old-fangled women with more modern ones, the arrangement would be left incomplete. If one is unable to create a new bridge between the inner and outer worlds, it would be impossible to propose social contacts anew.

There was a great scarcity of skilled mothers/nurses fit to bring up the vanguard of New Bengal resplendent with the Light of Europe. This regret has been expressed by many people in many ways – for instance, by Michael Madhusudan Dutt (1824–1873). The same Michael Madhusudan who would, in later times, write *Birangana*, was given a gold medal in 1842 by the jury of Hindu College for writing a meaningful essay on 'Narishikshar Gurutwa' ('The Importance of Female Education'). In that essay, he had written:

> Many people have been unable to give up their belief in the existence of ghosts, notwithstanding the strong remonstrance of Reason, and the evidence of Science, because the impressions left on the mind by the idle tales heard or recited in the nursery could not be effaced! It is needless to dwell upon the numerous benefits a child may derive from an educated nurse. In a country like India, where the nurseship (if I may so call the office of a nurse) generally devolves on the mother, the importance of educating the females . . . is very great; for unless they are enlightened, they spread the infection of their ignorance in the minds of those they bring up. Extensive dissemination of knowledge amongst women is the surest way that leads a nation to civilization and refinement.[51]

Not one slogan worth taking into account was left out by him: 'logic', 'science', 'education', 'civilization', 'enlightenment', 'ignorance', 'diffusion of knowledge'. The undiluted substance of Michael Madhusudan's proposal is as follows. Women are a field of experimentation for the theories of filtration that were conceived by the occidental educationists Macaulay and Trevelyan. As soon as their ignorance is eradicated, the natives will get the total right to enter the public thoroughfare of knowledge and science. Many 'orthodox', old-timer contemporaries of Michael Madhusudan perhaps did not completely approve of his views. Even so, there seemed to be no objection to the selection of the word '*dhatri*' (midwife).

Sushilar Upakhyan is an incomparable example of how closely associated imperialism can be with patriarchy. In order to reinforce patriarchal discipline, the position of both higher- and lower-class women have been assessed to be lower than that of males. It was Madhusudan Mukhopadhyay's heartfelt desire that women's education should spread widely, but that did not mean that girls should aim to be the equals or rivals of males. Even the *Smriti* that is more forceful than all other *Smriti*s, the *Manusmriti*, does not approve of female freedom. The ideological back and forth surrounding this contraction and expansion is directly linked with the narrative strategy of *Sushilar Upakhyan*. Was the story of modern women's education linked to the folk style to give an indication that Hindu women were not harmed and the timeless Hindu heritage did not suffer any fissures due to the encroachment of the British? Whether consciously, the parameters of the narrative and its ideological battle array were constructed using the folk style. In Madhusudan Mukhopadhyay's book, the purity of the Hindu woman and the contribution of foreigners towards female education are mutually linked. *Sushilar Upakhyan* is replete with praise for the honest efforts of Christian missionaries. Not just Mrs Wilson, Hannah Catherine Mallens is also mentioned. Chandrakumar reads out Mallens' *Phulmoni o Karunar Bibaran* to Sushila.

This book, written for native Christian girls, was published four years before Pyarichand's *Alaler Ghare Dulal*, in 1852, through the aegis of the

Calcutta Christian Tract and Book Society. Within a short span of time, apart from English, translations of the book came out in various Indian languages. There is not just a mention but an influence of *Phulmoni o Karunar Bibaran* in *Sushilar Upakhyan* that is written in the Bengali folk style. There is not even a slender difference of opinion between Sushila and the narrator of the *Bibaran* (*Account*), the Christian missionary, well-wisher and counsellor of well-educated women, on the rituals they should practise during pregnancy. Radhakanta Deb and Madhusudan Mukhopadhyay were of the same opinion that even while abiding by one's Hinduism, one can learn something from 'highly civilized' people from other religions.

Although there was a debate between the orientalists and the occidentalists on the outline of Indian history, the two parties reached more or less the same conclusion about the medieval age in India: that the age of Islam was an era enveloped in impenetrable darkness and malpractices. And even if that was not true, the brilliance of that age gets concealed by the radiant hue of the British period. Both camps used the issue of the pathetic condition of the Hindu woman as a chief constituent of their enquiry on India. For the Evangelicals, the Utilitarians and the Liberals, oppressed Hindu women were symbols of the immaturity and backwardness of Hindu society; for the orientalists, they were signifiers of the tyranny of Islam and the decline of Hinduism. Bethune said in his inaugural lecture on the day his girls' school was founded: 'further, it was a hopeful reflection that the seclusion and the ignorance to which your females have been so long condemned do not belong to the oldest customs of your nation, that they are themselves innovations, brought in, as I believe, by a courtly imitation of your Mohammedan invaders.'[52] Madanmohan Tarkalankar wrote in the essay 'Stree Shiksha':

> When this country was invaded by the unruly infidels, at that time that oppression of the vile race had made us rue the ruin of our happiness and our wealth. . . . Due to the fear of the non-Hindus, the movement of women in public places and their pursuit of learning was obstructed completely.[53]

On the other side, in the opinion of Mill, it was not because of 'bad charactered non-Hindus' that practices incarcerating women inside the *zenana* had started in the Hindu society; superstitious Hindus had, since time immemorial, kept their women circumscribed within the periphery of the house. The conflict between the orientalists and the occidentalists did not get sorted out despite many efforts of those who tried to bring about an agreement – there was no reason for it to get patched up either. On the contrary, in the critical moments of imperialism, the unresolved conflict became even more forceful. Even women did not get left out of the arena of the conflict. The chronological progression of the nationalist consciousness changed the abstract image of 'Sushila'.

The Rebirth of Sushila

In the third edition of *Stree Shiksha Vidhayak* (1828), Gourmohan Vidyalankar appended a new chapter: 'A Dialogue between Two Women'. Both of them are uneducated, their language is similar – 'I have heard from my Thakurani Didi that no Shastra has ordained that girls become widows if they study.' Their dialogue is strewn with sentences and phrases like '*gatar shoga magira*' ('lazy-bodied dames'), '*madda dhneti chhnuri*' ('the obstinate tomboy'), '*hede dekho didi*' ('look here, o sister').[54] The verbs are refined, but the language of the two women is not at all refined. In *Sushilar Upakhyan* (1859), the illiterate, uneducated Duliya's wife – hearing whose critique of her husband Sushila is struck dumb – talks in the same manner. She refers to her husband-god as '*porarmukho antkurir byata*' ('that burnt-faced offspring of a barren woman'), '*mukhpora, mosto bhudo shorir*' ('burnt face, huge, pot-bellied') and '*durdashyi kalamukho . . . bhatar*' ('evil, unruly, black-faced husband').[55] She does not hesitate to decorate him with such appellations. But whatever the nature of the husband may be, it is the duty of the wife to remain prostrate humbly and submissively, close to his feet. The moment the meaning of this maxim enters through her ear, Duliya's wife's inner eye opens, and the 'rigidity' of her tongue gets wiped out without any further delay by Sushila's pedagogical proficiency. That very night, she entertains her drunken husband with sweet words in highfaluting, ostentatious language: 'Oh Soudamini's father, I am greatly distressed that you have not had a square meal during the entire day today. Now wash your hands and face quickly and please take your seat to have dinner.'[56] Duliya is overwhelmed by his wife's sweet address, and it does not take very long for him to change his ways. He leaves the bad company of his alcoholic friends, and between husband and wife, they incorporate beauty and prosperity within their household. 'If people observed them, they would have believed them to be *bhadralok*.'[57]

Almost fifty years after the composition of the narrative about how to fashion a *bhadramahila*, we hear Rabindranath Tagore's utterance of regret:

> Upon getting Dakshinaranjan Babu's *Thakurmar Jhuli*, I was afraid of opening it. I had a doubt that cadence might get left out in the face of the hard steel of modern Bengali. Previously, I have tried to get some educated girls who are also skilled in storytelling to write fairytales. But despite being a female hand, abetted by the magic of English pens, the tale is held intact but its beauty does not remain quite as such.[58]

Has the wheel started going round in the opposite direction? Have the very *bhadralok* who were all eager to give a 'language' to women due to being pained by the dearth of compatible companions and able guardians of children, now started lamenting the forgetfulness of language in women? In 1907, at the peak of the *Swadeshi* movement, Rabindranath's primary statement in the Foreword of *Thakurmar Jhuli* was: 'The tenderness, sweetness and beauty that there is in fairytales and in the weaving of words therein is inherently feminine.' The 'origin' of fairytales 'is maternal love in the entire land'; therefore, 'when Bengali boys hear fairytales, it is not as if they are just happy to hear fairytales – the melody of the perennial affection of all of Bengal enters through their young hearts and seems to immerse them in the *rasa* [flavour] of Bengal'.[59] That unadulterated flavour of all of Bengal has become scarce these days. In the changeover of education, girls have also almost forgotten their 'own' language. The entire group of grandmothers would become impoverished forever unless schools are opened for modern grandmothers, and one can retrieve the links with the mood and tenor of the older language. Rabindranath believed that because of losing the current of that older flavour, human beings had lost connection with their roots. They were becoming only focused on their self-interest and mentally corrupted.

Oriental educationists have reiterated continuously that Hindu society is 'afflicted with disease'; that without the counsel of western doctors, there is no chance for Hindus 'to heal their souls'. Was Rabindranath trying to say in reply that Hindus were never afflicted, and that it was the foreign 'doctors' who had made such a mess in the name of welfare and under the pretext of 'treatment'? Hindus, meaning high-caste Hindus, had sold themselves by imbibing the bizarre 'medicine' called 'education', and they had become lethargic – the greatest proof of their destitution was the extinction of language in women. Through which path and in what direction could dispirited Hindus proceed so that they could be awakened and cured of the disease that had been learnt and mastered from outside India? Let us go back to the source – there is no hope of rehabilitation without retrieval of the asset called the heart. Not only Rabindranath but many people had been saying this from the very instant of the rise of nationalism.

Describing an interaction between himself and an Irish gentleman whose 'nationalist Irish spirit . . . [had not got completely 'subsumed' by] the nationalist British spirit', Bhudeb Mukhopadhyay (1827–1894) had written on the first page of *Samajik Prabandha* (1892): 'If one loses something, one has to search for it to find it. Is not the effort to develop the national sentiment a research into this lost substance?'[60] Were women one of the targets of the gentlemen who were 'enthusiastic about developing the national sentiment'? Overwhelmed by a thirst for archaeological inquiry, would they break open the cage of the older 'school' and lock women up in the cage of a new 'school'? Would Sushila have to undergo a new birth to keep in abeyance the degradation of society and to touch it with a new spark of life in a 'novel' manner?

Sceptres versus Scriptures

> We are a dependent race. We are humiliated by others and therefore hopeful of respect at home. That is why we want to tell the English: O Englishmen, your weapons (*shastra*) are great but our scriptures (*shaastra*) are greater. You are the rulers; we are a superior race. By pretending that we have whatever we had once upon a time, we want to forget our humiliation and sorrow. . . . In this manner, in order to forget the agony of humiliation, we ourselves make that humiliation a permanent condition. It seems from certain attitudes that some people feel it is essential to embrace ancient ideals for our political advancement.[61]

The utterance is that of the youthful Rabindranath – an excerpt from the essay 'Hindu Vivaha', read out in the Science Association Hall in 1294 (Bengali calendar). Throughout the essay there is severe criticism of the *Manu Samhita*. Rabindranath's sarcasm and censure were showered on those brave men who did not retract from granting the status of superhuman truths to Manu's venomous utterances on womankind, in the name of native heritage. Intertwined within the mystery of the creation of this native heritage is the account of Sushila's rebirth. By slow degrees, Sushila was gradually fashioned into a perfect woman – first by foreign and then by native, orientalist scholars.

During the course of the research of these orientalist scholars, the emperor Ashoka was rediscovered in a new way. Work started in researching from many angles the reality and meaning of Buddhist oppression, and its contribution to Indian culture. A new dimension was appended in Sanskrit poetics, especially in discussions of Kalidas. Many new commentaries and interpretations that were centred on the Vedas, Upanishads and the *Gita* were initiated. The ancient feats of the greater *Bharatvarsha*, extending up to Sinhala, Java, Sumatra and Bali, became a subject of pride. The Hindu race that had been rendered into oblivion received a lesson in self-knowledge through orientalist theoreticians. They were recompensed for the loss of their pristine glory by pride.

The indomitable Eurocentric vision of the European orientalists had rendered the east into a counter-universe of the west, a reflected image of the occident. The western vision was narrow-minded in the literal sense. According to Edward Said (1935–2003), the author of *Orientalism* (1978), the business of orientalist theory had far less to do with the east than with 'us', meaning the western world.[62] The westerner has always attempted to find his own image in the mirror of the east, that looking glass which has, at every step, assured him about his beautiful form. To the orientalists, the static and inert east stood at the opposite axis of the dynamic, constantly volatile west. Despite numerous ups and downs, the entire pattern of lifestyle and bent of thought of the easterners remained unshaken. Without thinking in the abstract, if one were to delve a little deeper, one could easily sense the self-centredness of the westerners. The unique providential will that plays itself out in human life and controls human beings has manifested itself through the many forms of the basic impulse of the different civilizations. It is impossible for human beings with limited intelligence to comprehend wholly the differences in the oriental and occidental minds decreed by fate, and the mysteries and the hidden resolve of the Ultimate Power. No matter how incomprehensible that impenetrable mystery may be to the human intelligence, it does not take a lot of effort to understand that an image of the endless passivity of the ruled would be to the satisfaction to the rulers.

The first rank among the subsequent period of orientalists, after Jones and Colebrook, was Friedrich Max Mueller (1823–1900). A supporter of the 1848 revolution in his early youth, a spokesman for German racism and an orthodox devotee of Bismarck, Max Mueller was an opponent of the neoclassical thought of the eighteenth century and a contributor to the German Romantic movement. This romantic angst drew him towards India. When he was ten years old, a picture of men and women bathing at the *ghat*s of the Ganga in Varanasi in a school textbook had first aroused his curiosity about India. Before that, what he knew about India was that Indians are dark-skinned and that they burn their widows. This picture rectified his misconception, and he discovered that Indians are tall and handsome, and not at all ugly like the 'niggers'.[63] One never recovers from the stupor of the intimations of being enthralled with something in one's childhood. In course of time, India became the mainstay of Max Mueller's romantic imagination. On reaching the shores of India, his romantic yearning was fulfilled. He located the barbarians who were much sought after. He discovered that the Vedas are the descriptive legends of 'immaculate' 'human childhood'.[64] There is no way but to praise the prudence of the Directors of the East India Company. Way back in 1846, they entrusted Max Mueller with the responsibility of compiling and editing the *Rig Veda* along with Sayan's glossary. One does not know whether it was to reciprocate the debt of this patronage that Max Mueller wrote quite a few books and delivered quite a few lectures for British officials and ICS officers. Really speaking, he constructed that famous myth about 'Aryans' almost single-handedly. He gave a new dimension to the tale of the Aryans by transforming the suggestions and connotations of the extremely familiar, excessively used word.

Through the contributions of Max Mueller and his colleagues, the words Hindu–Brahman–Aryan–Indian got mutually intertwined. The bygone Golden Age of the Hindus got metamorphosed into the Golden Age of the Aryans. In the golden past, the Aryans were valiant, courageous, independent, civilized; through their benevolence and their spiritual greatness, they had civilized many barbaric races. And the Aryan women were diversely talented, unrestricted and learned.[65] We get to know suddenly at the end of the nineteenth century that although Aryanness no longer had the same spirit, Aryan blood still courses through our veins. Despite relentless decay, a vestige of Aryan pride still remained. No matter how impoverished the east might be in comparison to the worldly assets of the materialist west, no matter what shortages they had in terms of their food and dress, in matters of inner resources and spiritual consciousness, the eastern people were far more advanced.

Was it for no reason that in 1888, Rabindranath wrote in the poem 'Bangabir' (*Manasi*): 'How are we less than the English / It is a mistake to believe that we are lesser / Since Max Mueller pronounced us Aryas / We have given up all work / . . . [They have said] Manu was spiritual / And so have we resolved.'[66] Although one can find references to Gargi and Maitreyi in many writings before Max Mueller, the appellation of 'Aryan woman' got appended to their names ever since these writers became exceedingly conscious of the Aryan heritage. In the nationalist phase, orientalism got transformed into a sharpened weapon. Just as self-analysis that is dependent on others lacerates them, it creates deadly wounds likewise within the core of oneself. But with the intent of 'erasing their memories' of 'their own torture', the *bhadralok* 'plant deep-rootedly with their own hands in their native land' the cause for their humiliation, whose liability has to be borne by lower-class men and women irrespective of caste, class or creed. The ideal of the *sati* woman and the social responsibilities of Sushilas get transformed by the tension between *shastra* (arms) and *shaastra* (scriptures). This tension, of course, originates long back.

Rammohun Roy wrote *Sahamaran Bishaye Prabartak o Nibartaker Dwitiyo Sambad* (*Second Dialogue between the Proponent and Opponent about the Practice of Dying Together*), possibly published in 1818, in protest against the practice of *sati*. In the booklet, Rammohun's basic contention was: there is no powerful endorsement in the classics for the practice of husband and wife dying together. In fact, even in the *Manu Smriti*, as far as the duty of the widow is concerned, the injunction is only for her to remain single as long as she lives. Rammohun's mouthpiece, the *nibartak* (opponent), relies on Manu as his chief hope and says to the *prabartak* (proponent): Why do you not put a stop to witnessing the killing of women by appealing to the *Manu Smriti*, which says that women should undergo lifelong singlehood when the husband dies in order to demonstrate the conservation of celibacy?[67] The government's views regarding *sati* had got confirmed shape five years prior to the composition of Rammohun's *Dialogue*. And the collection of data in relation to *sati* had started three years earlier. It was not only in governmental discourse, but also in the discourse of both sides – native speakers for and against the motion of the practice of 'dying together' – that the classics were getting mixed up with the practice of *sati*. Women were but an occasion. The brutal practice of dressing them up in flames and using them as combustible material for cremation was a mere pretext for appropriately determining the logic of the classics. That was not all. While writing against the practice of burning by *sati*, Rammohun himself had sung eulogies of women by demonstrating that women were far more firm of conscience because they voluntarily embrace a simultaneous death with their husbands. In *Sahamaran Bishaye Prabartak o Nibartaker Dwitiyo Sambad*, he had made the opponent say:

> In the same country in which men almost die in hearing the name of death, women get ready to enter the funereal flames with the object of reaching their husbands due to the firmness of their souls. See this manifest before you, and then say that there is no firmness in their souls.[68]

There is the trace of a dilemma about *sati* in Rammohun's writing too. On the one hand, he says that women are helpless and simple-minded; that villainous people use muscle power and force on them, and push them into the fire. On the other hand, he says that self-willed *sati*s are portraits of constancy.[69] In later years, Rammohun's second statement got prioritized by many nationalist thinkers. *Sati* became a symbol of bravery. Even Bankimchandra's Kamalakanta (1875) who does not talk except in sarcasm loses his innate power of irony when he sits in divine contemplation of the *sati* woman:

> When I start thinking on the illustrious womankind, instantly the form of a woman who has a penchant to die with her husband awakens in my mindscape. I can see that the pyre is burning; the devoted wife sits within the flames by respectfully holding her husband's feet in her breast. Gradually, the fire spreads; it scorches one organ and then enters the next . . . there is no signifier of bodily pain. The face is happy. . . . Bravo to her endurance, love and devotion![70]

It is not only Kamalakanta but even the reader who gets enchanted by the incantations of *sati* sung by Kamalakanta/Bankimchandra, in the eulogies sung about women's capacity to suffer burns. But was it only Bankim? The same Rabindranath who had written 'Hindu Bibaha' ('Hindu Marriage') would cling to antiquity in the middle phase of his life in the hope of 'political' progress, and would write 'Bibaha' ('Katha', 1306, Bengali calendar) 'Ma Bhoi' (1902), 'Naibedya' (1308, Bengali calendar), 'Pracheen Sahitya' (1907), 'Sibaji Utsab' (1904) and much else. Vivekananda's 'Prachya o Pashchatya' ('Easternness and Westernness') would be published serially in the second and third year of the magazine *Udbodhan* (1306–08, Bengali calendar). His opinion about why the chastity of women is desirable is as follows:

> If the chastity of women is destroyed, no children are born and the entire race becomes extinct. There is no corresponding harm in men marrying forty times – on the other hand, it breeds generations. For women, no more than one is acceptable simultaneously . . . as a result, there is barrenness.[71]

Brahmabandhab Upadhyay (1861–1907), who was first a Brahmo and later took initiation as a Protestant, subsequently created a balance between Vedanta and the Roman Catholic faith and became a 'Vedanticatholic', and ultimately performed penance to take refuge in the Vedic fold, would write in a prefatory letter to the *Swaraj* magazine:

> We seem to have lost the link and are wandering like people who have undergone a memory lapse . . . the sages have affixed the glory of the established Hindu society . . . to its festivals and ceremonies, its fairs and amusements, its rituals and practices, to the pride and honour of one's clan, the feats of fathers and forefathers, and the self-sacrifice of chaste wives. In our *Swaraj* magazine, we will paint a lucid picture of all these heroic tales.[72]

Strong pride in one's own race also influenced the curriculum for girls. In 1893, Mataji Maharani Tapaswini established the Mahakali Pathshala – it started with merely thirty students, but the female student population reached 450 by 1903. At that time, so many girls did not study in any school in Calcutta, not even in Bethune School. The names of some of the books published under the sponsorship of Mahakali Pathshala are: *Sadhvi Samachar*, *Stutimala*, *Shibpujapaddhati*. In the *pathshala*, girls were initiated in the ideals of devoted wifehood, and made aware of the chaste duties of Hindu women. Although the spirit of Hindutva became more and more fiery, the Christian missionaries did not entirely give up hope. Stunned and rendered sceptical by the Sepoy Mutiny of 1857, different religious groups got down to work together. One result of their enterprise was 'Streelok o Balakbalikadiger Nimitto' (For the Cause of Women and Boys and Girls'), published in *Jyotyiringan*, the monthly journal of the Calcutta Tract Society from 1859 onwards. In the first year, *Biranganar Upakhyan* (*The Brave Woman's Tale*) came out serially; it was the primary target of that narrative to prove the disagreeableness of Hindu *dharma*. It was written in the section on Ahalya: 'How horrific are the characters of the gods and goddesses mentioned in the Hindu classics!'[73] A poem titled 'Janmabhoomi' was published in the December issue of 1869. There are some unique exemplars of the use of similes in this poem. Dependent India is compared to a Hindu widow. The reason for Bharat's widowed state is the indescribable torture by the Muslims: 'Subjugated by the barbarians for centuries / Your sons have lost courage and strength.'[74] It is India's unending luck that that age no longer exists. Because remarriage of the Hindu widow is illegal, widowed India is still without a husband. Despite that, thanks to the magnanimous elder brother-in-law, implying the British, her poverty has abated to a great extent: 'He is a kind elder brother-in-law indeed / By sheer good fortune / He rears all your children with care.'[75]

Despite the benevolence of the elder brother-in-law, the self-reproach of the Hindu widow does not get eradicated. The more one's self-torture increases, the more it 'produces' the 'everlasting greatness' of Hindu society.[76] Its signature has remained in many an upper-class, nationalist thought and deed, dream and scheme, deliberation and art. To achieve political improvement, in eulogizing the 'everlasting greatness', the 'Sushilas' had to be configured in a new pattern. After circling the outside and inside, the *bhadralok* came and stood in the *andarmahal* (inner quarters). They saw that although the world outside had come under the clutches of foreigners, the 'home' had not yet gone out of their hands. The essence of the old-fashioned customs and practices had been salvaged by the women in the inner quarters. The world of their thought and belief was not yet totally 'polluted' and 'distorted' by the outside world. The marital devotion of the *sati* seemed to be the signifier of the 'authentic native heritage'. The image of the *sati* woman, decorated with glory, was enriched by many constituents taken from both the classes – upper and lower. That image of the woman unsullied by sin became the mirror image of the pre-colonial past. Through her agency was expressed the nostalgia for the lost past. Along with that, the *sati* was also the representation of Shakti. For the revival of society, one would have to take the initiation of Shakti from her. In other words, a special political dimension was attributed to the notion of *satitva*.

In *Sushilar Upakhyan*, Sushila was the instrument for maintaining the reproduction of social relations – to her was apportioned the role of the midwife. When the time came for breaking the relations of production, Sushila was summoned again. But her social role did not get transformed at all – she just got promoted from a mother to a mother goddess. The country that was greatly sprouting tributes to the mother converted patriarchal discipline, behind which discipline there was a lot of western contribution in the colonial age, into a weapon of rebellion against imperialism. There was not much of a difference in this law during the Gandhian era. Is there not a close relation between this 'novel' yet 'ancient' imaginative idol of Sushila of the nationalist phase with the exuberance of Rabindranath regarding fairytales? Did not the end of colonial 'disorderliness' and the dream of reinstating 'order' work at the core of upper-class nationalist thought? Is there not a structural similarity between that and the fairytale? Did Rabindranath himself not write a fairytale while sitting down to write an introduction? If one were to say that it was because of this similarity that intellectuals were able to welcome *Thakurmar Jhuli* so warmly at that time, it would not be too off the mark.

The Game of Aims

Six boys and girls have sat down to play the game, 'What we will be when we grow up' ('Ke ki hobo khela'). By just hearing the name of the game, one can make out that the six have gathered at one place so that they can voice to each other, by way of play, their individual thoughts on the future. The first one says that he will cross 'rivers, rivulets and faraway seas' to become a great merchant. The shopkeeping intelligence of the second boy is strong; he will not stop short of being the greatest shopkeeper in the country. The third boy does not want to be content by just buying and selling goods – his vision extends much further. He wants to become the owner of a big factory; in the 'chambers of that factory, thousands and lakhs of weavers, potters and blacksmiths would work'. Why should the fourth boy lag behind? His ambition is to compete with the capitalist and become a landlord. 'A thousand ploughs would work for me', and his granary would always remain full. The fifth boy is the most intelligent – he had known the essential matter from a tender age. No wish will be fulfilled if he does not have money in his pocket. He wants to be the owner of a bank. No matter who or what the others are – merchant, shopkeeper, capitalist or landowner – in order to take loans they would all have to come to him. He is quite pleased to think of this.

Through this play, *Ke Ki Hobo Khela* (*Khokakhukur Khela*, 1909[77]), not only do we get to understand the imagined future of these five boys but also that of Dakshinaranjan Mitra Majumdar. Dakshinaranjan's desire was that his intended readers – that is, respectable children of honest clans – should be replete with wealth and respect. Let them not get absorbed in the trivial illusions of a job but extend the periphery of their aspirations. Let them construct shops, factories and mines, and conduct business and commerce in order to hold the reins of the country's economy. And let those who are illiterate, those who inhabit the world outside books, who are the sons of carpenters, blacksmiths, potters, weavers and peasant farmers, remain as they are; let them labour in dingy rooms and work the plough in farms and fields. Did Dakshinaranjan want to suggest the national configuration of the future Bharat in his play, *Ke Ki Hobo Khela*?

It has already been stated that the dramatis personae in the play are six. If shops, factories, farms, fields and banks all go into the hands of the *bhadralok* boys, what then remains for the last character of the play, the girl? After letting people know what their aspirations are successively, the prospective helmsmen of the nation speak out in a unified voice: 'Each one of us will become very great! / What, brother, does one have to do in order to become very great? / . . . Cultivate a good heart and a healthy body, and study hard / You will all then grow up and be great!'[78] The word 'all' has been rendered plural through the glory of the community to which that glory is due. The two words 'study hard' explain that in 'First Boy, Last Boy', 'Charu o Haru' and in story after story, Dakshinaranjan has repeatedly articulated the much-heard maxim in order to reassure students who are burdened by studies: 'Those who study / Travel in cars and carriages.' The game 'Ke Ki Hobo Khela' is no exception. But the trouble has been caused by the last character in the play. At the beginning of the twentieth century, the bounds of education have considerably overstepped the earlier threshold. Women, at least a fraction of women in the higher classes, have come within the purview of this boundary. According to the maxim, women have fulfilled the condition of travelling in cars and carriages – in other words, that of growing up to be worthy. But will they gain that entitlement? The girl-child, the only one of her kind in the game 'What I will be when I grow up', has answered on behalf of Dakshinaranjan: 'How many great things you will do / When you grow up / And Dada / Won't I grow up? / I will keep coming then, Dada / To everybody's homes, gracefully / And keep seeing your homes 'again and again' / . . . I will feed the darlings of the houses, / . . . / Everyone will address me as "*Lokkhiti*" (O, dear one).'[79] There is no doubt that the girl is Sushila. Even her Gopal Dadas, therefore, admit this: '*Lokkhiti*! *Lokkhiti* sister – she has come to play / *Lokkhiti*! *Lokkhiti* sister, in fact, she has won!'[80] The reiterative use of the word '*lokkhi*' (good girl) elucidates that there are no different kinds of goodness for girls – consequently, one does not need more than one appellation for good girls. One can be a 'Gopal' in several ways, but Sushila is a single unit. She has nothing to do but to repeatedly generate both housework and physical effort. It would be adequate for the Sushilas to just emulate the unwavering exemplars of the everlasting greatness of Hindu society: Sati–Savitri, Sita–Behula. In this manner, under the camouflage of letting them win the 'What I will be when I grow up' game, the Gopals defeat the Sushilas.

In the book *Khokakhukur Khela*, there is another play of the same kind: *Bhai-bon*. There, the brothers declare with chests swollen with pride: 'How we will capture, beat, bruise, tear, and much else will we do!' And the quiet, docile sisters announce in a soft, gentle tone: 'We will always hold dear in our hearts / Our male progeny.'[81] Certainly modest by nature, simpleton Sushilas are the favourites of their fathers: 'Let me go and put my arms around my father's neck and extract my share of kisses from him!'[82]

The position of girls in Bengali juvenile literature is indeed very secondary. How many stories could be written about Sushilas who have been almost confined within the same compartment for ages immemorial? Even then, in the age under discussion, was there no writer who tried to hear the inhibited voice of girls and wanted to talk about those who inhabit the margins?

King/Queen

'Once there was a king / He punished me that day / . . . Who punished me like that? / Do you know who that king was?'[83] Although the question sounds like a riddle, the person who asks the question knows very well that those who have played into the hands of this king will understand the meaning of his puzzle. The sway of this king's kingdom extends across the globe, his glory is endless and his subjects are uncountable. One of the subjects in the poem removes himself quietly from the king's hearing and describes his experience to the sufferers. Early in the morning one day, he had climbed up the pomegranate tree to see how the lord dances. The branch broke suddenly, and due to this fault, he was banned from picking guavas, going to watch the *rathyatra* and eating sweetmeats made of flattened rice. The king seemed to have been eagerly awaiting an opportunity so that wherever he sensed some change, he could appear with his staff in hand. Who was this king?

According to Satishchandra Chakrabarti's injunction, those who are attentive to the formation of the child's character may or may not know the king, but those on whom some surveillance is going on every day will not take a moment to recognize him. Children would always know the name and address of the supreme god of the child's kingdom, meaning the father. Perhaps as a strategy of self-defence, the child narrator of Rabindranath's 'Raja o Rani' (*Shishu Bholanath*, 1922) does not narrate the account of getting punished directly but through a riddle. The patrons of patriarchy do not perceive much need for hiding or covering up.

In his book *Santaner Charitragathan*, too, Satishchandra Chakrabarti narrated the story of the king and the queen, and counselled that the family regimen should be structured along the lines of the regimen of the kingdom. Satishchandra was no exception – this decree was perpetuated by many people one after another. One can hardly count the innumerable times that readers of Bengali children's literature have had to heed this injunction. Satishchandra's 'Raja' and the 'Raja' of Rabindranath's child narrator are made in the same mould – both are diligent guardians of their subjects. But does the 'Rani' of 'Raja o Rani' observe the injunction of Satishchandra? Does she 'aid and abet' the Raja with her 'body, mind and words'?

The narrator of 'Raja o Rani' lets us know about his 'Rani':

> Once there was a queen / I follow all that she says / After hearing about the punishment / She just looked at me. / She did not utter anything / Just lowered her face / She went to her own room / And locked herself in for the day. / Neither did she eat / Nor did she go to see the chariot / She took me in her lap / When my punishment period was over. / Her voice was choking / Her eyes were red / Who that queen was / I know, I know, I know.[84]

In the poem, the 'queen' does not dismiss the king's command; she does not appeal to the 'king' on behalf of his 'subject'. Instead, she extends the ambit of the punishment and shares with the wretched 'subject' the desrepute of living inside a prison. Despite assisting the 'Raja' in word and deed, does Rabindranath's 'Rani' not support him from within? Although she outwardly serves the cause of discipline on the outside, does she suffer in her heart of hearts by suppressing her feelings?

By fusing the three words '*kaya*' ('body'), '*mon*' ('mind') and '*bakya*' ('word'), Satishchandra directed that it is the earnest duty of mothers to be obedient followers of fathers. By erasing the middle word '*mon*' (mind) from the compound word, Rabindranath deconstructed the grace of the ideal portrait of domesticity ingrained in the compound word. He demonstrated that the subtle perception of writers like Satishchandra had never paid much heed to the substance called women's hearts. They had not only believed the question of the wishes and disinclinations of mothers to be irrelevant, but also those of children. Within the patriarchal system, everybody – man and woman – is a prisoner, and subservient to phallic control.

The poems in Rabindranath's *Shishu* (1903) and *Shishu Bholanath* (1922) are private conversations between two prisoners. Taking advantage of his father's absence, the boy goes on babbling about whatever he feels like with his mother. He knows that unlike others, his mother will not dismiss his words as gibberish. Although the elders of the world and the venerable fathers and father surrogates who are replete with reprimands may not pay heed to his words, his mother is always there. He will not get another attentive listener like his mother. Seeing that all tasks are carried out by the wish of the lord and master, the same lord and master might assume his group of subjects to be dumb. But the subjects let it be known at every opportunity that if they are dumb, the lords and masters are far more deaf. In Rabindranath's poems, the very same 'children' and 'girls' who are garrulous with one and all and yet well-known as silent, carry on a dialogue and discussion among themselves on the possibility of making a copulative compound of silence–deafness under the pretext of telling a story, and share some fun and laughter.

The boys of *Shishu* and *Shishu Bholanath* are not alone; their community, too, is something to reckon with. At least they would have no objection to welcoming Kanchan, the hero of Sibram Chakraborty's *Baari Theke Paaliye*. This very Kanchan had given an assessment after doing a comparative analysis of his father and mother:

> Chanakya has said . . . '*Lalayet panchabarshani*' . . . recites the father. Its sum and substance is that one must start beating a boy soon after the age of five up to the age of sixteen, and go on beating them repeatedly. It is only then that the boy would grow up to be a man. . . . In the desert called Baba, Ma is the only oasis.[85]

Rabindranath's child characters too have this haven in the midst of the desert by the name of the mother as their only refuge. The narrator of *Shishu Bholanath* says in a tone of regret: 'I wish, mother, that you could be the *duorani* [the neglected queen of the king].'[86] The context of the *duorani* inevitably enters his self-composed story, 'Raja o Rani'. In the opinion of the narrator, it is far better to go into exile with the *duorani* than to stay with the Raja. By doing that, at least one would get a respite from the control of the insufferable Raja, and also always have the Rani close at hand. Is it that the child narrator of *Shishu Bholanath* voluntarily seeks to be Buddhu–Bhutum (the two princes who were converted to a monkey and an owl and sent away with their *duorani* mothers by the king, in an eponymous story in Dakshinaranjan's *Thakurmar*

Jhuli) – a sort of Buddhu–Bhutum who would not erase his distinguishing features through a price or temptation, and not bring back the 'royal regimen'? At the end of the poem 'Duorani', he warns his mother: 'When the night is hushed / I will bury my face in your chest / My eyes will shut with drowsiness / At that time, do not / Go away to Father, please!'[87]

Of whatever else there may be a scarcity in Bengali children's literature, there is no dearth of *duorani*s. Many narratives and short tales have been written around the unfortunate and deprived mother. We have seen Mintu's mother in Dinesh Mukhopadhyay's *Dukkhojoyir Jayajatra*. Jogindranath Sarkar's 'Jay Parajay' too is an account of a widowed mother and her son. Mohanlal of 'Jay Parajay' is not at all quiet, well-behaved and sensible like Mintu. In fact, he is the quite the opposite: extremely immodest and selfish. All the mother's distress is around him. The reason for Mohanlal's tastes and inclinations being extremely gross is that he was rendered fatherless at an 'exceedingly infant phase' and 'there was nobody to discipline him'.[88] Vidyasagar too had said there is an apprehension of boys becoming 'Bhubans' if they lose their fathers in early childhood and if they do not have an able person to manage them. Jogindranath Sarkar's hero, of course, has maintained his family's honour and his mother's dignity. He has restrained and rectified himself: 'Animality has been vanquished by godliness.'[89] At the root of his change of heart is the silent shedding of tears by the helpless widow: 'I felt really sorry when I saw Ma crying. I promised to myself that I will never do that which causes hurt to Ma.'[90] Ma's 'sullied face', tear-filled eyes', 'affection-filled embrace' and 'sweet advice' bring Mohanlal back in the direction of his predestined chamber – even the wish of the *duorani* gets fulfilled. In other words, the familiar account of the woman's subservience to her father in her childhood, to her husband in her youth and to her son in her old age is completed. On the other hand, Rabindranath's boys want to remain 'idiots', they have not the slightest desire to be 'social': 'Teach me your lesson of breaking a lock / That is finely set to tune / Even if I don't get anything else / Give me access to the sky / And a way of escape through the fields.'[91] There is only one appeal – let *Ma* be a companion of his endless journey of exile. Rabindranath's boys are drawn towards their sympathetic mothers – but is there not a going back within that move? Behind their eagerness, is there not a dormant desire to remove the father and grab his seat? From this pendulum movement is created the 'Birpurush'of *Shishu*, and the 'Khela Bhola' of *Shishu Bholanath*.

The boy in 'Khela Bhola' lets his mother know: 'Sometimes, Ma, the day comes / When I forget my play.'[92] When such a day comes, 'It sort of rings within my ear.' Leaving aside his game, he gazes far into somebody else's terrace and sees a little girl hanging out a sari in the sun. Immediately, he remembers the oft-heard stories of fairytales and thinks: 'This must be beyond the wilderness / I think to myself that this must be where the king's abode is.'[93] It is not difficult to understand that the boy's body is undergoing pubertal changes and that there is a budding sexual awareness. Beneath his intermittent abandoning of play and becoming sad is the nebulous pressure of sexual longing. He does not know the language with which to express his half-perceptible desire. He can only say: 'It sort of rings within my ear.' And he can suggest the state of his heart through stories of princes and the princesses, through the metaphor of fairytales. No wonder the thing called a 'fairytale' is an eyesore for writers like Satishchandra Chakrabarti. If Rabindranath had let it rest at declaring the onset of puberty, it would have made sense; but he struck an extreme blow with the poem without paying any heed to those who are squeamish about sex. The boy who abandons his play sees that even his mother forgets her work at times. 'What do you think, sitting silently? Pressed against the window pane?'[94] He observes that on the days that his mother forgets her work, in her hand there is a letter from the immigrant father. Immediately, the stories of fairytales flash in his mind. In those stories, between the prince and the princess stands the monster. Without this third individual, the conflicting triangular relationship cannot be forged. About his mother, immersed in anxiety over his father, he thinks:

> Which land are you a daughter of? / It seems that you are my mother / Of many ages / And from far away / Going near you, I touch your hand / You seem to be a mother who had gotten lost / . . . All play floats away / I wonder in what age / And in which land / At the shore of which sea your home was.[95]

In the last line of the poem, the manner of the address changes; the boy directly addresses his mother and says: 'I feel like going back / To that chamber in the unknown island / At dawn, you and I would go / On our boat with a sail.'[96]

In *Shishu*, the narrator of 'Chhotobaro' knows no word for 'growing up' except 'to be like his father'. Rabindranath lets us know in a mildly jocular manner that the boy's secret wish is not at all abnormal; in reality, too, it would happen exactly like that. The world of the child's imagination is not totally self-supported and self-created. He gleans the ingredients of his imagination from everywhere. Due to the strength of this material consciousness, the portraits emerging from Rabindranath's visualization of the child have proved to be credible and alive.

A *bhadralok* joint family comprises of other people apart from mother, father, brother, sister, kith and kin – there are also manservants and maids. Would the Gopals and Rakhals be enthused to compose fairytales about them?

Manservants–Maids

Children appeal to the Supreme God: 'Oh greatest God! You are the father of all – the rich as well as the poor. Just as you love us and are kind to us, please love the servants and maids of our house thus and be equally kind to them. In your eyes, we and they are all the same.'[97] This prayer is in the book *Saathi* (second edition, 1898), published by the Brahmo Samaj. The name of the author and the year of the first edition of *Prarthana Pustak* is unknown. But it does not seem that anybody will be eager to learn the name of the anonymous author – in the book *Saathi,* there is not a word that is new. The mental attitude of the *bhadralok* vis-a-vis servants and maids is like that of several other people. Most Bengali children's writers have said the same thing in a roundabout way about the 'people who work as domestic help'.

God is equitable – he will not deprive anyone of the blessing of an awareness of God. But if the consciousness of hierarchy is not firm in the material world, living souls will not understand the value of attaining freedom from hierarchy in the world hereafter. That does not mean, however, that it is always desirable for the differences to be pointed out. If that causes the hierarchical sense of people in the lower strata to get awakened, the respectable gentlefolk will be confronted with a great crisis. The spokesman of the writer in *Saathi* is very tender-hearted and softspoken: 'I do not at all like the idea of addressing maids and servants as *tui* [the informal second person address].'[98] You would remember that in *Shishushiksha*, *Part 3*, 91st edition, composed by Madanmohan Tarkalankar and revised by Ishwarchandra Vidyasagar, it was said by way of highlighting the qualities of well-behaved boys: 'They do not utter sharp words, even to servants and maids.'[99]

The writer of *Saathi*, of course, has exposed the hidden agenda of the lesson in courtesy:

> Do you know that sweet words do not cost money, yet they yield a lot of results? If you do not know it, why do you not get it tested by the slaves of the household? Whatever work your servants and maids do for you, in whatever manner, for some money, they will do it a lot better through sweet words.[100]

In other words, those who are careful spenders have to be sweet-tongued. It is not only money that gets saved through sweet words; one can win over servants and maids in three aspects – their bodies, minds and words. The writer in *Saathi* has explained:

> What made these servants develop such love for their masters? The only answer to this is 'Love and sweet behaviour.' The master used to think of the servant as one of his own kith and kin; the servant, too, therefore, worked hard for the master, thinking of him as a relative.[101]

In Bengali juvenile literature, there is no dearth of loyal '*puratan bhrityas*' ('old servants'). There are no specific differences among the lowly – across the board, they are all equally reliable and self-destructive. Some writers carry this one step ahead; there is no difference between Hemendra Kumar Ray's detective

Jayanta's servant Ramhari and his dog Bagha. Both are infinitely brave and profoundly loyal to their masters; their lives and souls are pledged to their masters. It is not only Hemendra Kumar Ray but many others who attribute equal value to domesticated animals and domestic servants.

But there are many servants and maids in the world who do not get charmed by the sweet words of their masters; in fact, without any rhyme or reason, they sometimes unleash sharp words on them. In *Sahaj Rachana Shiksha* (*Simple Lesson in Composition*), giving an introduction to a few firm rules about femininity in Bengali composition, Bankimchandra wrote:

> In non-Sanskritic words, adjectives that end with the feminine do not sound that good. . . . Instead of saying *sushila bou* [courteous wife] one should say *sushil bou* [Bengali] or *sushila bodhu* [Sanskritized Bengali]. Instead of saying *mukhara chakrani* [foul-mouthed servant woman], I'd rather say *mukhara dashi* [foul-mouthed maid].[102]

Because they follow the strong rules of femininity, the adjective *sushila* comes before *bodhu* and the adjective *mukhara* comes before *dashi*. In the 'Patralipi' chapter of *Sahaj Rachana Shiksha*, Bankimchandra had given the instruction: 'The daughters of Brahmans can all write *Debi* [goddess] after their names, it is only the Shudra girls who must write *Dashi* [servant girl].'[103]

When those who are supposed to remain dumb become garrulous, by what narrative strategy can that onslaught be stalled? If one makes servants who have unrestrained speech the victims of satire or farce, if one can make readers laugh at them rather than with them, no cracks and fissures are created in the social structure and the established status quo is maintained. Here are two quotations from two stories in Ashapurna Debi's early career: 'Babu seems to be Nawab Siraj-ud-daulah in person. Do you keep riding in cars and palanquins all day and night in your Katke district? You have the legs of a *chhotolok* – you will quickly go back and forth' ('Bhimsen Ghatotkach Sambad', *Half Holiday*, first published 1941).[104] 'Two sons of Brahmans of the Mahaprabhu living in their native land are gesticulating among themselves; perhaps such body language indicating objection is because the master has demanded the accounts of the domestic purchases' ('Keu Kom Jae Na' ['No Less'], *Half Holiday*).[105] There are some regulated signs for recognizing the Babu and servants: 'Seeing that he is ugly, dark and fat, they will surely think him to be a servant' ('Bodle Gelo Mot Ta' ['Reversal'], *Half Holiday*).[106]

It is not as if everyone unanimously accepted this understanding of signs and caste consciousness. There are counter-examples in Rabindranath's 'Khokababur Pratyabartan' (1298), Sukumar Roy's *Jhalapala* (1910), and even in Ashapurna Debi's later stories. The servant in the play *Jhalapala* (*Exasperated*), Ramkanai, is extremely devoted to his master, the zamindar. He is always attentive to his well-being or otherwise. In the zamindar's house at Jhingetola, there is a crowd of many kinds of parasitic characters. Some of them want to open a school with the support of the zamindar, some want to earn a few coins by singing songs about rescuing the country or by shameless flattery of the zamindar. The zamindar cannot at all tolerate the fellows, yet for the sake of simple civility due to people who belong to the same caste, he cannot express this frankly. At this critical moment in the play, Ramkanai enters. The zamindar is a gentleman, so what he says is different from what he feels inside. But Ramkanai has no such hindrance – he is a *chhotolok*. The zamindar is most pleased that he can kill the snake without breaking his stick. People would not malign him, yet he would be freed of this nuisance. What better solution could there be? Ramkanai is all set to free his master of all the irritants, but the zamindar greatly disapproves of coercion. He greatly fears the thing called defamation: 'Can't one do something so that they get up and go of their own accord? So that there is no backbiting about me?'[107] The sycophants grow exasperated at Ramkanai's sharp words; the zamindar still keeps silent. It is not difficult to understand that he indirectly supports it. Ramkanai does not excuse them as he talks to them; he carries on a repartee at the same level. Seeing that the servant is exceeding his limits due to the master's indulgence, the assembly gets infuriated. In order to pacify them, the zamindar intermittently says in a weak voice: 'O Rama – that is not the way to talk. Please respect the Babus as you talk to them'; or 'Rama, you shut up now – do not hinder the Babus.'[108] Seeing the audacity of an insignificant servant, the flatterers may get angry and protest, but it is not as though that due to this, they will abandon the company of the zamindar and go away. For the sake of self-interest, they have the capacity to digest any insult. The zamindar, therefore, utters his regret to himself: 'The servant fellow unleashes his abuses and everyone swallows them passively.'[109] To rescue himself from them, he takes refuge with his Kedarmama, who is a lawyer, hoping that his twisted intelligence will be able to set them right. Kedarmama comes and leaves but only after inciting the assemblage; vexed by him, it becomes impossible for them to stretch their arms and legs and stay on without a care in the zamindar's household. Whatever the zamindar had not been able to do despite trying, Kedarmama is able to achieve very easily. His greatest support in this, the chief weapon of accomplishing what he has resolved to do, is the same Ramkanai. He uses Ramakanai to instigate people and rag them: 'Let me go and provoke Rama now.'[110] Eventually, Kedarmama plays and wins the final round by getting Ramkanai disguised as a policeman. Fearing the police and the thought of having to go to prison, the parasitic group of flatterers put their tails between their legs and run away.

Almost throughout the play, Ramkanai is a subservient and obedient servant. He seems to have an inseparable bond with his master based on his self-interest. He is ostensibly greatly obliged by working according to the instructions of the zamindar and Kedarmama. Whatever presence of mind or ready wit he might have, in his habits he seems to be a mere passive instrument for the achievement of the objectives of his masters. The first impression of him might be that it is not only as if Ramkanai is caught in the web of an unequal relationship – he also has no complaint about or awareness of it. It might also seem that the only targets of his jokes, humour and quibbles are the opponents of the zamindar, and that he has no sense of aversion towards his venerable masters. But there is a change of mood in the last dialogue of the play. The last utterance of Ramkanai brings a new dimension to his character. When the Dulirams flee in order to avoid a confrontation with the police, Kedarmama claims for himself the entire credit of turning them out. In exchange, he gifts Ramkanai with a proverb: 'You saw Rama! This is what is called "Whatever is intelligence is strength." One must recognize people. After seeing the signs, the appropriate medication has to be given.'[111] In reply to that, like an ideal servant, Ramkanai agrees. He seems not to feel any grievance at not being given any credit, but he soon adds: 'Crows die in the storm, enhancing the miraculous powers of the fakir.' And this one utterance makes Ramkanai stand in the opposite camp to Kedarmama. The proverb used by Ramkanai negates the axiomatic truth used by Kedarmama. The representatives of high society come within the purview of his irony. They are those who instigate the Ramkanais, utilize hundred per cent of their intelligence, hard work and imaginative abilities, and after digesting all their achievements, swell with pride in taking all the credit. The resonance of Ramkanai's ironic utterance can also be seen in the choric song with which the play ends: 'Oh Chandicharan, / Why don't you die! / How dare you call a servant / To box the master's ears?'[112]

The household includes mother, father, son, daughter, servant and maid. One needs discipline for the functioning of the household; one needs to 'silently keep working at the base'. Chandranath Basu and his ilk had promised that once that task was accomplished, the Gopals and Rakhals would be 'able and authorized' to go outside the home. Have they been able to keep the honour of that authority?

Notes and References

1 Ishwarchandra Vidyasagar, *Barna Parichay, Part 2*, in *Bidyasagar Rachanasamagra*, Vol. 1, Calcutta, 1987, pp. 33–34.

2 Ibid., pp. 37–38.

3 Satishchandra Chakrabarti, *Santaner Charitragathan*, Calcutta, 1396 (Bengali calendar), p. 75.

4 Ibid., *Akkhyapatra*.

5 Ibid., p. 75.

6 Ibid., pp. 40–41.

7 Ibid., p. 42, pp. 11–12.

8 Ibid., p. 16.

9 Ibid., p. 69.

[10] Ibid., pp. 22, 25.
[11] Ibid., p. 74.
[12] Ibid., p. 75.
[13] Ibid., p. 8.
[14] Ibid., p. 74.
[15] Ibid..
[16] Ibid., p. 55.
[17] Ibid., p. 68.
[18] Rabindranath Tagore, '*Thakurmar Jhuli* Prasange', in *Dakshinaranjan Rachanasamagra*, Vol. 1, Calcutta, 1988, p. 4.
[19] Madhusudan Mukhopadhyay, *Sushilar Upakhyan*, reprinted in Supriyo Sarkar, ed., *College Street*, Calcutta, September–October 1986, p. 157.
[20] Biswanath Mukhopadhyay and Baridbaran Ghosh, 'Lekhak Parichiti', in Supriyo Sarkar, ed., *College Street*, Calcutta, September–October 1986, p. 249.
[21] Madhusudan Mukhopadhyay, *Sushilar Upakhyan*, p. 157.
[22] Ibid., p. 159.
[23] Ibid.
[24] Ibid., pp. 160–61.
[25] Rammohun Roy, *Sahamaran Bishaye Prabartak o Nibartaker Dwitiyo Sambad*, in Ajit Kumar Ghosh, ed., *Rammohun Rachanabali*, Calcutta: Haraf Prakashan, 1973, p. 202.
[26] Meredith Borthwick, *The Changing Role of Women in Bengal, 1849–1905*, Princeton: Princeton University Press, 1984, p. 28.
[27] Jogeshchandra Bagal, *Radhakanta Deb*, Calcutta, 1385 (Bengali calendar), pp. 30–32.
[28] Brajendranath Bandyopadhyay, *Gourmohan Vidyalankar, Radha Mohan Sen, Brajamohan Majumdar, Nilratna Haldar,* Calcutta, 1384 (Bengali calendar), p. 96.
[29] Jogeshchandra Bagal, 'History of the Bethune School and College (1849–1949)', in *Bethune College and School Centenary Volume (1849–1949)*, Calcutta, 1950, p. 107.
[30] Brajendranath Bandyopadhyay, *Jaygopal Tarkalankar, Madangopal Tarkalankar*, Calcutta, 1389 (Bengali calendar), pp. 49–50.
[31] Ibid., pp. 33–34.
[32] Ibid., p. 40.
[33] Ibid., p. 43.
[34] Madanmohan Tarkalankar, *Shishushiksha*, Vol. 2, revised by Ishwarchandra Vidyasagar, Calcutta, 1899, p. 15.
[35] Jogeshchandra Bagal, 'History of the Bethune School and College (1849–1949)', p. 23.
[36] Madhusudan Mukhopadhyay, *Sushilar Upakhyan*, reprinted in Supriyo Sarkar, ed., *College Street*, p. 161.
[37] Ibid., pp. 163–64.
[38] Ibid., p. 176.
[39] Meredith Borthwick, *The Changing Role of Women in Bengal 1849–1905*, pp. 83–84.
[40] Madhusudan Mukhopadhyay, *Sushilar Upakhyan*, reprinted in Supriyo Sarkar, ed., *College Street*, p. 164.
[41] Ibid., p. 174.
[42] Ibid., p. 176.
[43] Ibid., pp. 196, 202.
[44] Ibid., p. 202.
[45] Ibid., p. 212.
[46] Bharatchandra Shiromani and Jadunath Nyaypanchanan, trans., *Manusamhita*, Section 5, Shloka 154, Calcutta, 1336 (Bengali calendar), p. 469.
[47] Madhusudan Mukhopadhyay, *Sushilar Upakhyan*, reprinted in Supriyo Sarkar, ed., *College Street*, p. 232.
[48] Ibid., p. 199.
[49] Ibid., p. 229.

[50] Pyarichand Mitra, 'Bamatoshini', in *Pyarichand Rachanabali*, Calcutta, 1971, p. 591.
[51] Michael Madhusudan Dutt, 'An Essay on the Importance of Educating Hindu Females', in *Madhusudan Rachanabali*, Calcutta, 1983, p. 551.
[52] Jogeshchandra Bagal, 'History of the Bethune School and College (1849–1949)', in *Bethune College and School Centenary Volume (1849–1949)*, p. 108.
[53] Brajendranath Bandyopadhyay, *Jaygopal Tarkalankar, Madangopal Tarkalankar*, pp. 36–37.
[54] Brajendranath Bandyopadhyay, *Gourmohan Vidyalankar, Radhamohan Deb, Brajamohan Majumdar o Nilratna Haldar*, Calcutta, 1384 (Bengali calendar), pp. 13–15.
[55] Madhusudan Mukhopadhyay, *Sushilar Upakhyan*, reprinted in Supriyo Sarkar, ed., *College Street*, pp. 185–86.
[56] Ibid., p. 187.
[57] Ibid.
[58] Rabindranath Tagore, '*Thakurmar Jhuli* Prasange', in *Dakshinaranjan Rachanasamagra*, Vol. 1, p. 5.
[59] Ibid.
[60] Bhudeb Mukhopadhyay, *Samajik Prabandha*, Calcutta, 1981, p. 3.
[61] Rabindranath Tagore, 'Hindu Bibaha', *Samaaj*, in *Rabindra Rachanabali*, Vol. 12, Calcutta, 1960, pp. 415–16.
[62] Edward Said, *Orientalism*, reprint, London: Penguin, 1985, p. 12.
[63] Uma Chakravarti, 'Whatever Happened to the Vedic Dasis?', in Kumkum Sangari and Sudesh Vaid, eds, *Recasting Women: Essays in Colonial History*, New Delhi: Kali for Women, 1989, p. 81.
[64] Friedrich Max Mueller, *India: What Can It Teach Us?*, Delhi, 1961, pp. 99–101.
[65] Uma Chakravarti, 'Whatever Happened to the Vedic Dasis?', in Kumkum Sangari and Sudesh Vaid, eds, *Recasting Women*, p. 46.
[66] Rabindranath Tagore, 'Bangabir', *Manasi*, in *Rabindra Rachanabali*, Vol. 2, Calcutta, 1966, pp. 209–10.
[67] Rammohun Roy, *Sahamaran Bishaye Prabartak o Nibartaker Sambad*, in Ajit Kumar Ghosh (ed.), *Rammohun Rachanabali*, Vol. 2, p. 171.
[68] Ibid., p. 202.
[69] Latha Mani, 'Contentious Traditions: The Debate on *Sati* in Colonial India', in Kumkum Sangari and Sudesh Vaid, eds, *Recasting Women*, pp. 105–6.
[70] Bankimchandra Chattopadhyay, *Kamalakanta*, in Gopal Halder, ed., *Bankim Rachanasamagra*, Volume on Essays, Section 1, Calcutta, 1973, p. 140.
[71] Swami Vivekananda, 'Prachya o Pashchatya', in *Swami Vivekananda Vani o Rachana*, Calcutta, 1965, p. 196.
[72] Brahmabandhab Upadhyay, 'Anushthan Patra: Swaraj', in *Brahmabandhab Upadhyay Rachanasamagra*, Calcutta, 1987, p. 53.
[73] *Jyotoringan*, Calcutta, October 1869, p. 42.
[74] Ibid., p. 70.
[75] Ibid.
[76] Brahmabandhab Upadhyay, 'Anushthan Patra: Swaraj', in *Brahmabandhab Upadhyay Rachanasamagra*, p. 53.
[77] Dakshinaranjan Mitra Majumdar, *Ke Ki Hobo Khela, Khoka Khukur Khela*, in *Dakshinaranjan Rachanasamagra*, Vol. 2, Calcutta, 1388 (Bengali calendar), pp. 317–18.
[78] Ibid., p. 319.
[79] Ibid.
[80] Ibid.
[81] Dakshinaranjan Mitra Majumdar, *Bhai-bon, Khoka Khukur Khela*, in *Dakshinaranjan Rachanasamagra*, Vol. 2, p. 302.
[82] Ibid.
[83] Rabindranath Tagore, 'Raja o Rani', *Shishu Bholanath*, in *Rabindra Rachanabali*, Vol. 13, Calcutta, 1967, p. 91.

[84] Ibid., pp. 91–92.
[85] Sibram Chakraborty, *Baari Theke Paaliye*, in *Sibram Rachanabali*, Vol. 2, Calcutta, 1975, pp. 76, 78.
[86] Rabindranath Tagore, 'Duorani', *Shishu Bholanath*, in *Rabindra Rachanabali*, Vol. 13, Calcutta, 1967, p. 101.
[87] Ibid., p. 103.
[88] Jogindranath Sarkar, 'Jay Parajay', 'Chhobi o Golpo', in *Shishupathya Granthabali*, Calcutta, 1988, p. 180.
[89] Ibid., p. 192.
[90] Ibid., p. 183.
[91] Rabindranath Tagore, 'Baul', *Shishu Bholanath*, in *Rabindra Rachanabali*, Vol. 13, p. 95.
[92] Rabindranath Tagore, 'Khela Bhola', *Shishu Bholanath*, in *Rabindra Rachanabali*, Vol. 13, p. 85.
[93] Ibid.
[94] Ibid., p. 86.
[95] Ibid.
[96] Ibid.
[97] 'Agyata', *Saathi*, Calcutta, 1360 (Bengali calendar), p. 23.
[98] Ibid.
[99] Madanmohan Tarkalankar, *Shishushiksha*, Vol. 3, revised by Ishwarchandra Vidyasagar, Calcutta, 1900, p. 10.
[100] 'Agyata', *Saathi*, pp. 23–24.
[101] Ibid., p. 26.
[102] Bankimchandra Chattopadhyay, *Sahaj Rachana Shiksha*, in Gopal Halder, ed., *Bankim Rachanasamagra*, pp. 1192–93.
[103] Ibid., p. 1197.
[104] Ashapurna Debi, 'Bhimsen Ghatotkach Sambad', 'Half Holiday', in *Kishore Sahitya Samagra*, Vol. 1, Calcutta, 1390 (Bengali calendar), p. 169.
[105] Ashapurna Debi, 'Keu Kom Jae Na', 'Half Holiday', in *Kishore Sahitya Samagra*, Vol. 1, p. 140.
[106] Ashapurna Debi, 'Bodle Gelo Mot Ta', 'Half Holiday', in *Kishore Sahitya Samagra*, Vol. 1, p. 135.
[107] Sukumar Roy, *Jhalapala*, in Satya Chakrabarty (ed.), *Upendra Kishore – Sukumar Rachanasamagra*, Calcutta, 1983, p. 534.
[108] Ibid., pp. 533, 534.
[109] Ibid., p. 534.
[110] Ibid., p. 535.
[111] Ibid., p. 537.
[112] Ibid.

5

The White Man's Burden and the Black Man's Responsibility

Allan Quatermain is back in Africa once more, and with him are Sir Henry Curtis and Captain John Good. Nothing – not wealth, security or the comforts of a good life – has persuaded them to stay home. They are indifferent to the charms of a life that is prosperous but passionless. This does not mean that they are like any other traveller who travels to Africa simply to escape from the monotony of a predictable life, for a mere whiff of novelty. Nor have they come in search of money or fame. A 'motiveless' curiosity has drawn them from afar to this continent; it is Africa that has brought together this unlikely trio. The fifty-something veteran Quatermain, the practical Curtis and the affable Good – each one of them experiences in the depth of his heart an irrepressible pull Africawards.

The three Englishmen were first seen together in Africa in the late nineteenth century, in Rider Haggard's (1856–1925) *King Solomon's Mines* (1883); the sequel, *Allan Quatermain* (1887) records their second set of adventures. Of course, between these two appearances, Quatermain has changed a lot. His trip to Africa this time is neither for business nor quite for adventure.

Possessed by Africa

Quatermain's musings in the second novel reveal to the reader that his desire to go to Africa is fuelled by a simmering discontent. He lacks nothing, yet he knows not a moment of peace. An intolerable yet impenetrable perception of discontent torments him every moment. Some might attribute this 'unnatural' aspect of his psyche to his being oppressed by the prescriptions and proscriptions of society. It may be argued that Quatermain is not an exception; he is only a little more sensitive than the rest. The identities of all 'social' beings are inevitably split. Man has to discipline his natural propensities in order to sustain the social order. Innumerable laws and regulations have come into existence precisely in order to contain his excessive ambitions. Banished from the realm of the visible and the permissible, these forbidden desires settle themselves in the subconscious layers of the mind. Nor is it possible to unquestioningly accept the impositions and restrictions of society. However, even if he wishes to integrate himself into society, man is racked by secret and urgent longings that are apparently aimless but capable of incessant torment. It is not enough that these secret desires steal out of the dark caverns of the mind and reveal themselves in dreams when the 'conscious' mind is stilled; they even manifest themselves surreptitiously in so-called 'normal' behaviour. Besides, man continuously oversteps the boundaries of social control in art and in fantasy. Through fantasy, he lightens the unbearable burden of his life that is regulated by reason. Fantasy is the only way in which one can scramble the strictures of reason, break the strict linearity of cause and effect.

Quatermain would have had no trouble accepting this standard psychoanalytical reckoning related to the 'unconscious', for he too believes that at least ninety per cent of the so-called civilized person's mind is actually barbaric; as soon as the fine veneer of civilization flakes off, his primordial self reveals itself. Until he frees himself from this dominating, unduly privileged part of his consciousness, man cannot truly realize or understand himself fully. Quatermain visits Africa in search of this freedom. The crisis of civilization makes him turn to Africa; he is possessed by 'Africa'.

But whatever Quatermain may believe, his desire to be in Africa cannot be explained in purely psychological terms. Surely, it has a spatio-temporal dimension as well. What, then, is at the heart of his alienation? Is it an unspecified antagonism towards every code of civilization, or is it antipathy for the social system of which he is a part? Quatermain claims to hold the former view, yet his entire narrative is located in the context of nineteenth-century England. A little probing would reveal that a particular ideology deriving from that of modern industrial England functions as the ultimate value for Quatermain. This perspective is the sole arbiter by which he seeks to judge the various traditions, the cross-currents, and the flow and ebb of human civilization. The most complex of these signs in his personal semiotics is encoded in 'nature'. The very fluidity of capital (the soul of the mode of extraction of surplus known as 'capitalism') may itself be a cause for weakening the extreme rationality of the Newtonian universe, thereby smudging the neat picture of 'nature' that the new science supplied to the eighteenth- and nineteenth-century 'man of reason'. Quatermain seems utterly unaware of this.

Nature's Reason and the Nature of Reason

During the time of Quatermain, in England and Western Europe at least, the word 'nature' – or the particular idea associated with nature – had a different meaning and value. That idea has left a stamp on different categories – in fact, on opposing thoughts and beliefs – of that age. Its periphery had stretched so far during the eighteenth century itself that it became the most powerful theory not only in the natural sciences, but also in the field of the social sciences. Isaac Newton's (1642–1727) mechanics, the theoretical fulcrum to the explanation of absolute velocity developed in association with the Italian Galileo Galilee (1564–1642), provided special theoretical support to the ideology alongside various philosophical notions. Newton's mechanics held up an ideal of order to the theoretical pioneers of the eighteenth century. They learnt that there is not the slightest alteration in the laws of nature. Planets–stars–nebulae are bound within an impermeable system of rules. Nature does not tolerate the slightest laxity. If rules were violated by even a hair's breadth, the entire world would be destroyed. Newton's science not only acquainted us with the self-proven and infallible sources of nature, but also led us to a novel method for the search of knowledge. If one proceeded by that method, everything in the inanimate world would be accessible to human beings; dispelling the darkness of ignorance, everything would be illumined. The mutual dependence between nature and reason was the chief acknowledgement of this method. Just as nature is rationalistic, human beings too are governed by reason. The rationale of nature teaches us the nature of rationality. With the aid of his 'natural' perception of reason, man can configure his own world. Eradicating one by one the superstitions of many ages ingrained in man's mind, a rationalistic state is constructed either by demolishing entirely or changing the outer covers of the establishments and unjust systems that had been preserved through institutions or sanctified sites of ignorance. If one had to free oneself of self-deception and persecution or the ideals of self-sacrifice and forgiveness that had bound people in their coils for long, if one wanted to be involved with living, visible reality, one would have to be initiated by nature predicated on reason rather than be immersed in the experience or illusion of other-worldliness. One can learn the principles of balance and proportion and the methods of synchronization and grace from nature that is the epitome of moderation. There is no excess anywhere in nature. It is all determined by a pattern, an exact measure. Within it lie concealed all the ways of becoming successful in life. Man would not be able to reach any target unless he learns to follow the middle path by taking into account both sides. This implies that just as one can bring nature within one's control through the help of reason, similarly, the order of society can also be configured according to the rules of reason. The eighteenth century brought in its wake the mandate of the unopposed authority of reason.

Many theoreticians of that age summarized reason thus: instead of wasting time on unearthing rational interpretations of the spiritual world and instead of making real life insufferable in pursuit of the unattainable, one should address the question of how to make the world a little more livable. The principles of excellence of that period were constructed on the inseparable link between nature and reason. The ideological extent of these principles is, of course, very clear today. It is hardly necessary to reiterate that camouflaged under the theory of irrefutable supremacy of rationality, was the declaration of the supremacy of one class. There were many progressive aspects to the account of the advancement of that class, but man has had to pay a dear price for it – as is evident in the unceasing bloodshed, and a present that is full of sorrow, poverty and inequality. There was a huge deception in the promise on which modern rationality based its hope of human liberation because the word 'human', for all practical purpose, was used as a substitute for the signature of a particular class: the bourgeoisie. At that moment of transition, it was the bourgeois class that was the power or subject of history. At that revolutionary juncture of modernity, reason and science had got intertwined with capital and the self-interest of capital. Consequently, a special form and component of rationality that was spreading over society was gradually formed. According to the new law, whatever opposed the self-interest of capital was irrational.

This special kind of rationality, i.e. rationalism, wanted to dismiss, in one word, alternate possibilities, and suppress whatever opposing voices there were. Its success had two variations: either misappropriate other perspectives wholly or partially, or repress them somehow. It is no wonder that any substance would get classified into strata within the discipline of rationalism, and that they would become pure components of some catalogue or table. In fact, as time progressed it would be noticed that there was no fixed open space for man there – man had got transformed into a mere number. Actually, at the core of the rationalist ideology there is an inviolable paradox, an ultimate ambivalence. On the one hand, it is for dissemination; on the other, for preservation. On the one hand, it is eager to demolish all power that works against capital; on the other, it seems anxious to preserve the self-interest of capital by fair means or foul. In this great warp and woof, within this dilemma, rationalist observation gradually created the picture of a mechanized world where everything was perfectly coherent. There were no cracks and fissures; different components were interwoven within an enormous, undisputed plan. In the neatly structured arrangement, there was no gap anywhere. There was nothing that was incompatible or incongruent. Its simplicity was as perfect as it was satisfactory.

But the problem is that it is quite difficult to maintain unaltered positions; it is not only difficult but almost impossible. Capital, for which all this organization exists, repeatedly ruins the certainty of order. It upsets the infallibility of reason. This is because capital is by no means an immobile substance or worthless thing. Through it, a special image of social relations is formed. And, through many actions and reactions, cycles of conflict, those social relations evolve perpetually. Through capital's own rules a rival power is created, and one can see many crises at various levels in the rationalist theoretical framework. Are not some of the signs of those crises manifest in the thoughts and ideas of Quatermain?

Quatermain's Metaphysics

Let us now look at some of the binaries operative in Quatermain's approach:

England	⟷	Africa
culture/society/history	⟷	nature/chaos
work	⟷	play
rules and regulations	⟷	freedom from such constraints
light	⟷	darkness
order	⟷	disorder

– and so on. Of all these binaries, he privileges the second one, where 'nature' controls the rest. There is a dialectic running through the set of binaries; there is a demarcating line within them.

In Quatermain's eyes, all of Africa is afflicted by the supernatural, as if that continent is beyond the edge of reality – a magical space where there are no proper people living predictable and regulated lives. There is no glamour of civilization or external fanfare there; fashionable and cultured people do not have to get weighed down by pre-planned movement and fancy etiquette there. The natural abundance of Africa holds out a promise of freedom that is not to be had in the suffocating social world of England and its economy, where free choice is inseparable from strict work ethics. England, with its trimmed hedges, its cultivated fields of neat rows of crops, exhausts Quatermain. There is no food for excitement or pause for variety in its ordered nature. He desires instead the vast expanses of Africa stretching into the horizon, its dense jungles – nature that is not possessed by humans, nature wild in tooth and claw. According to Quatermain, nature in Africa is in its real sense 'organic' and untamed, and not humanized as it is in England; and because it is so, it has neither been exhausted nor distorted. Africa is as it must have been in that original moment of creation – suggesting that only he who dares to move back in time will reach Africa. It is a primordial source to which one may return only if one has unyielding determination. Only those who know how to transgress the border of history – to delete, one by one, all the signs of 'civilization' – may come into contact with her dark mystery. Bitten by the travel bug, one might spend a happy holiday there or even experience some heady excitement if one is simply addicted to adventure. But it is quite another thing to experience the primeval grandeur of Africa; that requires a rather special sort of mental orientation which not everyone has.

Quatermain's Africa is an imaginary land, a no-land or utopia. And that no-land is constructed as England's opposite. Thus, on the one hand, Africa is a symbol of Quatermain's unconscious – a land of absolute fulfilment 'created' out of death and love, woven from *eros* and *thanatos*. On the other hand, as a utopia that seeks to annihilate the claims of excellence of the 'superior' civilization, it is a straightforward reflection of England. Quatermain knows of many civilizations that have come up and disappeared in the sands of time. He also believes that the human mind is unchanging, that man's nature is essentially universal. With the help of this 'eternal verity', one may get out of the labyrinth of the changing world. With this metaphysical logic Quatermain tries to rid himself of self-corroding tendencies, besides wanting to overturn the genteel conventions of society. As though, if one does not overturn established conventions, it will not be possible to stage a return of the repressed. There is no other way for such a split existence to retrieve its lost wholeness.

At the heart of Quatermain's being is a great negativity, a deep contempt for England's material success. It is from the same moralistic impulse that he wishes to distance himself from history, dim the 'light' of civilization and drown himself in the unconscious. Quatermain, then, had come to Africa to erase himself. He was in search of absolute self-annihilation. Extreme anarchy was what he desired, and a lack of knowledge or unawareness was what he aspired to. He wanted to seek refuge in a world of non-knowledge and non-consciousness. Despite being the citizen of an optimistic, exuberant England, he was weighed down by a burden of despair. Quatermain is a reminder that it is darkest under the flame of the wick. That is why his search for self is just another name for self-extinction.

Quatermain does not aim for a gradual ascent through a rationalist, step-by-step progression, and therefore, it is not incumbent on him to be forever on his guard. There is nothing that keeps him from plunging into anarchy. Quatermain is an irrationalist; he does not consider the complications of reason to be within his purview. As might be expected, this kind of thinking is fundamentally flawed. 'History' and 'nature', both function as binaries; there is no scope for any exchange between the two categories. Thus the land-mass called Africa becomes for him a place without history, without geography. If Africa had not been conceptualized in this disjunctive, unrelated fashion, it could not have been presented as a pure, blank sign. That is, this construct has been placed outside of history precisely in order to critique history itself. However, it is inevitable for all reflections on nature to be bound up inextricably with history. But can one speak of this blankness within the restrictive parameters of human language? Imagination is necessarily mediated by language and all language bears the imprint of social exchange. Pure or absolute fantasy is therefore a chimera. If Quatermain erases all historical markers from Africa, he brings them back into the realm of history through language. On that blank sign called Africa, he adds various other signs of his own. His enterprise is thus riven by an irresolvable contradiction. By introducing history, he disrupts the diurnal rhythm of that ceaseless sameness which in his view is the very essence of unpolluted Africa.

Is there any specific reason for Quatermain's return to Africa? He has heard (rumours, so far) that in a remote pocket of Africa there are white men who have no contact with the rest of Africa. This region is a great deviation in the land of black people. It is all the more attractive because it is unexpected. This incredible minority of whites, as also the conjecture that these white men had come to Africa in some pre-historic era, fascinates Quatermain. (Who knows, they might have been in Africa even before the advent of blacks!)

At this point, it might be worth recapitulating the inspiration behind the starting point of Rider Haggard's *King Solomon's Mines*. In 1871, Karl Mauch came upon the ruins of ancient Zimbabwe. Europeans were thunderstruck by this sign of civilization in the dark continent. A new theory was set in motion to explain the mystery of the origin of Africa's civilization: the ruins were traced to the Biblical king Solomon's golden land of Ophir. The newfound civilization was thus attributed to the race of white men. The first refutations of this myth – from archaeologists – were to come only in 1906.[1] According to Jacques Derrida (1930–2004), the blatant lie propagated by the government that whites had been in South Africa prior to the blacks was a signature of '*homo politicus europeans*'.[2] It was a blatant display of the arrogance (or stupidity) of Europeans. Rider Haggard obviously had not the least doubt about the myth; he would not otherwise have written *King Solomon's Mines* a good fourteen years after the 'discovery' of the ruins of Zimbabwe.

Although both the novels have Quatermain as the hero, has he not undergone a change in the interim? Quatermain now wishes to move away from the whites. He has come to Africa precisely to distance himself from the whites. Does his quest for 'the heart of whiteness' within Africa, then, still make him one with his race? Instead of creating a split, does it not bind him in a secret thread of unity? Is he not trapped in his own metaphysics? The very history from which he seeks to free himself pursues him – but he seems unconscious of the irony.

Quatermain and his friends find refuge in the middle of Africa in the house of a missionary named Mister Mackenzie. He is thrilled by the surroundings of the mission, for it is a veritable simulacrum of England herself. The mission garden bears the imprint of human hands, human labour; it is a flawless picture of order. Grown from seeds brought all the way from England, there are lines of English trees, and apples, strawberries, tomatoes and cucumbers, in abundance. Thanks to the generous fertility of the African soil and its waters, it has been possible to bring into being and nourish this microcosm of England. Quatermain is pleased with the missionary sahib's enterprise in a 'home' conjured up in an alien land. But he seems to be quite indifferent, or at least unaware, as to whether this mini-England is in any way destroying his dream of an 'untainted' Africa. Does Quatermain continue to be prejudiced in favour of the familiar, his own known environment? Does he wish to return to England, then, even while he is in the midst of Africa? But in that case, 'history-less' Africa enters a different frame of reference; a different history is superimposed on her own. At this point, we might suspect that any indications we have thus far received against the discourse of rationality are actually superficial. In Quatermain's ideology, there is a conclusive statement that runs parallel to his nihilism. He seems to be bound in a secret pact with the very ideology against which he crusades. It is worth reiterating that he is not an exception: one may find many of his kind in nineteenth-century England, both in reality and in fiction.

Culture/Anarchy

A new crisis had shown up in the bourgeois ideology of that period. Utilitarian guidance would not work any more. It was progressively becoming clear that one would not be able to maintain peace and stability in society by parroting the slogan of 'The greatest good of the greatest number'. Bentham's Utilitarian theory was getting discarded from the experiences of daily life. In order to control this serious problem, it became necessary to exploit the legacy of Romantic Humanism – a theory that was constructed by merging the thought of the conservative Edmund Burke (1729–1797) with that of German Idealism, which went through the hands of the Romantic poet Samuel Taylor Coleridge (1772–1834) and was spread in the mind-set of society through Carlyle, Disraeli, Arnold and Ruskin. The writings of various thinkers within this literary current expressed an intense aversion to bourgeois social relations. They were all more or less vocal about the subject of man's degradation. But despite the aversion and hostility towards modern customs and principles, almost no question was raised about the legitimacy of capital in their idealist discussions. Ultimately, they did not express anything close to a fundamental objection to capital. With the union of Positivism and Romantic Humanism, this theory brought in its wake, a proposal of amicable settlement. By putting the resources of Romantic thought to use, by using the theoretical structure of metaphysics and the semi-feudal model, this new ideology devised a logic of the legitimate propriety of bourgeois ownership.[3] Nobody would say that everyone did this work fully consciously. Whether it happened consciously or unconsciously, either way the consequence was the same.

At the end of the third decade of the nineteenth century, a vivid example of this can be seen in the effort of John Stuart Mill. By linking Bentham with Coleridge mechanically, by combining realism with imagination, Utilitarianism with Romanticism, he wanted to make up for the shortfall on both sides. Of this effort at compromise, the most famous example is *Culture and Anarchy* (1869) by Matthew Arnold, the son of Dr Thomas Arnold who was the principal of Rugby School. The basic trend of thought during that period and all of its ideological crisis – designated as 'culture and anarchy' – are contained in that work. At a historically transitional moment, the trend of 'culture and anarchy' gave literary evidence of a directional change in England's bourgeois ideology. The new ideology was much more effective because it was able to keep pace with the transformed route of capital. England's economics has been configured through many stages, many metamorphoses – from trade capital to business capital, from business capital to investment capital. If the capital in our bank gets merged with business capital, the place of individual competition is replaced by monopolistic authority. Consequently, the theory of the sole importance of the individual gradually sounds more and more hollow – that there is a huge deceit in liberal ethical ideology gets exposed before many.

In the opinion of Matthew Arnold, the collective was much greater than the individual. For the welfare of the individual, man's will and propensity had to be brought under control and linked to the interest of the collective. It meant that the days of *laissez-faire* – acting according to one's will – were over. The target of the new, good tidings of Matthew Arnold was the bourgeois class. He wanted that they should relinquish the cover of narrow self-interest and take up the reins of society. He wished to let their supremacy spread across all rungs of society. There was nothing to be hoped for from the aristocratic community; history had left them behind. And the people of the working class were not at all mature-minded. They had no talent on the basis of which they could offer leadership; they lacked intellectual ability. They only knew how to raise a tumult and subvert regimented systems. In order to control that anarchy, it was necessary to spread culture. According to God's decree, there is a master–slave relationship between the bourgeoisie and the working class. The serious responsibility of improving the working class and making them cultured would therefore have to be assumed by the middle class. If the workers did not have faith in the middle class, a great catastrophe and extreme lawlessness would show up in society. In order to prevent the disintegration of society and a collective disaster, it was necessary to reinforce the position of the middle class. But Matthew Arnold knew very well that just any member of the bourgeois class would not be able to fulfil that very sacred duty. Some extraordinary, ideal human beings were the only ones he could depend on. In his opinion, only those who had crossed the threshold of their class, who had sacrificed one's individual rights to the needs of all or the interest of the nation, were ideal. For him, the nation was the last resort of the integration of society. So only he who dedicated himself to his nation reached a higher self, after transcending the triviality of his everyday self. Only he who emerged after tearing asunder the mesh of his immediate relationships was pious, unattached and cultured in the real sense. Only he had the ability to expose and distinguish the grain from the chaff to people permeated by darkness. The combination of a few moral qualities created the cultured mind. Morality has no class character – it is indiscriminating and impartial. Consequently, whichever class it comes from, it has been able to de-class itself. For it, the great meeting point called 'culture' is open. Matthew Arnold believed that it was possible to resolve class conflict only through the dissemination of culture.[4]

It may be recalled that in a meeting organized by *The Boys' Own Paper*, which started its triumphal journey in 1897, someone in the management of the Religious Tract Society designated the British empire as the successor of the ancient kingdom of Israel. *Culture and Anarchy* was published that very year, and it contained the same refrain. Matthew Arnold also gave place to Hebraism next to Hellenism. His aim was the fusion of the two ideals of Greece and Israel, looking in opposing directions. He wanted to balance the spontaneity of consciousness with the determination of conscience, one's commitment to duty and obedience next to beauty and radiance. In his opinion, the Hebrew heritage was being disseminated and embraced through the Christian faith. But due to various evil influences and the movements of ill-omened stars, that pure legacy was getting contaminated and the appeal of Christianity was gradually fading away. If the Christian faith did not become useful to the age as a result, it would be difficult to preserve its core. If one did not camouflage the Hebrew principles of excellence with a Hellenistic wrapping, its objective would not be fulfilled.[5] The real meaning of this was that the more culture was broadcasted, the more unopposed and absolute would be the power of the bourgeois class. It is hardly necessary to state that in this way, one could internalize other perspectives all the more.

In literature as well as in reality, the alternate ideals of the nation proposed by Matthew Arnold can be found in various faces and characters of human beings. They continue to carry the great message of culture as though they were the couriers of the nation. It spreads in different directions, through many nations, beyond the crossings of oceans and mountains, from the peripheries of the world to more peripheral regions – for example, through David Livingstone (1813–1873) and Henry Stanley (1841–1934) who dedicated themselves heart and soul to work as emissaries of 'civilization'. It was they who showed us the path of entrance into the heart of Africa. Livingstone's prop was the voice of Christ, the redeemer of mankind; for Stanley, it was the patronage of Leopold the Second, king of Belgium. The remark of Bishop Desmond Tutu (1931–) of South Africa, a severe critic of racial discrimination, about the English who came from nowhere and settled down is notable: 'When the missionaries first came to Africa, the ownership of the land was ours. They said, "Let us pray." We shut our eyes. When we opened them, we saw that we had the Bible in our hands and the land was in their control.' Livingstone, coming from a poor family, had had to enter a factory as a worker while he was still boy; and Stanley was a penniless orphan. Africa had brought worldwide fame to both. Many others before and after them had set out on victorious expeditions to capture newer and newer parts of the globe. Of them, the major names were Richard Burton, John Speke, James Grant and Samuel White Baker. Not only that, almost all the explorers of the new worlds have documented descriptions of their experiences. Travelogues like Livingstone's *Missionary Travels* (1857), Burton's *Lake Regions of Central Africa* (1861), Speke's *Discovery of the Source of the Nile* (1864) and Baker's *Albert Nyanza* (1866) became extremely popular. Within a few months of being published, the sales figure of Livingstone's *Missionary Travels* was 70,000 copies. Stanley's *In Darkest Africa*, which saw many editions, sold 1,50,000 copies just in English. Many of them also wrote adventure tales for adolescents – like Baker's *Cast Up by the Sea* (1866) and Stanley's *My Calulu: Prince, King and Slave* (1889).[6] These extraordinarily intrepid expeditioners wove their adventure stories with narratives of imperialist expansion.

The Welsh theorist Raymond Williams (1921–1988) has shown how the meaning and connotations of the word 'civilization' started changing from the end of the 'Age of Reason', the enlightened eighteenth century. It was used as an antonym of 'barbarism' as a reaction to neo-classical ideology. The Romantics of the nineteenth century presented another term, 'culture', against the ideals of 'progress' and 'civilization', and its meaning moved further away from cultivation or production.[7] But no matter in what sense the words 'civilization' and 'culture' were used, whatever subtle differences there were between the two words, not much difference was perceived as far as the people in the colonies were concerned. Was there not a group of people in England too who were not vulnerable to this so-called 'culture' and 'civilization'?

The Nation's Messengers

An example of this is *Deep Down: A Tale of the Cornish Mines* (1868) – a novel by Robert Ballantyne (1825–94) of *Coral Island* fame – which contains a detailed description of the mines in Cornwall. The description is rendered special and credible through many minutiae. The monthly income from the Botalac mines is about one thousand pounds a year. It is doubtful whether a worker of that mine, David Trevarore, gets paid ten shillings for his labour for a whole week. But he has no regret or accusation in his mind. Although his forehead is furrowed and his body gets drenched in perspiration while working his spade in semi-darkness under the earth, one corner of his mouth perpetually displays the faint shadow of a smile. His mind, free from all ties, soars above – in the realm of the sun, in meadows of light.

We know that according to the theory of Matthew Arnold, two harbingers of civilization, two inevitable conditions of man's full blossoming, are 'sweet' and 'light'. Those ideals of beauty and radiance seem to be second nature to David Trevarore. No matter the wants in his life, there is no bitterness in his mind. A happy ambience grows around him wherever he goes. It is not just David but even children who feel proud to be able to work in the mine. Their chest swells with pride at getting the opportunity to do back-breaking work. They do not retreat even as they know that their bodies will get destroyed within a short period. The reality and cruelty of child labour is somewhat camouflaged through the myth that the natives of Cornwall are hardworking and courageous from their very birth.

The education of the Methodist church propagated by the disciples of John Wesley has completely transformed David. Without demanding anything for himself, he can give of himself without any compunction. One recalls that for Matthew Arnold, the Christian faith was like a special antidote. There was no other elixir that was as useful for directing society towards restoring its health and for making men aware of their subservience. In Ballantyne's novel, alongside the worker David, there is a young doctor, Oliver Tremboth. He is both quick-witted and kind-hearted. Whoever comes close to him gets influenced by him. In fact, under his counsel and that of one of his local clergymen, even those who indulge in corrupt practices undergo a change of heart. Oliver seems to be a benchmark. With his blessings, even those who are socially ostracized regain some sense and become genuine social beings.

The sum and substance of Ballantyne's novel is that there is no basic opposition or conflict between work and capital. If amiable relations between the worker and the master remain intact, there is no fear; all problems are bound to get resolved. There is no fault in the system; if one can hold the reins of the administration, all the confusion will be resolved. The similarity between the ideology of Matthew Arnold and Robert Ballantyne is no coincidence. Arnold's theory was born at a critical historical juncture and a brilliant character like Oliver was created. And what about our Allan Quatermain? Whatever be the differences between them, is he not eventually an incarnation of Oliver? Do the good tidings about 'culture' not spread through him also? And if that is so, who are the objects of the good tidings? Is there any character comparable to Ballantyne's David in Rider Haggard's novel?

Rider Haggard dedicated the novel *Allan Quatermain* to his son. On the dedicatory page, he wrote that the various feats of Quatermain would inspire the next generation of youth just as it would inspire his son. Inspired by Quatermain, they would progress step by step and reach the pinnacle of success – that is, they would become full-fledged English gentlemen. Without any hesitation Haggard wrote that there is no rank higher than the status of an English gentleman; that this is what every young Englishman should aspire towards. Yet, at the beginning of the novel, there is a critique of English genteel society in Quatermain's voice. On hindsight, it might seem that there is an opposition between the commentary of the author and the speaker. But if one advances a little, that shadow of a doubt gets dispelled.

Father–Son

When the novel opens, we get to know that Quatermain has just lost his son, his support in life, for whom he had written *King Solomon's Mines*. His grief at the loss absolutely overwhelms Quatermain. This unexpected blow intensifies the suppressed discontent in his mind – and so he turns to Africa.

In the first chapter, almost as soon as he reaches Africa, he runs into Umslopogaas (a Zulu chief who had been a fellow-adventurer in the past). Umslopogaas comes running up to him as soon as he recognizes Quatermain, bows to him repeatedly in greeting and garlands him with terms of effusive praise. Not only that – he addresses Quatermain as 'father'. The honorific consistently occurs in his speech, as though it is the most apposite word to express his joy at meeting Quatermain. Does this mean that the grieving Quatermain finds a son in the depths of Africa? Will Umslopogaas – the very embodiment of subjection, the noble savage celebrated by the Romantics – make whole the yawning loss of a son? Instead of the English boy, will this elderly African become the object of Quatermain's paternal affection?

Quatermain behaves with Umslopogaas much like the 'ideal father' of nineteenth-century England, i.e. he is affectionate or stern as befits the occasion. He does not indulge him excessively yet does not neglect him. As for Umslopogaas, he is ready to give up his life for his 'father', his lord. He is ever-attentive, ready to carry out the least and many of Quatermain's orders. There is no doubt or reproach in his mind in this regard. The impotent condition of slavery does not distress him. It is as though the relationship between him and Quatermain is as 'natural' as several immutable laws of nature. If it was otherwise, there would be reason for some surprise or objection. What is the mystery of the deep veneration of Umslopogaas, a black man, for Quatermain, a white man come from outside Africa? Has he been mesmerized by Quatermain's bravery, his valour? But Umslopogaas too is a great warrior (even Quatermain is obliged to praise his skill and presence of mind). Does an invisible skein of power bind his consciousness? Is this relationship of power responsible for the complex of fear and devotion, of resentment and respect, that comes to mark his psyche?

White–Black

At the moment of Quatermain's meeting with Umslopogaas, two new categories – 'white' and 'black' – are added to the novel's already existing binaries. The difference in skin colour is arguably the most visible to the eye, and, therefore, they become operative as the two most dominant signs in the narrative. From the Preface to *Allan Quatermain*, we learn that Quatermain is on the side of darkness in the fight between light and darkness. But when it comes to white men and black men, in every instance he goes against his own logic.

His approach and behaviour, as also his description of natural beauty, reveal an excessive bias towards white as against black. Thus, in describing the mountains of Kenya, the word white is penned repeatedly. The lofty 'white grandeur' of the snow-capped mountains of Kenya dazzles him. He himself acknowledges that he does not have the skill of language to describe such a rare sight. Quatermain's modesty is undoubtedly praiseworthy, but is it not actually attention-seeking? Does it not conceal a sense of arrogance? Otherwise, why, in describing the mountains of Kenya, does he keep returning to its glittering, snowy-white peaks?

Quatermain has not the least doubt that whites are far superior to blacks – most certainly in terms of knowledge, but the inhabitants of Africa also lag a thousand leagues behind in matters of law and ethics. The Africans are orphaned children and the sahibs from distant lands are their refuge. If they accept without protest the sahibs' 'selfless' service, compassion and generosity, it is they who stand to gain ultimately. Anyone who does not understand this 'simple' truth becomes, in Quatermain's eyes, an enemy of 'civilization'. He

From *Allan Quatermain*

is ever-ready to offer all sorts of good advice to rid the blacks of their moral confusion. But after all, he too is human. When words fail, he (however unwillingly) has to take up the gun. And so the path walked by Quatermain and his ilk is reddened with the blood of blacks.

Umslopogaas is intelligent; he has been able to survive by bonding with and unquestioningly casting his lot with the sahibs. He is present in this trail of unending massacre not only to save the sahibs, but also to save himself. Umslopogaas' predecessor and prototype may be found in *King Solomon's Mines* in Umbopo – also a Zulu, and a devotee of the white man. In describing him, Quatermain frequently adds that Umbopo was not as dark as the others; in fact he is so light-skinned that he could pass for a white. Clearly, Umbopo is an ideal African in Quatermain's eyes: he is superior to his fellow blacks in intelligence and in his sense of morality because he unhesitatingly accepts the master role of the whites – his 'dusky' skin is an indicator of this moral excellence, a sign of his unquestioning obedience. (Later, Quatermain commends him for his dog-like fidelity.) While the colour of Umbopo's skin may be as dark as any black man's, the colour of his heart had already undergone a change. No wonder Capt. John Good had remarked (on seeing him bow before Quatermain) that his sense of morality was far ahead that of the average black man. The main point of Good's remark is that while not everyone has the good fortune of being born with white skin, why should one not have the 'freedom' of donning a white mask over a black face?

Quatermain and his crew have come with the promise of European 'enlightment' to black and 'dark' Africa, its sharp radiance reflected in the description of Kenya's snow-peaks. Is there not, after all, a link between the white grandeur of the mountains and the white grandeur of Europe? The more 'humanized' the terrain of Africa – its soil, water and landscape – becomes, the more eroded stands Quatermain's initial conception of Africa. And, along with this, as various parts of Africa come within the reach of Quatermain and his friends, Africa gets intertwined in a special history – a history filled with treachery and betrayals, a cruel history. No one is let off in the perpetual poisoning and detoxifying processes of colonial power.

The narrator of Rider Haggard's *Allan Quatermain* dies a hero's death in Africa. At the very outset he had let us know that in the primal forests of Africa there are many barbaric men whose ruthlessness matches that of the political economy (the capitalist system of which he is a part); yet they are essentially simple, with no contradiction between their word and deed. Embittered and exhausted by a devious and fragmented England, Quatermain had wanted to travel to a world that was 'harmonious'. And, as we have said earlier, one suspects that this desire to travel was in effect a death wish; the conclusion of the novel does not leave this in doubt. It is as if Quatermain gets into a frenzy over self-destruction and the joy of overwhelming devastation – as though

Africa is a site that fulfils his thirst for blood. Yet he continuously convinces himself throughout the novel that he is not as bloodthirsty as the savages; that his body does not respond to the maddening, pulsating rhythm of drums as do theirs; and that he is not incited into a devilish frenzy by music as they are. That is to say, Quatermain cannot entirely forget himself, dissolve himself in oblivion; something holds him back. As a result, he ends up fighting on behalf of the very political economy that he hates so much. He fights on behalf of 'capital', 'science' and 'rationality'.

At the end of the novel, after a bloody struggle, Sir Henry Curtis becomes the king of the white people in the heart of Africa – in the land called Zu-vendis. Zu-vendis is already far more advanced in terms of architecture, sculpture, statecraft, practically in every respect, than the rest of Africa; the entry of the trio adds to this splendour with the many advances in technology that they introduce. However, as soon as Curtis becomes king, he initiates an exhaustive search and seals off all entry-points into Zu-vendis. He believes that when primitive and unrefined people enter into 'civilization', greed, addiction to alcohol, new diseases and distractions such as guns and gunpowder – the many accomplishments of civilization – inevitably gain entry too. To ensure that the inhabitants of Zu-vendis remain aloof from these dangers, the cautious Curtis cuts off all relationships with the outside world, with the world at large. It is possible to consider this sealing off of Zu-vendis as a symbolic act. It suggests that unless one can fence the borders of the colony, unless one knows how to fend off all possible rivals in the game, it is impossible to sustain a colonial state. We know, of course, of the unceasing warfare between rival colonial powers, the price of which was paid by the colonized people.

Tales of Heroism

One account of such rivalry is the novel *Westward Ho!* (1855) by Charles Kingsley (1819–1875), author of *The Water Babies*. The subject of the narrative is the conflict between Spain and England, which was focused on the huge land-mass of America. The novel is written in a passionate style, in support of England. Kingsley does not have the slightest doubt about the legitimacy of England's authority over America. Every section of the novel demonstrates extreme hostility towards Spain. Roman Catholic Spain seems to be a stranglehold of all kinds of immoral practices and superstition, while Protestant England is the personification of honesty and civil behaviour.

By vocation, Kingsley himself was a religious preacher. He had written many articles and pamphlets about several contemporary social issues. The discontent among the masses and the mutinous uprising of 1840 pained him as much as it got him worried. He emphatically declared the need for social reform, especially for improving the conditions of the working class. In 1848, he joined the supporters of 'Christian Socialism' – a group tauntingly referred to as 'Christians with muscle power'. Kingsley, of course, did not like this appellation. Instead, he chose a different title for himself: 'a belligerent Christian'. He was involved with a paper called *Politics for the People*, which was run, along with other people, by Matthew Arnold's friend and the author of *Tom Brown's School Days*, Thomas Hughes (1822–1895).

No matter how much he disliked the title 'Christians with muscle power', there was no way but to admit that there was not the slightest trace of lack of manliness in Kingsley's prose. He seemed to have held a pen to demonstrate fictionalizing of the proverb, 'Might is right'. The hero of *Westward Ho!*, Amius Leigh, is the representative of England, and the ruler of England is Queen Elizabeth. Perhaps he is not intelligent or an erudite scholar, but he is courageous and honest. He has the will power to confront any adverse circumstance. He does not indulge himself by succumbing to temptation. He does not neglect his duty even for a moment. It is as though Amius is protected by his natural ethical sense like an invisible amulet and armour that is hardly noticeable. The brilliance of beauty and well-being lights up his radiantly healthy face.

According to Kingsley, in the conflict between enlightenment and darkness, the auspicious and the inauspicious in this revolutionary phase of history, just as it was inevitable that England would emerge victorious and Spain would meet its downfall, so it was predetermined that heroes with a fully developed sense of ethics would surface. It was as though people like him had rescued Western Europe from the darkness of the middle ages to the light of the modern period in order to observe a divine decree. And it was they who had made feasible England's supremacy all over the world. It was through their contribution that the path of unrestricted trade and free colonializing had been made easy for England. At the dawn of modernity, in the glorious age of Elizabeth I (1533–1603), it seemed as if not only Europe but the whole world had welcomed without reservations the torchbearers of freedom, culture and modern science.

In English colonial literature, there is no dearth of tales of heroism. William Henry Kingston (1814–80) wrote a book called *Blue Jackets: or Chips of the Old Block* in 1854, which narrated the incomparable feats of the English navy. British naval soldiers had taken part in various extraordinary expeditions all over the world, starting with defeating the Spanish Armada. They raised aloft the Union Jack in innumerable places, including Aden, Syria, China, Burma, Borneo, Africa, Latin America and the Northern Pole. In 1891, a compilation of poems was published under the editorship of William Ernest Henley (1849–1903), titled *Lyra Heroica: A Book of Verse for Boys*. The naming of the book in Latin is noticeable. In the introduction, the editor declares that it is his objective to inspire young minds with patriotism. Reading the poems would infuse in them a fiery spirit, and their youthful hearts would start dancing with a radiant joy – such was the editor's intent. In the book replete with eulogies of the grand achievements of England, just as Henley's poems were filled with unstinted eulogies of England, there were poems by famous poets like Thomas Babington Macaulay (1800–1859) and the Nobel laureate Rudyard Kipling (1865–1936). It is not difficult to gauge the subject and substance of the poems from their titles. One of Macaulay's poems is called 'The Armada' and one of Kipling's, 'The Flag of England'. The essence of what Macaulay and Kipling have to say is that through the ambassadorship of England, peace and stability are getting established far and wide. The same assurance is pronounced in Kingsley's *Westward Ho!* The basic reason for the war between Spain and England was not religious. Camouflaged by the blessings and assurances of writers like Kingsley, a new narrative was being fashioned – a narrative encompassing the primitive accumulation of wealth in England in the initial stages of its capitalism and, simultaneously, an all-encompassing disaster in various colonies.

In 1492, when Christopher Columbus (1451–1506) reached America, the land of plenty, in search of the golden Indies, a new epoch began in the history of man. Under the pressure of this new history, the people of the colonies lost one thing after another. At some places, an entire community of people were wiped off the face of the earth forever. In some others, their language–religion–rituals–customs–culture were all demolished and uprooted. Right from the beginning, the masters of the colonies emphasized moral indoctrination of the natives of the colonies. Just as the colonial powers named various countries anew, similarly they transformed the names, languages and religions of the people, and wanted to draw them into their own jurisdiction. The unsolicited guests were determined to make 'human beings' out of the 'barbaric' 'semi-humans'; they resolved to indoctrinate them with an evolved world-view. All they wanted in return was unconditional authority over all their wealth and assets. Indeed, this was also necessary for moulding the national life of the various colonies according to the European prototype, and to link the inhabitants of the colonies with the 'fundamental' current of human thought. It was as though the cyclical trend of human history had been fixed from earlier to gradually unveil an obscure, divine identity; there was no way out for the colonial subjects but to be linked with this current. By the logic of this gradual exposure, they had to bind the natives of Africa, run the slave trade with great authority, and send off more than twenty lakh people from Africa to America between 1680 and 1786. At another level of unveiling, the masters unfastened with their own hands the chains that tied them.

The movement for abolition of the practice of slavery started under the leadership of the leader of the Clapham community, the mentor of the Evangelicals and one of the chief supporters of English education in India: William Wilberforce. By that time, of course, the surplus capital necessary for England's expansion of industry had been accumulated. There was not much economic hazard or hindrance in demonstrating compassion to the slaves. Moreover, America was no longer under England's control. If the practice of slavery was abolished, England would be able to progress further as compared to rival nations dependent on the colonial slave economy. It would hasten the progress of the world's most industrially advanced nation. Observing the diktat of history, the colonies should have remained eternally grateful, therefore, but the problem developed exactly here. Due to the ingratitude of the 'uneducated', this extensive organization was almost sabotaged. Protests started to be constantly organized against the Victorian saviour/consumer. People of the Zulu, Ashanti and Matabele races, and natives of Ethiopia, Buganti and Sudan were repeatedly involved in battles with them. On the one hand, there was the disgruntled working class of their own nation; on the other, there was the community of malcontent people in the colonies. How much would the 'poor' ruling community of England have to manage?

A Brave New World

Writers such as Rider Haggard and other contributors to *The Boys' Own Paper* (started in 1879) stand witness to the attempt to keep pace with the changing times. Before Rider Haggard there was the unparalleled George Alfred Henty (1832–1902), whose work marked a break in English juvenile literature. Henty was a journalist in the first phase of his career, making a mark for himself for live dispatches sent from the battlefield. As a special correspondent, he travelled wherever there was a war – to Russia, Africa, Spain, India and the Balkans. Later, working on this store of war experience, he began writing a series of 'historical novels' for boys. His first novel, *Out on the Pampas, or the Young Stellar*, came out in 1871. He continued writing uninterruptedly till his death at the turn of the century. The titles below give a glimpse of the contents of Henty's books: *By Conduct and Courage: A Story of the Days of Nelson*, *With Cortez in Mexico*, *With Kitchener in Sudan*, *With Clive in India*, *At the Point of the Bayonet*, *A Tale of the Mahratta War*, *By England's Aid*, *For Name and Fame* and so on. Up to the beginning of the First World War, i.e. 1914, his books recorded a sale of 25 million copies. In terms of success, he beat just about every contemporary writer for children, including R.M. Ballantyne (1825–1894) and Kingston.

William Henry Kingston (1818–1880) started writing in 1860, and within thirty years, had produced more than 150 books for children. Additionally, he was the editor of various children's magazines like *The Colonist*, *The Colonial Magazine and East India Review* and the *Union Jack*. Many of his books were published under the auspices of the Society for the Promotion of Christian Knowledge. Kingston was also a committee member of the Society for the Promotion of Colonization which had as its objective the removal of unemployment from England. A lecture delivered by him at a meeting of that Society on 1 January 1949 gives us a fair idea of his views. He said that the Lord had placed two major burdens on the race of Anglo-Saxons: the spread of civilization and that of the Christian faith. All hitherto uninhabited regions of the world had been reserved by the ever-merciful Lord for the faithful (the believing Anglo-Saxon). Therefore, if one were to send people to various colonies across the world, one would be twice blessed: fulfilling the Lord's will and, at the same time, dealing with the problem of unemployment – thus forestalling the possibility of another destructive Chartist revolution. This would ensure that the workers of the nation do not get swayed by wrong ideas, and that the 'fallen' colonized get blessed by following the ordained path of the Lord.

Kingston's political objectives were quite explicit: export the internal conflicts of England to various colonies, make the colonists work at minimum wages, send goods 'made in England' to the markets in the colonies, and also take care of England's social 'problems' by planting members of the undesirable working class on distant shores. Thus an intricate matrix of economics, politics and sociology is at the heart of Allan Quatermain's spiritual crisis. Kingston's clarion call may lack the subtlety of Rider Haggard's narrative but their objectives are remarkably similar. The baton of the editorship of the *Union Jack* passed from Kingston to Alfred Henty in 1890, marking another chapter in the annals of children's literature.

In Henty's 'historical novel', one can hardly see missionaries; in lieu of them, there are those who invest their capital in industry and trade, and civil as well as military authorities. Between them, of course, the military authorities gain the greatest importance. Although there are detailed descriptions of military exploits in Henty's novel, its objective was not to construct tales of valour. He actually desired that battles and mutinies should end in the colonies, and that England's undisputed supremacy should remain intact. Trade and industry should get extended, local industries should be built, natural resources should be deployed – but all this in order to satisfy England's selfish requirements. It is not surprising that Henty should have emphasized the economic side of imperialism. He was explicitly involved in various trade ventures of the colony; he was one of the major shareholders of the Transval Gold Mining Estates Company of West Africa.

In Henty's novel *With Clive in India* (1884), Charlie Marriott is sent by his mother's uncle to India to carve his destiny. Charlie's great uncle knows very well that the fortune of even downright wretches could take a turn for the better if they got a job in the East India Company. All that was needed was enterprise and courage. Charlie saves his great uncle's honour. At the end of the novel, he returns to his country after becoming the owner of abundant wealth. As a reward for his heroism, he receives substantial wealth. Through the power of both, he becomes a Member of Parliament. Along with the account of war, Henty does not fail to mention the figures of Charlie's income. Charlie stays in India for just a handful of years. However, that was the time for the trader's measuring rod to get transformed into the king's sceptre. Charlie gets involved with many expeditions of Lord Clive. He participates in battles against Dupleix in southern India and against Siraj-ud-Daulah in Bengal. Charlie is not just an ideal soldier – his customs and conventions are worthy of emulation. On one hand, his skill as a soldier, and on the other, his steadfast devotion to British law and ethics make him the favourite of senior officers as well as his subordinates. What is more, even Indians do not hesitate to honour him.

Black Slave – White Slave Dialectic

On his way to India, Charlie saves an Irish youth named Tim Kelly by endangering his own life. In a reciprocal gesture, Tim seems to literally sign a bond of slavery to Charlie. He becomes his trusted servant and supremely servile attendant. Tim is not very sharp-witted. His manner, movements and attire are quite comic. But in spite of that, or perhaps because of that, Charlie cherishes an affectionate attachment for him.

Charlie encourages the spread of education: he appoints a teacher to learn the native language and masters the language very quickly. But despite trying many times over, Tim cannot progress beyond a few common words. Moreover, Tim nurses in his heart a great contempt for Indians. He has a few fixed catch-phrases for Indians: 'black ape', 'black heretic', 'nigger', 'black crook', 'creature from Hell', etc. But Charlie is noble-minded and much above all this. One never hears him utter a sentence expressing racial hatred. That does not mean that Charlie has any objection to Tim's contemptuous utterances. Not once does he ask Tim to restrain himself; contrarily, he keeps indulging him. Tim's words provide him with raw material for laughter. It is as though Tim is a comedian, and an object of patronage and entertainment, for the Charlies who are born into noble dynasties. But is there any specific intent in representing Tim as belonging to Irish stock? If we desire to know the correct answer, we would have to turn our attention to another Irish character in the novel.

Abandoning an English regiment, the fellow had joined the French forces. But the nature of the traitorous Irish is so despicable that even the French could not tolerate him; they became resentful and exasperated by his behaviour. This implies that there is a total of two roles accorded to the Irish in Henty's *With Clive in India*: either they are souls dedicated to the English, like Tim Kelly, or they are mutinous and traitorous. If they dedicate themselves to the service of the English, the Irish will get blessed by the compassion and generosity of their masters. If they do not want to be such, and if there is a dearth of adequate politeness and pliability in them, they will have to become

William Blake, *A Negro Hung Alive by the Ribs to a Gallows*, 1796

the target of English anger and bullets for 'appropriate' reasons. If one knows the history of England's connection with Ireland, one would easily understand the history of the formation of these binary roles. One would understand the dialectics of the relationship between the black slave and the white slave. It is noticeable that through Tim Kelly, a white slave, many curses and abuses are uttered about black people. There is a structural similarity between the social status of the black slave and the white slave; if that similarity becomes obvious to them, it would be quite difficult for the English to safeguard their

William Blake, *Flagellation of a Female Samboe Slave*, 1793

mastery. Is the same anxiety not working behind the effort to create differences between the two races? Henty's novel has a detailed 'description' of the 'Black Hole of Calcutta'. This 'black hole' or 'dark pit' is a symbol of the 'lamentable stupidity' and 'indescribable brutality' of the Indians.

The 'advanced' countries of Western Europe have always safeguarded clear differences between word and deed. They have manoeuvred a dual code – one for their own nation and another for the colonies – with great skill. They have paid lip service to humanism, conceptualized and formed many strategies for human rights, and led crusades. On the other hand, for the people in the colonies, they have devised methods that have abolished all their rights. They have never been flustered by the possibility that there may be a contradiction between the two. Also, it was necessary to manage the lower classes within. Consequently, the word 'human being' started acquiring a dual connotation. In the native context, the word is used in place of a class, and from the perspective of the world, it is a substitute for the 'white man'.

As long as people like Tim Kelly experience the pride and arrogance of having been born white, the masters can have a field day. In Henty's novel, there is another character of the same class besides Tim: Hussain. Hussain once mixed some poison in Charlie's food after taking a bribe, but his death sentence had got condoned through Charlie's intervention. Charlie's patronage and unbounded compassion transforms Hussain into a different human being. Like Tim, he too becomes an absolute devotee and a most humble servant of Charlie. No matter in what contempt Tim might hold the black man, he does not face any trouble in accepting Hussain as a friend. This implies that unconditionally acknowledging the authority of the rulers of the upper class would be of equal help and benefit for the lower strata of the nation and its colonies. They would get bound in cordiality and amicable brotherhood, and come closer to each other. This is the sum and substance of Henty's moral tale.

It is not just slaves in the literal sense, like Hussain and Tim, but also a feudal Raja who is impressed by Charlie's qualities. Charlie's martial skills, alertness and British sense of 'lawfulness' takes the Raja and the inhabitants of that state from darkness to enlightenment. The Raja is not willing to take a step without consulting Charlie. He has got to know that on the one hand, it would be difficult to save his throne without the patronage of the British; on the other hand, it would not be possible to become 'proper' human beings. The grateful chieftain endows Charlie with plentiful wealth. Charlie, who has been inspired by the example of Robert Clive, knows very well that it is a custom to take offerings from local rulers in return for good counselling.

Master–Servant Dialectic

In the novel *With Clive in India*, through Charlie, the people of England are made to stand before the inhabitants of the colony as illustrations and models of humanity. And in reality, after getting thwarted and cornered from all four sides, this deviant ideal gets transmitted in the consciousness of the natives. One will have to grow up and be adults, and to be adults entails becoming the shadows of the oppressors – this gradually becomes their preoccupation and obsession. The ideals of the oppressors spread virtually over their entire consciousness. The ideals of the rulers cover the entire range of their hearts, thought and existence. Just as they lose the ability to see themselves as distinct and independent of the existence of the rulers, similarly they start seeing themselves through the eyes of the rulers.

The ideal of submissiveness in English literature has been upheld in many ways and through the medium of several characters: David Trevarore, Umslopogaas, Tim Kelly, Hussain. Cornish, African, Irish, Indian or Latin American – whatever be their race, there is no difference among them by way of character. If one goes back a little, one can find Man Friday in Daniel Defoe's (1660–1731) novel *Robinson Crusoe* (1719); going back a little further, one meets Ariel in Shakespeare's *Tempest* (1611). Along with this, mentors have spread in various regions of the world through various names, guises and appearances to enlighten us that the right perspective is to see through the eyes of rulers, and that there is no alternate path or method of self-exploration for the ruled. There is a radical similarity somewhere between Prospero in *The Tempest*, Robinson Crusoe, Amius, Oliver, Charlie and Quatermain. It was not for nothing that the life-force of modern education in India, Macaulay, had said: 'Hand over *Robinson Crusoe* to boys. This one book equals all of grammar, figures of speech and logic.' Of course, Shakespeare's play or Defoe's novel is much more complex and profound than the novels of Kingsley, Ballantyne, Henty or Rider Haggard. But we must also remember that one can see the gradual increase of power in these kinds of characters only from the commencement of a particular phase of history of English literature.

The writings of Kingsley, Ballantyne and Henty are one-dimensional and even from beginning to end. No matter what ups and downs or turns there may be in the story, there is no variety in the construction of the narrative, and no deviation in tone and gesture. For example, Henty's prose has no vibrations; there is no rise and fall. There is unopposed dominance of one voice and one view. The whites belonging to civilized society speak in one language and in the same manner. And no matter what characters like Tim or Hussain do or say, they are actually passive and voiceless – they have no perspective of their own. In colonial literature, the independence of the servant gets obliterated in the master–slave dialectic.

In Henty's novel, even the adolescent Charlie talks like an adult. Subsequently, there are two possible reactions from the reader. Elders may not think the adolescent version believable – on the other hand, even elders might think it fit for immature adolescents. The youthful Charlie's solemn and measured speech and gestures are indicative of the supremacy of adult language. But because a young man talks in this language, the claim of its gravity is reduced at least to a certain extent. In colonial discourse, however much there may be an effort to represent stratified society as beneficial, the picture of a stable balance of power is bound to get threatened time and again. Many attestations of such disaster have remained in real life, and in the context and corpus of literature.

As in Henty's writing, so too in the novels of Edgar Wallace (1875–1932) and Edgar Rice Burroughs (1875–1950), the one-dimensionality and pliability of tone are suggestive of colonial pride and power. But there is a cloak of civility about Henty's novel, of which there is not even a trace in the writing of the two Edgars. One must remember that at the beginning of the twentieth century, in the whirlpool of many crises, the appearance of imperialism was gradually acquiring intensity; the days of Henty's cosmetic gentility were almost at an end.

In 1900, a magazine named *Boys of Our Empire* (1900–1903) started to appear, in which the life stories and multifarious feats of individuals were published under the title 'Empire Champions'. These champions included Evelyn Baring, Lord Curzon and Cecil Rhodes. In the words of Rabindranath Tagore, the '*imperial bayu-grostho*' ('empire-crazed') Cecil John Rhodes had broached the 'native' problem in South Africa's Cape House Assembly as follows: 'One should behave with the natives in a way that it seems they are minor children and immature and the whites are older and responsible, the guardians of helpless children.' He clearly stated that there was a need to perpetrate in South Africa the kind of arbitrary rule that had been firmly established in India.

Both the Edgars were straightforward like Cecil Rhodes; their writing was not cloaked or veiled, and there was no trace of disrepute or guilt. In Edgar Wallace's novel *Sandy the Kingmaker*, when the African protagonist addresses Sanders as 'Oh white man', the annoyed Sanders says: 'If someone addresses me as white, I can't hear it. This is because in this country, "white" means "owner" and when a black man addresses me like this as "Oh white man", I get infuriated.' Sanders' well-considered opinion is that if there is any indication of an old civilization in Africa, that must have been acquired from outside. The ancient Romans had civilized one region of Africa to some extent. Although that effort turned out to be more or less futile, there was no room for doubt about England's success. Did Rider Haggard not intend to say the same in *King Solomon's Mines* and *Allan Quatermain*, although in a roundabout way?

Edgar Rice Burroughs wrote a total of twenty-one novels in thirty-three years, between 1911 and 1944. The name of the hero in all of them was Tarzan. The literal meaning of 'Tarzan' is white-skinned. Although he grows up in the company of apes in the jungles of Africa, he has an aristocrat's blood. By birth, he is the scion of a distinguished family of English lords. In his first novel, *Tarzan of the Apes* (1914), Burroughs wanted to demonstrate that the natural temperament of aristocratic people cannot be repressed by the adversity of circumstance, that one cannot suppress a fire by hurling ash on it. Burroughs' serialized narratives seem to be a fictional representation of Social Darwinism. Charles Darwin (1809–1882) had exposed the 'natural' differences between the 'civilized' and the 'barbaric'. In his book *The Descent of Man* (1871), he had instilled a scientific reverence for the notion of progressive and backward races. So how does the fiery Tarzan, bearer of the views of Darwin and his successors, treat the blacks?

Tarzan keeps a notice hanging outside his home that reads: 'This is the home of Tarzan, the destroyer of animals and black men. Do not damage Tarzan's property. Tarzan is watching everything.' The aggressive face of imperialism becomes clear through the severity of Sanders' or Tarzan's tone, and the horror of their brutal actions. In course of time, through the evolution of imperialism, the novels of the two Edgars also show a change. Keeping pace with that evolution, the characters of supermen like Phantom Aranyadeb, Superman, Batman and the like would gradually be created successively on the model of Tarzan. And what about the famous Mowgli? Is there not an ideological kinship between Tarzan and the hero of *Jungle Book* by Rudyard Kipling, who won the Nobel Prize for Literature in 1907?

'It is the responsibility of white men to enable the evolution of black men': this arrogant utterance is by Kipling. About Kipling, Cecil Rhodes had said: 'After Disraeli, the person who had proved to the whole world with the greatest dexterity that the character of the British is genuine and untarnished, that it does not rust or gather dust, was Kipling.' In 1895, while welcoming Kipling to Cape Town, Edgar Wallace had said: 'You are our favourite author, friend and patron.' In that welcome address, Wallace also designated Kipling as 'the poet of the cuss-word and the swear'.[8]

In 1913, the same Kipling wrote in a letter to Rider Haggard: 'Each one of the new extremist ideologies is a special kind of disease – they are not new ways of thinking.' One gets to know from Haggard's diary that Kipling believed it was the Jews who were at the core of all the problems that were surfacing in remote Russia. Of course, Kipling was in favour of using the words 'trade union' in place of 'Jews'. By writing a letter to *The Times*, Rider Haggard appealed to Kipling that they needed to make their countrymen aware of the Bolshevik menace. Later, the two of them formed an association called the Liberty League with this objective. It is worth mentioning in this connection that in his early life, Haggard was the secretary of the Governor of Natal in South Africa. It is not at all surprising that mentors of colonialism like Haggard and Kipling should have had doubts and fears about democracy in their minds.

Kipling was born in India and he had a considerable acquaintance with the people of India. Perhaps he also had an obscure but real attraction for them. This self-contradiction manifested itself over and over again in him. For instance, in *The Jungle Book* (first edition 1894, second edition 1895), Mowgli grows up in the jungle surrounded by animals like Baloo, Bagheera and Sher-Khan. The wise Baloo teaches Mowgli the etiquette and customs of the jungle. Among many norms and directives, the most fundamental is that needless killing of human beings is an unforgivable offence. The inhabitants of the jungle know from experience that mishaps occur if they commit such an act: human beings enter the jungle to take revenge. Within a short while, inevitably, white men arrive there on the backs of elephants, wielding guns.

In Rudyard Kipling's imagination, the jungle is a symbol for *Bharatvarsha*, rendered invincible by its forests. On the one hand, he wants India's primitive purity to be preserved exactly as it is. On the other, he wants its transformation. But the very people who would bring about the transformation would taint its purity. Caught in this dilemma, just as Kipling portrays the picture of a jungle that is assaulted from all four sides, so he shows how the inside of the jungle is transformed under the leadership of Mowgli, a human being. Even if he wants to remove it from history, Kipling's jungle repeatedly gets intertwined with history. In the wicked attraction of history, there seem to be many ominous signs. For instance, the apes are about to seize leadership.

Monkeys and apes have no originality; they have no restraint, norms or ethics. Even their language is borrowed from others. They have a great lack of patience. As a result, their thought process is also not structured. Apes have neither intelligence nor bodily strength. They have no ability but to emulate others. They have coined a proverb to placate themselves: 'What apes think today, the inhabitants of the jungle will think tomorrow.' I hope it is not difficult now to recognize who these apes are. There is no doubt that through them, Kipling has tried to portray the Bengali *bhadralok*. Did he fear a possible rival for civilized Europeans among them? Of course, Mowgli does not have to undertake much trouble to subdue the insolent, worthless apes. Along with animals and other creatures, some naturalized human beings also live inside the jungle – for example, the Gonds. They know well that it is only the white people who can radically disrupt the order of the jungle. Intimidated by the power of the foreigners, the animals and human beings of the jungle have become peace-loving. Throughout the jungle, the rule of law prevails.

There was no impediment in the way of Kipling, a devotee of discipline and rules, to cooperate with the pioneer of the Boy Scout movement, Baden Powell. And Baden Powell dedicated his *Wolf Cub's Handbook* to Kipling. This episode of mutual give and take is memorable. The same Kipling had written the 'Recessional' during the diamond jubilee of the reign of Empress Victoria. In this eulogy, published on 22 June 1897, although England's glory is documented in a traditional manner, there seems to be a tone of ambivalence. The moral of the 'Recessional' is: 'Lest we Forget! Lest we Forget!' Kipling's cautionary statement is: 'If the powerful English suffer from egotism, God will not forgive them.' Of course, not much time elapsed before he himself forgot this cautionary statement.

Worker – Colonial Subject – Woman

What was the position of women in this literature created to illuminate and inspire English youth? Along with the binaries of light–darkness and good–evil, one could easily add a third category: man–woman. In the words of Quatermain in *King Solomon's Mines*: 'Women are women, all the world over, whatever their colour.' As she lies dying, Foulata, a black woman in the novel, is made to say, 'I love him [Capt. John Good], and . . . I am glad to die because I know that he cannot cumber his life with such as me, for the sun cannot mate with the darkness, nor the white man with the black.' In the eyes of these writers a woman is always 'weak', standing at the other pole of male heroism. However, while they may lack 'intelligence' or 'courage', women have the capacity to seduce men from the rough path of duty and destroy their objectives. Innumerable works of fiction emphasize, through a range of strategies, that woman is indeed the doorway to hell. Men are thus allowed to have a natural distrust of or inherent hostility towards women. Only the woman who happily accepts subjecthood at the hands of a man is acceptable. This material written for young readers comprises tales of heroism and glory; it also naturalizes an exclusively male-centred perspective, making it the only perspective without any alternative to patriarchy. After all, the colonial writer had to fend off the three-pronged 'evil' of labour unrest, the anti-colonial struggle and a long history of women's movements.

To sum up, the colonial discourse of heroism had three main objects – a homegrown class – i.e. the working class, the colonial subject and women. It was imperative to push these three kinds of subalterns into the margins of the colonial discourse, and necessary to transform them into a unified category. Yet it would be wrong to say that the voices of marginal subjects were not at all heard in colonial fiction.

In *The Tempest*, Shakespeare's Prospero has another servant besides Ariel: Caliban. Caliban is the one who does not accept unquestioningly the supremacy of the outsider Prospero. Rather, he curses Prospero in the very tongue that the latter has taught him. Knowing that he has been deceived, the angry Caliban's language acquires an intensity and life of its own. There are many Calibans scattered all over the globe; during the colonial era a new literature came into being in the many lands inhabited by these Calibans. Did not that literature arise out of the Ariel–Caliban conflict, from a dialectic of contrapuntal notes?

> *Caliban* . . . This island's mine, by Sycorax, my mother,
> Which thou takest from me. When thou camest first,
> Thou strokedst me and madest much of me . . .
> . . . and then I loved thee wouldst give me
> Water with berries in't, and teach me how
> To name the bigger light, and how the less,
> That burn by day and night
> And show'd thee all the qualities o' the isle,
> The fresh springs, brine-pits, barren place and fertile:

> . . . Cursed be I that did so! All the charms
> Of Sycorax, toads, beetles, bats, light on you!
> . . . For I am all the subjects that you have,
> Which first was mine own king . . .
> and here you stay me
> In this hard rock, whiles you do keep from me
> The rest o' the island.
>
> *Prospero*: . . . I pitied thee
> Took pains to make thee speak
> . . . I endowed thy purposes
> With words that made them known. But thy vile race,
> Though thou didst learn, had that in't which good natures
> Could not abide to be with; therefore wast thou
> Deservedly confined into this rock,
> Who hadst deserved more than a prison.
> Thou most lying slave
> Whom stripes may move, not kindness! I have used thee,
> Filth as thou art, with human care and lodged thee
> In mine own cell, till thou didst seek to violate
> The honour of my child.[9]

Although the Prosperos have always wanted to confine the vile race of Calibans either in prisons or 'into rock', the Calibans have intermittently loosened their shackles and escaped from their pens. In the course of wandering from place to place, one Caliban comes to the native land of another. The encounter between these two Calibans is full of dramatic possibilities. When either of them stands before the other like a mirror image and sees his own visage, will he perhaps shrink back in fear and shame? It is hard to predict what will happen when one of them sees his reflection in the other.

From early in the twentieth century, the Calibans of Bengal started saying quite emphatically that they will *not* be *bhadra*, they will *not* be wise; that they will observe the world from various perspectives; they will become 'human' with their share of vice and virtue, joy and sorrow, ascent and descent, etc. Bengali children's literature was no exception to this movement. The number of 'eccentric' and 'whimsical' characters rose alarmingly; driven by wanderlust, they abandoned hearth and home in response to the call of the open road.

'If only I were a Bedouin instead!'

Rabindranath Tagore wrote in his essay 'Bidyasagarcharit', delivered as a lecture in Emerald Theatre in 1895 (13 Shraban of 1302, Bengali calendar):

> In Part I of his *Barna Parichay*, Vidyasagar gives us the example of a conscientious

> boy who does whatever his parents bid him to do. But when Ishwarchandra was himself of Gopal's age, he resembled Rakhal more than he did Gopal. Far from obeying his father's command, he, in fact, did the opposite of whatever his father asked him. . . . There is no dearth of Gopals amongst the meek race of Bengalis. The allegation about the weak character of the Bengali race might be rectified if there were an outbreak of unruly boys like Rakhal and his creator, Ishwarchandra. The well brought-up boys will no doubt pass their examinations, get good jobs and earn a lot of dowry during their marriage, but one can hope for a lot for the motherland from the mischievous, disobedient, restless boys.[10]

Note the use of the word 'weak' in this extract from Rabindranath's essay on Vidyasagar. The Bengali's emaciated physique and ill health has been long lamented. In 1823, Rammohan wrote to the king of England: 'the natives of Bengal, wanting vigour of body and adverse to active exertion, remained during the whole period of the Mohammedan conquest, faithful to the existing Government, although their property was often plundered, their religion insulted, and their blood wantonly shed'.[11] The feeble body of the Bengali becomes a marker of his subservience; when a new order came into being, a new dimension was added to that symbol.[12] Standing out among the tribe of parasitical bootlickers who suck up to the sahibs, there are those who may be emaciated in their frame but robust in their strength of character. [13]

In children's literature, there are two kinds of characters who redeem the Bengali from 'culpability' for his 'weak character'. The first kind are those who are pushed into leaving their homes, persecuted by a father or father-figure. More intractable and obdurate than their peers, they torment their guardians no end – such is Kanchan in Sibram Chakraborty's (1903–1980) *Baari Theke Paaliye* (1937) or Bhombol in Khagendranath Mitra's (1896–1978) *Bhombol Sardar* (first edition 1937, second edition 1955, third edition 1975, fourth edition 1978). They rebel against the suffocating world of *Barna Parichay*. The second kind are those who are provoked by the 'fetters of fate' and enraged by the regimented monotony of their lives. At any given moment, they are ready to sail off for the unknown. Such is Shankar in Bibhutibhushan Bandyopadhyay's (1894–1950) *Chander Pahar* (1942), or Bimal and Kumar, the two companions in Hemendra Kumar Ray's (1888–1936) *Sonar Paharer Jatri*. In both cases, the catalogue of names can easily be extended for the same idea is reiterated in novel after novel. Bengali children's literature abounds in serious critiques of both kinds of life – the regimented and the passive. Did not the creator of Gopal–Rakhal, Vidyasagar himself, cry shame upon the advocates of the 'weak, trivial, heartless, lazy, arrogant' type, and did he not, 'as he aged, move away gradually [from] the entire unhealthy web of Bengal's narrow-mindedness to a silent and distant solitude'?[14]

The narrator comments on the reckless Shankar of *Chander Pahar*:

> [his] heart flies to far away places in the world – right in the midst of countless reckless actions . . . although he has never considered that what could happen to boys from other countries is inconceivable for Bengali boys. They are born to be schoolmasters, clerks, doctors or lawyers. There is little hope of their crossing over into untrodden paths in unknown realms.[15]

Bimal, the hero of Hemendra Kumar Ray's *Sonar Paharer Jatri*, does not waste his time on sociological explanations of the eternal indolence of the middle class. Instead, he says:

> A scent of adventure runs through our blood, our veins and the core of our heart; in spite of being born into the tribe of home-loving Bengalis, we seek kinship with the universal man. We do not desire wealth, status or fame. We only yearn to plunge into the whirlpool of events, feed on perpetual excitement; drown ourselves in ever-changing scenes of beauty. We crave for a dynamic life whose rushing torrents sweep us in a dangerous celebration of its momentum.[16]

Although few in number, there are some novels in which otherwise undistinguished, peace-loving people unwittingly get embroiled in all kinds of terrible happenings – like Sureshwar in Bibhutibhushan Bandyopadhyay's *Maraner Danka Baje* (1940). In describing Sureshwar, the narrator informs us:

> There are a kind of people who are thrilled at the prospect of facing new challenges in faraway lands – Sureshwar is not quite one of them. He is an ordinary, home-loving type, content, like other run-of-the-mill Bengali *bhadralok*, to hold on to his regular and safe job and stolidly fulfilling his domestic duties.[17]

We have noted that Haggard's Allan Quatermain also had a deep distaste for respectable society and its venerable members. But there is a world of difference between a successful Englishman and a successful, *bhadralok* Bengali! Because of the difference in their status, although the revulsion of Shankar and Quatermain may seem the same, their ennui has only superficial similarities. From the perspective of character, there is a huge difference between them. A close reading shows that most of these adventure-driven Bengali youth do not have any familial bonds or domestic responsibilities. For instance, Bimal and Kumar are well-to-do individuals with no strings attached, and that is why, perhaps, they can head for the outdoors with little or no qualms. Jayanta and Manik in Hemendra Kumar Ray's *Jayanter Kirti* 'are both orphans, and therefore free. . . . Both have some parental property, so their independence is not threatened.' Even if parents and other relatives are mentioned in certain places, their role is virtually negligible. It is not just that the familial context is only implied, but as though one cannot create realistic and credible adventure-loving Bengali characters without suppressing the familial context. The suppression becomes an indicator of the impossible claims of the 'family' in modern Bengali life.

As for those who refuse to be confined to a placid existence within a secure domesticity and are ready to face any trial, do they really expand the worlds that they choose to inhabit? At the end of the mental journey, is there any radical change? To answer this, one would first need to know how they survey the unknown world and its inhabitants.

'To know the unknown . . .'

It is remarkable how a majority of the texts draw on the same pool of vocabulary to describe people in faraway places. Let us assemble a few examples in chronological order. First, some opinions on Africa:

- 'The appearance of the Man [*sic*] was fat and stout, his complexion jet black, the face like a stupid ghost'; 'the mien of the people was dark like Yama the God of death, and the animal was like a huge rhinoceros – their fight was a very weird affair'.[18]
- 'With the settling of the white men from Europe in this country, they [the Africans] have reformed to a large extent, but how can they amend their nature?'[19]
- 'His complexion was charcoal black like ebony and his two eyes were . . . amazingly bright and ferocious like a wild animal's. He was snub-nosed like a monkey. And his teeth protruded in disarray like those of a fleshless corpse.'
- 'The Ristersveld mountain range is not the Himalayas, the mountain-king with a divine soul. Like the ancient Masai, Zulu, and Matabo tribes of this land, its soul is cruel, barbaric and cannibalistic.'[20]
- 'A Mulatto is a strange race that is a cross-breed between a Europen and a Negro or some other non-white race. Mulattos do not have brains . . . but that apart, there are many instances of their extraordinary physical strength.'[21]
- 'Like monsters, [the Negroes] gleefully ate the half-burnt meat'; 'After coming in contact with the civilized people of the city, Congo was simultaneously appointed as our cook and servant.'[22]

About America, it has been said:

- 'Ferocious beasts lived inside these inaccessible and dense forests, a large mountain kingdom that was more arid than an uninhabited desert.' The 'red man' of America fared no better: 'Whenever those cruel eyes would be hiding amidst nooks and crannies, identifying us, a volley of stinging bullets would be fired on us'.[23]

Of Myanmar:

- 'A pair of fiery, huge, hungry eyes stared fixedly ahead! Beside it was an ugly horrible man – he wore a feather cap on his head.'[24]

If we now move to Nepal:

- 'A small, flat nose, tiny peering eyes, the eyebrows non-existent! Stocky, short, dusky. . . . This is how lower-class Nepali thugs look like!'[25]

Of the Khyber in the west of India:

- 'Armed, ferocious, hordes of bandits roam here. They are uneducated, uncivilized, cruel.'[26]

Of the east of India:

- 'Perhaps it is a deed of some ancestors of the uncivilized Khasias'; 'it would be best if we could leave this country of monsters at the crack of dawn'.[27]
- 'The country is as inaccessible as its inhabitants are vicious and uncivilized. The English have marginal authority there. The uncivilized inhabitants near Kohima are somewhat controllable; however, they are yet to come fully under English rule. They would however studiously avoid the English after experiencing a few displays of their power.'[28]

Of China:

- 'The flat, yellow face of the Chinese man puckered up to become even more repulsive, the eyes seemed to come out of their sockets. Inside the blue, overturned lips, the teeth appeared in a grimace.' Or: 'One could see two yellow, flat, ugly faces one after another. The two faces bared whole hosts of teeth and were recurrently cackling like a hyena.'[29]

In the Philippines:

- people have 'a crude, flattened nose, large rolling eyes, springy hair and huge teeth. . . . Although human in appearance, they are but wild beasts transformed.' Later, the narrator avers: 'I am not the sort of fellow to cower before such brutes; I shall flatten out hordes of them if I use my rifle. I work in the military department – get it?'[30]

And much closer to home, about the farmers and peasants of the Sundarbans:

- '[they] could hardly contain their joy having come upon three civilized beings like us'.[31]

One cannot but wonder at the aplomb with which words like 'uncivilized', 'wild', 'uneducated', 'barbaric', 'demonic', 'black messenger of death (*yamadoot*)' and 'cannibal' have been used by diverse writers in the context of other races and the subalterns of one's own race. Did not the Calibans of Bengal know that an intentionally configured anagram of 'cannibal' made up the word 'Caliban'? To a lesser or greater extent, an attitude of contempt towards the suppressed races is to be found in all writers of children's literature. Writers like Khagendranath Mitra (*Africar Jangale*, adapted from Ballantyne's *The Gorilla Hunters*) or Dhirendralal Dhar (1913–1991) (*Jakher Jangale*) are no exception in this catalogue. These adventure stories, written for adolescents who are a part of *bhadralok* society, come across as fairytales in different garb. The Bimals and Kumars of these stories substitute for the Nilkamals and Lalkamals of *Thakurmar Jhuli*, and demonic Africans or some other wild creatures replace the monsters and fiends of the fairytales. It is just that, you do not find any princesses in these adventure fairytales.

It is not as if there is a difference of world-view between the writer/narrator and their protagonists, or a touch of irony anywhere in the texts; when it comes to spewing the venom of racial hatred, they all speak in one voice. In almost all the novels, irrespective of where the Bengalis go in search of excitement – Africa, Latin America, China, Burma or India – and the unfamiliar people they come in contact with, the protagonist merely skims the surface of that unknown world, bypassing it with extreme arrogance. He disregards the possibility of being acquainted with different customs, preoccupations and ideas. Consequently, he is untouched by the opposition between the known and the unknown. The familiar world he has left behind seems to spill over and appropriate the unknown world and its anonymous inhabitants. Through such safe absorption, the Bengali *bhadralok*'s semiotic system remains intact. A writer of the stature of Bibhutibhushan Bandyopadhyay is content to describe only the natural beauty of Africa. Shankar, in *Chander Pahar*, goes to Rhodesia, but there is no mention of apartheid and the terrible oppression of the blacks. Therefore, those who declare ceremoniously that they are rebellious and bohemian by nature are in effect afraid to face themselves. While wishing to be freed of any commitment to measure themselves in accordance with the standards of other people, they do not promote any alternative vision of life.

It can be said that the heroes of Bengali adventure fiction actually never leave home. Notwithstanding the innumerable suspense-filled accounts of calamities and their resolutions of heroes groping their way through unknown regions, in fact, they internalize the outside. I have argued that according to Vidyasagar's precepts, there are two autonomous domains and two distinct slots allotted to 'Rakhal' and 'Gopal', so that they are the inhabitants of two disparate worlds. In most adventure stories, such a clearcut division is absent: 'Rakhal' and 'Gopal' get inextricably intertwined all the time – a 'Gopal' seems to forever generate from a 'Rakhal'. Let us now acquaint ourselves with the 'Gopals'.

Black Skins, White Masks

Satyacharan Chakrabarty's story 'O Baba Re' (*Katamundur Deshe*, 1936) has all the coordinates of the English-educated, Hindu, middle-class Bengali hero:

> Aurobindo Ray was the son of a Baidya; his father was an England-returned magistrate. Having traversed many countries with his father from his boyhood, and having lived with sahibs, he had applied himself to his studies and become highly educated; simultaneously, his temperament had also become like the sahibs – courageous, reckless, daredevil and desperate.[32]

All the markers of English-educated, upper-caste, middle-class Bengalis are present in the story. In Manoranjan Chakrabarty's *Bomar Bhoye Burma Tyaag*, the gentleman-narrator who abandons Burma knows that although there is a road by the name of Pelel Road which leads to Manipur, only 'ladies and gentlemen, that is, the white-skinned' are permitted to enter there; simultaneously, he also knows that 'a few Indians who can prove themselves to be gentlemen are also allowed to go in'. This conscious sinner salutes the sahib camp commander and says, 'Sahib, although we are coolies, we are somewhat respectable coolies.'[33] Does that mean that Bengali gentlemen are a special brand of porters for English gentlemen?

Hiran Basu, the hero of Sachindra Majumdar's *Bhagyer Likhan*, is introduced to a 'fearless' English youth Meryl and his friend Nucel. Overwhelmed by Hiran's athletic, muscular physique, and later, finding evidence of his courage, Meryl is overwhelmed and tells his friend Nucel in an aside: 'Bose is white'.[34] Does the weak-bodied, mentally infirm Bengali claim that the man who is brawny, even if he be brown, is of the same genus as whites?

In Satyacharan Chakrabarty's 'O Baba Re', there is an excellent example of a sahib-aping mind-set. It has a female protagonist, Meera – a rare exception in Bengali adventure stories that are virtually denuded of women – who travels alone through the difficult terrain of the Deccan. Unparalleled in her courage as Meera is, she is after all a woman; the hero Aurobindo is obliged to disguise himself as a 'local' in order to save her from danger. Confronting the disguised Aurobindo, Meera is startled into asking in Hindi: '*Tum kaun? Kya mangta*?' ('Who are you? What do you want'?) Aurobindo replies, 'Memsa'b?' The mutation of language, the sudden shift from Bengali to Hindi, shows how much the *bhadramahila* as well as the *bhadralok* have internalized the tone in which the sahib speaks to a servant. The ways of speech constructed and used by the sahibs to display power in relation to people from other regions are exploited not just by Bengali *bhadralok*, but also by *bhadramahila*s. Do they want to educate the poor people of India in the 'wise teachableness' of the anonymous essayist of *Tattwabodhini Patrika*?

Binay, the hero of Nripendra Krishna Chattopadhyay's *Bijay Abhijaan,* hopes to become a member of the civil service 'in the near future'; in addition, 'his curiosity about life is as vibrant as that of European boys'. Does not Bibhuti-bhushan's Shankar also say that he has moulded himself according to the ideals of Livingstone, Stanley, Harry Johnston, Marco Polo, Robinson Crusoe – and, inspired by them, taken upon himself the pledge of daredevilry? Most of Shankar's ideal men were deeply involved in the business of expanding the empire; many uncovered one part of the globe after another only for indiscriminate destruction. In Hemendra Kumar Ray's *Jakher Dhon,* Kumar is eager to retreat to an uninhabited island *á la* Robinson Crusoe. The same catalogue of exceptionally intrepid men could have the names of Columbus and Vasco da Gama; somewhere, there might also be a mention of Colonel Suresh Biswas.

One could go on, for Bengali children's literature is replete with similar instances; a considerable portion of this literature documents the obsequeousness of the Bengali *bhadralok*. These examples are almost like expert commentaries on archetypal Bengali characteristics by Thomas Babington Macaulay, the advocate of English education. In his essay 'Warren Hastings' (1841), Macaulay had catalogued in detail and with great alacrity:

> The Bengali generally has a fragile physical constitution, almost feminine; in almost exact parallels, in a similar delayed tempo, the Bengali body and mind is narrativized; such is the state of their mind and body that bravery, independence, or honesty are not within their grasp. The slight body of the Bengali is unsuitable for any sort of manly resistance; however, just as the bull has it horns, the lion its deadly paws, the bee its sting, the Bengali too has one crucial weapon of defence, 'deceit'.[35]

Macaulay had already written in his essay, 'Lord Clive' (1840): 'Bengalis are perhaps renowned throughout the world because of their hospitality to foreigners, their ability to willingly become slaves, their talent in fighting amongst themselves, their garrulousness and their own natures.'[36] Macaulay, the man who had brought the Bengali a global platform by introducing the race to English education, himself proposed this 'anthropological' decision – the best solution for the Bengali would be perpetual servility.

In the English adventure stories of the Victorian age, imperialism is taught by way of storytelling; in the Bengali adventure stories, the parrot's cage of Tagore's *Totakahini* becomes all-expansive. Naturally, the two most important signs are 'white' and 'black'. The colour of the skin is of prime importance; it overshadows facial features, physique or health. Moreover, 'whiteness' becomes a signifier of morality, an indication of intelligence and ability, a marker of civilization. Satyacharan Chakrabarty can thus happily write in 'O Baba Re': 'He went right into the interior of the Deccan after hearing that there was a white boy from a civilized community who was living among wild, uncivilized people.'[37] By the same logic, he who is black is not only ugly, but also wicked, as in Hemendra Kumar Ray's *Aabar Jakher Dhon*: 'He was gesticulating and talking to two jet black, goonda-like fellows.'[38] The black–white divide is to be found even in writers like Khagendranath Mitra. In the novel *Bhombol Sardar*, Bhombol still remembers the horrid, big, black face of the fellow who has ruined his uncle; seeing a boy named Keshto, Bhombol thinks: 'Keshto looks exactly like his name, as if all the blackness of a touchstone had burst forth from his face'; and, 'the moral hierarchy between the elder and younger aunts is reinforced by the difference in their skin colour'. The elder aunt of one of Bhombol's friends, whose caste prejudices are very pronounced, is described thus: 'The colour of her skin was glossy.' About the younger aunt who does not believe in the same kind of petty untouchability, whose words and actions assuage the restlessness in Bhombol's mind, it is said: 'He considered how white the soles of her feet were! Her two white shell bangles somehow mingled with the rounded fairness of her hands.'[39] Undoubtedly, there is a long history of colour prejudice in the subcontinent, and behind the racist outlook lie habits and customs of many generations. A new dimension is added to this colour awareness in the colonial era. 'White' and 'black' get more deeply entrenched as soon as configurations are constituted vis-à-vis the ruler and the ruled.

It is but natural, then, that as one becomes 'civilized', the skin also pales, as in Pyarimohan Sengupta's *Kafrider Desh Africa-e*: 'The man who acted as master to the people of that country had a clean appearance, his body was also well-built. Among the black, uncivilized fellows, he appeared quite good-looking.'[40] One comes across such descriptions of African 'natives' in many English writers, including Rider Haggard. One might assume that inspired (and therefore led astray) by literary heavyweights like Kingston, Ballantyne, Henty, Haggard, Kipling or Wallace, and confounded by their propaganda, the Bengali writer unthinkingly filled pages with racist remarks. But that would be doing injustice to the Bengali genius. Even while granting the impact of literary mediation, one can still question how the writers were able to internalize so well – in over half a century of writing – the unflinching insolence and racist arrogance of their colonial masters. Despite being objectified in the same discourse of representation with few exceptions, Bengali writers did not resist being coopted in its dissemination without the slightest compunction. Surely, the 'evil influence' of 'foreign literatures' is not entirely to blame.

One must remember that there is – or bound to be – a fundamental difference between the liberal attitude of the English ruler and that of the Bengali *bhadralok*. In colonial literatures, there is no doubt that the history of the people in the colonies is wiped out; literature, in that sense, is a printed medium of colonial pride and power. But if the same method is applied to the literature of any colony, does it not mean that along with other colonies, some of its own history is also erased to a certain extent? Alongside dismissing the inhabitants of Africa and South America, do not the colonized Bengalis also reject themselves? Is there no interpolated self-contempt lurking within their contemptuous regard for other Calibans? In the numerous texts we have referred to, it is suggested that there is no real cause for anxiety because in the proximity of the white man, even wild people are educated and groomed. Although much blood is spilt in the 'civilizing' process, the uncivilized races only stand to benefit in the exchange because, 'unless the earth is irrigated by different kinds of bloodshed, civilization does not spread'.[41] Unless some of India's own history – bloody, sweaty and filthy – was voluntarily suppressed, could this ungrudging complicity in the destruction of other races by the colonial powers have been taken for granted?

The Gopal–Rakhal Dialectic

Although an indispensable part of it, the middle-class Bengali was unable to completely integrate into the colonial system. Consequently, from the very moment of his birth, his consciousness was split into two. To sustain the oppressive system, the ruler and the ruled have to be demarcated. The paradox of respect versus disrespect made the relationship between the English and the Bengali *bhadralok* even more complex. Wherever the difference between self and the other cannot be erased even while absorbing the other, a crisis of identity is inevitable.

No system of signs, for either the ruler or the ruled, can be completely stable; they supplement and complement each other. Therefore, when Macaulay, that magnanimous founder of modern education says that there is no other race in history which deserves to be governed by aliens more than the Bengalis, he means that by virtue of their nature and habits, these tamed creatures are ideally placed to be burdened with the yoke of slavery. Or, when Kipling taunts the Bengali babus by means of the proven imitativeness of the '*bandarlog*' in *Jungle Book*, they graft this alternative potential in order to comfort themselves. For in the ultimate analysis, 'Gopal' and 'Rakhal' are not mutually exclusive archetypes. Although possessed of a distinctive selfhood, they are manifestations of an undivided consciousness, simultaneously identical yet unrelated, alike yet independent. There is not only a 'Gopal' within 'Rakhal' but a dormant 'Rakhal' in every 'Gopal', because it is not possible for any 'Gopal' to be an unqualified 'Gopal'. An endless conflict with the self, a never-ending dilemma, works itself out perceptibly or unconsciously; the nature of the conflict changes with time and becomes explicit only at an explosive moment.

That is why in the adventure stories that are filled with details of 'Gopals' in the guise of 'Rakhals', one can, at times, hear other words too. Even in a grotesquely racist text like *Bhagyer Likhan*, one comes across statements like: 'The Khasiyas were noticed by [the Welsh priests] not to make sahibs of the uncivilized creatures, but in order to bring the immense wealth of these regions under their control.'[42] In *Ratnadwiper Bibhishikha*, where it is a matter of regret that God has scattered immeasurable riches among those 'beast-men' (*narapashu*) who do not value the natural qualities of minerals, we have: 'Keep your western science to yourself. What do the people of Europe know, and when did they ever learn anything? . . . And we forget our own culture and ape them in everything we do!'[43] In the essay 'Shaada Ghushi ar Kaalo Ghushi' ('White Punch and Black Punch'), Hemendra Kumar Ray writes:

> The fight between black and white is an age-old battle . . . now the whites have coined a new term – 'coloured races' . . . – the Chinese, the Japanese, the Tartars, the Indian and the Negroid, have been pushed into the same slot. In a way, it has done some good . . . a bond of unity will be forged among all non-white races.[44]

In most writers, including Hemendra Kumar Ray, however, there are not too many signs of the 'bond of unity'.

The hero of Nripendra Krishna Chattopadhyay's *Bijay Abhijaan*, Binay who believes that 'Such a great man's [Burmese] servant must be no mean person himself . . . the children of respected homes in Europe were forever anxious to talk to Napoleon's valet', also asks:

> Why is man moving away from the heart of nature in the lure of becoming civilized? These engines, hinges, gadgets – the tireless rotation of hundreds and thousands of machines – will they ever give him the peace of mind he desired? Man does not care today that the moon rises in the sky; he has forgotten to read and interpret the silent music which resonates from the very flowers and the very grasses of the wilderness.[45]

The topic for such a 'forgotten' message is furnished in many novels – there are countless mentions of the words of enlightened *rishi*s, of ancient Vedic texts and philosophies. Thus there is a litany of achievements in *Ratnadwiper Bibhishikha*:

> We are the descendants of the Aryan rishis who have knowledge of all the three eras. And to imagine that we pride ourselves in the westerner's education! . . . Our country was once the model of the world in (its) knowledge, education, wealth and culture. Our Vedas, Vedantas, Upanishads; our law, numericals, Patanjal; our Charaka, Sushruta, astrology – how would they understand the value of these?

Yet the same novel 'testifies' that no less than the American governor of Ratnadwip feels flattered to be introduced to the descendants of the Aryan rishis:

> The American governor melted like butter. As it is, they are known to greatly venerate the ancient sages of India. . . . After researching on the sages, they have discovered a lot of wondrous things. They are particularly aware that the cerebral machinery of these Bengalis who eat rice and *ghee* is extraordinary- otherwise, how could Jagadish Bose bring about a revolution in the world by inventing the wireless telegraph?[46]

The wisdom of the Aryans and the brains of the Bengali are not certified by just anybody or by somebody belonging to the uncivilized races, but by a person of pure American breed. This is a wonderful give-and-take relationship: because the westerners are civilized, only they understand, at least in part, the worth of the Indian civilization; similarly, civilized Indians do not have any qualms about acknowledging the wealth of western civilization.

An unparalleled example can be found in a detective story by Hemendra Kumar Ray. In the story, Jayanta assumes a disguise in order to go to the neighbourhood of *goonda*s; he takes off his *dhoti* and dons a *lungi*, sports a beard, and wears a cap. Thus, without saying anything overtly, by a mere exchange of signs, Hemendra Kumar identifies the *goonda*s with Muslims. A clandestine complicity persists between the anti-imperialist 'Rakhal' and Gopal who is nurtured on the imperialist philosophy.

Yet another kind of myth – constructed to some extent by the west, in an attempt to liberate a consciousness that is in the clutches of the 'other' and in order to demolish western ideals – places ascetic and steadfast India on the opposite pole of the materialistic, hedonistic west. In this process, the idea of the self also gets destroyed. In one phase of colonialism it was said that instead of dreaming about transcendence, Indians should come down to earth. In another phase it was iterated that without meditating on worshipping plenitude, there was no hope of regaining lost ground. In many writings for children – in fact, in several adventure stories – there is brazen propaganda of India's everlasting glory, eternal achievements and spiritual wealth. Bibhutibhushan Bandyopadhyay's writings, too, bear the stamp of this 'Hindu nationalism'. Sanat, the hero of *Hiramanik Jwale* (1946), musing on Southeast Asia, says: 'There must have been Hindu colonies there too . . . it is but India's child'. And saluting his 'all-conquering ancestors', he says: 'Bless us so that your almost vanquished, weak descendants may renew themselves according to the ideals of the same strength and spirit . . . that resided in you, and make India worthy of her name in the theater of the world.'[47] And what is the fate of the unruly boy? The bold hero of Swapanburo's (1902–1993) *Beparoa* (1928), Naru, ends up as 'the secretary of the Ramakrishana Muth (in the USA). He has found a spiritual anchor there.'[48] That this historical trajectory of Hindu communalism is alive and well is proved by the market for these stories: most of the stories discussed above sell as much today as they did at the beginning of the twentieth century.

As exemplars of the abstemious Aryan ideal, it is seen that in almost all instances of Bengali adventure stories, the heroes are not greedy for material benefits. Their quest is motiveless. In contrast, bad characters, like the vile and avaricious people of Hemendra Kumar Ray's *Jakher Dhon*, are devoid of ethics and discrimination precisely because they are attracted towards precious objects. They are also sworn enemies of good people like Bimal and Kumar. Those who turn away from domesticity do not express the slightest desire for worldly gain; they seem to dutifully duplicate the unattached Indian saint. In *Chander Pahar*, Bibhutibhushan writes: 'Shankar had an introspective heart with a love for beauty, (after all he is a son of Bengal, not a ruthless, self-seeking prospector like Alvarez)'; 'He [Shankar] had no desire for diamonds. The straw huts of Bengal, the shaded, peaceful, rural lanes, the small rivulets, the chatter of familiar birds were all aspects of a distant and unreal dreamscape; no African mine of diamonds was more precious than that land.'[49] One recalls, in this context, Mrityunjoy in Rabindrath's short story 'Guptadhon' (1907). At the end of the story, he too experiences a thirst for human habitation – 'what is underneath the radiant and open sky', 'the air perfumed with the scent of leaves and grass' – more valuable than all the treasures of the world. When nature beckons generously, Mrityunjoy frees himself from the irrepressible lust for gold that has been driving him hither and thither all these days. On the other hand, in English adventure stories, writers like Alfred Henty never forget to inform us about the exact income and expenditure of their heroes; they have not come to the colonies for the mere thrill of travel. In Rider Haggard's *King Solomon's Mines* (in a chapter entitled 'We Abandon Hope'), even in an extremely perilous situation, Quatermain has enough presence of mind to stuff his pockets with gems from the treasure trove. And what about Bibhutibhushan's Shankar? Well, he does get a few chunks of diamonds, but it happens almost by chance. The British government's wrathful stroke fell upon only two books for children, and they were confiscated: *Phooljhuri* (1933) and *Marujatri* (1939). Both were written by Bimal Sen. He had to serve his term in prison for his anti-British conduct. The breathlessly exciting novel *Marujatri* was the story of three rebellious young men of that tumultuous age.

The 'Rakhals' in Bengali literature, those 'Rakhals' who do not want to be linked with the 'Gopals' in any way, even those who seek a new world in the real sense of the word, cannot create a new world – all that they do is to wear themselves out peregrinating. Like Tarapada in Rabindranath's '*Atithi*' (1895), they are satisfied in partaking of the generous hospitality of creation. Tarapada leaves his village 'without any mental conflict' – it is not possible to bind him within any ties of affection. He perennially experiences in his pulse an attraction and a deep bonding with the whole of the universe. His brief but intense involvement with the zamindar Motilal Babu and his family appears to be a prelude to an English education, marriage and 'settling down'. The generous-minded Motilal Babu and his wife Annapurna adopt the innocent boy. Tarapada's memory is very strong anyway; moreover, he gets involved in learning English with undivided concentration. Annapurna proposes to her husband the marriage of their daughter Charu with Tarapada. But Tarapada is not the prince of a fairytale; he disdainfully leaves behind the princess and half the kingdom. Before 'the conspiratorial bond(age) of love, affection and friendship' can overwhelm him, he takes to the roads once again at the call of the 'aloof and indifferent cosmic mother earth' (*vishwaprithibi*). Tarapada does not want to get hemmed in by the enclosures of *bhadralok* society; he does not want to get confined by the tedium of the four walls of a happy but restrictive domesticity. But although there appears to be a temporal dimension alongside the spatial to Tarapada's incessantly moving on, is not the movement subsumed in a stasis? Is there not an insinuation of death in this goalless quest? The parameters of Bengali *bhadralok* life were so delimited in the colonial period that despite every effort, it was difficult to construct an alternative paradigm. An uncompromising attitude, therefore, becomes a euphemism for renunciation; an intense detachment develops into a deep apathy; and the rebellious figure turns into a fugitive, a wayfarer. It is a movement that is isolated from time and society. In other words, its only tempo is that of a purposeless journey; its only promise is the solace offered by nature. We may now appreciate why, in the children's world created by many writers including Rabindranath, death recurs so frequently. Restless and indomitable boys who are oppressed by a cruel regimen are compelled to take leave of the world because they do not have any means of escape. The death of Naga in Manik Bandyopadhyay's (1908–1956) novel *Majhir Chhele* (1940) might seem unexpected or gratuitous, but one may uncover the infallible logic of history in such 'accidents'. A terrible disenchantment overshadows Bengali children's literature – much of it is haunted by the sorrow of bidding a final farewell.

Ashok, the hero of Khagendranath Mitra's *Ajaana Desher Pathe* (1938), had wanted to comprehend the reason for the helplessness of Bengali life. When the warrant of death awaits him inside a cruel desert on the way to Palestine, he keeps thinking of the great voyagers of the world:

> They have discovered one country after another. They have never hesitated to suffer great hardships or even lay down their lives for it. But what was the aim of all this? Fame, and the enhancement of wealth on behalf of their own country. But why was he embracing such misery? He was only a young man of no consequence belonging to a dependent nation.[50]

Ashok decides that he would purposelessly wander around without keeping any objective before him, because his only asset was the joy of being an itinerant. While going to Baku, he is informed that there has been a great mutiny in Russia: 'The king has been dethroned, there is anarchy all around.' But Ashok is killed in an accident even before he can reach Russia. Behind his sudden death is not only the rationale of the novel, but the infallible logic of history.

Are there any characters in Bengali children's literature who do not want to accept, in the social sense of the term, the divine ordinance of death, and want to demolish the conflict-ridden compound of Gopal–Rakhal? The hero of Nihar Ranjan Gupta's (1911–1986) *Shankar* (1942) breaks out of middle-class constraints to mingle effortlessly with the workers. The headstrong Shankar has always spoken out against the oppression of the poor by the rich. He believes that only the 'organized strength of the poor' can wipe out the ugly gap between the rich and the poor. What is Shankar's role in arousing this 'organized strength'? He believes that 'These uneducated, dumb brethren will have to be imbued with language. . . . One will have to soothe with hope the pain of these oppressed, shattered hearts.'[51] In his eyes, the working class appears to be not the subject but the object of history; at best, they are entitled to the compassion of conscientious *bhadralok* like himself. The suspicion gets confirmed on reading what is said in the novel regarding one of those on whom lay the blessing of permanently settled land under the grace of colonial rule:

'He was the zamindar of the village. Instead of resisting all the oppression and giving shelter to all, he was, in fact, encouraging injustice.'[52] Towards the end of the novel, it is almost inevitable that Shankar wears a *khadi dhoti*, sports a Gandhi cap on his head, and moves away from the role of a belligerent working-class leader to become a Gandhian. There is no doubt that the novel was born out of the tension between the Gandhian philosophy and the leftist politics of the 1940s. In continuity of being linked with the leftist movement, Sukanta Bhattacharya (1926–1947) wrote the line: 'The drums of the rich are made of the skins of the poor'[53] in his *Mithe–Karaa* (*Bitter Sweet*). Has the leftist children's literature in Bengali, as a whole, been able to move out of the conflicting compound of Gopal–Rakhal? In this context, it is worthwhile to mention that in the novel *Shankar*, every brilliant and arrogant character is 'fair and ruddy'. Later, Nihar Ranjan Gupta wrote quite a few anti-communist novels for adolescents, like *Raktamukhi Dragon*, *Nishir Daak*, etc. Is there not a single character in Bengali juvenile literature who is different in an original and fundamental way?

Let us return to Khagendranath Mitra's *Bhombol Sardar*. Bhombol escapes from home many a time, and gets caught each time. From boyhood, his ambition has been to be a worker at Tatanagar. The world around him hinders him at every step, but it is difficult to suppress him because he is self-willed and daring. Even Bhombol's uncle, the zamindar's deputy, does not succeed in taming him – and Bhombol sets off yet again. He walks through villages that have been slumbering for a thousand years. He sees poverty and oppression; there is no sign of any organized resistance; everything seems axiomatic and inevitable like the rules of nature. At the end of the novel, Bhombol reaches Tatanagar; he stares wide-eyed and in breathless excitement at the city in the distance, lit up by electric lights. His wide-eyed vision seems to say that the agenda the Bengali *bhadralok* have been drafting from the day of their birth, now needs to be rewritten – from scratch. Will Bhombol succeed in initiating such a traumatic change, or will he be just another incarnation of Nihar Ranjan Gupta's Shankar? Only the course of history will be able to answer this.

Notes and References

1 Patrick Brantlinger, 'Victorians and Africans: The Genealogy of the Myth of the Subcontinent', *Critical Inquiry*, Vol. 12, No. 1, Chicago University Press, 1985, pp. 196–98.

2 Jacques Derrida, 'Regismus Lastward', *Critical Inquiry*, Vol. 12, No. 1, Chicago University Press, 1985, p. 294.

3 Terry Eagleton, *Criticism and Ideology*, London, 1976, pp. 102–10.

4 Matthew Arnold, *Culture and Anarchy*, London, 1963, pp. 83–84.

5 Eagleton, *Criticism and Ideology*, p. 109.

6 Brantlinger, 'Victorians and Africans', p. 176.

7 Raymond Williams, *Key Words*, Glasgow, 1981, pp. 48–49, 77–80.

8 *Penguin Book of Quotations*, Harmondsworth: Penguin, 1977.

9 William Shakespeare, *The Tempest*, Act I, Scene 2. In connection with Ariel and Caliban's

dilemma of friendship, see Sibaji Bandyopadhyay, 'A Memorandum on Amnesia', *Sibaji Bandyopadhyay Reader*, Delhi, 2012, pp. 105–44.

10 Rabindranath Tagore, 'Bidyasagarcharit', *Charitrapuja*, in *Rabindra Rachanabali*, Vol. 4, Calcutta, 1965, p. 488.

11 Rammohun Roy, 'Appeal to the King in Council', in Ajit Kumar Ghosh, ed., *Rammohun Rachanabali*, Vol. 4, Calcutta, 1973, p. 508.

12 Tanika Sarkar, 'Hindu Conjugality and Nationalism in Late Nineteenth Century Bengal' (unpublished).

13 Rabindranath Tagore, 'Bidyasagarcharit', *Charitrapuja*, in *Rabindra Rachanabali*, pp. 481, 490.

14 Ibid., p. 501.

15 Bibhutibhushan Bandyopadhyay, *Chander Pahar*, in *Bibhuti Rachanabali*, Vol. 1, Calcutta, 1982, p. 4.

16 Hemendra Kumar Ray, *Sonar Paharer Jatri*, in *Hemendra Kumar Ray Rachanabali*, Calcutta, 1983, pp. 29–30.

17 Bibhutibhushan Bandyopadhyay, *Maraner Danka Baje*, in *Bibhuti Rachanabali*, Vol. 9, Calcutta, 1976, pp. 85–86.

18 Pyarimohan Sengupta, *Kafrider Desh Africa-e*, adapted from Kingston's *Adventures in Africa*, Calcutta, 1922, p. 8.

19 Satyacharan Chakrabarty, *Rakshasher Deshe, Chhotoder Galposanchayan*, Calcutta, 1926, p. 11.

20 Bibhutibhushan Bandyopadhyay, *Chander Pahar*, in *Bibhuti Rachanabali*, Vol. 1, p. 38.

21 Sachindra Majumdar, *Pather Bandhu*, Calcutta, 1980, pp. 34–35.

22 Jyotishchandra Chakrabarti, *Rakshushe Africa*, Calcutta, 1981, p. 37.

23 Hemendra Kumar Ray, *Suryanagarir Guptadhan*, Calcutta, 1979, p. 18.

24 Nihar Ranjan Gupta, *Bisher Teer*, Calcutta, 1984, p. 36.

25 Shailabala Ghoshjaya, *Jaipataka*, Calcutta, 1985, p. 52.

26 Sunirmal Basu, 'Jibanta Kankal', in *Jibanta Kankal*, Calcutta, 1988, p. 7.

27 Narayan Gangopadhyay and Nimai Bandyopadhyay, *Bibhishikhar Mukhe*, Calcutta, 1984, pp. 47, 58.

28 Sachindra Majumdar, *Bhagyer Likhan*, Calcutta, 1980, p. 21.

29 Nihar Ranjan Gupta, *Raktamukhi Dragon*, Calcutta, 1984, pp. 70, 78.

30 Ashutosh Bandyopadhyay, *Ratnadwiper Bibhishikha*, Calcutta, 1980, pp. 54–55.

31 Chandrakanta Datta Saraswati Bidyabhushan, *Sundarbaner Shikari*, Calcutta, 1980, p. 34.

32 Satyacharan Chakrabarty, 'O Baba Re', in *Katamunder Deshe*, Calcutta, 1976, p. 23.

33 Manoranjan Chakrabarty, *Bomar Bhoye Burma Tyaag*, Calcutta, 1984, pp. 82, 105.

34 Sachindra Majumdar, *Bhagyer Likhan*, Calcutta, 1980, p. 64.

35 Thomas Babington Macaulay, 'Warren Hastings', in *Critical and Historical Essaays*, Vol. 1; first published in *Edinburgh Review*, London, October 1841, p. 173.

36 Thomas Babington Macaulay, 'Lord Clive', in *Critical and Historical Essays*, Vol. 1; first published in *Edinburgh Review*, January 1940, pp. 23–24.

37 Satyacharan Chakrabarty, 'O Baba Re', in *Katamunder Deshe*, p. 36.

38 Hemendra Kumar Ray, *Abar Jakher Dhon*, Calcutta, 1982, p. 27.

39 Khagendranath Mitra, *Bhombol Sardar*, Calcutta, 1970, p. 43.

40 Pyarimohan Sengupta, *Kafrider Desh Africa-e*, p. 10.

41 Sachindra Majumdar, *Bhagyer Likhan*, p. 35.

42 Ibid., p. 30.

43 Ashutosh Bandyopadhyay, *Ratnadwiper Bibhishika*, p. 24.

44 Hemendra Kumar Ray, 'Shaada Ghushi ar Kaalo Ghushi', 'Madhuchhatra', in *Hemendra Kumar Ray Rachanabali*, Vol. 5, Calcutta, 1983, p. 295.

45 Nripendra Krishna Chattopadhyay, *Bijay Abhijaan*, Calcutta, 1980, p. 21.

46 Ashutosh Bandyopadhyay, *Ratnadwiper Bibhishikha*, p. 24.

47 Bibhutibhushan Bandyopadhyay, *Hiramanik Jwale*, in *Bibhutibhushan Rachanabali*, Vol. 1, Calcutta, 1389 (Bengali calendar), p. 323.

[48] Swapanburo, *Beparoa*, Calcutta, 1928, p. 62.
[49] Bibhutibhushan Bandyopadhyay, *Chander Pahar*, in *Bibhuti Rachanabali*, Vol. 1, p. 36.
[50] Khagendranath Mitra, *Ajaana Desher Pathe*, Calcutta, 1938, p. 45.
[51] Nihar Ranjan Gupta, *Shankar*, Vol. 1, in *Kishore Sahityasamagra*, Vol. 2, Calcutta, 1387 (Bengali calendar), p. 36.
[52] Nihar Ranjan Gupta, *Shankar*, Vol. 2, in *Kishore Sahityasamagra*, Vol. 3, Calcutta, 1387 (Bengali calendar), p. 33.
[53] Sukanta Bhattacharya, 'Purano Dhandha', *Mithe–Karaa*, in *Sukanta Samagra*, Calcutta, 1375 (Bengali calendar), p. 181.

6

Sound versus Echo: The Poetics of Rejection

To Comprehend or Not

The 'Apologia' with which *Abol Tabol* begins does not resemble other similar prefaces or introductions in language or thought, in shape or character. Through his jibes in it, Sukumar Roy makes it known to his readers that his book is not for everybody. 'It is a whimsy book, not for those who are unfit to enjoy it.'[1] In other words, the incredible wonderland of *Abol Tabol* is an interdict for those who are bereft of the pleasures of whimsy and those who are incapable of comprehending the essence of the absurd. Unless one acquires an entry permit, one is not allowed to venture into this 'realm of gibberish'. Sukumar Roy reverts to a similar argument in the poem with which *Abol Tabol* ends: 'Today dear brother before I depart / I will say whatever comes to my heart / No matter that it has no meaning / Or that it doesn't reach everyone's understanding.'[2]

It is as though Sukumar Roy knows pretty well that although his language is spontaneous and lucid, his work is not easily digestible. The remaining verses of *Abol Tabol* are framed by the 'Apologia' and the 'end poem' wherein, one by one, strange beings appear. But all those disciples of the philosophy of the absurd or maniacs driven by strange urges have inside them a general belief. As Satyajit Ray has commented, 'because cobwebs swing in the skies, there are cavities on the surface of the wood', and because he is a believer of such strange wisdom, 'the fabulator or the dealer of the magical shadows has to find a place in such a world as much as the discoverer of photoscope, the uncle of Chandidas, or the big boss of the Head Office'.[3] The list can be extended effortlessly and one can add to it those excessively circumspect among them who are heedful: the king who sits on the slab of brick red from the sun, the quack, the theoretician who expounds, and many others. But in the minds of almost all these idiosyncratic or quirky individuals, there exists a regret about something – a complaint about the world as it is.

There seems to be an acute absence of someone who can fathom the sorrows eating into the soul of the 'old man of wood'; there is not a single individual who can make sense of his deep thoughts: 'Who is there to grasp the inner implication of all this?' The state of the big boss of the Head Office is also the same; his anger at people in his office climbs heights, the language of reprimand becomes increasingly sharp, because his subordinates fail to comprehend the glory and nobility of his moustache. Thus the wrestler who suffers from bodily ache from contesting with shadows, regretfully lets it be known: 'No one knows all these things / No one understands a thing / No one goes round and round / Running after shadows like me.'

At the conclusion of the poem 'Shabdhan!' ('Be Warned!'), the ever-wary man suffering from hypochondria, irritated at the sceptical Pyalaram for refusing to lend a ear to his unsolicited advice, declares: 'Those reluctant to heed any advice with regard to how to go about or what to eat / Will learn to their bitter cost what the price of such imperviousness is.' And the reddened-by-sun king seated on a pile of bricks, unable to resolve or find a solution to an abstruse puzzle, has the same complaint. There is no one who can gauge the meaning of the question that is slowly eating him away, devastating him: 'Who is there to listen to the problem that is rotating in all the corners of my brain?' The quack who is an expert at curing diseases is naturally eager to experiment his easily acquired expertise on those living human beings. But will he be able to fulfil his dreams by experimenting on those ignorant patients who will not let him be? Like Nandi of the neighbouring village, there is no dearth of scheming patients in this world. That is why, by adopting a contrary pose, the quack wishes to discover a pretext by which he can utterly knock down his reluctant patients. The old brahman, placing the *chador* around his neck and eager to hold forth to Shyamadas all kinds of abstruse sayings in the poem 'Saying is Explaining' or 'Bujhiye Bola', is furious to find the listener restless and totally lacking in desire for knowledge. He shouts: 'Theoretical wisdom does not enter the brain no matter how much I shout into his ears / It makes me want to pull hard the ears of the obstinate.'

All such characters pronounce the same thing in different ways and in such a roundabout fashion that no one understands them; no one listens to what they have to say. The world is indifferent to them – has turned its face away; it does not reckon their valuable sayings in any way, no matter how much they weave with words or attempt to break through the mystery of creation or have an inherent desire to do good to the world. The teller is present and the matter for telling is piling up, but there is no audience; the sender has all good intentions to send the message across but the receiver is impervious. Therefore these lonely, helpless beings are furious. They, of course, know that behind the refusal to acknowledge or to hear, there is an inter-relationship of intention and action, of cause and effect. And only those who are incorrigibly stupid and insensitive they keep their ears shut. The tellers are ready to see if pulling hard at the ears of such a hypothetical audience brings some beneficial results. But the problem is that it is very difficult to get hold of those proverbial 'ears', both in the literal and the metaphorical sense.

Adding strength to the bitter lament for the immense indifference shown towards the angry and unhappy residents of this unreasonable world is Sukumar Roy's emphatic pronouncement in *Abol Tabol*, where he declares that the book is not for everybody's comprehension; that it is not possible for all and sundry to enjoy the pleasures of the absurd or the bizarre. One would have to understand the two kinds of unreasonableness, else one would never be able to trace the *fons et origo* of all the fun in *Abol Tabol*. Not only that, we would not be able to discern the double sense which the very title of the book implies. The inception of *Abol Tabol* lies in the verse wherein Sukumar Roy extends an invitation to all those whimsical, mad people, drunk in fantasy, hearkening others to drown themselves equally in the fountains of the fantastic with ringing bells. In this context, the words *Abol Tabol* come to mean the strange ways of the world, a wrong and confusing method of keeping measure, and an adherence to an impossible rhythmic pattern. The same argument is held forth in the last eponymous poem, 'Abol Tabol': 'There is nothing prohibitive here, brother / Nothing to bind you or to oppose you.'

On the other hand, when Shyamadas, in a state of fury, tired of all the theoretical prattle of the wisdom sayers and devastated by the weight of wordy arguments of reasonable exposition in verse, wants to dismiss altogether the substantial and clever argumentation and the display of rhetoric and difficult decisions arrived at by acute learning processes, takes resort to the expression '*abol tabol*' and declares, 'What did you say? All this rubbish, gibberish *abol tabol*?', the tenacious wise old man hits the ceiling in a fit of vile temper.

He is the very person who would like to fill Shyamadas's brain with all kinds of wondrous theories by hitting the head with a hard nail, and can no longer contain himself when Shyamadas ventures to give him the slip or prepares to turn around and argue, his endurance having reached almost breaking point. The over-cautious, good Samaritan of the poem 'Shabdhan!' ('Be Warned!') also gets terribly angry over Pyalaram Biswas's obstinacy; he hates to be contradicted: 'Why must you all the time whine and disagree?' Even the woody old man, whose bald head has become heated and heavy with the burden of all kinds of convoluted problems – a huge mass of knowledge – even he, with his body full of perspiration, is angry about the argumentative nature of his antagonist and speaks out, 'Death be to you, you blind ass / You do not understand a thing but only dispute.' So it is not just the big boss whose moustache was stolen, but all these men who do not pay heed to another living soul or give a damn about any advice/opinion, and would like everybody to submit to them in unison and without a murmur, who are actually fond of only those sycophants who are the 'Yes Sir' types.

If the receiver, whether inclined to or not, was to quietly keep etched in his mind both the message and the speech of the sender, there would be no hassle. The professors of learning have undertaken the task of brainwashing, keeping in mind the total mental and physical welfare of their pupils. Whatever else they may be, Sukumar Roy's theoreticians cannot stand the sight of the disputants. Although they continually complain that the world is deaf, as a matter of fact, it is they who cannot hear. The philosophical theorists assume that the world would go to the dogs if the immutable pattern of truth, deeply ingrained in their minds, were ever so little unsettled. These self-enlightened beings not only stumble deep into the labyrinth of illusions of their own making, but also mislead others. A quiet certitude, that does not admit any apertures of disbelief, fills their minds with a sense of plenitude. They stand firm on the strength of such belief, can throw to the winds all the counter-arguments of their opponents.

Driven by unity of perception, Sukumar Roy's theoreticians draw the perimeters of knowledge with such unerring precision that it would be well-nigh impossible to either restrict or extend its boundaries or alter its pattern. They consider everything lying outside the prescribed perimeters as lacking in reasonableness and superfluous. One can, in this regard, recall 'Bidyabojhai Babumashai', the gentleman literally weighed down with learning, in the poem 'Jibaner Hishab' ('Life's Reckoning') belonging to Sukumar Roy's collection of verses titled *Khai-Khai*. Babumashai's self-satisfied, neat and sophisticated mind is filled with compassion on seeing that the boatman is unable to answer his many scientific queries, like: 'Why does the sun rise in the sky?' or 'Why does the moon wax and wane with ebb and flow of tide?' or 'What are the reasons behind the flood tide?' Stunned by the infinite ignorance of the boatman, this being of immeasurable learning calculates the gains and losses of the boatman's lived existence, and declares that three-quarters of his life has gone waste. Other self-centered theorists like Babumashai also firmly believe that in the hapless desire to raise themselves, wretched boatmen have no other option but to turn to them. Why? Simple: only the theoretician is a bearer of the beacon of progress. And that means one would have to unhesitatingly submit to the superiority of his knowledge – whence any attempt to gain access to the theoretician's field of learning would mean total sublimation of one's self, the abandonment of all that one regards as inalienably belonging to oneself. If one acknowledges the veracity of the theoretician's wisdom, then one would of necessity also have to acknowledge his power, because knowledge is entangled with power: power and knowledge, knowledge and power are indivisibly linked or interconnected.

The 'Fetish' of Sentence and Thought

We may not resolve all the problems by discounting the many characters of *Abol Tabol* as redundant, obsessive and somewhat neurotic. For, behind the appearance of all such neurotic gentlemen lurk the visages of familiar human types – types that in the real world of men do not induce amusement. Nor are these men mere creations of fantasy; these strange men are our neighbours. To take the argument further, we may declare that though poetic creations, these men are actually caricatures (or exaggerated semblances) of the long-faced humbugs that exist among us. In fact they are rather a latent version of the same and therefore more recognizable than those already known to us. By saying this, would the whole exercise become improper or indecorous or, worse, implausible?

According to Jibanananda Das, 'What emerges as truth in the world of Sukumar Roy's *Abol Tabol,* while not being either the world as we know it or its reflection, is nevertheless as familiar and as authentic.'[4] Does the more real and more recognizable world of *Abol Tabol* make us discern perceptively this shadowy world of our everyday existence and lead us to the core of its complex truth – all the more because it is so familiar to us? Unlike the fly-swatting clerk, we can expose reality without blindly imitating the external world. It is quite possible to extract a plausible account of the 'real' without trying to reflect reality mechanically. And this is not only the teaching of surrealist art, but also of realist art. At least the proponents of surrealism did not espouse the opinion that the idea of 'nonsense' is totally rubbish, a mere frivolity, a kind of light-heartedness – sharp without substance and quite unfit to find a seat in the august hall of poetry. The rule of remaining connected while being in a state of disconnect or being related to the material world when totally separate and vice-versa – such small symptoms of the poetics of surrealism, such examples may indeed be discovered in nonsense rhyme if one really searches for it. The topsy-turvy world of Sukumar Roy's *Abol Tabol*, while not being estranged from the real world, is an arrogant and daring version of an almost independent autonomous world. If we have to examine the means or the various skills upon which the construction of this world depends, we would have to take note of the way Sukumar Roy succeeded in breaking out of the impenetrable and tightly knit web of deceit made up of words and sounds, and how he managed to cope with all the verbal twists and turns, refuting one set of words with another.

If we place the two poems titled 'Saying Is Explaining' and 'Science Education' ('Bujhiye Bola' and 'Bigyan Shiksha') alongside, we will immediately detect a similarity. For, the theoretician of 'Saying Is Explaining', taking hold of Shyamadas by the scruff of his neck, reiterates like a parrot into his ear technical terms like the material world ('*bastupinda*'), the five elements ('*panchabhuta*'),

Illustration by Sukumar Roy in *Abol Tabol*: 'Bujhiye Bola' ('Saying Is Explaining')

the world of phenomena ('*prapanchamaya*') and so on and so forth, and sets out to expound upon complicated theories as to why the sap collects at the root of the Tree of Life or why there is a turmoil in the primary elements. On the other hand, the scientist of 'Science Education' tries to analyse the nature of intelligence that a little boy is endowed with by measuring the amount of dilution or corruption of his brain matter through a self-styled photoscopic machine. Adopting a scientifically valid method, the great man of learning would like to map the rate of the boy's improvement by first placing a magnet over his skull and then observing its reflection with the help of a bamboo stick, adding up the velocity with the help of a brick. The illustration alongside the poem, drawn by Sukumar Roy himself, shows a little boy clenching his two small fists, his wide mouth agape with pain, indicating that he in no way wants to act as a guinea pig in the terrible experiment.

About the use of words like 'magnet', 'reflect' and 'velocity', Subir Roy Chowdhury comments: 'Those English words have bestowed upon the scientist a gravity befitting his profession.' On the other hand, if Bengali words had been used instead of the English, the desired purpose would not have been served. All the fun would have been lost if instead of 'magnet', the Bengali word '*chumbak*' had been used as placed on top of the skull, though the rhythm of the verse would have remained intact.[5] Using a similar argument one can say that if philosophical terms like 'material world', 'five elements' and such had not been made use of in the poem 'Saying is Explaining', the poem would not

Illustration by Sukumar Roy in *Abol Tabol*: 'Bigyan Shiksha' ('Science Education')

have been so amusing. All such technical terminology in English or in Sanskrit, belonging to either science or philosophy, become in Sukumar Roy's hands a quarry of amusement, a storehouse of laughter, because he has put to use the fine and not-so-easily-discernible ancillary field of operation of the same words, indicating how in certain usage, the same words could become autonomous, self–referential and move beyond meaning, devolving into a cacophony of sounds; how these can then become weapons in the hands of knowledge theorists. Thus he points to a particular historical trajectory of language use.

The waywardness and the tyranny of language freed of any obligation to reason or thought, or sound escaping the boundaries of sense, are the subject/s of Sukumar Roy's essay on 'The Tyranny of Language' ('Bhashar Atyachar'). In order to demonstrate how the overwhelming weight of the cacophony of sounds, induced by an intoxication with its inherent autonomy, both debilitates thinking and clouds perception, Ray chooses his examples from sources in both western science and Indian philosophy. He says:

> We do not consider it worthwhile to investigate what Darwin's theory of evolution or progressive development is. However, it is not as if we do not adopt the expressions, such as 'evolution' or 'development', in the manner of an expert and, if necessary, discreetly venture an opinion or two. There are many who would like to inject gravity into their personal discourse by deploying such bombastic words as Life-force ('*Pran*'), Absolute Reason ('*Karan*'), Logos ('*Sabdabrahma*'), the Golden

> Womb ('*Hironaygarbha*'), '*Sugun*', '*Nigun*', Being and Nature ('*Purush–Prakriti*'). But who takes note of the fact that the thought the word had at one time encapsulated has long since cast off its covering and escaped? The more we get habituated to words, the more we reiterate, repeat them with ease like parrots, the more does thought retrace its steps and takes into account its mistakes.[6]

Along with the above Sukumar Roy came to realize that the reason why men are content to accept the governance of the state without knowing the principles underlying its system is the same as their taking secure refuge in high-sounding words without giving due weight to the value of human goal-oriented thought.[7] To him, both regimented thinking and language bereft of thought were, in equal measure, interdependent and indistinguishable. The proposed subject of his essay 'Doiban Dayam' ('Gift of the Gods') was the fetishism of sentence and thought.[8]

Now the question remains, what is the secret power hidden in words like 'magnet' or 'five elements' that not only overcomes the narrator but also takes the audience into captivity, if by chance they are found on the wrong foot? Wherein lie the origins of the power that can create a magic web out of the sonority of words, and make the audience surrender sense and reason? These terms or words are used far more by those theorists of persuasion ('Saying Is Explaining') and the scientists ('Science Education') who have invented the photoscope than by them, i.e. the actual users of words. At a glance, it may appear that these terms have been used by men consciously and intentionally; but actually the men themselves are mere playthings, they have no control over either words or sounds – rather, they are captive to and enslaved by those. And the sounds in themselves are not reflective of matter; they are hollow and empty. A hollow pit becoming entangled with sounds has led to the creation of a string of words where the words become the authoritative subject. Bereft of verbs, they are autotelic or 'mythical' – whose command the narrator is obliged to follow.

Attached to the poem 'Narad! Narad!' in *Abol Tabol* is an illustration of two fisticuffing warriors. Placing the picture alongside the poem, one begins to recognize a bit more clearly the character of these two brave wordsmiths – the '*bakyabagishes*'. Really speaking , in most cases, Sukumar Roy's illustrations compliment the poems. But just as the pictures are not mere cowardly submission to the meaning of the poem or its blind imitation, so too the additional data and signs or meanings the pictures might convey do not violate the main argument of the poem. In point of fact, the readerly material attains completion in the word-and-picture combine. The two eloquent warriors of 'Narad! Narad!' are standing with clenched fists and gnashing their teeth, their frames about to burst in fury, and their hair on edge. Both are dressed in *dhuti*, the traditional attire; one of them is barefooted, the other is in socks and boots.

Illustration by Sukumar Roy in *Abol Tabol*: 'Narad! Narad!'

The holy thread adorns the bare body of the person mentioned first, aggressively revealing his brahmanical arrogance. The second person sports a *kurta* (shirt), and his moustache is taut with agitation. Both have entered the arena of battle to prove that one is no less than the other. Tightening their belts and clapping their hands, they make a huge racket, concocting strange excuses for a fight: like snoring nightlong making a hideous sound, or mistaking the colour white for red.

They brawl raising their voices to the highest pitch and making use of the choicest of phrases. The pure undiluted language of their mother tongue, Bengali, simply cannot do – in order to express proper anger while attacking or retaliating, they sprinkle English words whenever they can or use a mixed vocabulary in constructing sentences. One of them even takes recourse to words in Hindi. It is not without reason that he presumes that the belting phrase '*choprao tum*' would hit the ears more powerfully and cause more pain than the soft-sounding Bengali expression, '*tumi chup karo*'. Simultaneously, it serves the purpose of humiliating the opponent by emulation of a tone generally used by the British when addressing the lower orders. No matter that they boast to the skies that they would physically vanquish the other in physical combat, their boast is related actually to the power of eloquence. They would overcome each other by the ammunition of sheer words; in this, both are determined and their main weapon in this respect, in fact, their main resource, is the English language. But if, in one sense, words like 'stupid', 'speakti not', 'I don't care', 'Sando', 'All-Right-Come-on-Fight' – both flashy and jocular – help in ejecting the harsh feelings their minds mutually harbour towards each other, in another, the accumulated secret power of the words link them indissolubly, making both the warriors of words come under its spell. Therefore, it is not surprising that if one regrets that he cannot teach the other a proper lesson due to the absence of an uncle, the other threatens to call the police, and in no time, the two warring antagonists resolve all their differences – like leeches vanquished by a dash of salt. They leave for their respective homes, having balanced their accounts, saying, 'It doesn't matter, it's all right, how do you do and good night!'

Neither of them dares enter the field of disputation he himself had created. When peace is won by sweet words like 'Very, very sorry, would you like some sweets?', one of them goes on to declare, 'Why, I am not angry at all!' Then, could it all have been simply a posture of rage, a charade or make-believe? However, it is important to know that the quarrel would have failed to take off if it had not been conducted in this strange language – mixing bits of English expressions with Bengali – else the grammar of argumentation would have remained weak or faulty. And there is no escape from the ambit of such grammar rules even if one were ignorant about their nature. Our very universe of thought is captive to the English language. The colonized gentlemen or the *bhadralok* has no right or power to ignore the stark authority of this new universe of language; they have no option but to consciously respond to it. In fact, lack of minimum expertise in English disqualifies one from getting an entry permit into the arena of power. If one is not able to acquire a certificate in the knowledge of English, one has to confront a 'No admission, very busy' notice hanging right in front of one's nose, even when plenty of jobs are available in the Dhurrumtollah office region.

Has the figure of the warrior of words – replete with sacred thread and bare foot, the utterer of 'Narad, Narad' – been conjured up by mixing and matching the theorist of persuasion ('Saying Is Explaining') and the scientist of boot-clad feet (an adherent of the 'Science Education')? Has he been created by combining rhetoric with objective scientific knowledge? Was Sukumar Roy trying to draw our attention to this hotchpotch of a theory: a product of our affecting a wondrous mélange of wisdom of the east and the west? If the settled discourse of the *bhadralok* society owes its inception to this myth of synthesis, and if this very myth becomes the target of Sukumar Roy's attack, we can with confidence refer to Sukumar Roy's literary experiments as counter-discourse. But that it is impossible for counter-discourse to shake off the shadow or gain absolute freedom from the established and ongoing discourse is amply demonstrated in our many social debates, as well as in our art and literature. And, like many others, even Sukumar Roy could not free himself entirely from its contagion, despite the gravity of his habitual 'scientific temper' and the clarity of his vision; he could not completely escape its authority or its jurisdiction.

Past–Future Synthesis

We are not likely to know the kind of strategies Sukumar Roy had to muster or adopt, still less comprehend their character, in order to withstand the pressures of society or prepare a rejoinder for countering those. We cannot gauge the extent of influence environment may have exerted on his creative energies if we ignore or bypass 'Image of the Past' ('Atiter Chhobi'), the poem he had written either on commission or otherwise.[9] This poem was distributed in the form of a small booklet among a gathering of small children assembled to celebrate the *Magh Utsab* week on 25 Magh 1329 (Bengali calendar). In it Sukumar Roy reveals his fidelity to the form of historical narrative with its clearly demarcated stages, which had acquired a stable status from the nineteenth century onwards – the poem being nothing more than a child-friendly version of an officially sanctioned and eminently flattering account of the history of India. The text, however, is remarkably free of either any mention or proof of the country's plural realities, its infinite structural differences and internal divisiveness. In 'Image of the Past' the history of India is presented in the form of a smooth and closed narrative with a clearly discernible beginning, middle and end. The ancient classical age, the dark middle ages, and the gradual enlightenment and a new awakening – the Indian historical narrative is thus an abject fashioning of a western historical model. So that the picture of the past begins with the brahmanical sanskrit hymn: 'Such a time there was in Bharat / When the minds of the humans were totally free.' The ancient sages, by lighting the lamp of enlightenment, were able to uncover the unfathomable mysteries that had hitherto lain buried in the abyss of darkness. These sages were in deep meditation aspiring to reach the state of the blessed, in the belief and assurance that all human beings were partakers of the divine – in other words, the children of God. No argument about the clash between the Aryans and non-Aryans finds place in such a narrative. What is also erased is how the ancient brahmanical culture, in its 'large-heartedness' and 'extreme compassion', extirpated the root and branch of other cultures. Then comes the phase of regret or remorse: of how that great tradition had become distorted, how the children of the divine had undergone a disastrous fall from grace – all this leading to an unending saga of lament: 'Through the Wheels of Time, alas / how terribly bad times have befallen us!' The brahman has forgotten his calling, his mind is emptied of all queries. Everybody has taken shelter in the enchanting sleep of forgetfulness. And the country has divided itself into many *varna*s and classes. The dangerous reasoning of separateness has loosened the thread of an inter-racial unity that had hitherto kept the country together.

The belief that at one time in the remote past everything had been perfect, and that the incomparable harmony or grace that was, had been destroyed by some machination, continued to occupy Sukumar Roy's thinking for an extended period of time – though in a weakened form. Earlier, in the essay 'The Tyranny of Language', he had written: 'Although a reasonable system built upon the rule of law had been established in society, it is hardly worth recalling or producing ample evidence of how, in course of time, arrogance and an illegitimate aggrandizement of territories have led to the overcoming of that simple commonsense among generations of men.'[10]

After this humiliating second act, in 'Image of the Past' begins the third and the last one. And it is now, despite the fact the country is overcome by a pall of ignorance and so many races have dug their presence in its indigenous soil – with India silently surrendering both its physical wealth and its self-respect to external powers in the process – that we witness the signs of a new awakening and the horizons of a new dawn. Rammohun Roy is the high priest for initiating us into these new rites. By gathering classical wisdom, by blending the newly arrived knowledge of the west with the wisdom of the ancients, here and elsewhere, he began a revolution pursuing which India may yet regain the lost core of its divine knowledge. 'In this land of Bharat will / the songs of divine knowledge be sung again.' The restoration of uninterrupted links with the past projected the future in terms of an image of the past. The great learned men of the Brahmo Samaj worked to bring about that much awaited future inspired by the example of a pilgrim with a mission, like Rammohun. Sukumar Roy does not evade, completely, the topic of the mutual conflict of opinion and strategy among Ramachandra Bidyabagish, Devendranath Thakur, Keshabchandra Sen, Vijoykrishna Goswami and others like them. However, as far as possible, he accomplishes this in muted tones and with minimum elaboration.

The poem ends with a fervent appeal to the new worshippers of egalitarianism to come forward and restore equal rights to humanity through an enhancement of the revolutionary potential of the Brahmo Samaj. 'Would the door to worship remain permanently shut?' he plaintively asks. When scrutinized, one notices that nowhere in the poem are there arguments against the classical brahmanical culture, nor is there a single mention of Gautama Buddha. One could even say that the Buddha is drowned or, rather, has been made to attain his *nirvana* amidst the glory of the Absolute. But even more alarming is the omission of Islam – about which there is not a word. Therefore, it is easy to relegate the period of Islamic rule to the insufferable, dark middle ages. This deliberate silence induces a link between the spiritual crisis of the country and the 'great catastrophe' following the forcible entry, and the rule and culture, of the Mussalmans. Although there is a mention of the word '*fakir*' in relation to Devendranath, no separate weight or value is given to it. We also find that while ruing foreign rule, Sukumar Roy refrains from making any connection between that and the message of new wisdom from the west. In fact, such problems do not engage him in the least or cause him even a semblance of a headache. For him, power and knowledge are intrinsically intertwined, each dependent on the other, and therefore not problematic – his understanding not being any different from other such liberal, reasonable gentlemen of the times. Nevertheless a faint contrary voice finds its way into such a platitudinous pattern of progress. In the two penultimate lines of the poem – 'Is there no ray of hope anywhere / I ask, giving others beseeching looks' – we can gauge the clear presence of scepticism as the sound of deep sighs, though hushed, enters the ears. And in this change of tone, this alteration, in the final lines of the poem, there is a retraction, unsettling somewhat the very foundational reasoning of the poem – bringing it even closer to the mainstream Sukumar Roy and building a secret bridge of unity of intention among all his writings.

The latent pessimism that makes its appearance inside the poem is less propelled by an internal impulse than by some external compulsion, there being direct though unrelated, extra-textual evidence for this: the secret personal letter Sukumar Roy wrote on the night of 23 August 1920, before embarking on the 'Image of the Past'. He was compelled to write the letter in order to calm the agitation raging within his aggrieved mind on that night of a personal psychological crisis. Rather than communicate with another person, he chose to come to terms with himself and pen the urgent letter. Satyajit Ray has revealed to us that although the letter was ostensibly addressed to his friend Prasanta Mahalanobis, it was delivered to him three whole years later, after Sukumar Roy's death – reaching Mahalanobis through Sukumar Roy's wife.[11] And the precious letter entered the public domain 62 years after it was composed, in 1982! It may be said, therefore, that it was not a letter in the strict, literal sense of the term. Rather, we may regard it as a testimony, a reliable and valued historical document of the fact that, for Sukumar Roy, the universe of belief had collapsed, and the foundation of a traditionally held and practised culture had become unstable.[12] Roy wrote:

> I have for long felt in my mind that all my social activities are not in sync with my mental attitude and that all this does not benefit me in the least, rather it does me immense harm. I do not know why I have remained connected with these all this time. Perhaps it has been out of sheer habit.[13]

That evening, on the eve of giving a talk at Brahmo Samaj Mandir, he had a strange experience. Having come prepared to give a talk on a specific topic, he found himself speaking on something completely contrary. It seemed as if his tone had suddenly changed. He recalled:

> I had begun with one or two ideas central to my talk when I realized to my horrible shock that I did not believe in a single word I was about to utter – that is to say, I did not have the strength of conviction in what I was going to say. I did not even for a moment really believe in ideas of hope, happiness and an optimistic scenario.

> The reason I repeated them so often, so emphatically was because the desire to believe was strong within me, but in actual fact, what I believed in were quite the opposite: rampant, morbid and out and out pessimism. What I had wanted to say was that it is so easy, so natural to preserve a life of contentment. . . . Instead I heard myself saying that the hope that burns brightly like a lamp within us has become extinguished, the source of happiness forever closed, and that no one can entertain any hope now, nor set any store by for the future etc. As I spoke, I thought, how strange are my utterances yet how true of my inner being in every word I utter. I felt that some connectivity had come asunder. I am unable to relay to you that strange and depressing experience – how I came to understand clearly – almost immediately I got up to speak – that so many cherished illusions I harboured in my heart were coming apart, and that I had never been able to make much use of, not now not ever of all this talk of happiness, of pleasure and such buzz around us.[14]

Sukumar Roy added that he has no time to wait, all the delaying must come to an end, he has to do what has to be done. And all that had to be done – at least one of them – was to write. But what kind of writing was that going to be? Soon after submitting this deposition to himself, the poem 'Sabdakalpadrum' makes its appearance in the Aswin edition of *Sandesh*, followed, one after the other, by 'Baburam Sapure', 'Thash Goru', 'Sadhe ki Bole Gadha?' 'Ekushe Ain', 'Bombagarer Raja', 'Obak Kando', 'Bhalo re Bhalo', 'Palowan', 'Jalakujo Sangbad', 'Nacher Batik', poems of such variety and then stories like 'Dashur Khapami', 'Sabjanta Dada', 'Ukiler Buddhi' and 'Heshoram Hushiarer Diary'. And in 1329 (1922) was serialized, in *Sandesh*, *Ha-ja-ba-ra-la*, which was written in the same year as the last poem of *Abol Tabol*. Whether or not some of these literary pieces were executed prior to his writing the letter, what remains indisputable is that his testament or deed did, in truth, spell out the true character of his writings. Addressing his statistician friend, Sukumar Roy wrote: 'I have the faith that despite your propensity for the so called logical, you would be able to enter my universe of illogicality with compassion and do what is proper.'[15] Making 'illogicality' a weapon to attack abstract reasoning, moreover to critique the school of thought that induces a structured view of the world, was a task Roy took upon himself, long before he essayed his personal memoirs.

Feigning Anger

The play *Sabdakalpadrum* (in the manuscript it is referred to as *Srisabdakalpadrum*) and the essay 'The Tyranny of Language' were both written in the same year, 1915.[16] The essay has a direct relationship with the play. Moreover the two plays written at about the same time as *Sabdakalpadrum*, i.e. *Bhabuk Sabha*, published in Aswin 1321 (1914) of *Prabashi*, and *Chalachittachanchari*, also bear a close link with it. The subject matter of all the three plays is the onslaught of sound free of sense, rather, 'unsubstantiated feelings'. Just as the Dada or the mentor of the Wise in *Bhabuk Sabha* bestows profundities upon the two novitiates while gasping and drowning in the sea of contemplation, saying, 'Meaning is at the root of all mischief', similarly, the Master of *Sabdakalpadrum* provides his disciples with counsel that 'one must break into bits, the fangs of those live words in whom is latent a dangerous dynamism, root them out as their meanings keep jelling'. According to the Master's 'Ultimate Mantra', one will have to repeat *ad infinitum*, '*Gou, Gabou, Gabon*'. Again, in *Chalachittachanchari*, in order to demonstrate the excellence of the method of self-reflexive verbal ruptures and show the unique aesthetic pleasure that can be extracted from a simple word, Srikhandadev chooses the word 'goru'. The Master of *Sabdakalpadrum* knows only too well what a potent weapon a cacophony of sounds can be; the way it can bring both the devoted pupils and the devotion-loving gods into submission. 'See how in course of time the hands and feet become frozen with words / and how the hard impregnable words strike the head like a rod.' Although the Master, along with his pupils, is able to travel towards the final goal (Heaven itself), it all comes undone due to a faulty beginning. Even though Brihaspati, Narad, Aswini or Indra leave them alone, Viswakarma spoils the entire game. To Viswakarma, the first stanza of Kalidas' *Raghubangshakavya* contains a self-evident truth that he is not willing to budge from. Viswakarma's motto thus is: 'The word and its meaning are always and constantly at play – so says Kalidas.' Hence he remains unperturbed, no matter how much the Master and his pupils loudly chant '*Gou, Gabou, Gabon*'. He stands up to oppose any attempt at invalidating this interactive verbal meaning: 'What do you think – will the proud not be humbled? / Will the smouldering fire not rear its head? / Have not the trumpets of revolt started sounding / If there are sounds, will there not be echoes?' Viswakarma's sharp verbal arrow strikes hard and with deadly efficiency. The Master can hardly withstand its blow. And with such a sound as '*drum*', the Master along with his pupils tumble from paradise, their desire to reach their ultimate goal ending abruptly thus.

Raising the topic of the tyranny of sounds bereft of sense in his plays, poems and stories was not merely a simple linguistic ploy for Sukumar Roy. His aim was to examine how inflated and dispossessed sounds have overcome our consciousness, how language itself has lost its intrinsic value. Just as one needs to adequately gauge the power of a dominant discourse in order to disregard its institutional supremacy, one needs must also have the ability to produce a powerful counter-discourse. Sukumar Roy fulfilled these two conditions with equal dexterity. We can unhesitatingly bestow upon him the appellation of 'Viswakarma's infallible weapon' because of the kind of counter-discourse we come across in his writings. By assaulting an apparently organized and orderly patterned milieu with a cacophony of meaningless sounds, his special '*sab-*

dakalpadrum' prised open its hidden incoherence. In the play *Sabdakalpadrum*, piteous cries pierce the ears of Viswakarma from every quarter. Irritated and furious at the difficulties underlying any attempt to break out of the binding incoherence of language, he puts forward the question: 'In the darkness of the night / behind the formless volley of noise / the overheated breath of whose suppressed revenge / raves, in a state of delirium?'

No matter with how much pomp and fanfare the core argument is relayed, if one could shut the ears to all the trumpeting of sounds, one would recognize them as ravings. Similarly, if one could resist being overcome by the eloquence of words, one would succeed in identifying the latent 'heated breaths' and 'suppressed curses'. Sukumar Roy's intention was to dispel the dangerous spell cast by such sonority; to protect himself and others from the aggressive onslaught of mere words. And for this he had to design many clever strategies, many kinds of inversions, as well as play many tricks.

He invented a game he called 'feigning anger', and in this game lay hidden one of the keys to his artistic design. Lila Majumdar writes:

> So many new games would appear in Tatai's [Sukumar Roy's] head – among them was, 'feigning anger'. Perhaps he would be angry with someone and was unable to do anything about it. Or he would not actually be angry at all, though he could have been, and in such case he would be obliged to invent it. Which meant imagining a situation in which his opponent was appropriately put to shame, and how this could raise laughter in those playing the game.[17]

In the literature of Sukumar Roy, we come across many such different kinds of 'anger games' or inventions of anger. Just as his compulsion to devise 'anger' was strong, his creative skills were endless. One cannot but wonder at the infinite variety of his inventions and the dexterity of their deployment in the play *Sabdakalpadrum*. One cannot but be astonished at the display of his creative strategies – their easy and smooth crisscrossing over the text. On the one hand, there is the language of the Master and his disciples, whose style and tone, though not altogether strange, are nevertheless not fully credible. As a result, despite the fact that the Master and his pupils retain full faith in the theories thus expounded, these become an object of laughter to the reader. As if, unknowingly, Guruji & Co. have dug their own graves. On the other hand, Viswakarma, the spokesman for the author, directly criticizes the Guruji's theoretical pretensions and declares the writer's intention without prevarication. But the play has another character besides the loud-mouthed Viswakarma – one who works quietly, secretly and stealthily, and makes unexpected appearances in the discourse of the Guruji and his adherents; who does not allow the completion of their theoretical disputations and repeatedly resists them, thus disrupting the harmony of their discourses. By secretly subverting the argument, by striking at its foundational premises, Sukumar accomplishes his task from within the play itself, weaving his critique into its verbal texture. Whence, though less visible and a simpleton as compared to Viswakarma, the second character of the clumsy Vishwambhar fulfils more astutely the writer's aims. He can more easily unravel the web of verbal deceit because he is less verbose – almost soundless. When the disciples of Guruji get angry at Vishwambhar's interruption of their master's speech, he suddenly blurts out, in utter disregard of the appropriateness of his remark, 'Must one latch on to Guruji's tail?' And almost immediately, another characteristic is added to the image of the Guruji visualized thus far in the play. In other words, Guruji appears to resemble a creature with a tail. Vishwambhar is such a simpleton, he hardly knows what to say when; unused to working in tandem with Guruji's rhythm, he disrupts the everyday routine of the ashram. Just as Guruji counters words with words, the unwarranted tone of Vishwambhar's voice subverts those very contrary and contradictory strategies.

Bhavadulal of *Chalachittachanchari* is but a refined version of Vishwambhar.[18] The latter had, like the figure of Moral Conscience, clearly stated the main theme of the play: 'Your minds would be in whirl if you were to listen to all such talk / some would comprehend the total meaning, some only half / (some would not understand at all) – but enough is enough, now put a full stop / why should one offload all the learning in the market place of the ordinary / or offload them at all?' But being a harmless goody, Bhavadulal has neither the desire nor the means to reveal the sum and substance of the play. There is hardly anyone around who possesses his kind of natural curiosity, it is even more rare to find someone with his indomitable thirst for knowledge. And yet, it is this quest for knowledge that has taken Bhavadulal to the court of equipoise of Ishaan–Satyaban – to the very heart of the abode of Srikhandadev. Finally, caught between these two antagonist forces, he has to face untold difficulties for no fault of his own.

Bhavadulal writes a book called *Chalachittachanchari* – and it is a wonder of a book – where he quotes with gratitude all that is worth learning or memorializing, besides documenting the facts of his own life. One is curious to know if any one of those who had dedicated their lives to composing the ultimate book of encyclopaedic knowledge during this luminous period of eighteenth-century European history (the Age of Enlightenment), could have even dreamt of a unique lexicon of wisdom such as *Chalachittachanchari*. But rather than encouraging Bhavadulal by praising him and applauding him for accomplishing the impossible, rather than showing immense gratitude to him for showering us with his generosity, people try desperately to destroy all that he has achieved. The irony is that they do not do this out of churlish envy; their tempers are aroused because of Bhavadulal's crass stupidity and they are ready to strike at him. The problem remains that although Bhavadulal pays attention to all that is being said and is eager more than ever to memorize everything worth knowing, whenever he tries to speak or write about them, he completely mixes them up and produces something grotesque and indecorous. For example, he is told that to argue is an entirely worthless piece of activity, that there is no substance to it. And as a solid proof of this, he is furnished with the example of the law of gravitation that drives the sun, moon and stars around their orbit, which, presumably, does not depend on the power of argumentation. But Bhavadulal confuses the issues in his attempt to repeat the problem in an orderly manner, and turns this infallible piece of wisdom into a hopeless piece of chicanery. He says: 'Look here, it is no use contradicting, can't you see that the law of gravitation propels everything by the help of argumentation – is that doing any good?' Bhavadulal, a disciple of the Lord of Guileless, has one patent answer whenever he is caught on the wrong foot by angry folks. Blundering idiot that he is, he says he is mentally deficient, and that ever since either a cat or a porcupine had bitten him as a child, he has been in this state. He is so far gone that he cannot distinguish between words that are similar sounding but vastly different in meaning, such as '*samiksha*' and '*makhika*', and often replaces one with the other in the most unbecoming manner, unknowingly devaluing the very concept of '*samiksha*' – or truth collectively expounded in Sankhya philosophy.

Satyasadhan, Ishan and Nikunja time and again warn their students that unless they give up their bad habit of arguing, there is no scope for their self-improvement. No matter how much disagreement they may have about other matters, in this respect at least, they have no disagreement; they are all equally against any argumentation. Vishwambhar had trailed behind when Guruji of Sabdakalpadrum, along with his pupils, was rushing towards paradise. As he was not able to utter the chant of the ascent in its totality, Guruji's speed faltered. Rajnish counsels Vishwambhar to recite the '*dhuk dhuk*' prayer in order to shed all gross prejudices. Instead of doing that, all of a sudden , Vishwambhar blurts out, 'I have been thinking . . .'. The very word 'thinking' – with such devastating implications – is enough to send shivers down everybody's spine. The Guruji is extremely displeased at the foolhardy manner in which thought is forced upon words. He rebukes Vishwambhar harshly, saying, 'They who confound people with meaning are themselves ghouls.' Guruji is derailed from his purpose by twin forces: the pressures exerted by Viswakarma from the top and being held back by worthless pupils like Vishwambhar. He is not able to reach paradise. Like many characters of *Abol Tabol*, the dramatis personae of the play regard their wisdom and self-understanding to be supreme, leaving no room for doubts or questions about this. The pattern of thinking they deem as reasonable, they cannot dream of upturning. No evidence to the contrary can unsettle their beliefs; rather than determine the authenticity of theory by reality, they do quite the opposite; they adjudicate reality by theory. Their resources being authoritative statements and rigid verbal patterns, Satyasadhan and his ilk may have experienced internal dilemmas; there is, however, no basic difference in the thought pattern to which they are all equally subservient. And to their opposite end exist the Bhavadulals who carry on their work silently. They quietly add the sentence: 'I do not say this for the sake of argument' while making the pronouncement that the law of gravitation cannot do much good if it works by 'force of argumentation'. And because the Bhavadulals do not cross swords with the Satyasadhans, they can deny the conditions imposed upon them by the latter's structured reasoning; and because they do not directly participate in a dialogue with them, they can dismiss with impunity the theoretical universe of the Satyasadhans, thus maintaining their identity as outsiders till the end.

The King (Raja) of *Abol Tabol* who sits with a slate in hand, perspiring profusely in frustration for not being able to find a solution to his puzzle in any book; the counsellor of the poem 'Shabdhan!' ('Be Warned!') who drives Pyalaram up the wall regarding the rules of medical science; the scientist of the poem 'Science Education' who wishes to examine a child's brain using scientific reasoning; the man of the poem 'Ki Mushkil!' ('What a Bother!') who is continuously involved in 'News of the World', and has a deep curiosity regarding which one among the sahibs commands high respect or prestige in government offices; the worshipper of wisdom who jots down all knowledgeable matters in his notebook in the poem 'The Notebook' – all of them are of the same ilk as Satyasadhan, the author of '*Samya–Nirghanta*', the linguist Srikhandadev, the author of *Sabdartha-khandika*, or the Guruji who had composed '*Sabda-Samhita*'. They all have a profound respect and exhibit an undying devotion to the printed word, or the book. Thus, against Satyasadhan's work that is devoted to the pursuit of different kinds of scientific knowledge, such as law, science or the notebooks, resides its opposite: Bhavadulal's *Chalachittachanchari*. This book becomes an imperfect reflection or a distorted replica of Satyasadhan's '*Samya–Nirghanta*', '*Siddhantsa–Visuddhika*', or Srikhandadev's *Sabdartha-khandika*'. By obliquely reflecting the absurdity of Bhavadulal hoarding all kinds of knowledge, it highlights the grotesque aspect of their (Satyasadhan and the like) endeavours. In the inimitable language of Bhavadulal, '*Samya–Nirghanta*' becomes '*Samya–Ghanta*' and '*Siddhanta–Visuddhika*' becomes '*Siddhawa–Visuchika*'. By changing just a few words around, antonyms are created, and thus the division of the lexicon – '*Sabdakalpadrum*' – takes place. And it is this '*Sabdakalpadrum*' that lets out, rather subtly, that no matter how much antagonism exists between the Satyasadhans and Srikhandadevs, no matter how much hairsplitting is done over their fine differences, ultimately and centrally they inhabit the same verbal universe; that universe has much in common with our reality, though it may or may not be grounded in the material world.

Srikhandadev is a sharp critic of Satyasadhan's pedagogy. In his opinion, there is absolutely nothing to gain from parroting such old-fashioned techniques in this present age of ours, and unless one can disseminate knowledge through utilizing more advanced scientific method, all effort would come to naught. To Srikhandadev, the apostle of this newly awakened consciousness, the dictionary of modern psychological truth lies indisputably, of course, in a few hard-to-pronounce English words. The more incomprehensible these are, the more relevant they seem to be: like 'meta-psychological principles', 'graduated psycho-thesis of phonetic forms', 'Pal's extra-cyclical equilibrium', etc. His ideal unity of knowledge lies in this kind of holistic symmetry; an elixir wrought out of the confluence of eastern and western knowledge systems. It is therefore that the pupils in the school of Srikhandadev have to cultivate difficult classical texts like, *Aieskhanda Paddhati* or *Lokashta Prakaran*, alongside impenetrable subjects like 'synnecous cosmopaedia'.

The esoteric names given to the various disciplines are gathered from pseudo-Latin terms, meaningless English words and even weighty Sanskrit compounds. The stage direction of students sitting in a semi-circle in Srikhandadev's room in the ashram reads like this: 'On one corner there are strange instruments and charts that make no sense.' On the other hand, no matter how backward they are as regarded by Srikhandadev, the socialist goal-oriented Satysadhans (practitioners of truth) are believers of a similar hotchpotch theory. Although they think that Srikhandadev dishes out scientific nonsense in the name of education, their own curriculum is but a version of the same. To them all endeavour, thought or meditation, rather, the entire existence, is valued in terms of the certificates issued in English by the sahibs: the final reach of all their ambitions.

They catch hold of Ramapada, a student in Srikhandadev's school, and lecture him, saying, 'Look, you must always refrain from publicizing yourself', while they themselves, no doubt, either directly or indirectly never forget to mention they are the sahib's favourites and objects of their praise. Besotted by the idea of his own uniqueness, Satyasadhan lets it be known that Fauson Sahib had himself certified him as 'second to none' in learning, wisdom, knowledge, enthusiasm and moral probity. Nikunja, unwilling to be left behind, claims that his paternal cousin had sung for the Governor-General. But Ishan, the person whose envy against Satyasadhan is not that covert – and because it is not so, it is not difficult to gauge that the group is about to fall apart – reveals that the journal *Bengali* had this to say about his three-volume English epic: 'In Memorium', 'O Mandhata', 'O Mores': 'We congratulate the distinguished author of the monumental production (Double demy octavo, 974 pages) who is evidently in possession of a stupendous amount of astounding information.' Ishan, of course, fails to see that his book is being commended for its bulk rather than its quality, and that information rather than poetic value is the subject of praise. Moreover, the Ishans of the world fail to grasp that the word 'stupendous' has an auditory affinity with the word 'stupid'.

Sukumar Roy, time and again, in his various writings, pointed to the Bengalis as being Anglophiles. In a book for children titled *Sri Gobindokatha*, he had written: 'The Sahibs here know me well / If you wish I can produce a certificate.' In the play *The Spiteful Female* (*Hingshuti*), one among those Anglophile Bengali females dreams that a *memsahib* (an English lady) had given her a doll – and her joy at receiving the doll from a *memsahib*, albeit in a dream, is absolute. In the play *Jhalapala*, a sycophant, listening to a song sung by Kewalchand, an admirer of the zamindar, lamenting within an India in a state of captivity, cries out in apprehension, 'It's seditious!' – while Gheturam is very irritated at all such display of rebelliousness, fearing the worst for the future of his maternal cousin in the service of the British government. And the great Panditmashai who is wont to display his knowledge of English to his students, through the Bengali translation of the phrase 'I go up, You go down', having an inkling of what the word 'seditious' implies, shudders at the mere sound of the word. Each and every such person, overwhelmed by an universal Anglophilia, is not only desirous of praise and encouragement from the sahibs, but also curls up like a worm in constant fear of them. Therefore, it is no surprise that Somprakash is the ideal disciple of those committed to socialism, who apprehends, little by little and in small doses, the heart-rending sobs and entreaties about him when his feelings are roused to the hilt. He drops the names of western scholars at every opportunity, is thrilled to bits by the realization that his ideas more than match theirs. No matter how strange the course of man's thoughts may appear, there remains nothing mysterious about them when one recalls the two pregnant expressions, 'heredity' and 'environment'. Everything instantly becomes crystal-clear, fluid and transparent like water. And in this context, the significance of the dual influence of 'heredity' and 'environment' acquires a tremendous reach. It also points to the way in which during the periods – pre-colonial and colonial – the two levels of our existence were shaped, how various resources had come together and formed our diverse and complex mentality.

Sukumar Roy was not content with merely pointing out the phenomenon; he tried to reveal its implication as clearly as he could by referring to a devastating comment made by Bhavadulal. When Somprakash asks Bhavadulal, 'You know, of course, who was Herbert Spencer', without batting an eyelid he replies nonchalantly. 'Oh, yes, I believe in Herbert and Spencer, sneezes, lizards, ghosts and goblins all.' It is to be noted that the logical status of the answer does not match the logical status of the question. Whereas Somprakash would like to know whether Bhavadulal has heard of Herbert Spencer, Bhavadulal not only disconnects the two words Herbert and Spencer, he extends the list to proudly display the extent of his beliefs. Thus, by demonstrating a shift from one logical paradigm to another through the example of Bhavadulal, Sukumar Roy points out that rather than arriving at knowledge or adjudicating or measuring the validity of an argument, the Satyaprakashes of this world are in the habit of accepting everything effortlessly as if with a sense of inevitability; that the so-called enlightened gentlemen of the western world are characteristically habituated to wholesale consumption of knowledge rather than a diligent application for the acquisition of wisdom. We may, in this connection, recall the uncle who is neurotic about science in the play *Abak Jalpan*. He offers all kinds of scientific information to the thirsty traveller rather than assuage his thirst by offering him a sip of water. He knows all that there is to know about 'hydrophobia' or the fear of water. Nevertheless, giving a detailed description of what befell the unfortunate Baidyanath when bitten by a dog, he goes on:

> Poor soul [Baidyanath] was unable to take a sip of water. His throat got choked at a single drop – such problem! I had to get hold of an exorcist and make him consume medicines mixed with *dhatura* [bitter], and had to get rid of the poison in his system by reciting spells – only then was he able to swallow a drop of liquid. It happens!

These people need both scientific knowledge as well as indigenous medicines, both quacks as well as those knowledgeable in the science of healing. They have to have all kinds of remedies near at hand, as one never knows when what may come handy. In his essay 'The Tyranny of Language' ('Bhashar Atyachar'), Sukumar Roy wrote:

> When theory for the sake of aesthetics gets firmly ensconced in figurative language or else assumes an absurd character, like that of 'Hing, Ting, Chhat', then in the imagination of our future generation, theory could easily become synonymous with whatever one desires, such as poetry, history or scientific experiments.[19]

In this context many of Sukumar Roy's writings, alongside 'The Tyranny of Language', may be seen as linked to Rabindranath's poem 'Hing Ting Chhat' in his *Sonar Tori* collection. And we may note how there too, the sublime sounds of senseless words devastate the processes of thought. How with the help of high-sounding words like 'evolution'/'revolution' or attraction/repulsion', it is possible to produce a bizarre explanation of an equally bizarre dream experienced by Habuchandra Bhup, and render everything crystal-clear leaving no misgivings in the mind of anyone. In the dream analysis of the dimunitive-sized Pandit from Gaur with a bald pate and an emaciated frame, scientific and theoretical terms like atom, molecule or the magnetic field reside comfortably beside the name of Shiva, '*Trinayan*', '*Jeebshakti*', '*Shivshakti*', '*Trambak*' etc. He has an extraordinary skill, this Pandit, an effortless ability for the creation of a grotesque mélange out of ingredients belonging to the wisdom of the east and the west. As in the writings of Sukumar Roy, in Rabindranath Tagore's works too, we witness the coalescing of western science and Indian philosophy. It is therefore necessary that the two be regarded as constituent parts of the theoretical universe of Satyasadhans; leaving out either would be tantamount to destabilization of meaning, rendering the thought-system problematic.

Quack disciples of the western philosophers who have surpassed the skills of their progenitors are a minor but nevertheless important marker of the identity of Rabindranath's 'Gauriya Pandits', the native masters of learning; no matter how small the instrument is, its ability to churn out sounds is remarkable. The dubious attempts at scientific explanation of Hindu thought, its sense of things, habits and rituals, initiated by 'orientalism' of the nineteenth century, continue to this day. Whether the arguments Rabindranath marshals, in his 'Hing Ting Chhat', is an attack on Chandranath Bosu or not, contextually his debates with Bosu became very popular. Some years prior to his composition of 'Hing Ting Chhat', Rabindranath had criticized Hindu conservatism, blind belief in Hindu faith, the edicts of Manu, and the promotion of an unquestioning acceptance of ancient prejudices by the likes of Chandranath Bosu in his essay, 'The Hindu Marriage'. He had said:

> We have acquired many 'sentiments' from our English education . . . which have inspired many patriotic people to authenticate the antiquity and the indigenity of these sentiments deriding their opponents for their distorted mentality induced by foreign education. These patriots are able to discern and rescue, with their sharp hawk-like eyes, new theoretical- scientific formulations like Evolution, Natural Selection, Magnetism etc., from the web of complex thoughts of our ancient poets. Wrapped in the illusory disguise of Magnetism, many unsubstantiated opinions, meaningless rituals of our Aryan ancestors intrigue to find a place next to science. In contemporary times, Psychic Force – a word of obscure origins – has been trying to occupy the position of Magnetism.[20]

Echoing a somewhat similar idea, Sukumar Roy, in his essay, 'Doiban Dayam', had written: 'When the bogey of science takes recourse to praising the glory of spurious practice of keeping a long tuft of hair and the supposed spiritual properties of water from the Ganges, then it is no surprise that providence would claim to have a scientific pedigree.'[21] And in the essay on 'The Tyranny of Language', Roy wrote that no matter how vague our ideas are about the real identity or the signature of terms like Indian thought, the indigenous identity of a nation or the shape of Hinduism, we so easily apply them to art, literature, to our apparel and habits, our faith in and our respect for those verbal utterances are not one bit lessened or become contrary.[22] Therefore, on the one hand, the myth of the greatness of Hinduism thrives on the careful analysis accorded to it by western rational philosophy; on the other, it also distorts our ideas about the reality on the ground: that the cruel oppression encouraged by Hindu philosophy actually leads to a dangerous cover-up. Both Sukumar Roy and Rabindranath Tagore direct our attention to how *langue* or prescribed speech could result in establishing an eternal discourse; they critique the feebleness of our thinking processes and attempt to bring our attention back to the reality that lies hidden under the covering of myth.

In the play *Jhalapala*, Kewalchand, by means of his un-rhythmic song, 'Lament for India', tells us: 'Alas that the golden land of Bharat has succumbed to such a terrible calamity / the land about whose greatness plentiful evidence abound / And today that land is being ignored and is the subject of every body's ridicule.' In another song, he grieves about 'what we have been reduced to in this fallen times!' One could interpret the 'what have we been reduced to' in two ways, to mean: how the uncommon power associated with brahmanism has disappeared, or, even more, the pride of the Aryan race has simply evaporated. The progeny of those universally acclaimed learned men are now crawling on their bellies like worms, hiccupping and working their fat off at offices. The image of India's past, so gloriously presented in the poem 'Image of the Past' or 'Atiter Chhobi', is attacked through the collection of sounds, the rhythm and stance of these two songs – as if by a pair of pincers.

In the play *Lakshmaner Shaktishel* or *The Mythological Missile of Lakshman*, peeping from behind the cover of the *Ramayana*'s sanctified heroes – Ram–Lakshman–Hanuman–Vibhishan and such others – are the deserving assistants or followers of the time-tested ideals of ancient Hinduism, like the gentlemen who are fated to wriggle on the earth like worms, the *bhadralok*![23] The play opens with the description of a royal dream: Ram dreams that Ravan is dead, even though in his wildest dreams Ram could not have imagined that he would have the courage to defeat Ravan. But coming to know that Ravan's death was due to his slipping and falling off a tall palm-tree, Ram and his companions become elated at the prospect of annihilation of the enemy. But almost immediately they come to learn through a messenger that Ravan was not only alive, proving the royal dream to be a lie, but was, together with his party, advancing towards Ram's fortress amidst great fanfare and creating much clamour. One slowly comes to realize that not only Ram but others in his camp, like Sugriv, Hanuman, etc., are all equally afraid of something like a war. No matter how much Ram boasts – 'Like moth drawn to the flame / like spice singed in oil' – in imitation of the long-lined blank verse, *Meghnadbadh Kavya*, of Michael Madhusudhan Dutt – and despite the extent to which Sugriv and Vibhishan show off their might, no ne has the courage to confront Ravan. They sit down to confabulate at the slightest opportunity, and go on to devise many schemes and intrigues, but all the bang ends in a whimper! That a condolence meeting has to be held in case they all die is something Vibhishan cannot forget. Those with a gift of the gab, who have the skill to demolish their opponents with verbal power, would rather curse and berate than force Ravan into submission through physical assault.

In the writings of Sukumar Roy, characters like those above appear in many guises. In the 'Khai Khai' poem, 'the man with ifs and buts' declares proudly: 'I growl and go after them / and then retreat with tail between my legs.' In the poem 'Narad Narad', the two warriors each retreat to their own shelter after making much noise. And the two contestants of 'Jhalapala', Gheturam and Duliram, are but variations of the two warriors of 'Narad, Narad'. The narrator of the poem 'Baburam Sapure' demands of the snake-charmer a snake that has no fangs, which cannot see or move, and does not bite anyone. He would like to demonstrate his prowess by killing such a harmless, timid creature and finds no peace till he can teach it a lesson by bringing the rod fiercely down its head. After all the ruckus in *Sabdakalpadrum*, such as, 'Go after him – Help, help – My god', etc., the advice, 'Come let's leave – he is girding his loins' is sent out. All such individuals desire a quiet and peaceful life; they are forever looking for how to avoid all kinds of trouble and somehow continue to exist.

In *The Mythological Missile of Lakshman*, because it plays on the Bengali gentlemen's relying on the truth of the *Ramayana* to authenticate their love for ancient culture, and because it introduces into the epic, landscape and characters emulating the ideal, loving narrator of the poem 'Shabdhan!' or 'Be Warned!', who gently treads on the earth – on the one hand, the enormous gap between the upright characters of the *Ramayana* and their spineless imitators become the occasion for uproarious laughter, and on the other, the nature of the new Hindu middle class, basking in the glory of the Aryans, is also exposed. Even in Michael Madhusudan's epic, *Meghnadbad Kabya*, neither Ram nor Lakshman are Ravan or Indrajeet's equals. And though a recipient of unstinted blessings of the gods and armed with innumerable arsenals, Lakshman of Michael's epic, not unlike his *Ramayana* original, does not dare face Meghnad in a direct confrontation; rather, he slays him in an unjust battle.

There is no doubt that Michael's sympathies are with the demons; to him Ram and his followers are objects of contempt, at the most pity. But Sukumar Roy does not spare even Ravan of his sarcasm; he is unwilling to leave out anyone from his ridicule, as when Sugriv abandons the contest and Ravan cries out, 'Shame! Shame!', or when he filches Lakshman's pocket after the latter is incapacitated by the mythological missile. Ram and Ravan resemble each other more than they appear different. When the two emissaries of Yama come to fetch the dead Lakshman's soul, they get frightened out of their wits at the sight of Vibhishan: 'When defeat is most certain / Is it wise to wage a war?' And they get perturbed at the prospect of losing the job they fancy. When Hanuman places the Gandhamadan mountain on the head of Yama, the skies seem to fall over the heads of his two emissaries and they loudly lament, 'O Yama you rascal, you have cheated us / we have yet to collect the thirteenth anna of our salaries'. These quiet, dependent beings who rely on their jobs are modelled on the much familiar type of civilized gentlemen. Sukumar Roy seeks to endanger the logic and grammar of the lives of the Gopals and their likes from all quarters of the society of the time.

The Self and Its Annihilation

Not just Sukumar but many others, along with him, join in the game of taking the grammatical apart; in the forefront of these so-called anti-Gopals are Rabindranath, Abanindranath and Sibram Chakraborty. Like Sukumar Roy, they too are experts in upturning the civilized and sensible word sequence. But this does not mean that they all adopt the same strategy for countering words with antonyms, or that there is no difference in the political significance of their colourful inversions. Nevertheless, despite their distinct individual stances, in certain contexts they evince a sameness of mental attitude with regard to Hinduism . Even Abanindranath, whose paintings were for the most part coloured by 'the mist of Indian thought', and whose *Rajkahini* may as well be seen as a delightful children's version of Todd's tales of Rajput heroes, that very Abanindranath wrote in his book on Bengali rituals (*Banglar Bratakatha*, 1350):

> Behind the liberal, open-hearted stance of Hindu dharma lies an extreme narrow-mindedness – there is no scope for individuals to pursue their individual beliefs, rather all are brought under the stranglehold of priests and the Brahmins and for this the Scriptures act as an engulfing network of prohibitions'.[24]

As for Sibram Chakraborty, he is forever virulently against the Hindu dharma. The first edition of his eloquent satire on the 'new Hindus', 'Moscow versus Pondicherry', bears the title 'Today and Tomorrow' (1929). In it he says:

> We regard ourselves as the fortunate children of the world, it is through us that all the prosperity in the world would come about – we are the tallest of all, the most loved creatures on earth – it is so nice to think in this way! It is but natural to feel inhibited about waging an assault on such honeyed dreams, because in actual fact there is very little sweetness, rather we suffer from a great deal of sting – this futile pride, this easy self-satisfaction, this deadening illusion – the time has come to free ourselves from all of this. In the process of getting to know the truth about oneself we may hurt our self pride and cause ourselves pain and yet it is very important to be thus self-critical.[25]

Sibram has in this respect provided us with an important clue: self-knowledge requires self-annihilation. Sukumar's characters want nothing more than this: Pagla Dashu, Vishwambhar and Bhavadulal provide us with a text that demonstrates how to strike at the honeycomb and still escape being stung. Sibram's unfailing weapon for this is the pun. Those who wish to mesmerize the audience with a spell of sonorous sounds are also partial towards punning – a verbal ornament of ridicule. By the use of this particular ornament, they aim to show that no matter the difference in intention and meaning of words, it is possible to tie them up simply by the affinity of their sounds, and consistency of meaning is achieved through this magical kinship of words. The myth merchants, basking in the glory of auditory fame, believe that 'it is futile to desperately go after significance or unnecessarily aggravate one's headache cogitating over nation, time, or history – all meaning is hidden in the sound'. There is no cause for anxiety once one learns how to unravel that hidden secret. But there those who want to destabilize myths, apply puns or irony for quite a contrary purpose. Sibram Chakraborty belongs to this second group. And one cannot but concede that his love for puns at times becomes contrapuntal to his writing. But for the most part, the sense permeating the sound unfailingly reaches its destination. A few examples from 'Moscow versus Pondicherry' may suffice: 'Sangha means *Sanghatik* (or dangerous)'; 'Ah yes! I am that Brahma – the All-knowing'. This self-perception, fairly common, induced by a certain sense of self-gratification, has not been rendered invalid in our country; nothing proves this more than the habitual response to being stepped on the toes by those famous adherents of a philosophy that equates the soul with the Supreme Being. They show no mercy towards those who come in the way of their privileges: 'From Superman to Super-mania'; 'No one denies that Rabindranath had no "art" or "artificiality" in him; or that there was a lot of "pose" in his success to his "position" and that an extremely generous "purse" aided the development of his personality.'[26]

Many self-proclaimed megalomaniacs appear in the stories Sibram wrote for children. But he was not a person to spare others like the father, the teacher and the official – all of whom had his unqualified attention. In this context, it is worth quoting stories like: 'The Eternal Red Tape', 'Pig Means Piglets', 'Running Away from Home', 'The Great Sage's Nirvana', 'The Birth of the Gods', and, finally, 'Farewell to the Pundits' (or learned men). 'Hargobinder Jogbal' ('The Yogic Power of Haragobindo') is a story dealing with megalomaniacs. 'Come repeat the mantra – the magical power of the words takes you nowhere; the physical power of yoga can.' Listening to this utterance of Haragobindo, the first-person narrator of the story muses, 'The gentleman must have gone to Sri Aurobindo Ashram and now, after losing his mind, he has come back home instead of going to Ranchi.' He not only muses thus, he even lets the following words slip inadvertently out of his mouth: 'Instead of going to Pondicherry you have achieved Pindochari or given up the ghost!'[27] Most of the simple-minded narrators of Sibram's stories are Bhavadulal's kinsmen.

In the writings of Sibram and Sukumar Roy especially, the deconstruction of self is achieved primarily through the medium of pleasurable sounds. Their eternal self-dissolution breaks down the fortress of sounds, and inserts into the narrative ways of escape. However, neither Sibram nor Sukumar give an indication about the escape route, it is futile to ask them the address of an abstract imaginary world. It is the job of the Bhavadulals of this earth to rouse our suspicions or feel at odds about those edicts of society that have been accepted as irrefutable. They are the living images of contradiction who go about proving the underlying falseness behind direct experience, or what is regarded as self-evident. And in this way the Bhavadulals discover truth in what is palpably bizarre. Manabendra Bandyopadhyay remarks: 'Dashu's or Bhavadulal's eccentricities or stupidities are philosophical investigations, they are a means to enjoy life and to know it better.'[28]

Next to the stupid or moronic Bhavadulal and the mad Dashu is Vishwambhar and Hijibijbij and other characters belonging to *Ha-ja-ba-ra-la*'s nonsense world. Is Dashu really mad or Bhavadulal really stupid, or are they only pretending to be so? Just as it is impossible to determine what is what, there is no satisfactory explanation as to why Hijibijbij throws up his hands and feet at the slightest pretext, and laughs loudly for no apparent reason at all. They only disrupt the rhythm, prise open the apparent symmetry, in order to reveal all the knotty problems. That Sukumar Roy had a soft corner for them is revealed in this remark of Lila Majumdar: 'Dada [Sukumar Roy] would write plays, he taught people how to act, but he generally would keep the main part for himself. By main I mean the one that is most stupid or ignorant. There was no one matching Dada for taking on the role of Hadaram or the imbecile.' When, in the play *Chalachittachanchari*, Srikhandadev and Satyasadhan enter into a fierce argument, Bhavadulal does not directly participate in it; he merely interrupts, saying, 'Good heavens! It's getting late!' Satyasadhan screams in irritation, 'Why are you interrupting us?' But this kind of intrusion, the insertion of a gap in the dialogue, are the peculiar characteristics of Sukumar's poetics. The interruptions, the apparently harmless assaults, do not allow the narrative, which may have acquired such smooth and pleasing contours in the hands of those like Satyasadhan, to achieve any final closure. And because of this, all the suppressed incongruities of the established and dominant discourse that have not been allowed to surface – all the contrary stances towards society that have not been given their due recognition – all these become important in Sukumar Roy's writings. Farce is Bhavadulal's stratagem for affecting a separate identity while maintaining an intimate relationship with the preceptors of society, and for remaining involved with the world around him in a way in which he can avoid being reduced to an outsider.

Are such jesters totally absent in the writings of Rabindranath or Abanindranath? In *Lipika*, Rabindranath himself takes on the persona of a jester. He says, 'I can neither hit out nor demolish, in the arena of providence I can only laugh.'[29] Of course, all the frolic and banter of the jester are not pure or innocent; intermixed in them are puns of anger and sadness. The outcast clown has only one vow – to act the buffoon. The knowledge that he would incur the

Mythical prince with broken umbrella, illustration from *Shey* by Rabindranath Tagore

displeasure of the king does not prevent him from appearing as a slanderer in *Totakahini*. And only by taking cues from the jester/slanderer are we able to reach Rabindranath and Abanindranath's theory of the child.

The Child and Meditation on Childhood

Rabindranath himself provides us with a description of what had urged him to write *Shishu Bholanath*:

> For some time now I have spent my days [in America] suffocated by the poisonous gas of inhospitable suspicion, and have remained captive to the darkness induced by the blind pursuit of material gain. I began to write *Shishu Bholanath* the minute I could escape the grasp of American materialism . . . much like a freed prisoner who runs to the sea side in order to breathe in the air of freedom. I drowned myself in child's play, rode on the crest of waves of children's games so that my thoughts were chastened, my mind rendered pure and free.[30]

This was true not only of *Shishu Bholanath*; time and again, throughout his life, Rabindranath, fed up with the external world, would turn his gaze on the child and become extremely eager to enter into the world of childhood fantasy.

Therefore, in Rabindra-literature, the essential image of the child is a creation of the mingling and matching of external pressure and inner urgency. So that while the particular child is pure, free of all kinds of sins as well as solitary, it is at the same time compassionate, open-minded and far-seeing. In the self-created world of the child there is, however, no place for workaholics. The old do not have the wherewithal to know the perimeters of the child's mind because the child does not accept the grammar of the crooked and broken universe of the elders. It creates an audacious anti-world in opposition to the world of the elders – a world where all desires are fulfilled and another order of truth or the land of more-than-truth resides.

Rabindranath and Abanindranath had given another name to this world or the land of 'more-truth'. In 'Stories' and 'Jorasankor Dhare' ('Alongside the Precincts of Jorasanko'), Rabindranath had called this non-country *poristhan* (fairyland), as nothing was impossible in the land of fairies. And the impossible can become possible because there is no final pause in the place; in its ceaseless movement, it is forever pulsating. The curiosity of the child has no bounds, his questions know no end. The child has no sense of discrimination, it has no use for market values; it does not either get caught or surrender to any situation. Since it knows how to become detached, its interest or enthusiasm continues unabated. It takes equal pleasure in destroying and creating – the diver plunges into the ocean in search of pearls, the merchant sets sail his ship on the river in the hope of wealth, but the child goes on playing on the banks of the world-ocean. He has no illusions, hence he can forget – which is why his other name is Bholanath or Shiva, the god of forgetfulness. In fact Shiva's fiery persona or *rudraroop* is but an expression of his child-entity. And therefore Rabindranath's entreaty to the child-god Bholanath: 'O Bholanath, take me into the fold of your frenetic dancers (the *tandavs*), make me your devotee, bestow freedom among destruction forever and ever, protect "playing" by freeing it from all kinds of restrictions and inhibitions.'[31]

In the literary career of Rabindranath, there was no exception to this imaginary – only a change in perspective, in tandem with different historical moments. Amal of 'Dakghar' or 'Post Office' is the embodiment of this imaginary. He is as pure as his name suggests; none of the dirt or grime of the world touch him. Nonetheless, in a place where the striving and calculating people manage to keep themselves alive and remain in the pink of health, he happens to be the sole person suffering from an incurable disease. The Amals of this world are the emblems of a form of grace whose purity is unsustainable in this cruel world of ours. They have to either disappear from the earth like Phatik of 'Chhuti' and the parrot of *Totakahini*, or keep drifting in the air like Tarapada of 'Atithi' or Sukumar of *Shey*.

But the question remains: why, time and again, does Rabindranath feel compelled to assume a child's voice in order to voice his own thoughts? He himself says, 'Why did I have to pen the poems of *Shishu Bholanath* – certainly not for others but for my own sake.'[32] But can one explain his continuous preoccupation with childhood by attaching the tag of romantic artist to him? It is without doubt that Amal–Sukumar's makebelieve world, and later, that of the hero of *Tong Ling* (Lila Majumdar's novel) are indeed testimonies against the materialistic world such as it is; the other name for which is art. And it is art that is the sole protective talisman of the marginalized Rakhals of this world – a place for their final refuge. But would we be fair towards the Rakhals, not do them grave injustice, by misunderstanding their artistic creed if we merely seek the aid of western romantic theory?

A Preface to Departure

In 'Shishur Jibon' ('A Child's Life'), a poem belonging to the volume *Shishu Bholanath*, Rabindranath says: 'Let the promise of turning into a child be rekindled in my heart / let the wind pick up sails freed of worries / I will rip the mask off the visage of the future in one wrench / and glimpse the same at time present.'[33] But for which face of the future in the present did Rabindranath wish to tear off the mask in the children's literature he wrote during his last days? By then all his faith in European civilization had taken a severe beating; 'It was gradually revealed to him that the function of the beacon of European civilization was not ushering in enlightenment in strange lands, but igniting the fire of destruction.'[34] Standing at the precinct of the present and ripping off the mask covering the face of the past at one blow, Rabindranath prised open the big lie encoded in the 'promise' of European 'civilization'. 'Thus Europe revealed its ugly clenched teeth amidst the thorns it strewed along the path to civilization / I know what civilization can be but today I only see the impurities and humiliation endured / the sole purpose of such civilization which people have taken refuge in, being repression of human beings.'[35] When, during the World War II, fascism was preparing for a holocaust the world over, Rabindranath wrote *Chelebela* (*Childhood Days*), *Golpo Sholpo* (*Stories*) and, some time earlier, *Shey* (*The Other*), *Khapchara* (*Misfit*) and *Charra* (*Rhymes*). These works militate fiercely against the so-called rational order,[36] and in his last efforts in children's literature, the news of snub-nosed, mustachioed gentlemen (of war posters) effortlessly enters the world of discourse as does news of World War II, the oppression of the ryots and topics such as the plight of women. Is Rabindranath trying to tell us that the time has come to leave behind the world of new childhood we had made an entry into at the advent of the nineteenth century, with its blessings of 'civilization'? Is there not some link between *Sabhyatar Sankat* (*Crisis of Civilization*) and the final phase of his meditation on childhood? The intense crisis problematizes his linguistic consciousness and, in the bargain, opens out to him the world of visual images. At the fag end of his life, not only does the very foundation of his belief in the ideal of reform become unstable, but a grave doubt about his own creativity makes its appearance. In the twenty poems belonging to *Janmadin-e* (*Birthday*), written at about the same time as *Golpo Sholpo* or *Stories*, he says: 'I would think, that innumerable stray sounds have become free / defying rules governing the sentences / having adopted the free voice of those lacking in sense and intelligence / Breaking free of this prison house of meaning / it has bestowed an ironic laughter on pure literature.'[37] Because of the suspicion or discomfiture with high literature, the prose of *Shey* is extremely self-conscious, the main argument of the book being language itself. But where lies freedom from all this? This is hinted in the dedicatory verse to *Shey*: 'Where the disreputable society lies, there only will the wretched social outcast find his freedom.'[38] Does this mean that an era has truly come to an end, and that rather than fill the mouths of the so-called idiots with words, the time has come for us to learn language from the ignoramus? And is the ability to do that easily acquired? Besides, would excessive eagerness not lead to carelessness? Thus Sukumar Roy, in his deep aversion to the quiet, settled life of the *bhadralok*, had also gazed at the domain of those who are disreputable, and had made the infamous and the low-born stand up and oppose the much-esteemed Gopals.

In the play *Bhabuk Sabha* (*Assembly of Thinkers*), when an elderly thinker gets into a temper at the disturbance caused by a cacophony of sounds produced by a gathering of 'greenhorns', and loses his sleep, one of the youthful thinkers, aiming at calming him down, says: 'Sleep, did you say? How absurd! You make me dumbfounded! You hadn't gone to sleep at all – merely drowned yourself in thought. Only the base – the grocer, the oilman and the peasant – fall asleep, but you and me – the thinkers – live in the world of thought!' Thus it is presumed that indulging in thought or the pursuit of pleasure is reserved only for the upper strata of society; these are not available and are even interdict for those belonging to the lower strata, for the base and the mean. Nevertheless, in the poems of *Abol Tabol* or *Khai-Khai*, it is the base and the mean, or those inhabiting the margins of the genteel society, who gain the upper hand. And they act as an antidote to the self-satisfaction, sense of certitude and arrogance of the upper-class.

The ignorant boatman of 'Life's Reckoning', a poem included in the *Khai-Khai* volume, overwhelms the Babumashai, already overburdened with learning, by venturing a single question – while he himself is not knocked down by the weight of Babu's erudition. The boatman asks the simple question, 'Do you know how to swim?' Not a word escapes the gentleman's lips. The learned gentleman had never in his life imagined he would have something to learn from the illiterate boatman. The poor and helpless boatman's simple query, 'Do you know how to swim?' not only literally astounds the gentleman, but the sharp edge of the question actually creates a sense of conflict with the established and acceptable discourse. So far Babumashai had led a secure and unhindered existence under the shelter of the reigning discourse; now he is thoroughly unnerved by the sudden onslaught that leaves him without a pillar of support. He loses his voice and is reduced to silence. In the poem 'Tejiyan' ('The Spirited Man'), in the same volume, the man who had walked about with his shoes creaking, red-faced, humming-and-hawing in a display of temper, abusing and kicking people at random, has to, at last, accept defeat at the hands of the sweeper Harusardar and his bucket – a simple sweeper's innocuous bucket is enough to silence all his vaunting. When the king, seated on the red-hot bricks, cannot fathom the meaning of the difficult riddle, a thin-looking water-carrier comes and solves the problem with his common sense. Of course Ramkanai of the play *Jhalapala* remains the most shining example of persons belonging to the lower class in the literature of Sukumar Roy.

Although it is true that both Rabindranath Tagore and Sukumar Roy had in their writings given an honourable place to the vulgar or the common people, this does not mean that they had directly entered the world of those who are audible or spoken of, or that they had even tried to do that. The one person who could break free of the bounds of the established discourse in his desire to radically alter the nature of the language of the privileged was Abanindranath Tagore. And it is not coincidental that compared with other members of the Tagore family, the maids and servants of the household have a more prominent place in his memoirs. In his writings 'we continually move downwards to the lived life of the lower order, the universe of the maids and servants, the grooms and the guardsmen – and we come and stand in a space outside our familiar genteel lifestyle and habitation'. For the sake of making portraits, Abanindranath gazed at 'life in motion' which had thus far not been part of the literary consciousness.[39] The more he became antagonistic towards the established literary standards, the more was there a change in the style and content of his writings. Beginning with 'Shakuntala', through *Khirer Putul*, *Rajkahini*, *Nalak*, *Buro Angla* and *Alor Phulki*, he arrived at the world of the folk-theatre – the *jatra*. In his desire to hearken back to the origins of language, as far as he could, he removed self-referential words from the vocabulary in order to make place for indigenous sounds. Abanindranath had no faith in Bankimchandra's injunctions – given in *Sahaj Rachana Shiksha* or 'Easy Way to Compose' – that the sounds and words used by the vulgar and the villagers must not be practised;[40] rather, his devotion to that which is simple and accessible pulled him towards language that was banned. In his writings, constructions of Hindi, Urdu and Oriya words mix and mingle with *prakrit* or the popular language. And, in this way, one kind of ludicrous mannerism gets entangled with another, and Abanindranath falls into the trap of a species of elaborate figuration in order to avoid another. Rabindranath, in his composition *Shey*, points to the need of skill even when dealing with the strange and the fantastic, for 'it is easy to make a scattered and unorganized semblance of the absurd'. But Abanindranath was not inclined to pay heed to such warnings, no matter where they came from. He created brilliant fireworks of words according to his whim. He no doubt wanted everyone to participate in his festival of words – there was no question of any discrimination so far the right of entry to his literary domain went. But it so happened that, in course of time, he slowly moved away from the historical and got enmeshed in a self-created language-system. And that pilgrimage which progressed from history to hysteria could not have been worthwhile. The luxury of self-indulgence and the chaos of words trapped him in his own space; try as he might, he could not escape the self-centered world of Gopals. Though Abanindranath had always wanted to get away, the address of his desired destination remained forever unknown to him. In the language of his Chaidada, one can say, 'It does not look as if we can continue with the tale, Abubabu! Imagination has turned hysterical – has been babbling nonsense throughout the night!'[41] As Abanindranath continued with his writing, the structure became increasingly loose. The fun of narrating the popular and his temperament of a raconteur made him lose all sense of proportion. The kind of heightened pleasure that a decorous, compact and patterned prose can give is well illustrated in Upendra Kishore Roy Chowdhury's *Tuntuni's Book* (1910), *Goopy Gayen Bagha Bayen*, and Gyanadanandini Debi's *Tak Duma Dum, Dum*. Abanindranath's *Khirer Putul* and *Buro Angla* can be added to this list. Ishan, angry at Bhavadulal's seemingly irrelevant nonsense and continuous bragging, shouts out, 'Why Sir – uttering all such nonsense?' Even the anti-grammatical nonsense has to contain some grammar, else it would be literally akin to 'preaching to the dumb'.

Sukumar Roy did not break free of grammatical rules in order to satisfy his curiosity about language theory or indulge in a game of words. Alongside an acute linguistic consciousness, he possessed a firm knowledge of the temporal and a deep sense of the historical. There is a four-lined poem in the notebook he had given seven different names to: 'Dots and Dashes', 'Redundant', 'Stray', 'Worthless', 'Just like that' 'Draft', 'Journal'. The poem may be easily taken as a key to understanding the nature of his creative skill. 'If the mind chooses to get mesmerized by pleasure / then listen to the discourse on the theory of play in this world of material reality / as reality resides in the material world / squeeze its juice and you'll find it packed with honey as in a honeycomb.' A recourse to the theory of play in the material world bestowed to the writings of Sukumar Roy a unity of subject matter and structure, sense and utterance. We can learn the art of dismantling the grammatical structure and an authentic poetics of rejection from Sukumar Roy, the grammarian of nonsense. At the least, he did not encourage either cynicism or masochism in the name of rejection or self-dissolution.

Just as it had been impossible to restrain Pagla Dashu by scolding him, similarly, it had not been possible to finally suppress Bhavadulal. At the end of *Chalachittachanchari*, Bhavadulal warns with a ringing voice that even if one were to tear the pages of the play into bits, he was not a person to be subdued. 'You've torn the pages of my exercise book – so what? I will write it all over again – my book – bound in red morocco.' Bhavadulal or Pagla Dashu and the students of both *Chalachittachanchari* and *Jhalapala* are comparable to the Hijibijbijs of *Ha-ja-ba-ra-la*. The strange being's name is an amalgam of Hijibiji and Bijbij. Laughter continually bubbles within their being and rises to the surface. The role played by Pagla Dashu in the courtyard of the school is matched by Hijibijbij's in *Ha-ja-ba-ra-la*'s court of law.

Sukumar Roy had translated the poem dealing with justice in Lewis Carroll's *Alice in Wonderland* as 'Judgement'. He described how an ignorant village bumpkin had taught a clever lawyer a lesson in the story 'Lawyer's Wit'. Among the central topics of the play *Jhalapala* is the relationship between the zamindar's lawyer-uncle and the servant Ramkanai. In the story *Ha-ja-ba-ra-la*, a clever fox makes its appearance in the garb of a black-coated lawyer. In that criminal court, however, the judge is present, so is the pleader and there are witnesses galore; only the accused is absent. There is no question that the law court scene of *Ha-ja-ba-ra-la* closely imitates the one in *Alice in Wonderland*, but it also contains Hijibijbij. And this creature suddenly comes out with the statement, 'I have seen many judges – all of them are myopic', and goes on giggling. One never knows what the amusement is about or why, and it does not help in preserving gravity proper to law courts either. And along with this, we come to realize that just as witnesses can be bought cheaply to keep cases going, one can get hold of anyone – even someone like the bald-headed simpleton (Nyara) – and make him stand on the dock as an accused. According to the constitution of the law, there ought to be a judge, lawyers, witnesses, the accused and a complainant plaintiff. Once these are in place, there is no need to worry and one does not have to go deep into any problem. Is it any surprise therefore that when the boy of *Ha-ja-ba-ra-la* wakes up, his elderly uncle, the representative of society, reminds him about learning the grammar rules? The other elderly uncle has hardly any time to pay attention to the boy's recounting of his dreams. That is why the boy says regretfully, 'Man becomes such a dullard as he gets older that he does not want to believe in anything. You are still young so I can depend on you and say all this.'

Another clue to the literature of Sukumar Roy lies hidden in this last comment. His target audience are not those grim-faced dullards but the young ones who are not as yet spent, and who have no hesitation in responding to the new. Because he could remain true to the language of children, be faithful to their unique idioms by using words like '*chhayachor chotolok*' (the mean cheat), '*michkemi*' (making mischief), '*chittire*' (specimen), in the stories of

Pagla Dashu and 'Recurring Decimal' in *Lakshmaner Shaktishel*, and because he was conscious of how different the manner of a child's speech is to an adult's, his literature could never become literature for children in the truest sense. Alongside, he was able to create an alternative grammar opposite to that established by the elders. The significance of the reflected image being that those who cherish the absurd can claim affinity with the young, who still have the guts to dress up reality in very many new ways.

Lila Majumdar has written that once someone had given three saplings to the three daughters of the house, and

> when the buds blossomed, it was seen that both Suroma Mashi and Sukholata's trees sported beautiful blue flowers whereas Khushi's flowers were totally white. Khushi's eyes welled up with tears, everyone tried to comfort her saying, why white flowers are also pretty. When Khushi woke up next morning she found her tree covered with flowers of all kinds of hues, and was she elated – no one could touch her then! When after many days the drops of colours at the roots of the trees came to our notice, we understood that Tatai [Sukumar Roy] had poured colour over the flowers overnight.

Not everyone has the ability to render white flowers red, to pour colour over this colourless earth and make it resplendent or have the longing to fashion a parallel universe. Besides, this kind of point of view is even rarer in a society where the young are hardly given any importance, and the relationship they have with their elders is one of obedience. Sri Kakeswar Kuchkuch's advertisement in *Ha-ja-ba-ra-la* reads, 'Children half-price' – translated into Bengali, it reads 'children at half-price'. Sukumar Roy was perhaps reneging the cause of these half-priced children in his writings.

Because the Pagla Dashus or Bhavadulals of this world can, by turning reality's established explanatory paradigm on its head, create a free or boundless space, and because nothing is certain in that space, its possibilities are also boundless. And we can discover some signatures of that world of limitless possibilities in many poems belonging to *Abol Tabol* and *Khai-Khai*. Although that world does not work according to set rules, it does not mean one can do as one pleases there. And it is not Sukumar Roy's intention to provide an anarchistic counsel. In the poem 'Khichuri', he declares his aversion to grammar and claims he has no understanding of Hanshjaru' s activities (why, for instance, he sauntered into the forest), but soon after he goes on to expound the mystery of creating strange compound words – *dhare-muro-sandhi*, a forcible conjunction of words. The world of *Abol Tabol is* free; it has tremendous scope for play, but that game too is conducted according to some underlying rules.

It is worth noting that many who are the objects of Sukumar's ridicule are weak in mathematics. The teacher of *Jhalapala* recites seven times fourteen is fifty-three, Nandalal gets a big zero in his math exams; on the contrary, Pagla

Dashu's brain cells work with alacrity when it comes to working out difficult sums, especially long multiplication and division. In fact, arithmetic is the one thing that cannot be learned by rote, and Pagla Dashu with his mischievous intelligence can overcome anyone in problems related to sums. The boy called Tabu, appearing in the poem 'Kajer Lok' of *Khai-Khai*, is not at all afraid of sums. 'Study science, you'll become world wise, your life's journey become smooth / by computing you'll realize that this unfortunate world is subject to rules and regulations.' It is not possible for the person who wrote such lines to have encouraged irrationality. In the poem 'Abujh' of *Khai-Khai*, an example of a poem written by the person who advises Shyamadas to give up the 'bad habit of arguing' and savour his poetic creations silently, runs like this: 'Shashadhar drinks wine frantically in the funeral grounds.' Ishan's song 'Catch, catch etc.' in *Chalachittachanchari* is of the same kind. In 'Kabel's Letter', Sukumar Roy shows how the rejection of sense and becoming captive to alliteration and internal rhyming may result in prose which is full of ridiculous mannerism or empty bombast. On the other hand, he amply demonstrates how proficient he himself is in the use of poetic alliteration in his poem on 'Barnamala-Tatwa' ('Theory of Alphabets'). He was extremely aware how the mind becomes befuddled by nebulous sounds. Many of his poems, plays and prose bear testimony to this truth. Therefore, it is no surprise that the role of sound in his writings is different.

We may discover how a new-fangled Banglatin language had been fashioned out of combining Bangla and Latin words, if we examine the key to the origin of the compounds, such as in the diary of 'Heshoram Hushiar' – like Hanglatheoriam, Lagbagnis, Gomratheriam, etc. Heshoram is compelled to tag Latin words to Bengali words in order to maintain the gravity and importance befitting a scientific enquiry, and to preserve the sobriety of professionalism. In fact, Heshoram's Bengali *bhadralok* identity unfailingly becomes clear not only because of his use of Bengali in half of his words, but for his attaching Latin terms to them.

Sukumar Roy experiments with all kinds of ways in which verbs can be used and played with in his poems, such as 'Sabdakalpadrum' from *Abol Tabol*, and 'Darer Kabita', 'Porar Hisheb', 'Khai, Khai' and 'Pakapaki' from *Khai-Khai*. As there is a literal description of eating in the poem 'Khai, Khai', so also is there its figurative dimension – the words '*kala khao*' ('have a banana') are inserted in the middle of the poem in order to imply both the literal and metaphorical aspects of the meanings of the words. In the long list of things to eat are idiomatic expressions like '*Ghol khaoa*', '*Noon khaoa*', etc., and alongside are given instances of '*Mahajaner shud khaoa*' or the moneylender's extraction of interest, '*ghush khaoa*' or the policemen's taking of bribes, '*tara khaoa*' or the turning away of street beggars, '*din ane din khaoa*' or making do with what one earns. In Sukumar Roy's writings, there is an easy traffic between the sound and the image, and also the other way around. The poem 'Burir Bari' or 'Old Woman's House' in *Abol Tabol* affords an excellent example of a sound image. Sankho Ghosh says, 'The image of the "doddering" ("*thure-thure*") old woman's dilapidated ("*jhure-jhure*") brick house is entirely made up of verbal sounds.' It is rare to find in Bengali poetry another such extraordinarily realistic picture of an old woman's cottage, drawn by the help of onomatopoeia. There is such a prolific use of the 'h' alphabet in the sixteen-line-long poem that one can almost get a sense of the precarious condition of the hut, and the reader is 'afraid to rest his arm on it lest it collapses'. 'We can see so many huts along the way to Kolkata that are fit to be tied up by strings or held together by sharp nails!'[42]

In the fantasy world of *Ha-ja-ba-ra-la*, the hyper-real or 'more-true' world of the young boy, where he is left free and nothing is forbidden to him, where the handkerchief is transformed into a cat, people age or get younger at will, and no one has an address or a location, we see some moving illustrations of verbal eloquence. Such as: 'One has the scathe the other gets the scorn', or 'What does the lunatic not say, what does the goat not munch', or 'Crocodile tears' – and by such means the story is made to advance literally. In 'Chobi-o-Golpo' ('Picture-and-Story'), we get an example of the same kind of exercise. It is because he recognized the nature of Bengali language so distinctly that we find almost an incessant use of onomatopoeic sounds in Sukumar's writings. In this sense, both in terms of their continuous use and variety, only Rabindranath is his equal. 'There may exist a difference in language use as also the choice of words between those who are educated and those who are not, nevertheless he [Sukumar Roy] wanted us to be conscious that the two classes of people did not veer away from the resources of language or its unhindered flow.'[43] The compulsion behind giving in his poetry an honourable place to those who belong to the lower orders and those living on the margins of society is the same as that which made Sukumar move towards the use of popular language, and helped him acknowledge the true character of the Bengali language.

In his counter-discourse, with respect to both the subject and structure, the rules and conventions, the rituals and behaviour of the civil society become a quarry of amusement; they become the object of ridicule, a source of the comic for those who have been hitherto at society's beck and call and have obeyed its injunctions at every turn. Sukumar's mode of 'seeing things differently', 'the disjunctions at the heart of arrangement of thought' – in other words, his method of pointing out the drawbacks of those elders constantly criticizing others – create many strange and comical situations, and lend to amusement arising out of a cacophony of sounds.[44] And thus we get in *Abol Tabol* the description of somersault as a prescription for the common cold, the ritual of painting the feet with *alta* on the night of the full moon, the sight of the huge pumpkin creature, the strange and the oddball, the griffin's calf. The hookah-shaped sickly resident of Bengal and other such strange beings, also available in the curious tale of the kingdom of Bombagarh – alongside which are the description of a doddering old woman living inside a dilapidated hut about to collapse, and all kinds of news of the land of Shiva in the grip of stagnation.

Despite long illness, Sukumar kept unquenched the passion of his spirit, his determination and ability to experience this universe with all the senses. The poem he wrote prior to 'when all his work were done', emerges as a world redolent with immense possibilities of the confluence of colour, sound and visual beauty: there the waterfall leaps over, intoxicated by the sound of music; flowers blossom involuntarily in the landscape of the empty sky; the drum or the *tabla* gives out '*dhai, dhapa dhap*' sounds; the greedy elephant throws up his limbs into the void. It is a place where you can obtain the 'cold moonlight of bygone days' and a bouquet made out of 'horses' eggs'!

Notes and References

1 Sukumar Roy, *Abol Tabol*, in Satya Chakrabarti, ed., *Upendra Kishore – Sukumar Rachanasamagra*, Calcutta, 1983, p. 420.

2 Ibid., p. 433.

3 Satyajit Ray, 'Bhumika' ('Preface'), in Sukumar Roy, *Samagra Shishusahitya*, Vol. 1, Calcutta, 1973, p. 3.

4 Jibanananda Das, 'Patrabali', in *Jibanananda Daser Patrabali*, compiled by Dinenkumar Bosu, Calcutta, 1981, p. 19.

5 Subir Roy Chowdhury, 'Dhvani theke Drishye: Sukumar Royer Shabdatatwa', in Pabitra Sarkar, ed., *Sukumar Parikrama*, Calcutta, 1989, p. 133.

6 Sukumar Roy, 'Bhashar Atyachar', in *Barnamalatatwa o Vividha Prabandha*, Calcutta, 1363 (Bengali calendar), pp. 20–21.

7 Ibid., p. 20.

8 Ibid.; Sukumar Roy, 'Doiben Dayam', in *Barnamalatatwa o Vividha Prabandha*, p. 53.

9 Sukumar Roy, 'Atiter Chhobi', in Satya Chakrabarti, ed., *Upendra Kishore – Sukumar Rachanasamagra*, pp. 442–44.

10 Sukumar Roy, 'Bhashar Atyachar', in *Barnamalatatwa o Vividha Prabandha*, p. 20.

11 Satyajit Ray, 'Bhumika', 'Bileter Chiti o Ar Ekti', in *Ekhon*, Saradiya Sankha, 1389 (Bengali calendar), p. 114.

12 Ibid., p. 115.

13 Ibid., p. 170.

14 Ibid., pp. 171–72.

15 Ibid., p. 170.

16 Sukumar Roy, *Sabdakalpadrum*, in *Rachanasamagra*, pp. 554–59.

17 Lila Majumdar, 'Sukumar Roy', in *Lila Majumdar Rachanabali*, Vol. 3, Calcutta, 1981, pp. 92–93.

18 Sukumar Roy, *Chalachittachanchari*, in *Rachanasamagra*, pp. 546–52.

19 Sukumar Roy, 'Bhassar Atyachar', in *Barnamalatatwa o Vividha Prabandha*, p. 23.

20 Rabindranath Tagore, 'Hindubibaha', 'Samaj', in *Rabindra Rachanabali*, Vol. 12, Calcutta, 1370 (Bengali calendar), p. 425.

21 Sukumar Roy, 'Doiben Dayam' in *Barnamalatatwa o Vividha Prabandha*, p. 60.

22 Sukumar Roy, 'Bhasar Atyachar', in *Barnamalatatta o Vividha Prabandha*, p. 22.

23 Sukumar Roy, 'Lakshmaner Shaktishel', in *Rachanasamagra*, pp. 538–42.

24 Abanindranath Tagore, *Banglar Bratakatha*, Calcutta, 1350 (Bengali calendar), pp. 11–12.

25 Sibram Chakraborty, *Moscow banam Pondicherry*, Calcutta, 1980, p. 11.

[26] Ibid., pp. 43, 29, 23.

[27] Sibram Chakraborty, *Haragobinder Jogbal*, in *Sibram Rachanasamagra*, Vol. 1, Calcutta, 1985, p. 95.

[28] Manabendra Bandyopadhyay, 'Shake the Bottle! Shake the Bottle!', in *Prastutiparba*, special edition on Sukumar Roy, Calcutta, 1985, p. 140.

[29] Rabindranath Tagore, *Bidushuk* and *Lipika*, in *Rabindra Rachanabali*, Vol. 26, Calcutta, 1970, p. 125.

[30] Rabindranath Tagore, *Paschim-Jatrir Diary*, in *Rabindra Rachanabali*, Vol. 19, pp. 404–05.

[31] Rabindranath Tagore, *Shishu Bholanath*, in *Rabindra Rachanabali*, Vol. 13, Calcutta, 1967, pp. 65–66.

[32] Rabindranath Tagore, *Paschim-Jatrir Diary*, in *Rabindra Rachanabali*, Vol. 19, p. 404.

[33] Rabindranath Tagore, 'Shishur Jiban', in *Rabindra Rachanabali*, Vol. 13, p. 67.

[34] Rabindranath Tagore, 'Kalantar', in *Rabindra Rachanabali*, Vol. 24 , Calcutta, 1970, p. 250.

[35] Rabindranath Tagore, 'Dhangsha' in *Golpo Sholpo*, *Rabindra Rachanabali*, Vol. 26, Calcutta, 1970, p. 355.

[36] Manabendra Bandyopadhyay, *Rabindranath: Shishu Sahitya*, Calcutta, 1377 (Bengali calendar), p. 71.

[37] Rabindranath Tagore, 'Janmadin-e', in *Kabita Sankhya*, *Rabindra Rachanabali*, Vol. 25, pp. 90–91.

[38] Rabindranath Tagore, 'Utsarga' and *Shey*, in *Rabindra Rachanabali*, Vol. 26, p. 184.

[39] Sankho Ghosh, 'Kalpanar Hysteria', in *Kalpanar Hysteria*, Calcutta, 1984, p. 26.

[40] Bankimchandra Chattopadhyay, *Sahaj Rachana Shiksha*, in Gopal Haldar, ed., *Bankim Rachanasa*, Vol. 1, Calcutta, 1973, p. 1191.

[41] Abanindranath Tagore, *Chaidadar Golpo*, in *Abanindra Rachanabali*, Vol. 3, Calcutta, 1976, p. 573.

[42] Sankho Ghosh, 'Ashambhaber Chhanda', in *Kalpanar Hysteria*, p. 128.

[43] Subir Roy Chowdhury, 'Dhvani theke Drishye: Sukumar Royer Shabdatatwa', in Pabitra Sarkar, ed., *Sukumar Parikrama*, p. 137.

[44] Rabindranath Tagore, 'Bhumika', *Pagla Dashu*, in Sukumar Roy, *Samagra Shishusahitya*, Calcutta , 1973, p. 1.

Epilogue

> The bough that was all but bare yesterday
> Doth burst today with blossoms[1]

Seventy-five years after *Barna Parichay* came *Sahaj Path*; the infertile, arid desert became prolific with beauty and sensitivity.

From the perspective of their time of publication (first published in 1930), *Sahaj Path* is a contemporary of *Shey*. There is no doubt that whatever motivated Rabindranath to write *Shishu*, *Shishu Bholanath* and *Shey* also inspired him to write *Sahaj Path*. In the hands of Rabindranath who was a votary of childhood, even a textbook became a book for amusement. As they graduate from *Barna Parichay* to *Sahaj Path*, children who have been rendered anxious by the reprimands of adults heave a sigh of relief. In it, nobody repeats the refrain of 'study, study', or asks children to pull up their socks and gear up to become adults. Instead, it holds up a light of perception. Children see with amazement how flowers become butterflies, the flame of a lamp acquires wings and transforms into fireflies, the stagnant water of a pond spreads smoky wings and wanders into the sky. In the first two parts of *Sahaj Path*, there are only three references to studies. Although *ya*, *ra*, *la* and *ba* sit at home, the narrator extends his wings and flies away into the sky. 'Uncle raises both hands and pleads to him to stop / For he must go to school and thus come down for now'[2] – but could his wanderings through the firmament be curbed by that? 'I say, O uncle, you shout and scream in vain / I've risen to the sky and become a cloud.'[3] In Part 2 of *Sahaj Path*, Binu dreams that Calcutta can no longer be contained within Calcutta – the city has suddenly woken up and started to run rapidly, goodness knows in which direction. And along with that, 'Our school runs swiftly / So run the arithmetic and grammar texts.' [4] Binu chooses the metaphor of a bird to describe the plight of the maps on the walls of the school that walks so fast: 'The maps get fidgety on the walls / As though they were birds beating their wings.'[5] In *Sahaj Path*, Part 4, the curious narrator, on seeing a caged parrot, wants to know if the bird flies. Of course, the bird does not fly: 'It has fetters on its feet.' But it used to fly once upon a time: 'It was earlier in the woods. There was a river in the wood; it used to go and drink water by itself.'[6] Within the description of nature in *Sahaj Path* are fused memories of that liberated but stupid, wild but self-controlled bird. Rabindranath's chief query is, 'If a flower blossomed in the woods, why is the bird not there?' The sky of *Sahaj Path* is strewn with that 'There was a bird'. In the hard, disciplined world of *Barna Parichay*, there is no question of wasting one's time by viewing natural scenery. Madanmohan Tarkalankar's *Shishushiksha* (1850) and Jogindranath Sarkar's *Hashikhushi* (1897) do contain descriptions of nature and animals, but basically, there is no similarity between these two books and *Sahaj Path*. The bird in the rhyme 'All the birds twitter' and the bird of *Sahaj Path* are of different kinds. Buddhadeb Basu wrote:

> Characters have been expressed in each of its lines, the most innocent pronouncement of the greatest attainment of prophecy. At an age when learning 'ka' and 'kha' is enough, *Sahaj Path* initiates one into a taste for literature; because of this one book, I consider the luck of the Bengali child worthy of envy by the world.[7]

Basu certainly realized that in the rhythmical, beautiful language of *Sahaj Path*, the soul of the child has been captured most substantially. The pure and indiscriminate beauty of the child's mind has found expression through the magic of Rabindranath's pen. The Bengali child *per se* can respond, therefore, to this simple harmony and can easily be close in spirit with a simple, eager and sympathetic child narrator. But does the child narrator really not have a specified social identity or standing?

'It is morning. The washerman comes. There is Loka the washerman.'[8] Whoever has said this must have learnt in the meanwhile that although people of the likes of the washerman may be older, it is acceptable not to use[9] any form of respectful address for them; it does not particularly impair formality. And how does one address guests belonging to one's own class? 'Come, come, Gour – come in. Hey Koulu – run and get a stool' (the use of the formal and informal 'you' distinguishes them).[10] It is not very clear whether Koulu is the servant of the house or a young boy. Either way, it is clear from different lessons that the child narrator is a person belonging to the upper class – the way he observes natural and human life is governed almost entirely by his class position. He gazes and surveys the outside world and the flow of people in a detached way: 'So many people walk on the road. Bullocks pull so many carts. There goes Bhola the gardener';[11] 'The old maid brings water';[12] 'Hey Kailash! I want curds . . . the milkman did not deliver curds'.[13] It is thus very natural that the boy would unwittingly and of his own accord imbibe the customs and codes of the society in which he is growing up. But does he have even an iota of awareness that this relationship between classes is not in the least 'normal'? Or is it that he has meanwhile presumed that they, the class who work, and he, are inhabitants of different worlds? They will meet every day, exchange words, but that is about all; he will never get lost in the crowd of those who have to labour for a living. In Himani Bandyopadhyay's opinion, in lesson after lesson in *Sahaj Path*, the boy is made conversant with his 'specified' social role; the sense and belief that the arrangement is permanent, as unchangeable and infallible as the laws of nature, are embedded within the description of nature.[14] For instance: 'The day has rolled on. The fields stretch endlessly. A breeze blows intermittently like a blazing fire. Dust flies in the distance. Chuni the gardener draws up water from the well and the dove calls "Ghu ghu."'[15] Chuni the gardener is bound within the everyday cycle of nature, as though the dove will keep calling in the same pitch forever and he will mechanically go on drawing water – that is what is appropriate and normal.

But the organization is not really permanent. If the Paran Mandals act a little too mulish, this natural equilibrium could get ruined. In the second part of *Sahaj Path* is the tale of the honest herder Uddhab Mandal who has been sold out by his liabilities of debt. Rabindranth has not concealed the zamindar Durlabhbabu's oppression or cruelty or anything. But the solution to the problem appears at an intensely critical moment in the story: Durlabhbabu's warm-hearted aunt. On the day of Uddhab's daughter's wedding, she arrives unsolicited at his house. Presenting a gold necklace and a hundred-rupee note to his daughter, she says: 'This is your dowry.' In return, she has just one request to Uddhab: 'Durlabh insulted you yesterday; please do not bear that in mind.'[16] Besides, all zamindars are not as stone-hearted as Durlabh; if Sanjay Sen had not been there, who would have looked after the blind Kunjabihari? 'The zamindar of the district is Sanjay Sen: he gives him two handfuls of grain morning and evening.'[17]

In the prose extract of the second part of *Sahaj Path*, one cannot locate the child narrator of the first part. His place is taken up by busybodied individuals who are masters – adults with grave airs. The pliable and moderate tone of the first part is missing; the voice is far more high-pitched. Will the gentle-mannered boy of the first part who is engrossed in dreams eventually be in the same predicament? In the second part, one hears intermittently: 'Tell Indu that there should be no flaw in her hospitality. . . Tell Rangu the bearer that he should keep his trunk in his room';[18] 'Let our servant Kanta eat something quickly';[19] 'Please rake up the fire in the oven. Let the cook not put any chillies in my gravy';[20] 'Srishtidhar, find and get the umbrella – it will be very distressing otherwise';[21] 'Let Banchha quickly get me a cup of tea and a few biscuits'.[22] When the 'wretches' ostracized from society find 'liberation' in their 'unknown neighbourhoods', will they still clutch on to their older practices and ways of life?

In *Barna Parichay*, the devoted student Gopal was the ideal boy. Now, his place has been snatched by the Rakhal who is on the run from school and possessed by his dreams. On the one hand, he observes how flowers, butterflies, the flames of a lamp, fireflies and water get transformed into clouds, and asks of himself: 'Will what I nurture in my mind never happen?'[23] On the other, there is no reservation or query in his mind about the form of social relations. On the one hand, there is endless alteration of form and just becoming; on the other, there is a state that is free of worry and calmly static. The same dilemma that destabilizes the world of Rakhal and Gopal also maintains the balance of power in the world. It keeps unbroken the composite of the world's dilemmas. If worldly-minded Gopals were not there, would the death of Rakhals' dreams be possible? Or would the Rakhals who reach out for the distant meet the Gopals again if they did not have some bond of attachment for their homes? That colonial age does not exist any more; but have the futile voyages of those who want to strive for the far and beyond stopped even today?

Notes and References

1 Rabindranath Tagore, 'Lesson 7', *Sahaj Path, Part 1*, in *Rabindra Rachanabali: Achalit Sangraha*, Vol. 2, Calcutta, 1975, p. 621.
2 Rabindranath Tagore, 'Lesson 8', ibid., p. 623.
3 Ibid.
4 Rabindranath Tagore, 'Lesson 11', *Sahaj Path, Part 2*, in *Rabindra Rachanabali: Achalit Sangraha*, Vol. 2, p. 638.
5 Ibid.
6 Rabindranath Tagore, 'Lesson 4', *Sahaj Path, Part 1*, p. 617.
7 Buddhadeb Basu, 'Bangla Shishusahitya', in *Sahityacharcha*, Calcutta, 1981, pp. 68–70.
8 Rabindranath Tagore, 'Lesson 8', *Sahaj Path, Part 1*, p. 622.
9 Ibid.
10 Rabindranath Tagore, 'Lesson 9', *Sahaj Path, Part 1*, p. 623.
11 Rabindranath Tagore, 'Lesson 2', ibid., p. 615.
12 Rabindranath Tagore, 'Lesson 4', ibid., p. 617.
13 Rabindranath Tagore, 'Lesson 7', ibid., p. 621.
14 Himani Bandyopadhyay, 'The Mirror of Class: Class Subjectivity and Politics in Nineteenth Century Bengal', *Economic and Political Weekly*, Vol. XIV, No. 19, Bombay, 13 May 1989.
15 Rabindranath Tagore, 'Lesson 5', *Sahaj Path, Part 1*, p. 618.
16 Rabindranath Tagore, 'Lesson 13', *Sahaj Path, Part 2*, p. 644.
17 Ibid.
18 Rabindranath Tagore, 'Lesson 4', *Sahaj Path, Part 1*, p. 629.
19 Rabindranath Tagore, 'Lesson 6', ibid., p. 631.
20 Rabindranath Tagore, 'Lesson 8', ibid., p. 633.
21 Rabindranath Tagore, 'Lesson 9', ibid., p. 633.
22 Rabindranath Tagore, 'Lesson 10', ibid., p. 635.
23 Ibid.

Select Bibliography

Bengali

Books and Articles

Anonymous, 1360 (Bengali calendar), *Satheee*, Calcutta.

Ashapurna Debi, 1390 (Bengali calendar), 'Half Holiday', in *Kishore Sahitya Samagra,* Vol. 1, Calcutta.

Bandyopadhyay, Ashutosh, 1980, *Ratnadwiper Bibhishika*, Calcutta.

Bandyopadhyay, Bibhutibhushan, 1389 (Bengali calendar), *Chander Pahar*, in *Bibhuti Rachanabali,* Vol. 9, Calcutta.

———, 1389 (Bengali calendar), *Maraner Danka Baje*, in *Bibhuti Rachanabali,* Vol. 9, Calcutta.

———, 1389 (Bengali calendar), *Hiramanik Jale*, in *Bibhuti Rachanabali,* Vol. 9, Calcutta.

Bhattacharya, Chandroday Bidyabinod, 1893, *Sunitisandarbha*, Calcutta.

Bhattacharya, Sukanta, 1375 (Bengali calendar), *Mithe–Karaa*, in *Sukanta Samagra*, Calcutta.

Bhowmik, Haripada, ed., 1987, *Sekaler Sambad Patre Calcutta – Samachar Darpan, 1818–1822,* Calcutta.

Chakrabarty, Manoranjan, 1984, *Bomar Bhoye Burma Tyaag*, Calcutta.

Chakrabarty, Satyacharan, 1343 (Bengali calendar), *Katamunder Deshe*, Calcutta.

Chakraborty, Sibram, 1983, *Baari Theke Paaliye*, in *Sibram Rachanabali*, Vol. 2, Calcutta.

———, 1985, *Sibram Rachanasamagra*, Vols 1 and 2, Calcutta.

Chandrakanta, Saraswati Bidyabhushan, 1980, *Sundarbaner Shikari*, Calcutta.

Chattopadhyay, Bankimchandra, 1973, *Sahaj Rachana Shiksha*, in Gopal Haldar, ed., *Bankim Rachanasamagra*, Calcutta.

Chattopadhyay, Nripendra Kishore, 1985, *Udashi Babar Akhra*, Calcutta.

———, 1985, *Bijoy Abhijan,* Calcutta.

Deb, Narendra, 1944, *Parag o Renu*, Calcutta.

Dhar, Dhirendralal, 1945, *Jakher Jangale*, Calcutta.

Dutta, Akshay Kumar, 1876, *Charupath*, Calcutta.

Gangopadhyay, Mohanlal, 1932, *Boarding School*, Calcutta.

Gangopadhyay, Narayan and Nimai Bandyopadhyay, 1988, *Bibhishikar Mukhe*, Calcutta.

Gupta, Nihar Ranjan, 1387 (Bengali calendar), *Shankar, Part 1*, in *Kishore Sahityasamagra*, Vol. 2, Calcutta.
———, 1387 (Bengali calendar), *Shankar, Part 2*, in *Kishore Sahityasamagra*, Vol. 3, Calcutta.
———, 1984, *Bisher Teer,* Calcutta.
———, 1984, *Raktamukhi Dragon,* Calcutta.
Majumdar, Lila, 1984, 'Badyinather Bori', in *Lila Majumdar Rachanabali*, Vol. 1, Calcutta.
Majumdar, Sachindra, 1980, *Pather Bandhu*, Calcutta.
Mitra, Khagendranath, 1939, *Ajana Desher Pathe,* Calcutta.
———, 1972, *Bhombol Sardar,* Calcutta.
Mitra, Pyarichand, 1971, *Bamatoshini*, in *Pyarichand Rachanabali,* Calcutta.
Mitra Majumdar, Dakshinaranjan, 1388 (Bengali calendar), *Thakurmar Jhuli*, in *Dakshinaranjan Rachanasamagra*, Vol. 1, Calcutta.
———, 1388 (Bengali calendar), 'First Boy Last Boy', in *Dakshinaranjan Rachanasamagra*, Vol. 1, Calcutta.
———, 1388 (Bengali calendar), *Thandidir Thole*, in *Dakshinaranjan Rachanasamagra*, Vol. 1, Calcutta.
———, 1388 (Bengali calendar), *Thakurdadar Jhuli*, in *Dakshinaranjan Rachanasamagra*, Vol. 2, Calcutta.
———, 1388 (Bengali calendar), *Khokakhukur Khela*, in *Dakshinaranjan Rachanasamagra*, Vol. 2, Calcutta.
———, 1388 (Bengali calendar), 'Charu o Haru', in *Dakshinaranjan Rachanasamagra*, Vol. 2, Calcutta.
Mukhopadhyay, Dinesh, 1981, *Dukhajayir Jayajatra*, Calcutta.
———, 1985, *Tepantarer Math*, Calcutta.
Mukhopadhyay, Madhusudan, 1393 (Bengali calendar), *Sushilar Upakhyan*, *College Street*, Festival edition, Calcutta.
Mullens, Hannah Catherine, 1387 (Bengali calendar), *Phulmoni o Karunar Bibaran*, Calcutta.
Ray, Hemendra Kumar, 1983, *Jakher Dhon*, in *Hemendra Kumar Ray Rachanabali,* Vol. 1, Calcutta.
———, 1983, *Sonar Paharer Jatri*, in *Hemendra Kumar Ray Rachanabali,* Vol. 5, Calcutta.
———, 1983, 'Madhuchhatra', in *Hemendra Kumar Ray Rachanabali,* Vol. 5, Calcutta.
———, 1984, *Jayanter Kirti,* Calcutta.
———, 1984, *Abar Jakher Dhon,* Calcutta.
Roy, Sukumar, 1983, *Abol Tabol*, in Satya Chakrabarti, ed., *Upendra Kishore – Sukumar Rachanasamagra*, Calcutta.
———, 1983, *Khai-Khai*, in Satya Chakrabarti, ed., *Upendra Kishore – Sukumar Rachanasamagra*, Calcutta.
———, 1983, *Pagla Dashu*, in Satya Chakrabarti, ed., *Upendra Kishore – Sukumar Rachanasamagra*, Calcutta.
———, 1983, *Ananyo Golpo*, in Satya Chakrabarti, ed., *Upendra Kishore – Sukumar Rachanasamagra*, Calcutta.
———, 1983, *Jhalapala*, in Satya Chakrabarti, ed., *Upendra Kishore – Sukumar Rachanasamagra*, Calcutta.
———, 1983, *Lakshmaner Shaktishel*, in Satya Chakrabarti, ed., *Upendra Kishore – Sukumar Rachanasamagra*, Calcutta.

———, 1983, *Abak Jalpan*, in Satya Chakrabarti, ed., *Upendra Kishore – Sukumar Rachanasamagra*, Calcutta.
———, 1983, *Hingshuti*, in Satya Chakrabarti, ed., *Upendra Kishore – Sukumar Rachanasamagra*, Calcutta.
———, 1983, *Chalachittachanchari*, in Satya Chakrabarti, ed., *Upendra Kishore – Sukumar Rachanasamagra*, Calcutta.
———, 1983, *Bhabuk Sabha*, in Satya Chakrabarti, ed., *Upendra Kishore – Sukumar Rachanasamagra*, Calcutta.
———, 1983, *Sabdakalpadrum*, in Satya Chakrabarti, ed., *Upendra Kishore – Sukumar Rachanasamagra*, Calcutta.
———, 1983, *Atiter Chhobi*, in Satya Chakrabarti, ed., *Upendra Kishore – Sukumar Rachanasamagra*, Calcutta.
———, 1983, *Ha-ja-ba-ra-la*, in Satya Chakrabarti, ed., *Upendra Kishore – Sukumar Rachanasamagra*, Calcutta.
Sarkar, Jogindranath, 1988, *Shishupathya Granthabali*, Calcutta.
———, 1989, *Hashikhushi*, Calcutta.
Sen, Nikhilesh, 1980, *Romanchokar Kahini*, Calcutta.
Sengupta, Achintya Kumar, 1981, *Dui Bhai*, Calcutta.
Sengupta, Pyarimohan, 1329 (Bengali calendar), *Kafrider Desh Africa-e*, Calcutta.
Sinha, Ashalata, 1985, 'Oder Bibek Buddhi', in *Rangin Akash*, Calcutta.
Swapanburo, 1928, *Beparoa*, Calcutta.
Tagore, Abanindranath, 1976, *Chaidadar Golpo*, in *Abanindra Rachanabali*, Vol. 3, Calcutta.
———, 1980, *Shib Saudagar*, in *Abanindra Rachanabali*, Vol. 5, Calcutta.
Tagore, Rabindranath, 1967, *Shishu Bholanath*, in *Rabindra Rachanabali*, Vol. 13, Calcutta.
———, 1970, *Lipika*, in *Rabindra Rachanabali*, Vol. 26, Calcutta.
———, 1970, *Shey*, in *Rabindra Rachanabali*, Vol. 26, Calcutta.
———, 1970, *Golpo Sholpo*, in *Rabindra Rachanabali*, Vol. 26, Calcutta.
———, 1971, *Shishu*, in *Rabindra Rachanabali*, Vol. 9, Calcutta.
Tarkalankar, Madanmohan and Ishwarchandra Vidyasagar, 1899, *Shishushiksha, Part 2.*
———, 1900, *Shishushiksha, Part 3.*
Vidyasagar, Ishwarchandra, 1987, *Barna Parichay, Vols 1 and 2,* in *Bidyasagar Rachanasamagra*, Vol. 1, Calcutta.
———, 1987, *Nitibodh*, in *Bidyasagar Rachanasamagra*, Vol. 1, Calcutta.
———, 1987, *Charitabali*, in *Bidyasagar Rachanasamagra*, Vol. 1, Calcutta.
———, 1987, *Jibancharit*, in *Bidyasagar Rachanasamagra*, Vol. 1, Calcutta.
———, 1987, *Bodhoday*, in *Bidyasagar Rachanasamagra*, Vol. 1, Calcutta.

Supplementary Reading

Adhikari, Santosh Kumar, ed., 1392 (Bengali calendar), *Bidyasagarer Nirbachita Patrabali*, Calcutta.
———, 1970, *Bidyasagar*, Calcutta.
Anisuzzaman, 1971, *Muslim Manas o Bangla Sahitya, 1757–1918,* Calcutta.
Bandyopadhyay, Bhabanicharan, 1987, *Rachanasamagra,* Calcutta.
Bandyopadhyay, Brajendranath, 1355 (Bengali calendar), *Kolikata Sanskrit Colleger Itihas*, Vols 1 and 2, Calcutta.
———, 1383 (Bengali calendar), *Sahitya Sadhak Charitmala*, Vols 1 and 2, Calcutta.

Bandyopadhyay, Manabendra, 1377 (Bengali calendar), *Rabindranath: Shishu Sahitya*, Calcutta.

———, 1982, 'Tarzan Theke Tintin', in *Saradiya Parichoy*, Calcutta.

———, 1983, 'Calibaner Prithivi', *Shiladitya,* Calcutta.

———, 1393 (Bengali calendar), 'Antargata Alochana', in *Adhunik Bharatiyo Golpo* / 2, Calcutta.

———, 1990, *Stadhotar Sanskritir Biruddhe: Edward Camus Brafetter Kabita*, Calcutta.

Basu, Bani, ed., 1372 (Bengali calendar), *Banglar Shishu Sahitya: Granthapanji*, Calcutta.

Bhattacharya, France, 1978, '*Thakurmar Jhuli* o *Thakurdadar Jhuli*: Ekti Path', *Ekkhon* (Calcutta), June.

Bhattacharya, Pradyumna, 1382 (Bengali calendar), 'Samajer Matra ebong Tarashankarer Upanyas: Chaitali Ghurni', *Ekkhon* (Calcutta), Saradiya Sankhya.

Bhattacharya, Sabyasachi, 1396 (Bengali calendar), *Aupanibeshik Bharater Arthaniti: 1850–1947*, Calcutta.

Bhattacharya, Sourin, 1386 (Bengali calendar), 'Rammohuner Arthanaitik Chinta', *Anukta* (Calcutta), Baisakh–Aswin.

Chakrabarti, Satishchandra, 1396 (Bengali calendar), *Santaner Charitra Gathan*, Calcutta.

Chakrabarty, Sibkumar, 1387 (Bengali calendar), *Moscow Banam Pondicherry*, Calcutta.

Chattopadhyay, Bankimchandra, 1973, 'Bangadesher Krishak', *Vividha Prabandha* (second part), in Gopal Haldar, ed., *Bankim Rachanasamagra*, Calcutta.

———, 1973, 'Lokrahasya', in Gopal Haldar, ed., *Bankim Rachanasamagra*, Calcutta.

———, 1973, *Kamalakanta*, in Gopal Haldar, ed., *Bankim Rachanasamagra*, Calcutta.

Chattopadhyay, Saratchandra, 'Narir Mulyo', in *Sarat Sahitya Sangraha*, Vol. 9, Calcutta.

——— *Pather Dabi*, in *Sarat Sahitya Sangraha*, Vol. 13, Calcutta.

Chattopadhyay, Satishchandra, 1395 (Bengali calendar), *Bankim Jeebani*, Calcutta.

Choudhuri, Kesab, 1984, *Bharatyo Jatyotabader Bhitti o Swaroop*, Calcutta.

Chowdhury, Sirajul Islam, 1983, *Saratchandra o Samanatabad*, Calcutta.

Das, Sisir Kumar, ed., 1988, *Shatayu Sukumar*, Delhi.

Datta, Itima, 1986, *Rabindranather Shishusahitya o Shishu Charitra*, Calcutta.

Gangopadhyay, Asha, 1368 (Bengali calendar), *Bangla Shishu Sahityer Kromobikash*, Calcutta.

Gangopadhyay, Dwarakanath, 1371 (Bengali calendar), *Shishur Sadachar*, Calcutta.

Ghosh, Benoy, 1984, *Bidyasagar o Bangalisamaj*, Calcutta.

Ghosh, Benoy, ed., 1983, *Shamayik Patre Banglar Samajchitra*, Vol. 1, No. 6, Calcutta.

Ghosh, Manmathanath, 1331 (Bengali calendar), *Manishi Bholanath Chandra*, Calcutta.

Ghosh, Sankho, 1984, *Kalpanar Hysteria*, Calcutta.

Khan, Azaruddin and Ujjal Chattopadhyay, eds, 1974, *Bidyasagar Smarak Grantha*, Calcutta.

Majumdar, Lila, 1981, 'Sukumar Roy', in *Lila Majumdar Rachanabali*, Vol. 3, Calcutta.

Majumdar, Nepal, *Bharater Jatyota o Antarjatikata ebong Rabindranath*, Vol. 1, sixth part, Calcutta.

Mitra, Khagendranath, 1961, *Rabindra Shishu-Sahitya Parikrama*, Calcutta.

———, 1967, *Shatabdir Shishu Sahitya: 1818–1960*, Calcutta.

Mitra, Pyarichand, 1971, 'David Harer Jibancharit', in *Pyarichand Rachanabali*, Calcutta.

———, 1971, 'Etoddeshiya Streelokdigoker Purbabashta', in *Pyarichand Rachanabali*, Calcutta.

Mukhopadhyay, Bhudev, 1981, *Samajik Prabandha*, Calcutta.

Ray, Satyendranath, ed., 1389 (Bengali calendar), *Rabindranather Chintajagat*, Calcutta.

Roy, Benoybhushan, 1989, *Prasanga: David Hare,* Calcutta.

Roy, Rammohun, 1973, 'Sahamaran Bishoy Prabartak o Nibartak Sambad', in *Rammohun Rachanabali,* Calcutta.

———, 1973, 'Sahamaran Bishoy Prabartak o Nibartak Dwitiyo Sambad', in *Rammohun Rachanabali,* Calcutta.

Roy, Sukumar, 1363 (Bengali calendar), *Barnamalatatwa o Vividha Prabandha*, Calcutta.

Sarkar, Pabitra, 1392 (Bengali calendar), *Bhasha, Desh, Kal*, Calcutta.

Sarkar, Pabitra, ed., 1989, *Sukumar Parikrama*, Calcutta.

Shastri, Sibnath, 1977, *Ramtanu Lahiri o Tatkalin Banga Samaj*, Calcutta.

Shiromani, Bharatchandra and Jadunath Nyaypànchanan, trans., 1336 (Bengali calendar), *Manusamhita*, Calcutta.

Tagore, Abanindranath, 1350, *Banglar Broto*, Calcutta.

———, 1389, *Bageshwari Shilpa Prabandha*, Calcutta.

———, 1985, 'Apon Katha', in *Abanindra Rachanabali*, Vol. 1, Calcutta.

———, 1985, 'Gharoa', in *Abanindra Rachanabali*, Vol. 1, Calcutta.

———, 1985, 'Jorasankor Dhare', in *Abanindra Rachanabali*, Vol. 1, Calcutta.

Tagore, Rabindranath, 1960, 'Samaj', in *Rabindra Rachanabali*, Vol. 12, Calcutta.

———, 1960, 'Shiksha', in *Rabindra Rachanabali*, Vol. 12, Calcutta.

———, 1965, 'Bharatvarsha', in *Rabindra Rachanabali*, Vol. 4, Calcutta.

———, 1965, 'Charitra Puja', in *Rabindra Rachanabali*, Vol. 4, Calcutta.

———, 1965, 'Loksahitya', in *Rabindra Rachanabali*, Vol. 6, Calcutta.

———, 1965, 'Jibansmriti', in *Rabindra Rachanabali*, Vol. 17, Calcutta.

———, 1968, *Paschim-Jatrir Diary*, in *Rabindra Rachanabali*, Vol. 19, Calcutta.

———, 1969, 'Atmashakti', in *Rabindra Rachanabali*, Vol. 3, Calcutta.

———, 1969, 'Pracheen Sahitya', in *Rabindra Rachanabali*, Vol. 5, Calcutta.

———, 1970, 'Kalantar', in *Rabindra Rachanabali*, Vol. 24, Calcutta.

Umar, Badaruddin, 1983, *Chirasthayi Bandobaste Bangadesher Krishak*, Calcutta.

———, 1386, *Ishwarchandra Bidyasagar o Unish Shataker Bangali Samaj*, Calcutta.

Upadhyay, Brahmabandhav, 1987, *Rachanasamagra*, Calcutta.

Vidyasagar, Ishwarchandra, 1987, *Banglar Itihas*, in *Bidyasagar Rachanasamagra,* Vol. 1, Calcutta.

———, 1987, *Nishkritilabh Prayas*, in *Bidyasagar Rachanasamagra*, Vol. 2, Calcutta.

Vivekananda (Swami), 1371 (Bengali calendar), 'Prachya o Pashchatya', in *Swami Vivekanader Vani o Rachana*, Vol. 6, Calcutta.

English

I list here only the writings that have been of use in the making of this book. This bibliography is by no means a complete record of all the works and sources I have consulted. It indicates the substance and range of reading upon which I have formed my ideas. The dates indicate the years of publication of the editions consulted.

Primary Texts

Ballantyne, Robert M., 1868, *Deep Down: A Tale of the Cornish Mines*, London.
Burroughs, Edgar R., 1960, *Tarzan of the Apes*, London.
Carroll, Lewis, 1986, *The Complete Illustrated Works of Lewis Carroll*, London.
Defoe, Daniel, 1977, *Robinson Crusoe*, London.
Haggard, Henry Rider, 1969, *Allan Quatermain*, London.
———, 1976, *King Solomon's Mines*, Bombay.
Henley, William Ernest, 1921, *Lyra Heroica: A Book of Verse for Boys*, London.
Henty, George Alfred, 1901, *With Clive in India or Beginnings of an Empire*, London.
Hughes, Thomas, 1958, *Tom Brown's School Days*, Bombay.
Kingsley, Charles, 1953, *Westward Ho!*, London.
Kingston, William H.G., 1854, *Blue Jackets: Or Chips of The Old Block*, London.
Kipling, Rudyard, 1894, *The Jungle Book*, London.
———, 1978, *The Second Jungle Book*, London.
Sarkar, Pyari Charan, 1985, *The First Book of Reading*, Calcutta.
Shakespeare, William, 1968, *The Tempest*, London.
Wallace, Edgar, 1927, *Sandi, the King Maker*, London, 1927.

Other Texts

Adler, Alfred, *The Practice and Theory of Individual Psychology*, London.
Adorno, Theodor W. and Max Horkheimar, 1979, *Dialectics of Enlightenment*, London.
Althusser, Louis, 1969, *For Marx*, London.
———, 1971, *Lenin and Philosophy and other Essays*, London.
———, 1984, *Essays on Ideology*, London.
Althusser, Louis and E. Balibar, 1971, *Reading Capital*, London.
Amur, G.S. and S.K. Desai, eds, 1984, *Colonial Consciousness in Commonwealth Literature*, Bombay, 1984.
Andersen, Hans Christian, 1985, *The Complete Illustrated Stories of Hans Christian Andersen*, London.
Anderson, Perry, 1976, *Consideration in Western Marxism*, London.
———, 1976, *In The Tracks of Historical Materialism*, London.
Aries, Philippe, 1962, *Centuries of Childhood: A Social History of Family Life*, New York.
Arnold, Matthew, 1875, *Culture and Anarchy: Essays in Political and Social Criticism*, London.
Bagal, Jogesh Chandra, 1950, 'History of the Bethune School and College 1849–1949', *Bethune College and School Centenary Volume*, Calcutta.
Bagchi, Amiya Kumar, 1989, *Private Investment in India 1900–1939*, Bombay.
Bagchi, Jasodhara, 1975, 'Review of "The English Utilitarians and India"', *Nineteenth Century Studies* (editor: Alok Ray), No. 11, Calcutta, July.
———, 1991, 'Shakespeare in Loin Cloth: English Literature and the Early Nationalist Consciousness in Bengal', in Svati Joshi, ed., *Rethinking English: Essays in Literature, language, History*, New Delhi: Trianka, 1991.

Bakhtin, Mikhail, 1981, *Dialogic Imagination: Four Essays*, edited by M. Holquist, Texas.
———, 1984, *Rabelais and His World*, Bloomington, 1984.
Balibar, Etienne and Pierre Macherery, 1985, 'On Literature as an Ideological Form', in Robert Young, ed., *Untying the Text*, London.
Bannerji, Himani, 1988, 'The Politics of Representation: A Study of Class Struggle in the Political Theatre of West Bengal', unpublished Ph.D. thesis, OISE, Toronto.
———, 1989, 'Class Subjectivity and Politics in Nineteenth Century Bengal', *Economic and Political Weekly*, Vol. XXIV, No. 19, 13 May, Bombay.
Banerjea, Surendranath, 1975, 'Lord Macaulay and Higher Education in India', *Nineteenth Century Studies* (editor: Alok Ray), No. 9, Calcutta, January.
Barrett, Michéle, 1986, *Women's Oppression Today*, London.
Barrett, Michéle and Mary McIntosh, 1985, *The Anti-Social Family*, London.
Barthes, Roland, 1979, *Elements of Semiology*, New York.
———, 1984, *Writing Degree Zero*, London.
———, 1986, *Mythologies*, Glasgow.
Benjamin, Walter, 1982, *Illuminations*, Suffolk.
Bentham, Jeremy, 1968, *Collected Works of J. Bentham*, Vols. 1–6, London.
Berger, John, 1972, *Ways of Seeing*, Harmondsworth.
Berger, Peter and Thomas Luckmann, 1984, *The Social Construction of Reality*, Harmondsworth.
Bhabha, Homi K., 1985, 'Signs Taken for Wonders: Questions of Ambivalence and Authority Under a Tree Outside Delhi, May 1817', *Critical Inquiry* (editor: W.J.T. Mitchell), Vol. 12, No. 1, Autumn.
Bharadwaj, Krishna and Sudipta Kaviraj, eds, 1989, *Perspectives on Capitalism: Marx, Keynes, Schumpeter and Weber*, New Delhi.
Bhaskar, Roy, 1986, *Scientific Realism and Human Emancipation*, London.
Bhatnagar, Rashmi, 1986, 'Uses and Limits of Foucault: A Study of the Theme of Origins in Edward Said's "Orientalism"', *Social Scientist* (editor: Prabhat Patnaik), Vol. 16, No. 7, New Delhi.
Bhattacharya, Malini, 1975, 'A Utilitarian View of Literary Culture: Mill and the Westminister Review', *Nineteenth Century Studies* (editor: Alok Ray), No. 11, Calcutta, July 1975.
Bhattacharya, Sourin, 1973, 'Permanent Settlement and Rammohun Roy', *Nineteenth Century Studies* (editor: Alok Ray), No. 1, Calcutta.
Boden, Margaret A., 1979, *Piaget*, Glasgow.
Borthwick, Meredith, 1984, *The Changing Role of Women in Bengal 1849–1905*, Princeton.
Bose, N.K., 1985, *The Structure of Hindu Society*, New Delhi.
Bottomore, Tom, ed., 1985, *A Dictionary of Marxist Thought*, Oxford.
Brantlinger, Patrick, 1985, 'Victorians and Africans: The Genealogy of the Myth of the Dark Continent', *Critical Inquiry* (editor: W.J.T. Mitchell), Vol. 12, No. 1, Autumn.
Buckland, C.E., 1971, *Dictionary of Indian Biography*, Varanasi.
Carey, W.H., 1980, *The Good Old Days of Hon'ble John Company*, Calcutta.
Carpenter, Humphrey and Mari Prichard, 1984, *The Oxford Companion to Children's Literature*, Oxford.
Centre for Contemporary Cultural Studies, 1977, *On Ideology*, London.

Césaire, Aimé, 1972, *Discourse on Colonialism*, New York.

Chakravarty, J., 1977, *Studies in the Bengal Renaissance*, Calcutta.

Chakravorty Spivak, Gayatri, 1987, *In Other Worlds: Essays in Cultural Politics*, New York.

Chandra, Sudhir, 2011, *Dependence and Disillusionment: Emergence of National Consciousness in Later 19th Century India*, New Delhi.

Chatterjee, Bankimchandra, 'A Popular Literature for Bengal', 1940, in *English Writings*, edited by Brajendra Nath Bannerji and Sajani Kanta Das, Calcutta.

———, 1940, 'Bengali Literature', in *English Writings*, edited by Brajendra Nath Bannerji and Sajani Kanta Das, Calcutta.

Chatterjee, Kalyan K., 1976, *English Education in India: Issues and Opinions*, Meerut.

Chatterjee, Partha, 1984, *Bengal 1920–1947: The Land Question*, Vol. 1, Calcutta.

———, 1986, *Nationalist Thought and the Colonial World: A Derivative Discourse?*, Delhi.

Chatterjee, Ratnabali, 1990, *From Karkhana to the Studio: Changing Social Roles of Patron and Artist in Bengal*, New Delhi.

Chattopadhyay, Gautam, ed., 1978, *Bengal: Early Nineteenth Century: Selected Documents*, Calcutta.

Checkland, E.O.A. and S.G. Checkland, eds, 1974, *The Poor Law Report of 1834*, Harmondsworth.

Cohen, G.A., 1982, *Karl Marx's Theory of History: A Defence*, Oxford.

Collins, Richard *et al.*, eds, 1986, *Media, Culture and Society: A Critical Reader*, London.

Dasgupta, Anil Chandra, ed., 1959, *The Days of John Company: Selections from Calcutta Gazette*, Calcutta.

Deleuze, G., and F. Guattari, 1984, *Anti-Oedipus: Capitalism and Schizophrenia*, London.

Derrida, Jacques, 1980, *Of Grammatology*, Baltimore.

———, 1981, *Writing and Difference*, London.

———, 1985, 'Racism's Last Word', *Critical Inquiry* (editor: W.J.T. Mitchell), Vol. 12, No. 1, Autumn.

Desai, A.R., 1975, *Social Background of Indian Nationalism*, Bombay.

Dews, Peter, 1987, *Logics of Disintegration: Post Structuralist Thought and the Claims of Critical Theory*, London.

Dickens, Charles, 1958, *Hard Times*, Bombay.

Dixon, Bob, 1977, *Catching them Young 1: Sex, Race and Class in Children's Fiction*, Bristol.

———, 1978, *Catching them Young 2: Political Ideas in Children's Fiction*, Bristol.

Dorfman, Ariel, 1983, *The Empire's Old Clothes*, New York, 1983.

Dorfman, Ariel and Mattelart, 1984, *How to Read Donald Duck*, New York.

Duene, Patrick A., 1980, 'Boy's Literature and Idea of Empire, 1870–1914', *Victorian Studies*, Vol. 24, No. 1, London.

Duff, Alexander, 1975, 'The Early or Exclusively Oriental Period of Government Education in Bengal', *Nineteenth Century Studies* (editor: Alok Ray), No. 9, January.

Dutt, Michael Madhusudan, 1983, 'An Essay on the Importance of Educating Hindoo Females', *Madhusudan Rachanabali*, Calcutta.

———, 1983, 'The Anglo Saxon and the Hindu', *Madhusudan Rachanabali*, Calcutta.

Dutt, Romesh Chandra, 1874, *The Peasantry of Bengal*, Calcutta.

———, 1970, *The Economic History of India*, Vols I–II, New Delhi.
Eagleton, Terry, 1976, *Marxism and Literary Criticism*, London.
———, 1980, *Criticism and Ideology: A Study in Marxist Literary Theory*, London.
———, 1983, *Literary Theory: An Introduction*, Oxford.
———, 1986, *Against the Grain*, London.
———, 1987, *Walter Bengamin or Towards the Revolutionary Criticism*, London.
———, 1987, *The Functions of Criticism: From the Spectator to Post-structuralism*, London.
Eco, Umberto, 1984, *The Role of the Reader*, Bloomington.
Edwards, Michael, 1969, *British India 1772–1947*, London.
Ehrmann, Jacques, 'Homo Ludens Revisited', 1968, *Yale French Studies*, Vol. 41, New York.
Enzendberger, Hans M., 1974, *The Consciousness Industry: On Literature and Politics and the Media*, New York.
Fanon, Frantz, 1967, *A Dying Colonialism*, New York.
———, 1968, *The Wretched of the Earth*, New York.
———, 1968, *Black Skin White Masks*, New York.
Foucault, Michel, 1973, *The Birth of the Clinic: An Archaeology of Medical Perception*, New York.
———, 1980, *Power/Knowledge; Selected Interviews and other Writings 1972–1977*, New York.
———, 1982, *Discipline and Punish*, Harmondsworth.
———, 1983, *Order of Things*, London.
———, 1984, *Foucault Reader*, New York.
———, 1985, 'Order of Discourse', in Robert Young, ed., *Untying the Text: A Poststructuralist Reader*, New York.
———, 1985, *Madness and Civilization: A History of Insanity in the Age of Reason*, London.
Fowler, Roger, ed., 1987, *A Dictionary of Modern Critical Terms*, London.
Fox, Geoff *et al.*, eds, 1976, *Writers, Critics and Children*, New York.
Freire, Paulo, 1973, *Pedagogy of the Oppressed*, New York.
Galeano, Èduardo, 1974, *Open Veins of Latin America*, New York.
Ganguli, B.N., 1979, *Some Aspects of Classical Political Economy in the Nineteenth Century Indian Perspective*, New Delhi.
Gardella, Peter, 1986, 'From Possession to Compulsion: Religion, Şex and Madness in Popular Culture', *Social Research*, Vol. 53, No. 2, Summer.
Ghose, Lotika, 1950, 'Social and Educational Movements for Women and by Women', *Bethune College and School Centenary Volume*, Calcutta.
Ghosh, Aurobindo, 1973, *Bande Mataram*, Pondicherry.
———, 1985, *The Foundations of Indian Culture*, Pondicherry.
Gramsci, Antonio, 1982, *Selections from the Prison Notebook*, London.
———, 1985, *Selections from Cultural Writings*, London.
Greimas, A.J. and R. Francois, 1968, 'The Interaction of Semistic Constraints', *Yale French Studies*, No. 41, New York.
Guha, Arabinda, ed., 1971, *Unpublished Letters of Vidyasagar*, Calcutta.
Guha, Ranajit, 1981, *A Rule of Property for Bengal*, New Delhi.
———, 1988, *An Indian Historiography of India: A Nineteenth Century Agenda and Its Implications*, Calcutta.
Guha, Ranajit, ed., 1982–89, *Subaltern Studies*, Vols. I–IV, New Delhi.

Gunder Frank, Andre, 1974, *On Capitalist Underdevelopment*, Bombay.
Hauser, Arnold, 1968, *Social History of Arts*, Vols. 1–4, London.
Hegel, G.W.F., 1975, *Aesthetics: Lectures on Fine Arts*, Oxford.
———, 1979, *Phenomenology of Spirit*, Oxford.
Home Department, 1890, *Papers relating to discipline and moral training in schools and colleges in India, Selections from the Records of the Government of India, Home Department*, CCLXV, No. 8, Calcutta.
Huizinga, Johan, 1985, *Homo ludens: A Study of the Play Element in Culture*, Boston.
Jameson, Fredric, 1971, *Marxism and Form*, Princeton.
———, 1982, *The Political Unconscious: Narrative as a Socially Symbolic Act*, New York.
———, 1988, *The Ideologies of Theory: Essays*, Vols I–II, London.
Jamuna, K.A., ed., 1982, *Children's Literature in Indian Languages*, New Delhi.
Jan, Isabella, 1969, 'Children's Literature and Bourgeois Society Since 1860', *Yale French Studies* (New York), Vol. 43.
Jan Mohamed, Abdul R., 1985, 'The Economy of Manichean Allegory: The Function of Racial Difference in Colonialist Literature', *Critical Inquiry*, No. 1, Vol. 12, Autumn.
Jenks, Chris, ed., 1982, *The Sociology of Childhood: Essential Readings*, London.
Jones, William, 1984, *Discourses and Essays*, edited by Moni Bagchee, New Delhi.
Kaiser, Ernest, ed., 1977, *A Freedomways Reader*, Berlin.
Kakar, Sudhir, 1982, *The Inner World: A Psychoanalytic Study of Childhood and Society in India*, Delhi.
Kappeler, Susanne, 1986, *Pornography of Representation*, Oxford.
Kauffmann, Linda, ed., 1989, *Gender and Theory: Dialogues on Feminist Critisism*, Oxford.
Keating, P.J., 1979, *The Working Classes in Victorian Fiction*, London.
Kipling, Rudyard, 1916, *How Shakespeare Came to Write 'The Tempest'*, New York.
Kopf, David, 1969, *British Orientalism and Bengal Renaissance: Dynamics of Indian Modernization 1773–1835*, Calcutta.
Kosambi, D.D., 1986, *Myth and Reality*, New Delhi.
Kuha, Annette, 1985, *The Power of the Image: Essays on Representation and Sexuality*, London.
Kumar, Dharma and Tapan Raychaudhuri, eds, 1984, *The Cambridge Economic History of India*, 2 vols, New Delhi.
La Guma, Alex, ed., 1978, *Apartheid: A Collection of Writings on South African Racism by South Africans*, Berlin.
Laclau, Ernesto, 1977, *Politics and Ideology in Marxist Theory*, London.
Lorrain, Jorge, 1980, *The Concept of Ideology*, New Delhi.
Lenin, V.I., 1967, *On Literature and Art*, Moscow.
———, 1977, 'Materialism and Empiro-Criticism', in *Collected Works*, Vol. 14, Moscow.
———, 1977, 'Imperialism, the Highest Stage of Capitalism', in *Selected Works*, Vol. 1, Moscow.
Loomba, Ania, 1989, *Gender, Race in Renaissance Drama*, Manchester.
Lukács Georg, 1971, *Theory of the Novel*, London.
———, 1978, *Studies in European Realism*, London.
———, 1978, *History and Class Consciousness*, London.
Lunacharsky, Anatoli, 1981, *On Education: Selected Articles and Speeches*, Moscow.

Lynskey, Alan, 1976, *Children and Themes*, Oxford.
Macksey, Richard and Donato Eugenio, eds, 1982, *The Structuralist Controversy*, Baltimore.
Macaulay, T.B., 1835, *Minutes on Indian Education, dated 2nd February, 1835*, G.I.C.P.O., Calcutta.
Macpherson, C.B., 1972, *The Political Theory of Possessive Individualism: Hobbes to Locke*, Oxford.
Madge, Elliot Walter, 1967, *Henry Derozio: The Eurasian Poet and Reformer*, edited by Subir Roy Chowdhury, Calcutta.
Marcuse, Herbert, 1987, *Eros and Civilization: A Philosophical Enquiry into Freud*, London.
Marx, Karl, 1976, *The German Ideology*, in *Collected Works*, Vol. V, Moscow.
———, 1977, *Introduction to the Critique of Political Economy*, in *Selected Works*, Vol. I, Moscow.
———, 1977, *The Class Struggle in France*, in *Selected Works*, Vol. I, Moscow.
———, 1977, *The Eighteenth Brumaire of Louis Bonaparte*, in *Selected Works*, Vol. I, Moscow.
———, 1979, *Capital*, 3 vols, Harmondsworth.
Marx, Karl and Freidrich Engels, 1982, *Selected Correspondence*, Moscow.
Mészaros, Istvan, 1982, *Marx's Theory of Alienation*, London.
Mill, James, 1848, *The History of British India*, 2 vols, London.
Mill, James and John Stuart Mill, *James and John Stuart Mill on Education*, 1931, edited by F.A. Caveragh, Cambridge.
Mill, John Stuart, 1974, *Utilitarianism*, edited by M. Warnock, Glasgow.
Millet, Kate, 1970, *Sexual Politics*, New York.
Misra, B.B., 1961, *The Indian Middle Classes*, Oxford.
Mitra, Pyari Chand, 1979, *A Biographical Sketch of David Hare*, edited by Gouranga Gopal Sengupta, Calcutta.
Mittra, Kissory Chand, 1975, 'On the Progress of Education in Bengal', *Nineteenth Century Studies* (editor: Alok Ray), No. 9, Calcutta.
Moi, Toril, 1985, *Sexual/Textual Politics: Feminist Literary Theory*, London.
Mookerjee, Haris Chandra, 1975, 'Eighteen Fifty Seven', *Nineteenth Centuries Studies* (editor: Alok Ray), No. 12, Calcutta.
Newsinger, John, 1986, 'Lord Graystroke and Darkest Africa: The Politics of the Tarzan Stories', *Race and Class*, Vol. XXVIII, No. II, London.
O'Flaherty, W.D., 1984, *Dreams, Illusions and Other Realities*, Chicago.
Owen, Roger and Bob Sutchiffe, eds, 1980, *Studies in the Theory of Imperialism*, London.
Patnaik, Arun, 1987, 'Gramsci's Concept of Common Sense: Towards a Theory of Subaltern Conscious in Hegemony Processes', Occasional Paper 95, Centre for Studies in Social Sciences, Calcutta.
Piaget, Jean, 1972, *Psychology and Epistemology: Towards a Theory of Knowledge*, Singapore.
———, 1973, *The Child's Conception of the World*, London.
———, 1978, *The Language and Thought of the Child*, London.
Pradhan, Sudhi, ed., 1979–85, *Marxist Cultural Movement in India: Chronicles and Documents*, 3 vols, Calcutta.
Propp, V., 1970, *Morphology of the Folk Tale*, Texas.
Raltansi, Ali, ed., 1989, *Ideology, Method and Marx*, London.

Ray, Niharranjan and Pratulchandra Gupta, eds, 1957, *Hundred Years of the University of Calcutta*, Calcutta.
Raychaudhuri, Tapan, 1987, *Three Views of Europe in Neneteenth Century Bengal*, Calcutta.
Roy Chowdhury, Subir, 1975, 'The Governor and Guru', *Nineteenth Century Studies* (editor: Alok Ray), No. II, Calcutta.
Roy, Rammohun, 1973, 'Brief Remarks Regarding Modern Encroachment on the Ancient Right of Females', in *Rammohun Rachanabali*, edited by Ajit Kumar Ghosh, Calcutta.
Rodney, Walter, 1972, *How Europe Underdeveloped Africa*, London.
———, 1985, 'An Ideology of Difference', *Critical Inquiry*, Vol. 12, No. 1, Autumn.
Said, Edward W., 1976, *Orientalism*, London.
———, 1984, *The World, the Text and the Critic*, London.
Sandbrook, R. and R. Cohen, eds, 1975, *The Development of an African Working Class: Studies in Class Formation and Action*, London.
Sangari, Kumkum and Sudesh Vaid, eds, 1989, *Recasting Women*, New Delhi.
Sarkar, Sumit, 1973, *The Swadeshi Movement in Bengal 1903–1908*, New Delhi.
———, 1983, *Modern India 1885–1947*, New Delhi.
———, 1983, *Popular Movements and Middle Class Leadership in Late Colonial India: Perspective and Problems of History from Below*, Calcutta.
———, 1985, *A Critique of Colonial India*, Calcutta.
Sarkar, Susobhan, 1979, *On the Bengal Renaissance*, Calcutta.
———, 1983, *Towards Marx*, Calcutta.
Sarkar, Tanika, 1978, *Bengal 1928–1934: The Politics of Protest*, New Delhi.
———, 1989, 'Hindu Conjugality and Nationalism in Late 19th Century Bengal', in *Indian Women: Myth and Reality*, National Seminar Papers, School of Women's Studies, Jadavpur University, Calcutta.
Seeley, J.R., 1971, *The Expansion of England*, Chicago.
Sen, Amartya and Bernard Williams, eds, 1982, *Utilitarianism and Beyond*, Cambridge.
Sen, Asok, 1975, 'The Bengal Economy and Raja Rammohun Roy', in V.C. Joshi, ed., *Rammohun Roy and the Process of Modernization in India*, New Delhi.
———, 1977, *Ishwar Chandra Vidyasagar and His Elusive Milestone*, Calcutta.
Sharp, H., ed., 1920, *Selections from Education Records, Part I, 1781–1839*, Calcutta.
Shishkoff, Serge, 1976, 'The Structure of Fairy Tales: Propp versus Levi Strauss', *Dipositio*, Vol. 1, No. 3, Michigan.
Simon, Brian, 1960, *Studies in the History of Education 1780–1870*, London.
Smiles, Samuel, 1968, *Self Help*, London.
Smith, Adam, 1976, *An Enquiry into the Nature and Causes of the Wealth of Nations*, Vols I–II, Oxford.
Smith, Dorothy E., 1987, *The Everyday World as Problematic: A Feminist Sociology*, Toronto.
Stokes, Eric, 1985, *The English Utilitarians and India*, New Delhi.
Sunder Rajan, Rajeshwari, 1986, 'After Orientalism: Colonialism and English Literary Studies in India', *Social Scientist*, Vol. 16, No. 7, New Delhi.
Tagore, Rabindranath, 1977, 'King and Rebel', *Rabindra-Viksha-3*, Santiniketan.
———, 1985, *Nationalism*, Madras.
Tattvabhushan, Sitanath, 1904, *Social Reform in Bengal*, Calcutta.
Timpanaro, Sebastiano, 1980, *On Materialism*, London.
Tompkins, Jane P., 1980, *An Introduction to Reader Response Criticism*, London.

Trevelyan, Charles Edward, 1838, *On the Education of the People of India*, London.
Trevelyan, George Otto, 1978, *The Life and Letters of Lord Macaulay*, Vols I–II, Oxford.
Viswanathan, Gauri, 1985, *The Ideology of Literary Education in British India, 1813–1880*, unpublished Ph.D. thesis, Columbia University.
Volosinov, V.N., 1986, *Marxism and the Philosophy of Language*, Cambridge, Mass.
Williams, Raymond, 1979, *Marxism and Literature*, London.
———, 1980, *Problems in Materialism and Culture*, London.
———, 1981, *Keywords*, Glasgow.
———, 1982, *Culture and Society, 1780–1950,* London.
———, 1983, *Culture*, Glasgow.
Wood, Ellen Meiksins, 1986, *The Retreat from Class: A New 'True' Socialism*, London.

Index

Individuals, Institutions, Organizations and Movements

Books, Journals and Compositions